The Nineteenth-Century German Lied

The Nineteenth-Century German Lied

Lorraine Gorrell

AMADEUS PRESS
Reinhard G. Pauly, General Editor
Portland, Oregon

To my father and mother

Permission to reprint granted by:

Cambridge University Press to quote from *Richard Strauss: a chronicle of the early years 1864–1898* by Willi Schuh. Trans. Mary Whittall, 1982.

J. M. Dent to quote from *Schubert: A Documentary Biography*, edited by Otto Deutsch, 1946.

The Music Review to reprint material from "The Songs of Louis Spohr" by Lorraine Gorrell, 39:31–38, 1978.

The NATS Journal to reprint material from "Fanny Mendelssohn and Her Songs," 42:6–11, 1986.

Orpheus Publications Limited to reprint material from "Viewpoint: Composers and Singer," which appeared in *Music and Musicians, International* 37:59–60, 1989.

Penguin USA to quote from *The Portable Nietzsche*. Trans. & ed. Walter Kaufmann, 1987.

Yale University Press to quote from *Schumann as Critic* by Leon B. Plantinga, 1967.

ISBN 0-931340-59-4
Printed in Singapore

AMADEUS PRESS
9999 S.W. Wilshire, Suite 124
Portland, Oregon 97225

Library of Congress Cataloging-in-Publication Data

Gorrell, Lorraine.
   The nineteenth-century German lied / Lorraine Gorrell.
      p.   cm.
   Includes bibliographical references and indexes.
   ISBN 0-931340-59-4
   1. Songs, German--Germany--19th century--History and criticism.
   I. Title. II. Title: 19th-century German lied.
ML2829.4.G67   1993
782.42168'0943'09034--dc20   92-37138
                                                       CIP
                                                       MN

Contents

Illustrations

Acknowledgments

I am grateful to Winthrop University for faculty development funds and two Research Council grants, and to the Southern Regional Education Board for a travel grant to study collections in England and Germany. I would also like to thank Peggy Crouch, Professor Constance Kenna, Professor Willi Adams, the library staffs of Winthrop University, the Bodleian Library, the Library of Congress, and the Staatsbibliothek Preußischer Kulturbesitz, Musikabteilung (Berlin). To Reinhard Pauly, Karen Kirtley, and Carol Odlum of Amadeus Press, I owe a debt of gratitude for their care in editing this manuscript.

Most of all I am grateful to my family: to my daughter, Rachel, for her presence in the world and to my husband, Wilburn Newcomb, for his continued encouragement, suggestions, careful reading of the manuscript, and assistance with all matters relating to computers.

"Auch kleine Dinge"

I believe artists often do not know what they can do best: they are too conceited for that. Their attention is directed to something prouder than those little plants give promise of, which know how to grow up in actual perfection, new, rare, and beautiful, on their soil. The final excellency of their own garden and vineyard is superficially estimated by them.

—Nietzsche[1]

Although song has been prized throughout history, it has also been considered a slight genre by even its finest creators. Schumann thought his greatness as a composer could only be achieved by writing symphonies and operas. Yet he, like Schubert and Wolf, wrote songs of unsurpassing beauty which, of themselves, sealed his reputation for posterity. Song held a special delight for nineteenth-century composers and seemed to come from the most intimate, fragile space in their creative spirit. Their friends leave touching accounts of private performances by Schubert, Brahms, and Wolf as singers of their own songs. Schumann used the lied to meditate on his own interior world.

The lied, as a miniature genre, seemed to these composers to be insignificant when weighed against the massive forces of Beethoven's symphonies or Wagner's operas. In fact, its life was brief, and its delicate essence was lost when composers in the second half of the century began to orchestrate their songs, thereby subverting its intimate nature.

Perhaps the fate of the lied could have been predicted at its inception. Composers who followed Beethoven were overwhelmed by the magnitude and complexity of his contributions to the symphony, the concerto, the string quartet, and even opera. They defined their success in terms of the example he had set, yet the forces that shaped the emerging musical world of the nineteenth century had already broken Beethoven's mold.

THE VERBAL ERA

The nineteenth century was, in every way, a verbal age. Music periodicals flourished, and articulate composers were eager to write about themselves, their music, and their ideas: Schumann, Berlioz, and Hugo Wolf were critics for periodicals; Liszt wrote biographies of Chopin and Robert Franz; and many composers kept diaries, maintained voluminous correspondence, and wrote autobiographies. Some of these autobiographies are fascinating self-justifications of the composer, his ideas, and his struggles to be recognized. Wagner not only wrote an autobiography (with the assistance of his wife, Cosima) but also poured out hundreds of additional pages (now immortalized in a ten-volume collection), defining and justifying his revolutionary theories of art.

Even the great Beethoven reflected the verbal currents that would dominate the new century when he allowed words to invade that most abstract musical genre, the symphony. Other composers such as Mendelssohn and Mahler soon followed his lead. Symphonic works began to appear with printed programs: Berlioz's *Symphonie fantastique* had its own full-blown program, Franz Liszt wrote thirteen symphonic poems and two programmatic symphonies, and Strauss wrote highly graphic symphonic poems.

As we look back over this verbal century, we see that musical change occurred in song and in opera—both verbally oriented arts. The flowering of the nineteenth-century lied was made possible because of literary developments that began in the previous century. The eighteenth century had ended with an outpouring of lyric poetry that culminated in the works of Johann Wolfgang von Goethe (1749–1832). He was followed by other poets such as Joseph von Eichendorff (1788–1857), Friedrich Rückert (1788–1866), Heinrich Heine (1797–1856), and Eduard Mörike (1804–1875) who provided a wealth of lyric poetry for nineteenth-century composers.

The link between music and poetry, which composers have explored for hundreds of years, found a new vitality and meaning in the German lied. There was a desire on the part of many nineteenth-century artists to merge various arts, and the art song reflects a unique melding of poetry and music.

Some composers, such as Peter Cornelius, even wrote the poetry for their own songs. Ironically, two of the most verbally sophisticated composers, Schumann and Wolf, searched in vain for suitable texts that could be used in opera. They, along with Brahms, expended tremendous energy in their futile searches for "the right" opera text. The works that Schumann and Wolf finally set to music were singularly undramatic. Wagner, of course, solved this problem for himself by writing his own libretti.

For most composers of lieder, opera was not really a medium for their inspiration. Their gifts for finding intimate meaning and for exploring the hidden recesses of the soul did not necessarily coexist with the skills that opera composition required—histrionic expression on a grand scale. Brahms wrote no operas, and the operas of Schubert, Schumann, and Wolf were unsuccessful.

THE PIANO

But each of these four composers was wonderfully attuned to the possibilities provided by poetry, and at the same time, they were also given an expressive, rapidly developing new instrument, the piano, which could deliver a miniature orchestra of sound, simultaneously producing sonorous harmony and mellifluous melody. This instrument could create an atmosphere that enhanced poetic mood or even mimicked the meaning of words. It was no accident that three of the four also achieved success in writing for the piano as a solo instrument.

NO LONGER A FAMILY TRADITION

Music historians often observe that the nineteenth-century musician, unlike his predecessors, was not the progeny of great musical families who for generations passed on their musical knowledge to their offspring. Schumann was the son of a bookseller, Berlioz the son of a doctor, and Wolf was the child of a leather manufacturer. Perhaps the free treatment of musical form and the extension and eventual breakdown of tonal harmony was precipitated by the often haphazard musical education of many of the century's most notable musicians. Even musicians such as Frédéric Chopin, who began his musical studies at the age of six, were striving for unique sounds and harmonic colors that often made traditional modes of expression no longer sufficient.

The song, as a free miniature form, was ideal for this era. It demanded little sophistication in formal long-term development, and it flowered with the growing harmonic vocabulary that could be used for subtle word coloration. Often, it seems, the sheer originality of harmonic ideas became an end in itself. Bruckner is quoted as admiringly asking Wolf, "Where the devil did you get that chord from?" after he heard the opening of Wolf's song, "Seemanns Abschied" (The Sailor's Farewell).[2]

SOCIAL FORCES

Even the social climate was ideal for song. Prosperous middle-class ladies had the money to buy music, music periodicals, and musical instruments, such as the piano, harp, or guitar, and they had the leisure to learn to play and sing. Throughout Europe, accomplished young ladies hoped to improve their marital prospects by distinguishing themselves as amateur musicians and artists.

> "Do you play and sing, Miss Bennet?"
> "A little."
> "Oh!—some time or other we shall be happy to hear you. Our instrument is a capital one, probably superior to——. You shall try it some day. Do your sisters play and sing?"
> "One of them does."
> "Why did not you all learn? You ought all to have learned. The Miss Webbs all play, and their father has not so good an income as yours. Do you draw?"
> "No, not at all."
> "What, none of you?"
> "Not one."
> "That is very strange."
>
> *Pride and Prejudice*[3]

Prosperous young ladies might be expected to draw, play, and sing, but they were rarely given the opportunity to become professional musicians. Fanny Mendelssohn's father exhorted his brilliant daughter to remember that music was only an ornament for a truly feminine woman. A few women, however, did manage to achieve success as musicians: after Clara Schumann was left a widow with seven children to support, she became one of the most renowned pianists of her age.

NATIONALISM

The political world of the nineteenth century was in a state of revolutionary upheaval, but even this stimulated the development of opera and song. Nationalistic sentiment among German-speaking people spurred interest in their own folk poetry, folk music, myths, and history. Many of the legends about Teutonic heroes, as told in the Nibelungenlied (The Song of the Nibelung) from the thirteenth century, were examined by composers of the era: Heinrich Dorn (1804–1892) wrote an opera based on the Nibelungenlied in 1854; Fanny and Felix Mendelssohn discussed the saga's musical possibilities in their letters; Friedrich Hebbel (1813–1863), one of Germany's greatest dramatists, wrote a trilogy on the epic; and of course Wagner composed his momentous cycle of music dramas *Der Ring des Nibelungen*. Musicians "rediscovered" Bach and carefully studied his musical techniques. Composers such as Robert Schumann, Robert Franz, and Johannes Brahms explored the possibilities of traditional counterpoint and adapted some of these techniques in their songs. Brahms was so inspired by folk music that he collected and arranged both folk melodies and poems. The folk tradition also fertilized the musical ideas of Gustav Mahler in the second half of the century.

Hundreds of songs had been written by both major and minor composers in previous centuries, but it was not until the nineteenth century that a fortuitous set of circumstances converged to produce the unique genre that is now called the art song. Although the romantic lied was not to outlive its century, it influenced and changed composers' concept of songwriting throughout the Western world. Not only did the nineteenth-century German lied stimulate the development of other national styles of song, such as the French mélodie and the Italian lirica da camera, but song is now considered a significant musical medium, attracting the interest of many serious composers. The link between music and poetry, which composers have explored for hundreds of years, found a new vitality and musical vocabulary with the German lied.

Figure 1-1. Johann Wolfgang von Goethe. Courtesy of the Library of Congress.

CHAPTER ONE

Poetry and Music

The nineteenth-century German lied owes much of its origin and inspiration to German poetry. The lyric outpourings of the great Johann Wolfgang von Goethe and other poets of his age acted as a stimulus to song composers from Mozart in his "Das Veilchen" (The Violet) to Wolf in his over fifty settings of Goethe poetry.

The lied is generally defined as a genre that melded poetry and music into a unique relationship in which piano and voice were closely linked to the poetic phrase, and the melody, harmony, and rhythm of the music were crafted to reflect the meaning and mood of the poems they interpreted. Every song composer of the nineteenth century was highly individual in the use and relative emphasis of these various elements. But the uniting of two distinct arts, poetry and music, has generated much controversy and a great variety of opinions during the nineteenth and twentieth centuries, as poets, musicians, and critics tried to determine what constituted the most successful balance in this relationship. Composer Arnold Schoenberg, one of the many participants in the verbal battles on the subject, stakes out an extreme position in his essay "The Relationship to the Text."

> I discovered in several Schubert songs, well-known to me, that I had absolutely no idea what was going on in the poems on which they were based. But when I had read the poems it became clear to me that I had gained absolutely nothing for the understanding of the songs . . . since the poems did not make it necessary for me to change my conception of the musical interpretation. . . . On the contrary, . . . without knowing the poem, I had grasped the content, the real content, perhaps even more profoundly than if I had clung to the surface of the mere thoughts expressed in words. . . . Inspired by the sound of the first words of the text,

I ... composed many of my songs straight through to the end
without troubling myself in the slightest about the continuation
of the poetic events, without even grasping them in the ecstasy
of composing. . . . Only days later I thought of looking back to see
just what was the real poetic content of my song. . . . To my
greatest astonishment, . . . I had never done greater justice to the
poet than when, guided by my first direct contact with the sound
of the beginning, I divined everything that obviously had to
follow this first sound with inevitability. . . . It became clear to me
that the work of art is like every other complete organism. It is so
homogeneous in its composition that in every little detail it
reveals its truest, inmost essence.[1]

This lofty quotation, taken from Schoenberg's collection of essays
Style and Idea, obscures the actual "nuts and bolts" of setting text to
music. Schoenberg, in fact, minimized mechanical considerations in
songwriting by saying that "the outward correspondence between
music and text, as exhibited in declamation, tempo, and dynamics,
has but little to do with the inward correspondence and belongs to
the same stage of primitive imitation of nature as the copying of a
model."[2] Schoenberg, who considered poetry to be "an art still bound
to subject matter," valued the abstract nature of music and relegated
poetry to a secondary rôle within song composition.

Music historian Paul Henry Lang, also extolling the virtue of
musical profundity in song composition, nevertheless offers us a different perspective on Schubert's rôle in uniting text and music in
nineteenth-century song.

One can understand why ... the Lied reached its real
flourishing in the early romantic era—a literary era par
excellence in the history of music—for a song cannot be treated
in the same manner as an opera libretto; poetry has vested rights
in it that cannot be ignored. The eighteenth century neglected
the song as being incompatible with a purely musical approach
to vocal music. . . . Schubert . . . was far more creative in the
purely musical sense than any other song writer, with the occasional exception of Schumann and Brahms. Had he accepted the
romantic dictum of the poet's absolute supremacy, merely
providing music to the text, he would not have created the
modern song; but by consciously elevating such purely musical
elements as harmony and instrumental accompaniment to equal
importance with poem and melody, he brought to bear upon the
atmosphere of the song the force of an overwhelming musical
organism, a force sufficient to establish a balance between
poetry and music. . . . While there were many fine song composers after Schubert who divined the secret of the Lied, the

balance was gradually upset in favor of the literary element, thereby ending the history of the true song.[3]

Schumann, as music critic for the *Neue Zeitschrift für Musik*, was highly conscious of poetry's rôle in a song and praised composer Norbert Burgmüller because:

> His foremost concern is—as it should be with everyone—to recreate in a subtle musical realization the most delicate effects of the poem. Seldom does any connotation escape him; nor, if he has grasped it, does his interpretation of it miscarry.[4]

In a review of Robert Franz's songs, Schumann criticizes earlier songwriters because "the poem merely ran along beside [the music].... [Robert Franz] is interested in something other than music that merely sounds good or bad; he strives to recreate for us the real essence of the poem."[5]

Throughout the history of music, debate has raged over how much importance should be delegated to the text of a vocal composition. Composers such as Vincenzo Galilei (d. 1591) and Christoph Willibald Gluck (d. 1787) participated in reform movements that sought to place music at the service of the text. Mozart, on the other hand, expressed the opinion that the text was to be the handmaiden to music. The nineteenth-century German art song was a genre which linked poetry and music so closely that much criticism revolves around the quality of the poetry selected and the care with which this poetry is treated.

A composer may choose to enhance the meaning of words with his music and even emphasize the onomatopoetic quality of particular words. As soon as words become part of a musical composition, the listener's thoughts can be directed toward specific ideas. A few composers, such as Sergei Rachmaninoff, Ralph Vaughan Williams, Maurice Ravel, and Nicolay Medtner, have sometimes written for the voice as an abstract musical instrument without using words, but traditionally, words are as basic to vocal music as are melody and rhythm. Words call forth specific images in the mind of the listener and have definite meanings, so that when they are used in a musical composition, the music becomes less abstract than in purely instrumental music. While instrumental music may communicate general moods to its listeners, the words of a song can change the listener's thoughts directly.

Early composers of lieder such as Johann Friedrich Reichardt sometimes created musical "readings" of poems, simple settings in which music provided a background for the presentation of a poem. Goethe certainly enjoyed Reichardt's and Zelter's modest settings of his work, which highlighted the poetry without drawing too much attention to the music; the text was rarely dominated by its musical setting, and its interpretation by the music was limited to general mood or atmosphere.

In many early song settings, the poet is given a status equal to or greater than the composer's. When the song "Lenore" was published in 1798, the title page bore the inscription, "G. A. Buerger in Musik gesetzt von I. R. Zumsteeg," with Johann Zumsteeg's name printed in the same-sized typeface as the poet. In Zumsteeg's setting of "Die Büssende" (Repenting), a poem by Friedrich Leopold, a count, Breitkopf & Härtel printed the poet's name in larger typeface than the composer's.

But composers such as Schoenberg and Medtner have weighed

Figure 1-2. Decorative Cover to Johann Friedrich Reichardt's edition of *Lieder, Oden, Balladen und Romanzen* with poetry by Goethe.

in on the side of music. In his book, *The Muse and the Fashion*, the Russian composer Nicolay Medtner, also a composer of German song, made it clear that he was not taking dictation from the poet:

> Poetic text may beget purely musical song which flows along sometimes uniting itself with the text, but never forsaking its own musical bed.... The music ... of songs, that is entirely guided by the text and has no self-sufficient musical sense or content, naturally belongs to the domain of program music, since writing it was merely taking down dictation of the poetic text.[6]

Wolf's biographer, Ernest Newman, considered Wolf a great composer because he *did* take dictation from the poet. "He allowed the poet to prescribe for him the whole shape and colour of a song, down even to the smallest details."[7]

Music is potentially the more powerful force in the relationship of poetry and music, for it possesses the ability to enhance or obscure words; words most certainly find their clearest form of expression in the artistic mediums of poetry and prose. In the last quarter of the nineteenth century, composers such as Wolf chose to give more weight to poetry in this relationship. The history of the nineteenth-century lied is a story of how composers chose to balance the forces of poetry and music.

While usually honoring the rhythm and meter of a poem, the composer could also derive musical motives from the poetic structure. Beethoven permeated his setting of "Der Wachtelschlag" (The Quail's Song) with a motive extracted from the words "Fürchte Gott!" (Fear God), which were supposed to imitate the call of a quail (see Chapter 5 on Beethoven). Brahms stated that he would reflect on a poem for some time before he actually wrote a song. This allowed the text to stimulate his musical ideas; he often used the metrical structure of the poem for rhythmic guidance at the beginning of his songs.

Some critics have even questioned the right of musicians to set a fine poem to music. If a poem is itself a work of art, why should such a poem be set to music? The poem already exists as an independent entity. In a musical setting, the listener is locked into one reading of the poem—the composer's. Unlike Hugo Wolf or Robert Schumann, Gustav Mahler did not specifically seek to set the finest poetry to music. Mahler, however, was not expressing poetic nuance for piano and voice in the intimate setting of the recital hall. After he began to orchestrate his songs, he had to be sure that the poetry could be heard over a substantial orchestra. Although he created a sense of intimacy in his *Rückert Lieder* and the *Kindertotenlieder* (Songs on the Death of Children), he was working in a new medium on a much grander scale than were the art song composers. In his *Das Lied von der Erde* (The Song of the Earth), he used the voice to "declaim" the words and allowed the voice to be heard over a large orchestra by treating the poetry in an operatic manner. While he was directly inspired by words, he was not "limited" by words and was frequently at a loss to find words other than his own that suited his aim. In a letter to Arthur Seidl, Mahler stated:

> Whenever I plan a large musical structure, I always come to a point where I have to resort to "the word" as a vehicle for my musical idea. . . . In the last movement of my Second [symphony] I simply had to go through the whole of world literature, including the Bible, in search of the right word, the "Open Sesame"—and in the end had no choice but to find my own words for my thoughts and feelings.[8]

Mahler's views on choosing poetry for his songs are presented by his wife, Alma Mahler, in her *Memories and Letters*:

> It even seemed to him a profanity when composers ventured to set perfect poems to music; it was as if a sculptor chiselled a statue from marble and a painter came along and coloured it. He himself had only appropriated some few bits from the *Wunderhorn*—from earliest childhood his relationship to the book had been particularly close. The poems were not complete in themselves, but blocks of marble which anyone might make his own.[9]

Max Harrison uses similar words in his discussion of Brahms's songs:

> Certainly a perfect poem, just because of its completeness, can have little added to it by music. A poem or other text which attracts a composer suggests to him emotions that are only implicit in it but which he can make explicit with his music.[10]

On the other hand, many great poems such as Goethe's "Heidenröslein" (Heath Rose) are more famous in their musical setting than they are as poems. But the poem can still be appreciated for itself alone, and the multitude of various musical readings that this poem has inspired must indicate that other composers found their own meaning in it. Artistic questions such as this one have no real answer other than in the success of the results. Should we be deprived of Schubert's wonderful setting of Goethe's equally great poem "Wanderers Nachtlied" II (Wanderer's Night Song)? (This song is often identified by its first line of text "Über allen Gipfeln ist Ruh"—Over All the Mountaintops Is Peace. Schubert wrote two songs with the title "Wanderers Nachtlied." His "Wanderers Nachtlied" I, written in 1815, uses the Goethe poem which begins "Der du von dem Himmel bist"—You Who Are from Heaven; "Wanderers Nachtlied" II was written in 1822.)

Robert Schumann, a highly literate man, asked the opposite question: "Why select mediocre poetry that is certain to mirror itself in the music?"[11] This question also has no absolute answer other than in the musical responses it has elicited. Composers such as Schumann did choose excellent poetry for their songs, just as composers such as Brahms did not. Both made major contributions to the lied.

Schubert has inadvertently presented us with both sides of the coin. His choice of poetry ranged from great to banal. He set well over sixty of Goethe's poems to music, but his friendships with numerous obscure poets of his day account for many of the lesser poems that he also set to music. His close friend, Franz von Schober, for example, was the poet for Schubert's beloved "An die Musik" (To Music). Can a composer set a second-rate poem to music without writing a second-rate song? Schubert answered this question again and again with a flood of great songs. His monumental song cycle *Winterreise* (Winter Journey) was based on the popular, undistinguished poetry of Wilhelm Müller, yet Schubert set each poem with such individuality and depth of feeling that he succeeded, despite the quality of the poetry, in creating songs of overwhelming beauty. His sublime music communicates the universal ideas that can be found in the poetry without drawing attention to the weaknesses of the poem itself.

Schumann commented wryly that, though he was "not much over thirty when he died, . . . [Schubert] wrote an astonishing amount. . . . He would have eventually set the whole of German literature to music, and Telemann, who insisted that a proper composer should be able to set a public notice . . . to music, would have found his man in Schubert."[12] Schumann, actually a great admirer of Schubert, admitted that "wherever he reached, music gushed forth: Aeschylus and Klopstock, so reticent to be set to music, gave in to his hands, just as he drew forth the deepest qualities from the facile style of W. Müller and others."[13]

Schubert set to music some of the most notable writings of his age, poems by Goethe, Schiller, Hölty, Heine, and Rückert. Many of his finest songs unite this great poetry with subtle, illuminating musical settings. But these words no longer belong solely to the poet. Schubert's musical ideas stretch the time it takes to read the poem, and as he lingers on words of his choice, he may obscure the poem's

meter and rhyme schemes. As he combines stanzas and adds or sub-
tracts words and phrases to accommodate the musical structure,
Schubert is creating a new artistic entity. His "Wanderers Nachtlied"
II is such a song. He captures the entire mood of the famous poem as
well as the character of individual words in this polished gem. His
homophonic beginning conveys the calm of the opening words—
"Über allen Gipfeln ist Ruh" (Example 1-1). Shifting from half-note
and quarter-note values to eighths while retaining a slow harmonic
rhythm similar to the opening section, his piano figuration lends just
enough movement to the musical phrase to depict the subtle stirring
and rustling of the birds and leaves in the quiet forest and, at the same
time, suggests to the listener a more subtle meaning in the text
(Example 1-2). Schubert's music seems in perfect unity with the
words; it is simple, stately, and reflective. As he returns to a hymnlike
texture in the last lines of the song, "Warte nur, balde ruhest du auch"
(Only wait, soon you also will rest), Schubert mirrors Goethe's image
of nature's peace and promise of human rest, thereby returning to the

Example 1-1. Schubert, "Über allen Gipfeln ist Ruh" (Over All the
Mountaintops Is Peace), mm. 1–4.

Example 1-2. Schubert, "Über allen Gipfeln ist Ruh," mm. 5–7.

original mood in this brief through-composed song. The dirgelike rhythms at the beginning of "Wanderers Nachtlied," which are partially repeated in the last two bars of the song, have suggested to some listeners that Schubert was equating peace with death; he does use this same rhythmic pattern of a long note followed by two short notes in several songs dealing with the subject of death—most notably "Der Tod und das Mädchen" (Death and the Maiden) and "Der Jüngling und der Tod" (The Youth and Death).

Are some types of poetry more easily set to music? The nineteenth-century composers showed a definite preference for lyric poetry . . . but what kind of lyric poetry? Music historian Max Harrison suggests that

> the most suitable verses for a song writer, and those which give a composer the finest opportunities, are those leaving gaps in their expressive content, thus allowing a collaboration between words and notes.[14]

W. H. Auden and Chester Kallman, in their introduction to *An Elizabethan Song Book*, state that the poetry most suitable for musical setting has definite characteristics.

> The elements of the poetic vocabulary . . . which are best adapted for musical setting are those which require the least reflection to comprehend. . . . For example: interjections, which in one's mother tongue always sound onomatopoeic (fie, O, alas, adieu); imperatives; verbs of physical motion (going, coming, hasting, following, falling) or physical concomitants of emotions (laughing, weeping, frowning, sighing); adjectives denoting elementary qualities (bright, hard, green, sad); nouns denoting states of feeling (joy, love, rage, despair) or objects, the emotional associations of which are common to all, and strong (sea, night, moon, spring). On the other hand, complicated metaphors which, even if the words are heard, take time to understand and didactic messages which demand assent or dissent are unsuitable.[15]

A composer can choose to enhance, omit, or rearrange any aspect of his text. Schoenberg's view that he commanded an understanding of an entire poem in its first line is certainly extreme, but a poem does become the possession of the composer when he sets it to music. In *Dichterliebe* (Poet's Love), Schumann was tampering with Heine's *Lyrical Intermezzo* by selecting only sixteen of the sixty-five poems and by then arranging them in a different order. To complete their musical ideas, composers may find it necessary to repeat words or

Figure 1-3. Heinrich Heine. Photo print of drawing. Courtesy of the
Library of Congress.

phrases of the poem that had not been repeated by the poet.
Schubert, for example, repeats the refrain, "Meine Ruh ist hin . . ."
(My peace is gone) at the end of "Gretchen am Spinnrade"
(Gretchen at the Spinning Wheel) and thereby alters the formal
structure of Goethe's poem. Instead of ending at the climax of the
poem, "An seinen Küssen vergehen sollt" (expire under his kisses),
Schubert adds a denouement filled with pathos, misery, and reflection. He uses the refrain and the piano figuration—in this case, the
imitation of a spinning wheel—as unifying features in this song.[16]
Even Schubert's spinning-wheel figuration in the piano shows how
much liberty he has taken with Goethe's poem. Schubert, with his
amazing musical facility, has the spinning wheel stop in the middle of
the song as Margaret becomes lost in her thoughts of Faust; then, as
she regains her senses, Schubert has the spinning wheel hesitantly
begin again. Nowhere in the original play does Goethe indicate this
event, yet Schubert's imagination provided this unique vision. The
poem now belongs to Schubert.

Schubert's decision to change Goethe's formal organization of
the poem by repeating the refrain has changed the meaning and
intent of the poem. The composer must decide upon some formal
organization for the music, which may or may not coincide with the
poet's structural divisions.

The most common song form and one that was preferred by many
of the early lieder composers is strophic form; that is, each stanza of
text is sung to the same music (like a hymn—AAAA). Schubert's
"Seligkeit" (Bliss) is an example of a strophic lied. The simplicity of
this form works well when the poetry is conveying a single mood and
the composer is able to write music which transmits the general
character of that mood.

If, however, the composer wishes to portray specific nuances of
the text, then a less restrictive form is used. The composer may retain
the strophic skeleton of the music, varying either the melody, the
accompaniment, or both (A $A^1A^2A^3$, etc.). In "Vergebliches Ständchen" (The Fruitless Serenade), for example, Brahms varies the
piano figuration in each of the four stanzas and shifts from A major to
A minor in the third stanza (when the male character tells the female
character that he wants to come inside the house with her because he
is so cold that his love might die). The voice part remains almost the
same for all four stanzas except for the expected alterations that
occur when the music moves to A minor in stanza three and a slight
change in the voice part at the beginning of stanza four when the

female character flippantly responds to her admirer.

If a composer does not wish to repeat musical material but prefers to respond to every change in the text with new music, a song form called "through-composed" (ABCD, etc.) results. This form allows the composer great freedom to present the text in the most colorful or creative fashion, as in Schubert's "Erlkönig" (Erlking).

Another common song form in lieder is a three-sectioned (ternary) form with a contrasting middle section (ABA or ABA'). Brahms cast many of his songs, such as "Ständchen" (Serenade), in a three-part structure; the second stanza of Franz Kugler's poem is set to music that contrasts in key, figurations, and rhythms to the first and third stanzas of music. The returning A section of the song, using the third stanza of Kugler's poem, has the same voice line as stanza one, with a slightly different figuration in the accompaniment.

Some songs do not fit neatly into any of these categories. "Gretchen am Spinnrade," for example, with its verse and refrain structure (RARBRCR or ABACADA), is often called through-composed, but it could just as easily be described as a rondo, a form not generally associated with nineteenth-century vocal music. Robert Schumann's setting of "Und wüssten's die Blumen, die kleinen" (And If the Little Flowers Knew) is mostly strophic until he reaches the final stanza of text—AAAB. Fanny Mendelssohn set this same poem in a binary structure, using two stanzas of poetry for every one stanza of her music—ABAB.

We associate the works of particular poets with certain composers: Schumann with Heine and Eichendorff, Schubert with Goethe and Müller, Wolf with Mörike, Eichendorff, and Goethe. A composer's affinity for a particular poet reveals a subtle view of that composer's psyche; in fact, the character of a composer's music can often be associated with his inspiration from a particular poet. A reflective, introverted Schumann unveils his own dream world as he defines unfulfilled romantic longing in the intimacy of nature with Eichendorff's poems; Wolf's realism, humor, and subtle depiction of character are revealed in his choice of other, more direct Eichendorff poems. The composer can find kindred spirits in the poetic world that suit his musical language, or he can chose to impose upon a poem such a unique vision that some readers fail to find what they are sure was the intended meaning of the poetry.

The range of subject matter and emotion in the poetry selected by art song composers had a subtle effect on their songs. Some of the north German composers such as the Mendelssohns and Johannes

Brahms (until he wrote the *Four Serious Songs* at the end of his life) usually chose poetry that was lyrical in nature and expressed a slightly more limited emotional range than that explored by Wolf. The resulting songs were flowing, lyrical, and less distinctive in character than some of the songs of Wolf or Schubert. These composers tended to be less interested in highlighting individual words and phrases or in using extensive word-painting. Certainly both Schubert and Wolf wrote many songs that rhapsodized on Spring, love—both requited and unrequited—and beauty, but they also explored tough, bitter, more psychological topics in songs such as "Der Doppelgänger" (The Double) and the *Winterreise* songs of Schubert, and "Herr, was trägt der Boden hier" (Father, What Does This Ground Yield Here) or "Wie viele Zeit verlor ich" (How Much Time I Have Lost) of Wolf. Schumann also approached the darker side of human nature in some of his Heine settings.

Can a reputable composer misinterpret a poem? Jack Stein, in his provocative book *Poems and Music in the German Lied*, accuses Schumann, a composer with impressive literary credentials, of grossly misreading the Heine poem "Im Rhein, im heiligen Strome" (In the Rhine, in the Holy Stream) in *Dichterliebe*.[17] Stein also states that Schubert's "Der Doppelgänger" can be appreciated "only if [the listener] suppresses Heine altogether, for it is painfully wrong in its interpretation of the poem."[18] Elaine Brody and Robert Fowkes, on the other hand, state in *The German Lied and Its Poetry* that [in "Der Doppelgänger"] "Schubert surpasses many of his own extraordinary achievements. He changes the music to suit the text."[19] And Charles Osborne, in *The Concert Song Companion*, calls "Der Doppelgänger" "the greatest of all."[20] How can this song be so variously perceived? Since these reactions to "Der Doppelgänger" are from knowledgeable scholars, one must conclude that subjective responses and different criteria for judgment play a significant rôle in their evaluations.

We know that a composer can establish an appropriate mood for the text and can even imitate extramusical sounds such as bird calls. When words such as *heaven* are placed on a high note or *hell* on a low note, however, word-painting is no longer absolutely literal; a high note of itself does not make us think of heaven, although the combination of word and tone may. But how does a composer suggest irony? Was Schubert expressing irony in "Der Doppelgänger" when the piano echoes the vocal line after the phrase "wohnte mein Schatz" (lived my sweetheart) and "auf demselben Platz" (in the

same place), or is this merely a repeated musical motive? Schumann's
"Das ist ein Flöten und Geigen" (There Is a Fluting and Fiddling)
from *Dichterliebe* presents us with a stronger opportunity for finding
irony. As the lover observes his sweetheart dancing her wedding
dance with another man, the music reflects a jarring, noisy figure in
the left hand of the piano part. What about the performer's rôle in the
interpretation of the song? Certainly some choice and responsibility
for conveying irony must rest here.

Suppose Schumann or Schubert did not perceive the poet's
irony? Stein admits that Heine's poetry has not been universally
understood. Nevertheless, Schumann's lyrical, meditative gifts produce some of the most beautiful, expressive lieder.

Hugo Wolf is credited with great taste in his choice of poetry, in
conveying the most subtle shades of poetic meaning, and in slavishly
deferring to the poet. He always read a poem aloud before performing a song, and in lieder collections such as his settings of
Mörike's poetry, he places the poet's name above his own on the title
page. Yet Wolf is also credited with creating ideas where they did not
previously exist in a poem. In his discussion of Wolf's *Italienisches
Liederbuch* (Italian Songbook), based on a number of anonymous
poems translated into German by Paul Heyse, Wolf's biographer
Frank Walker states that

> taking these translations as a starting-point . . . the composer
> allowed his imagination to play about them freely. Often he
> imposed his own will upon the words, expressing by the
> virtuosity of his handling of the vocal line shades of meaning and
> emotion that certainly never occurred either to the unknown
> authors of the original Italian poems or to Heyse.[21]

A song must be examined on its own terms. It is not a poem or the
strict recitation of a poem; nor is it a purely abstract musical work
with no verbal association. It is a new medium with its own artistic
rules. Just as a novel that is made into a film creates a new and different artistic entity from the original novel, so a composer, in creating a song, uses text as only part of a new whole. The lied when considered as a unique entity provides a variety of often conflicting
answers to many of the artistic questions that have been posed about
the relationship between poetry and music. Schubert and Brahms
molded exquisite songs around mediocre poetry and created songs of
profundity and beauty. Schumann's musical meditations, relying on
the piano rather than the voice to establish mood and explore
uncharted musical territory, may often have explored more of his own

inner world than that of the poet. Wolf was thorougly attuned to every nuance of his chosen text so that rhythm, harmony, and melody are inseparably linked to the poetry. Each composer brilliantly yet uniquely defined the relationship of poetry and music in his own terms.

Figure 1-4. Title page to the second complete edition of Hugo Wolf's setting of Goethe's poetry. Wolf placed the poet's name above his own.

Politics and Poetry

The political defeat of Greece was the greatest failure of culture: for it has brought with it the revolting theory that one can foster culture only when one is armed to the teeth.

—Nietzsche[1]

Political freedom may be the true nourishment of poetry.
—Robert Schumann[2]

Composers, performers, painters, and philosophers have often been in the forefront of political movements and have thrust before the eyes of the public the compelling social and economic issues of their day. *Guernica* was Picasso's devastating protest against war, repression, and Fascism; Beaumarchais's controversial play *Le Mariage de Figaro* was banned because it dared to expose the aristocracy's abuse of the lower classes; and many of the poets and composers of the eighteenth and nineteenth centuries were caught up directly or indirectly in the political turmoil that typified revolution and nationalism. The poet Christian Daniel Schubart (1739–91), immortalized by Schubert in his setting of "Die Forelle," was imprisoned for ten years because of his political beliefs; composer Johann Friedrich Reichardt (1752–1814) lost his post as Kapellmeister to the court of Berlin because of his liberal ideas and sympathy for the French Revolution; the political writings of Heinrich Heine (1797–1856) were banned in Germany, and he was forced to live in exile for the last twenty-five years of his life. The visual and literary arts have an immediacy that has allowed them to communicate messages directly to the public. But music, with the assistance of words, has also participated in the political arena of its day.

HISTORICAL SETTING

We want to be careful about calling something German: in the first place, it is the language; but to understand this as an expression of the folk character is a mere phrase, and so far it has not been possible to do so with any people without fatal vagueness and figures of speech.

—Nietzsche[3]

Until the end of the eighteenth century, most German-speaking people had little sense of identity. They were scattered in disunited groups throughout a multitude of German principalities and in the Hapsburg empire. The Hapsburg empire itself consisted of a tremendous mixture of groups: Germans, Magyars, Italians, Czechs, Slovaks, Ruthenians, Rumanians, Serbs, Croatians, Slovenians, and Poles.

During the first half of the eighteenth century, the French culture was admired in many parts of continental Europe. The Russian court spoke French and mimicked French manners. Even the great Prussian conqueror Frederick the Great (1712–1786) wrote his hundreds of pages of military, philosophical, and literary works in French. He, like most of his intellectual contemporaries, considered his native language, German, to be crude and uncouth. Believing himself to be an enlightened despot, he had been shaped by the French philosophes. Yet his great military victories planted seeds of German identity and pride.

The new century began with tumult and change for all of Europe as it reeled from the effects of the French Revolution. In France itself, the chaos of the revolution made the nation vulnerable to a dictator: less than ten years after the revolution, Napoleon Bonaparte came to absolute power. And the European aristocracy had seen its worst fears realized—the revolt of the lower classes. They looked now with justified apprehension toward their populace, for the revolution of the French people gave hope to the downtrodden throughout Europe, and the ideal of the individual's right to freedom began to grow.

Figure 2-1. Friedrich Nietzsche. Reproduction of photograph in Karl Werckmeister, *Das Neunzehnte Jahrhundert in Bildnissen,* 1901, vol. 5, p. 585. Courtesy of the Library of Congress.

There were mixed reactions throughout Europe when Napoleon Bonaparte appeared on the stage. His brilliance as a military tactician and political leader temporarily blinded not only his own countrymen but many important foreigners, such as Goethe and Beethoven. Beethoven at first believed that Napoleon would defend the rights of man and free the oppressed peoples of Europe. But Caesar was ambitious. Napoleon declared himself emperor and continued to swallow up state after state, making it clear that his appetite for power was insatiable. German princes, who had at first fallen over one another in a rush to absorb their neighboring territories instead of opposing Bonaparte, were shocked to find not only themselves absorbed but even the "invincible" Prussian army crushed by French forces in the battles of Jena and Auerstädt in October of 1806. (Composer, music critic, and publisher Johann Karl Rellstab found himself financially ruined after the French entered Berlin and quartered many of their men and horses with him at his expense.)

After Napoleon expanded his empire to include much of Europe, national feelings of identity began to ripen. As Napoleon pressured them to participate in a continental system that was dominated by French interests, the various peoples of Europe began to resent the ascendancy of their French neighbors. Napoleon became a catalyst for a multitude of nationalistic movements.

ARTISTIC RENAISSANCE

Actually, the arts were already setting the stage for German nationalism in the late eighteenth century as German-speaking people began to experience a phenomenal literary and philosophical renaissance. Gotthold Lessing (1729–81) was one of the central figures at the beginning of this revival. He helped to steer German authors away from their stifling imitation of French literary models and awoke their interest in Shakespeare, Classical Greece, Rome, and their own heritage.

The bond of their common language became a rallying point in the writings of men like Johann Gottfried Herder (1744–1803) and Johann Gottlieb Fichte (1762–1814). Herder maintained that German-speaking people had a common spirit that was different from other peoples'. He believed that any group who spoke a common language also shared common ideals and evinced a spirit he

called "Volksgeist," a spirit of the people that mirrored their uniqueness. He maintained that, while no society was better than another,
each reflected its individual character. (Fichte took the next step and
claimed that Germans were better than other people.)

Herder's pursuit of Volksgeist led him to collect the folk poetry of
German-speaking people as well as poetry of other countries, which
he published in *Stimmen der Völker in Liedern* (Voices of People in
Songs), an important source of texts for the composers of the
nineteenth century. Brahms's song "Murrays Ermordung" (Murray's
Assassination), a Scottish folk poem, and "Ein Sonett," a poem from
the thirteenth century translated by Herder into German, came from
this collection—as did many others. Herder's involvement with folk
poetry captured the imagination of Germany's greatest literary
figure, Johann Wolfgang von Goethe, who wrote numerous poems
such as "Heidenröslein" in the folk idiom. Schubert's setting of this
poem has become as famous as the poem itself and has entered the
realm of folk song.

Sah ein Knab ein Röslein stehn,	A boy saw a little rose growing,
Röslein auf der Heiden,	A little rose on the heath.
War so jung und morgenschön	It was so young and morning fresh,
Lief er schnell, es nah zu sehn,	He ran up quickly to see it closely,
Sah's mit vielen Freuden,	He looked at it with great joy,
Röslein, Röslein, Röslein rot,	Little rose, little rose, little red rose,
Röslein auf der Heiden.	Little rose on the heath.
Knabe sprach: Ich breche dich,	The boy spoke: I will pick you,
Röslein auf der Heiden!	Little rose on the heath!
Röslein sprach: Ich steche dich,	The rose said: I will prick you
Dass du ewig denkst an mich,	So that you will always think of me,
Und ich will's nicht leiden.	And I will not suffer it.
Röslein, Röslein, Röslein rot,	Little rose, little rose, little red rose,
Röslein auf der Heiden.	Little rose on the heath.
Und der wilde Knabe brach	And the savage boy picked
's Röslein auf der Heiden;	The little rose on the heath;
Röslein wehrte sich und stach,	The rose fought and pricked him,
Half ihm doch kein Weh und Ach,	Cries of grief did not help her,
Musst es eben leiden.	She had to suffer.
Röslein, Röslein, Röslein rot,	Little rose, little rose, little red rose,
Röslein auf der Heiden.	Little rose on the heath.

Johann Ludwig Uhland (1787–1862) also wrote a number of
poems that mirror the simplicity of folk poetry so much that they, like
"Heidenröslein," have also been incorporated into the "canon" of

folk poetry. Many of his lyric poems were set to music by Brahms, Grieg, Liszt, Loewe, Mendelssohn, Hensel, Schubert, Schumann, and Strauss. Uhland, a political activist as well as a poet, was a member of the Frankfurt Assembly of 1848 which attempted to create a liberal German state.

Interest in folk poetry continued and even grew in the nineteenth century. In 1805, Achim von Arnim (1781–1831) and Clemens Brentano (1778–1842) published the first volume of *Des Knaben Wunderhorn* (The Youth's Magic Horn), a collection of folk lyrics (completed in 1808) that would prove to be of the greatest importance to song composers. This collection (although it was not always faithful to original sources nor was all the poetry genuine folk poetry) became a major source book for Felix Mendelssohn, Luise Reichardt, Robert Schumann, Johannes Brahms, Gustav Mahler, Richard Strauss, and Arnold Schoenberg. The Wunderhorn poetry is direct and filled with vitality and bite. Its topics deal with the essence of life: love—"Wer hat dies Liedlein erdacht?" (Who Invented This Little Song?); religion and humor—"Des Antonius von Padua Fischpredigt" (Anthony of Padua Preaches to the Fish); starvation—"Das irdische Leben" (Earthly Life); nature—"Betteley der Vögel" (The Begging Birds); war—"Revelge" (Reveille). A surprising number of poems relate to war: soldiers, deserters, absence from home and sweethearts. Certainly war was a subject with which the peasantry were well acquainted, for they were the helpless pawns of their rulers.

Ich armer Tamboursg'sell!
Man führt mich aus dem G'wölb!
Wär ich ein Tambour blieben,
Dürft ich nicht gefangen liegen.

O Galgen, du hohes Haus,
Du siehst so furchtbar aus!
Ich schau dich nicht mehr an,
Weil i weiss, dass i g'hör dran.

Wenn Soldaten vorbei marschiern,
Bei mir nit einquartiern.
Wenn sie fragen, wer i g'wesen bin:
Tambour von der Leibkompanie.

Gute Nacht, ihr Marmelstein,
Ihr Berg und Hügelein!
Gute Nacht, ihr Offzier,
Korporal und Musketier!

I, poor drummer boy,
They are leading me from my cell.
Had I remained a drummer
I would not be imprisoned.

O gallows, you tall house,
You look so terrible.
I will not look at you anymore,
Because I know, I belong on you.

When soldiers march by,
Who are not quartered with me,
When they ask who I was:
[I say:] Drummer from the main
    company.

Good night, marble stone,
Mountains and little hills.
Good night, officers,
Corporals, and musketeers.

Ich schrei mit heller Stimm:	I scream with a clear voice,
Von Euch ich Urlaub nimm!	I take my leave from you.
Von Euch ich Urlaub nimm!	I take my leave from you.
Gute Nacht! Gute Nacht.	Good night, good night.

("Der Tamboursg'sell" set by Gustav Mahler)

Dedicated to Goethe, and entirely German in origin, *Des Knaben Wunderhorn* raised German morale and fed nationalistic aspirations in the face of the conquering Napoleon. One of the collectors, Brentano, published a number of his own poems that were also used by song composers.

Other German scholars collected folk tales and examined the history of the German language. Jacob Grimm (1785–1863) and his brother Wilhelm (1786–1859) not only published their well-known *Kinder- und Hausmärchen* (Fairy tales), but they embarked on a dictionary of the German language that was so monumented in scope, it was not completed until 1960. Even these two gentle scholars were caught in the political ferment of their age. In 1830, they moved to Göttingen where Jacob was appointed professor and librarian, and Wilhelm was appointed assistant librarian. In 1837, however, they were summarily dismissed from their jobs and banished from Hanover because they had signed a protest after their new king nullified the constitution.

As German writers pursued their linguistic and intellectual identity, they also threw off what they considered to be the bonds of the French Enlightenment, an intellectual movement that had touted reliance on human reason, science, and progress from the past. Herder, like Jean-Jacques Rousseau, abhorred the Enlightenment's glorification of rationalism and artifice and, instead, commended the virtue and simplicity he believed resided in the common people. By asserting the primacy of feeling and intuition over reason, he and other German writers inaugurated the short-lived but significant movement that is now called "Sturm und Drang" (storm and stress), a term taken from the title of a play, (*Sturm und Drang*, 1776) by Friedrich Maximilian von Klinger (1752–1831).

The field of poetry was one of the first areas in which Sturm und Drang made itself felt. Poets began to counter the conventions of mid-eighteenth-century poetry where polish and elegance were considered at least as important as content. Already in the middle of the eighteenth century, the poet Gottlieb Klopstock (1724–1803) exposed what he called the "shallowness" of this approach.

Klopstock was a harbinger of Sturm und Drang, establishing his own fame in a religious epic, *Der Messias*, whose first cantos appeared anonymously in 1748 in the *Bremer Beiträge*. The work was filled with an emotionalism and fervor that marked the beginning of a new ideal: Klopstock's use of unrhymed hexameter and free verse provided an avenue for the young poets of his generation and the next. It became less important for poets to observe classical rules of composition, but it was highly crucial that they reveal their originality and genius by saying something profound and meaningful. Content now took precedence over form. Klopstock became important to many composers of the romantic era: Fanny Mendelssohn Hensel set to music his beautiful lyric poem "Die frühen Gräber" (Early Graves), and the noble hymn of praise "Dem Unendlichen" (To the Infinite God) was one of thirteen Klopstock poems that Schubert set.

Many writers participated at one time or another in the Sturm und Drang wave, including Johann Christian Friedrich Schiller (1759–1805) and Johann Wolfgang von Goethe. Goethe's international fame was first established in 1774 by his Sturm und Drang novel *Die Leiden des jungen Werthers* (The Sorrows of Young Werther). This novel highlighted the nature of the Sturm und Drang movement and stimulated young men all over Europe to imitate the character of Werther's dress, his emotionalism, and even his suicide in the face of unfulfilled love. Another famous product of Goethe's storm and stress period was his ballad "Erlkönig." A young child, riding through the woods with his father (the voice of reason), is frightened to death by the Erlking (mystical, irrational fear). Emotion triumphs over reason . . . tragically.

Wer reitet so spät durch Nacht und Wind?
Es ist der Vater mit seinem Kind;
Er hat den Knaben wohl in dem Arm,
Er fasst ihn sicher, er hält ihn warm.

"Mein Sohn, was birgst du so bang dein Gesicht?"
"Siehst, Vater, du den Erlkönig nicht?
Den Erlenkönig mit Kron und Schweif?"
"Mein Sohn, es ist ein Nebelstreif."

"Du liebes Kind, komm, geh mit mir!
Gar schöne Spiele spiel ich mit dir;
Manch bunte Blumen sind an dem Strand,

Who is riding so late through the night and the wind?
It is a father with his child;
He has the boy in his arms,
He holds him securely and keeps him warm.

"My son, why are you so anxiously hiding your face?"
"Don't you see the Erlking, father?"
"The Erlking with crown and train?"
"My son, it is a streak of mist."

"You lovely child, come with me.
I will play wonderful games with you.
Many colorful flowers grow on the shore,

Meine Mutter hat manch gülden Gewand."	My mother has many golden dresses."
"Mein Vater, mein Vater, und hörest du nicht, *Was Erlenkönig mir leise verspricht?"* *"Sei ruhig, bleibe ruhig, mein Kind:* *In dürren Blättern säuselt der Wind."*	"My father, my father, don't you hear What the Erlking is whispering to me?" "Be calm, remain calm, my child: It is only the wind whispering in the dry leaves."
"Willst, feiner Knabe, du mit mir gehn? *Meine Töchter sollen dich warten schön;* *Meine Töchter führen den nächtlichen Reihn* *Und wiegen und tanzen und singen dich ein."*	"Will you go with me, fine boy? My beautiful daughters will wait upon you: Every night my daughters lead the round dance, And will rock you and dance and sing to you."
"Mein Vater, mein Vater, und siehst du nicht dort *Erlkönigs Töchter am düstern Ort?"* *"Mein Sohn, mein Sohn, ich seh es genau:* *Es scheinen die alten Weiden so grau."*	"My father, my father, don't you see the Erlking's daughters There in the shadows?" "My son, my son, I see clearly: The old willows appear very gray."
"Ich liebe dich, mich reizt deine schöne Gestalt; *Und bist du nicht willig, so brauch ich Gewalt."* *"Mein Vater, mein Vater, jetzt fasst er mich an!* *Erlkönig hat mir ein Leids getan!"*	"I love you, your beautiful form entices me; And if you are not willing, I will use force." "My father, my father, he is grabbing me! The Erlking has hurt me!"
Dem Vater grauset's, er reitet geschwind, *Er hält in Armen das ächzende Kind,* *Erreicht den Hof mit Mühe und Not:* *In seinen Armen das Kind war tot.*	The father shudders, he rides swiftly, He holds the groaning child in his arms, He reaches the courtyard, weary and anxious; In his arms, the child was dead.

(A fascination with the supernatural and the fantastic was prevalent throughout Europe during this period. In the world of art, Henry Fuseli's *The Nightmare* [1781] pictures a frightening vision of the human mind, and Goya painted and etched a variety of demons and witches. A unique blend of German and French influences can be seen in the works of English writer Ann Radcliffe, particularly in her Gothic novel of 1794, *The Mysteries of Udolpho*.)

Goethe, an intellectual as well as a poetic giant, responded to a staggering array of changes that occurred during his long life of eighty-three years. His writing was always fresh, incorporating new literary modes while exhibiting a Mozart-like fluency and ease of style. He participated fully in the crosscurrents of his age and met many other great figures of his day.

By the end of the eighteenth century, the German-speaking world had living in its midst such eminent figures of literature, theater, philosophy, music, and theology as Goethe, Schiller, Immanuel Kant, Georg Wilhelm Friedrich Hegel (1770–1831), Ludwig van Beethoven, Friedrich Schleiermacher (1768–1834), and others. Cultural supremacy was no longer the sole province of the French! Surprisingly, the tiny court at Weimar had managed to attract an impressive number of these luminaries: Christoph Martin Wieland (1733–1813), Goethe, Schiller, and Herder all found a niche in the circle of the Dowager Duchess Anna Amalie, niece of Frederick the Great, and her son Karl August. Anna Amalie, like her uncle, was a talented musician as well as a patron of the arts.

Goethe's comfortable life among the aristocracy was sufficient to dampen any great feelings of revolutionary fervor. He enjoyed his economic prosperity and position of privilege and, like Voltaire, was able to justify the concept of an enlightened despot. In a letter to Bettina von Arnim, Beethoven contrasted his own view of social position with that of Goethe's in the following anecdote:

> Kings and princes can certainly create . . . titles, and hang on ribbons of various orders, but they cannot create great men. . . . Yesterday on the way home we [Beethoven and Goethe] met the whole Imperial family. . . . Goethe slipped away from me and stood to one side. Say what I would, I could not induce him to advance another step, so I pushed my hat on my head, buttoned up my overcoat, and went, arms folded, into the thickest of the crowd. . . . Duke Rudolph took off my hat, after the Empress had first greeted me. . . . Hat in hand, [Goethe] stood at the side, deeply bowing.[4]

In his protected environment, Goethe wrote a wealth of fine works that were to provide nineteenth-century lieder composers with some of their most beautiful texts. *Faust*, *Werther*, and *Wilhelm Meister* were wellsprings for song composers. In fact, more of Goethe's poetry was set to music than that of any other poet with the exception of Heinrich Heine, a member of the next literary generation. Goethe's contribution to the emerging German art song is actually too profound to measure. His poetry was, in itself, filled with music, yet it inspired another kind of music as well. Song composers from Johann Reichardt and Carl Zelter to Hugo Wolf and Richard Strauss were aroused to sing his verses. The subjective nature of his poetry, along with its fluid, lyrical beauties, became the soul of the lied.

Friedrich von Schiller, another literary Titan who, in the last part of his life, resided in Weimar, found himself less willing than Goethe to see the political status quo maintained. He had suffered injustice as a young man at the hands of the ruling aristocracy when he was forced by Duke Karl Eugen of Württemberg to attend military school and prepare for a career as a regimental surgeon. His early writings, and especially his Sturm und Drang play *Die Räuber* (The Robbers), exhibit his rebellious spirit. Some of his revolutionary dramas later attracted another artist who longed for the unification of his own fragmented country—the Italian composer Giuseppe Verdi. Verdi adapted several of Schiller's plays into operas: *Die Räuber* became *I masnadieri*, *Kabale und Liebe* became *Luisa Miller*, and *Don Carlos* became an opera of the same name. Gioacchino Rossini's final opera, *Guillaume Tell*, was also based on a Schiller play. Beethoven, of course, used part of Schiller's "An die Freude" in the last movement of the Ninth Symphony.

While Schiller's lyric poetry is considered the least successful of his literary output, his great essays, reflective poetry, and dramatic ballads were not easily set to music. Nevertheless, he appears to have been one of Schubert's favorite poets after Goethe and Wilhelm Müller: Schubert set forty-two poems by Schiller. Some of these lieder are very long and seem to bog down in musical graphics, yet "Gruppe aus dem Tartarus" (The Group in Tartarus) is one of his greatest songs.

Horch—wie Murmeln des empörten Meeres,	Listen—like the murmuring of an angry sea,
Wie durch hohler Felsen Becken weint ein Bach;	As a creek weeps through its hollow, rocky basin,
Stöhnt dort dumpfigtief ein schweres, leeres,	Sounds there a deep, heavy, empty Tormented groan
Qualerpresstes Ach!	
	Pain distorts
Schmerz verzerret	Their faces, despair opens
Ihr Gesicht—Verzweiflung sperret	Their cursing mouths.
Ihren Rachen fluchend auf.	Their eyes are empty—their gaze
Hohl sind ihre Augen, ihre Blicke	Peers fearfully on the bridge over
Spähen bang nach des Cocytus Brücke,	Cocytus,
Folgen tränend seinem Trauerlauf.	Following its sad course with tears.
Fragen sich einander ängstlich leise,	Fearfully they ask one another softly
Ob noch nicht Vollendung sei?	Whether there is no end.
Ewigkeit schwingt über ihnen Kreise,	Eternity oscillates over them in circles
Bricht die Sense des Saturns entzwei.	And breaks Saturn's scythe in two.

Nationalism was slow to manifest itself on the concert stage. Italian arias were a typical feature of a normal German concert program, while the blossoming German lied was only heard at home and was rarely performed in the concert hall until the 1830s.[5] German audiences continued to prefer French and Italian opera well into the beginning of the nineteenth century. Even Beethoven's great *Fidelio* was modeled on the French Revolutionary rescue opera. But when Carl Maria von Weber's *Der Freischütz* burst onto the German operatic stage in 1821, German romantic opera became a major force.

ROMANTICISM

I am made unlike any one I have ever met; I will even venture to say that I am like no one in the whole world. I may be no better, but at least I am different.

—Rousseau[6]

Fervent emotionalism and rejection of eighteenth-century rationalism, an appreciation for fairies and the fantastic, the cult of the individual and his isolation from society, a reveling in nature, a love of the past, and the glorification of romantic love were features of a movement called romanticism. The major manifestations of this movement were literary and occurred in the last half of the eighteenth century and the first quarter of the nineteenth. The writer Johann Paul Friedrich Richter (1763–1825), better known to his many admirers as Jean Paul, seemed to embody the extravagant fervor, passion, and humor of the era. The unrestrained feelings he expressed struck a responsive chord in such composers as Felix Mendelssohn, Fanny Mendelssohn Hensel, and Robert Schumann, who all read his works with enthusiasm. Novelist and musician E. T. A. Hoffmann (1776–1822) shared a rôle similar to Jean Paul's. Hoffmann was thoroughly a part of the romantic era, and although he did not participate directly in the development of the lied, his imaginative novels—filled with the mysterious and the grotesque— were an important part of the fabric of the period.

August Wilhelm Schlegel and his brother Friedrich propelled romanticism forward with their periodical, the *Athenäum* (1798– 1800), which became the vehicle for defining the movement's ideals. The Schlegels, who both had some of their poems set to music, were thoroughly immersed in the intellectual and social ferment of their society; their circle of friends and acquaintances, like Goethe's, was important to the intellectual growth of German culture. Novalis (1772–1801), Schleiermacher, Madame de Staël, Dorothea Veit—daughter of Moses Mendelssohn and eventually the wife of Friedrich Schlegel—Ludwig Tieck, the Grimm brothers, and Johann Friedrich Reichardt and his daughter Louise Reichardt were all part of this society.

The term *romantic* has caused considerable discussion and dispute among scholars when it is imposed on music. Historians rightly point out that those qualities which are defined as either classic or romantic can be found in all musical eras. Carl Dahlhaus in his comprehensive discussion of romanticism concludes that one might use romanticism to mean "a collective name without necessarily being reconstructable from an underlying structure or substance from which all of its elements derive."[7]

Romanticism is an important concept in the German art song since the lied is so closely wedded to the literary movements that preceded and paralleled it. All of the romantic literary themes are present in the lied: the artist as a wanderer cast out from society, a reveling in nature, a love of the past and the exotic (including the Greeks, the Romans, the Persians, Shakespeare, the Middle Ages), supernatural forces, ghosts, fairies (Loewe's "Erlkönig," "Elvershoh," [Elves' Mountain] and "Tom der Reimer"), and of course, love—the most popular topic of the lied.

The artist as an outsider, a wanderer, is a powerful, poignant theme in many of Schubert's songs. Both of his song cycles: *Winterreise* and *Die schöne Müllerin* (The Beautiful Miller Maid) exhaustively explore this subject. *Winterreise* begins with the words: "Fremd bin ich eingezogen, Fremd zieh ich wieder aus" (I came here a stranger, I depart a stranger). His song, "Der Wanderer" (The Wanderer), the second most popular lied in the nineteenth century after "Erlkönig," expresses the forlorn message "Ich bin ein Fremdling überall . . . 'Dort, wo du nicht bist, dort ist das Glück!' " (I am a stranger everywhere; "there, where you are not, there is happiness!").

The artist's love of nature is sometimes coupled with isolation from human society. The young miller in *Die schöne Müllerin* finds his only companion and friend to be a brook! The wanderer in *Winterreise* finds his emotions mirrored by the winter landscape. Yet the theme of nature as something joyful, something in which to rejoice, is also expressed over and over. Fanny Mendelssohn Hensel's last song sets Eichendorff's "Bergeslust" (Mountain Joy).

O Lust vom Berg zu schauen	O, what a joy to look from the mountain
weit über Wald und Strom,	Far over the forest and stream,
hoch über sich den blauen,	High above is the blue,
den klaren Himmelsdom,	The clear dome of heaven,
tief klaren Himmelsdom.	The deep, clear dome of heaven.
Vom Berge Vögel fliegen,	From the mountain, birds fly
und Wolken so geschwind,	And clouds flow by quickly.
Gedanken überfliegen	Thoughts fly over
die Vögel und den Wind.	The birds and the wind.
Die Wolken ziehn hernieder,	The clouds go down,
das Vöglein senkt sich gleich,	The bird sinks down also,
Gedanken gehn und Lieder	Thoughts and songs soar
bis in das Himmelreich,	Into heaven.
Gedanken gehn und Lieder	Thoughts and songs go
fort bis in's Himmelreich.	Straight to heaven.

Without any apparent conflict in the romantic mind, a growing sense of nationalism could coexist with a love of the exotic. Poets and musicians were fascinated with Oriental themes, poetic forms, and poets. Brahms, for example, set several of Daumer's translations of the fourteenth–century lyrical poet, Hafiz (Shamsuddin Mohammed). Goethe's and Marianne von Willemer's *West-östlicher Divan* (1819) was inspired by a German translation of Hafiz's poetry, and after reading this collection, other poets used the names of Suleika and Hafiz in their poems. The *Divan* poems were themselves set to music by many composers including Schubert, Mendelssohn, and Wolf. An Arabian poetic form, the ghazal, was also popular for a short time in Germany during this period, but the form was so difficult to manipulate, with its multiple repetitions of the same rhyme, that its popularity waned quickly despite the efforts of Rückert and other poets to promote its use. An acquaintance of Rückert, August von Platen (1796–1835), an excellent scholar in his own right as well as an antagonist of romanticism, published a volume of poems entitled *Ghasel* (1821). Schubert set one of his ghasals, "Du liebst mich nicht" (You Love Me Not), and Brahms set another, "Der Strom, der neben mir verrauschte" (The Stream Which Rushed by Me). Louis Spohr set to music a ghasal by Adil.

An interest in the exotic was accompanied by a growing admiration for Shakespeare. Herder was to awaken Goethe's admiration for Shakespeare in their first meeting, and Herder's important essay on Shakespeare stimulated interest among other German intellectuals as well. Increasing awareness of this English genius eventually culminated in a brilliant translation of Shakespeare's plays into German by August Wilhelm von Schlegel, Dorothea Tieck (daughter of Ludwig Tieck), and Graf W. H. Baudissin[8] that not only became the standard German version but also became a source of inspiration for the German art song. Schubert set several translations of poems by Shakespeare ("An Silvia" [To Silvia] and "Ständchen") as did Richard Strauss (*Drei Lieder der Ophelia*), Brahms (*Fünf Lieder der Ophelia*), Schumann ("Schlusslied des Narren"—Final Song of the Fool), and Wolf ("Lied des transferierten Zettel"—Song of the Exchanged Note).

Other important romantic poets for the lied were Joseph von Eichendorff and Friedrich Rückert. Master of thirty languages as well as professor of Oriental languages, Rückert wrote lyric poetry that was set to music by Schubert, Schumann, Mahler, Carl Loewe, and Brahms. Mahler, in particular, found inspiration in Rückert's work, and some historians suggest that it was Rückert's oriental mysticism, exemplified in such poems as "Nun seh' ich wohl" (Now I see) from the *Kindertotenlieder* that provides a link between Mahler and his cultivation of the oriental in his *Das Lied von der Erde*.[9] Rückert's fluency in handling all poetic forms including the ghasal resulted in a wealth of material for nineteenth-century song writers.

Ich atmet' einen linden Duft.	I breathed linden perfume,
Im Zimmer stand	In the room stood
Ein Zweig der Linde,	A branch of the linden tree
Ein Angebinde	A gift
Von lieber Hand.	From a beloved hand.
Wie lieblich war der Lindenduft!	How lovely was the linden's scent!
Wie lieblich ist der Lindenduft!	How lovely is the linden's scent!
Das Lindenreis	That sprig of linden
Brachst du gelinde;	you gently broke;
Ich atme leis	I lightly breathe
Im Duft der Linde	In the perfume of the linden,
Der Liebe linden Duft.	The perfume of love.

("Ich atmet' einen linden Duft" set by Gustav Mahler in 1902)

Rückert, politically responsive to his era, published a volume of poetry in 1814 that included sonnets opposing Napoleon.[10]

Eichendorff was acquainted with many prominent romantics of his day including Friedrich Schlegel, Achim von Arnim, and Clemens Brentano. His beautiful musings on night, moonlight, the rustling forest, and longing for the past are exquisitely reflected in Robert Schumann's *Liederkreis* (Song Cycle), Op. 39. Brahms, Wolf, and the Mendelssohns all cherished the great lyric beauty of Eichendorff's poetry.

Es war, als hätt' der Himmel	It was as if heaven
Die Erde still geküsst,	Quietly kissed the earth,
Dass sie im Blütenschimmer	So that earth, with her shimmering
Von ihm nun träumen müsst.	flowers,
	Must dream only of heaven.
Die Luft ging durch die Felder,	
Die Ähren wogten sacht,	The breeze went through the fields,
Es rauschten leis die Wälder,	The corn billowed gently,
So sternklar war die Nacht.	The forest rustled lightly,
	So clear and star-filled was the night.
Und meine Seele spannte	
Weit ihre Flügel aus,	And then my soul
Flog durch die stillen Lande,	Spread wide its wings,
Als flöge sie nach Haus.	Flew through the still land
	As if it were flying home.

("Mondnacht"—Moonlit Night, set by Robert Schumann in the *Liederkreis*)

The poetry of Heinrich Heine was a major source for the German lied. There are literally thousands of settings of his poems besides those of Schubert, Schumann, Loewe, Brahms, Liszt, Wagner, Strauss, the Mendelssohns, Wolf, and Franz. Ironically, Heine's contribution to the lied, this magnificent, uniquely German art genre, was viewed as anything but "German" during the Nazi era. Politics again assert themselves, this time on the dead. Heine, the political refugee of the nineteenth century became Heine, the "racially impure" of the twentieth century.

Schubert, in the last years of his life, set six of Heine's poems, which were published posthumously in a diverse collection of songs titled by the publisher, Haslinger, *Schwanengesang* (Swansong). Schubert's profound response to Heine's work set a standard for other composers that has rarely been equalled. Heine's *Lyrisches Intermezzo* (1822–23), a collection of sixty-five poems, became an important source for many composers. Robert Schumann selected and arranged sixteen of these poems for his famous cycle *Dichterliebe*. "Les deux grenadiers," Heine's French version of the noble "Die Grenadiere," even drove the anti-Semitic Wagner to song. Schumann's setting of the original German poem, which he called "Die beiden Grenadiere," is one of his most famous songs.

Nach Frankreich zogen zwei
  Grenadier',
Die waren in Russland gefangen.
Und als sie kamen ins deutsche
  Quartier,
Sie liessen die Köpfe hangen.

Da hörten sie beide die traurige Mär:
Dass Frankreich verloren gegangen,
Besiegt und geschlagen das tapfere
  Heer
Und der Kaiser, der Kaiser gefangen.

Da weinten zusammen die Grenadier'
Wohl ob der kläglichen Kunde.
Der eine sprach: "Wie weh wird mir,
Wie brennt meine alte Wunde!"

Der andre sprach: "Das Lied ist aus,
Auch ich möcht mit dir sterben,
Doch hab ich Weib und Kind zu Haus,
Die ohne mich verderben."

"Was schert mich Weib, was schert
  mich Kind,
Ich trage weit besser Verlangen;
Lass sie betteln gehn, wenn sie hungrig
  sind—
Mein Kaiser, mein Kaiser gefangen!

Gewähr mir, Bruder, eine Bitt':
Wenn ich jetzt sterben werde,
So nimm meine Leiche nach Frank-
  reich mit,
Begrab mich in Frankreichs Erde.

Das Ehrenkreuz am roten Band
Sollst du aufs Herz mir legen;
Die Flinte gib mir in die Hand,
Und gürt mir um den Degen.

So will ich liegen und horchen still,
Wie eine Schildwach', im Grabe,
Bis einst ich höre Kanonengebrüll
Und wiehernder Rosse Getrabe.

Dann reitet mein Kaiser wohl über
  mein Grab,
Viel Schwerter klirren und blitzen;
Dann steig ich gewaffnet hervor aus
  dem Grab—
Den Kaiser, den Kaiser zu schützen!"

To France were returning two
  grenadiers
Who had been prisoners in Russia.
And when they came to the German
  quarters,
They hung their heads.

They heard there the sad news
That France was lost,
Their courageous army conquered and
  beaten,
And the Emperor, the Emperor
  captured!

The grenadiers wept together
Over the sad news.
One said, "Oh woe is me,
How my old wounds burn!"

The other spoke: "the song is done.
I would die with you
But I have a wife and child at home,
Who will die without me."

"What do I care about wife or child!
I recognize a stronger claim;
Let them beg, if they are hungry—
My Emperor, my Emperor is captured!

Brother, grant me one favor:
If I die now,
Take my body to France.
Bury me in French soil.

My cross of honor with the red band
You must lay on my heart;
Put my rifle in my hand
And my sword next to me.

Thus will I lie and listen silently,
Like a sentry, in my grave,
Until I hear the cannon roar
And the neighing of trotting horses;

Then my Emperor will ride over my
  grave,
Swords clanking and flashing;
I will rise, fully armed from the grave—
My Emperor, my Emperor to defend."

This poem reflects Heine's admiration for Napoleon, an admiration he later tempered but never lost because of Napoleon's liberalization of laws pertaining to the Jews.

Heine's great lyric gift allowed him to portray with the utmost delicacy the most exquisite emotions, which he would then often ridicule or obliterate in a single phrase.

Wenn ich in deine Augen seh',	When I look into your eyes
So schwindet all mein Leid und Weh;	All my grief and pain disappears
Doch wenn ich küsse deinen Mund,	And when I kiss your lips
So werd' ich ganz und gar gesund.	Then I become completely well.
Wenn ich mich lehn' an deine Brust,	When I lie on your breast
Kommt's über mich wie Himmelslust;	Profound happiness comes over me,
Doch wenn du sprichst: Ich liebe dich!	But when you say: I love you
So muss ich weinen bitterlich.	Then I must weep bitterly.

("Wenn ich in deine Augen seh'" used by Schumann in *Dichterliebe*)

The beautiful simplicity of these four-line stanzas is fairly typical of Heine's style, influenced as it was by folk song. His use of cynicism and irony following images of lyrical beauty carries the real world into the poetic realm and foretells the end of romanticism. As one modern critic has said, "his poetic imagination creates a mood or a picture which his critical observation then rejects as not corresponding to reality."[11]

AFTER THE CONGRESS OF VIENNA

In 1815, the Congress of Vienna restored peace among the European governments but failed to address the nationalistic sentiments that were festering on the Continent. The reactionary Austrian minister, Metternich, fearing the secret societies and spirit of unrest that were growing in German universities, called a meeting of the amorphous German federation of states to which Austria belonged and intimidated its members into passing the Carlsbad Decrees (1819). These decrees successfully supressed the free exchange of ideas in the following years by censoring all books, magazines, and newspapers while at the same time placing government officials in the universities to keep watch over professors and students. Unrest and repression of free expression marked the following years.

THE REVOLUTION OF 1848

In 1848, revolution in France inspired insurrection in Hungary and Austria. Metternich resigned and the revolution spread to the German states. Although serfdom was abolished, the revolution itself was eventually suppressed. Musicians were, of course, not immune from the chaos and turmoil of the revolution. Robert and Clara Schumann, leaving their children behind, fled from Dresden during the uprising of 1849 to prevent Robert from being conscripted into the army. The singer Wilhelmine Schröder-Devrient was arrested in 1850 as she passed through Dresden because she had been sympathetic to the 1848 revolution. Richard Wagner, who participated in the Dresden uprising on the side of the rebels, was forced into exile from German territory, an exile which lasted until 1860.

The constant suppression of political freedom had taken its toll. Realism began to appear in both politics and literature. Poetic subject matter moved away from the dreamy and the ideal. The image of the drunken woman in Gottfried Keller's (1819–1890) "Das Köhlerweib ist trunken" (The Charcoal Woman Is Drunk), is lifelike and unvarnished with sentimentality.

Das Köhlerweib ist trunken	The charcoal woman is drunk
Und singt im Wald;	And singing in the woods;
Hört, wie die Stimme gellend	Listen, how piercingly her voice
Im Grünen hallt!	Resounds on the green!
Sie war die schönste Blume,	She was once the most beautiful flower,
Berühmt im Land;	Famous throughout the land,
Es warben Reich' und Arme	Both rich and poor courted her
Um ihre Hand.	For her hand in marriage.
Sie trat in Gürtelketten	With chains at her belt,
So stolz einher;	Proudly she walked around;
Den Bräutigam zu wählen,	To choose a husband
Viel ihr zu schwer.	Was much too hard.
Da hat sie überlistet	But she was outsmarted
Der rote Wein—	By red wine—
Wie müssen alle Dinge	How must all things
Vergänglich sein!	Be fleeting!
Das Köhlerweib ist trunken	The charcoal woman is drunk
Und singt im Wald;	And singing in the woods;
Wie durch die Dämmrung gellend	How piercingly through the twilight
Ihr Lied erschallt!	Her song resounds!

(Set by Hugo Wolf in 1890)

Figure 2-2. Alfred Rethel: *Dance of Death,* 1849. Woodcut. Courtesy of Bruckmann Verlag Bildarchiv, München.

Even Hugo Wolf's early poetic choices reflect an ambivalence to the romanticism of the past and a move toward the pragmatism of the present. When he chose poetry by Eichendorff or Goethe, poets of previous generations, he often chose their more realistic works. In "Der Musikant" (The Musician) by Eichendorff, for example, the musician is not entertaining hopeless love but rather humorously rejecting the advances of pretty girls because they are looking for husbands, and marriage would end his carefree life.

Hugo Wolf found his first major musical inspiration in the lyric poetry of Eduard Mörike. Mörike's romanticism is tempered with realism and humor, also pointing the way to the century's changing mood. It is no accident that of the more than sixty settings of his "Das verlassene Mägdlein"—including Schumann's beautiful setting, which he called "Das verlass'ne Mägdelein" (The Abandoned Girl)—it is Wolf's setting that best translates into music, with the aid of a harmonic vocabulary that has vastly expanded from that of his predecessors, the pathos, grayness, and futility of this realistic poem.

Früh, wann die Hähne krähn,	Early, when the cock crows,
Eh' die Sternlein schwinden,	Before the stars disappear,
Muss ich am Herde stehn,	I must stand at the hearth,
Muss Feuer zünden.	Must kindle the fire.
Schön ist der Flamme Schein,	The light of the flame is beautiful,
Es springen die Funken.	Sparks fly up,
Ich schaue so darein,	I look at them,
in Leid versunken.	Lost in grief.
Plötzlich, da kommt es mir,	Suddenly it comes to me,
Treuloser Knabe,	Faithless boy,
Dass ich die Nacht von dir	That all night, of you
Geträumet habe.	I have dreamed.
Träne auf Träne dann	Then tear after tear
Stürzet hernieder;	Rushes down;
So kommt der Tag heran—	So the day begins—
O ging' er wieder!	Oh, that it were over!

As the century continued, many poets lost the romantic illusion and fervor that had marked their predecessors' works.

Wolf also chose many folk poems that were highly realistic in subject matter:

Du sagst mir, dass ich kein Fürstin sei;	You tell me I'm no princess;
Auch du bist nicht auf Spaniens Thron entsprossen.	Well, you are not a descendant of Spanish royalty yourself!
Nein, Bester, stehst du auf bei Hahnenschrei,	No, my dear, you get up when the cock crows,
Fährst du aufs Feld und nicht in Staatskarossen.	You travel to the fields and not in a royal coach either.
Du spottest mein um meine Niedrigkeit,	You taunt me for my lowly station;
Doch Armut tut dem Adel nichts zuleid.	But poverty doesn't take away a noble spirit.
Du spottest, dass mir Krone fehlt und Wappen,	You taunt me because I have no crown or coat of arms;
Und fährst doch selber nur mit Schusters Rappen.	But you have to travel by means of your own feet.

(Set by Wolf in 1896 from the *Italienisches Liederbuch*)

Both Wolf and Richard Strauss also used poetry with sexual overtones, displaying a more realistic, less mystical view of love and the world. The graphic symbolism of Wolf's "Erstes Liebeslied eines Mädchens" (The Girl's First Love Song, by Mörike) leaves little to the imagination.

Was im Netze?	What's in the net?
Schau einmal! aber ich bin bange;	Look! But I am afraid;
Greif' ich einen süssen Aal?	Am I grabbing an eel?
Greif' ich eine Schlange?	Am I grabbing a snake?
Lieb' ist blinde Fischerin;	Love is a blind fishermaid.
Sagt dem Kinde,	Tell your child
Wo greift's hin?	Where to grab.
Schon schnellt mir's in Händen!	It already goes quickly in my hands!
Ach Jammer! O Lust!	Oh, misery! Oh, delight!
Mit Schmiegen und Wenden	With its nestling and turning,
Mir schlüpft's an die Brust.	It is sliding onto my breast.
Es beisst sich, O Wunder!	Amazing! It brazenly bites
Mir keck durch die Haut,	Its way through my skin,
Schiesst's Herze hinunter!	It shoots my heart down!
O Liebe, mir graut!	O love, I shudder!
Was thun, was beginnen?	What should I do, what's happening?
Das schaurige Ding,	The horrible thing
Es schnalzet dadrinnen,	Is snapping inside,
Es legt sich im Ring.	It's coiling.
Gift muss ich haben!	I must be poisoned!
Hier schleicht es herum,	It crawls around here,
Thut wonniglich graben	Blissfully digging
Und bringt mich noch um!	And killing me!

(Also, see Wolf's "Nimmersatte Liebe" [Insatiable Love] and "Begegnung" [The Meeting] and Strauss's "Heimliche Aufforderung" [Secret Request] and "Cäcilie".)

THE FRANCO-PRUSSIAN WAR
AND GERMAN UNIFICATION

The nationalistic aspirations of many German speaking-people were finally fulfilled in the last quarter of the nineteenth century when Bismarck precipitated war with France and, in 1871, succeeded in forming a German state with Prussia as its nucleus. The unification of Germany was greeted by many Germans such as Clara Schumann's daughter Eugenie with wild pride.

> We had been certain of the successful ending of the war . . . and this made us indescribably happy. Even as a child I had often realised with resentment that the Germans were treated with contempt in their own country by their cosmopolitan visitors. . . . Yet we Germans knew what we were worth, and that we ought to take our place with the great nations. . . . We knew that these were great times, and that the outcome for our Fatherland would be its rightful place, of which it had been deprived for centuries.[12]

Brahms, living in Vienna at this time, followed the unification movement with tremendous interest and excitement. An admirer of Bismarck, Brahms gloried in the unification movement and wrote *Triumphlied* to honor the German victory in the Franco-Prussian War. His musical antipode, Richard Wagner, was also exhilarated by the new German state and hurled graceless taunts at the defeated French. Ironically, this low point in French political affairs was offset by a dramatic musical rebirth in France, giving some credence to Friedrich Nietzsche's statement that "culture owes its peaks to politically weak ages." [13]

Nietzsche (1844–1900) had much to say about the political changes in Germany.

> Political superiority without any real human superiority is most harmful. One must seek to make amends for political superiority. To be ashamed of one's power. To use it in the most salutary way. Everybody thinks that the Germans may now rest on their moral and intellectual superiority. One seems to think that now it is time for something else, for the state. Till now, [the Germans were] for "art," etc. This is an ignominious misunderstanding; there are seeds for the most glorious development of man. And these must perish for the sake of the state? What, after all, is a state? . . . The only way to use the present kind of German power correctly is to comprehend the tremendous obligation which lies in it. Any slackening of cultural tasks would turn this power into the most revolting tyranny. [14]

There is a chilling foresight in that final sentence.

Nietzsche was actively involved in the musical life of his age. Not only was he a competent pianist, but he also had aspirations as a composer. He briefly admired the music of Brahms but eventually dismissed him as lacking inspiration. More than thirty years younger than Richard Wagner, Nietzsche at first acted as an apologist for Wagner's music and musical philosophy. Ultimately, their personalities and musical aesthetics diverged, and they became the most bitter adversaries. Even devoted Wagnerites such as Hugo Wolf nevertheless remained admirers of Nietzsche.

Nietzsche reflected in his philosophical writings many of the changes that marked the second half of the nineteenth century. The systematic documentation of evolutionary processes by Charles Darwin and terms such as "the survival of the fittest" could be translated into Nietzsche's glorification of the superman. Richard Wagner sought the German superman in his *Ring* Cycle. The grand scale on which Wagner worked—huge orchestras, a large stage, massive props, and the necessarily large voices that would carry over the increased orchestral sound—were the antithesis of the intimate art song. Mahler's *Das Lied von der Erde* (1907–08), which incorporates some of these Wagnerian characteristics, is no longer a lied of the recital hall but a grandiose declamation from the concert hall.

Nietzsche had little sympathy for democracy, equality, or the Christian concept of sin. Sometimes called a neopagan, Nietzsche extolled the physically strong, brave, sexually free human who affirms the life force by joyfully seeking self-realization. His influence on following generations was tremendous, spawning a diversity of sophisticated and simplistic responses that extended from Spengler's *Decline of the West* to the Nazi movement. Nietzsche denied the restrictions of nationalism, stating that "I am granted an eye beyond all merely local, merely nationally conditioned perspectives . . . I, the last anti-political German."[15] He strove to teach absolute independence of thought and denied the "true believer."

> You say, you believe in Zarathustra? But of what account is Zarathustra! You are my believers: but of what account are all believers! You had not yet sought yourselves: then did you find me. So do all believers; therefore all belief is of so little account.[16]

His writings, like those in the Bible, have been used to make political judgments and to prove absolutely opposite points of view.

While creating their rich inner worlds, artists are also buffeted by the economic condition of their country and themselves, the demands of their families, the wars that are being fought. The gentle Schubert only escaped being conscripted for military service because he was too short; he was less than five feet tall! Had he been drafted, the art song might be a quite different genre. Some artists have been forced to take a political position or were condemned in the eyes of the world because they did not. This was the case with Richard Strauss, whose musical reputation has been tarnished because of his failure to publicly repudiate the Nazi movement. Although he did not seek his position as president of the Reichsmusikkammer, he also did not refuse it. He was the father-in-law of a Jew and, therefore, the grandfather of Jewish children, and yet he ignored the plight of the Jews in Germany until it was too late. His desire to keep the great Jewish writer Stephan Zweig as his librettist also precipitated a number of crises. After Zweig told Strauss that it would no longer be possible for them to work together because he did not wish to be perceived as collaborating with the Nazi regime,

Strauss wrote the following letter on 17 June 1935:

> Dear Herr Zweig,
>
> Your letter of the 15th is driving me to distraction! This Jewish obstinacy! Enough to make an anti-Semite of a man! This pride of race, this feeling of solidarity! Do you believe that I am ever, in any of my actions, guided by the thought that I am "German" (perhaps, *qui le sait*)? Do you believe that Mozart composed as an "Aryan"? I know only two types of people: those with and those without talent.[17]

As it happened, this letter was intercepted by the Gestapo and caused the Nazis to force Strauss's resignation as president of Reichsmusikkammer. Some have considered Strauss to be as reprehensible as the rabid anti-Semite, Richard Wagner, simply because of Strauss's failure to act in one of history's blackest periods.

The arts and philosophy are often considered to be apolitical, existing in an idealistic realm of thought and experience more abstract than day-to-day realities and compromises. The artist may wish to say: "Lass, o Welt, o lass mich sein" (Let me be, world), but much of what was written by poets, writers, and composers demonstrates their intense involvement in the life of their times, both political and cultural. The German art song was influenced both directly and indirectly by the events that shaped the century in which it flourished. It was not isolated from the world, but it did make the world more bearable.

CHAPTER THREE

The Piano

The pianoforte is still the least studied and developed of all instruments; often one thinks that one is merely listening to a harp. . . . I hope that the time will come when the harp and the pianoforte will be treated as two entirely different instruments.
—Beethoven, 1796[1]

The composer names his songs "Lieder with Piano," and this is important. For the singing voice certainly is not sufficient in itself; it cannot carry out the task of interpretation unaided.
—Robert Schumann, 1843[2]

The piano is a fundamental player in the rise of the nineteenth-century German lied and represents a major factor in the lied's unique equation of voice, poetry, and piano accompaniment. Even the piano's late appearance on the musical scene as a viable musical instrument is an important factor in how and when the German art song developed.

Invented by the Italian Bartolomeo Cristofori at the beginning of the eighteenth century (he began work on this new instrument in 1698, and an 'arpicembalo' is catalogued in the Medici instrument collection in 1700),[3] the piano evolved from an outgrowth of the clavichord and the harpsichord to eventually become a responsive, sophisticated musical intrument with its own unique characteristics. Originally called a pianoforte (meaning soft-loud) because its dynamic level could be controlled by the fingers of the player, the instrument was first built by harpsichord, clavichord, or organ craftsmen. Most of the early instrument makers were Germans, some of whom moved to England and France to become part of the foundation of those nations' piano-building enterprises.

The piano did not gain acceptance among well-known composers until about 1770. Up to this time, its indistinct character and inefficient designs tempted few professional musicians to explore its possibilities.[4] Its tone was dull, and it was not able to produce a sound as loud as that of a large harpsichord.[5] Since some of the early piano makers, such as the French firm Érard, were also manufacturers of harps, Beethoven's statement comparing harps and pianos is not as strange as it might first appear. Monsieur Érard gave Beethoven one of his instruments in 1803, but Beethoven was so dissatisfied with this piano that he had it altered several times and eventually tried to give it away.[6]

As it became more flexible, expressive, and dynamically versatile in the last quarter of the eighteenth century, the piano gradually supplanted the clavichord and harpsichord as both a solo instrument and as an accompanying medium for songs. There was a growing awareness among composers that the piano could produce its own entirely new set of musical effects. The keyboard works of Wolfgang Amadeus Mozart (1756–1791), particularly his piano concerti, represented a major contribution to the growing repertory for this new instrument. Although Mozart showed little interest in writing solo songs, he did compose thirty-six lieder for piano and voice between 1767 and 1791, the most famous being "Das Veilchen" (The Violet) on a text by Goethe.

Mozart's contemporaries, Johann Friedrich Reichardt (1752–1814), Johann Zumsteeg (1760–1802), and Carl Zelter (1758–1832) were also writing songs with piano accompaniment during this period, and the simplicity of many of their piano parts reflects not only the modest status of song during this period but also the as yet unexplored rôle the piano could take in song (Examples 3-1a and 3-1b). The scene was being set for Schubert's over six hundred songs, which would represent a whole new vista for the piano and voice. Schubert's songs would become a major revelation to his successors.

Singing and piano playing were of great importance to the social life of the German middle class during the last half of the eighteenth century and throughout the nineteenth, particularly among girls and women. "Women were expected to cultivate 'feminine' instruments—instruments requiring no alteration in facial expression or physical demeanor. Accordingly, keyboard instruments such as the harpsichord and the piano were deemed especially desirable,

Das Blümchen.

Sih hier, mein liebes Mümchen,
Des jungen Frühlings Pracht.
Es ist das erste Blümchen,
Seit uns die Sonne lacht.

Ins Gras gebeugt und trauernd
Ob seiner Einsamkeit,
Auf einem Amor lauernd
Fand ich das Blümchen heut.

Du nimst es nicht? wie blöde?
Kanst du so grausam seyn?
Bald solt es mich, du spröde!
Daß ich's gepflücket, reun.

Doch nein! ich pflantz es Mümchen,
Dir an die holde Brust.
So stirbst du, erstes Blümchen,
Mit neidenswerther Lust.

Figure 3-1. Das Blümchen, by Johann Friedrich Reichardt.

1. I have loved, now I love the right one!
2. I have believed, now I have the right belief!

Example 3-1a. Zelter, "Gewohnt, getan" (To Do the Customary Thing), mm. 1–4.

Example 3-1b. Zumsteeg, "Ritter Toggenburg" (Knight Toggenburg), mm. 36–38.

all the more because they could be played at home."[7] Since young women frequently attained only a modest level of accomplishment on the piano, composers who wished to appeal to this market sought to write music that was within their capabilities. Many composers wrote songs that had very easy piano accompaniments and often doubled the voice part, either to add extra support for the voice or so that a song could even be performed as a piano solo, without a singer. It is somehow ironic that Felix Mendelssohn would later develop a genre which he called, "Lieder ohne Worte" or "Songs Without Words."

Most early lieder had accompaniments that were not idiomatically conceived for the piano and would work just as well on a harpsichord or clavichord. This was even true for some of the songs by the better-known art song composers, the Reichardts and Carl Zelter, head of the Berlin Singing Academy (Example 3-2; see also Examples 3-1a and 3-1b). Zelter, although a sophisticated musician, had little faith in the German public and refused to challenge its taste. His songwriting, while pleasant, was therefore mostly conventional.

The waves are parting, the horizon is approaching,

Example 3-2. Reichardt, "Glückliche Fahrt" (Happy Journey),
mm. 17–20.

By the end of the eighteenth century, the patronage of music and
musicians became less dominated by a cultivated aristocracy. The
growing middle class began to exhibit its cultural prowess as it entertained itself. Music was being written to include, not just young
women, but every member of the family and continued to be
conceived in a manner that would not tax the abilities of the amateur
musician (Example 3-3). A comparison of these early German songs
to Schubert's shows his to be all the more remarkable, for it is with
him that the intimate partnership of voice, piano, and poetry was
definitively achieved. The originality and unsurpassed beauty of his
songs illustrate Schubert's extraordinary contribution to vocal
literature.

The tooth, the tooth must come out, otherwise it will cause pain,
The tooth, the tooth must come out, and then Gustchen will get some cake,
The tooth, the tooth is out, it's hanging by a thread,

Example 3-3. Schulz, "Ein Lied in die Haushaltung zu singen" (A Song
to Sing at Home), mm. 5–6.

The middle class also provided a lucrative market for piano
manufacturers, music and magazine publishers, and music teachers.
Loesser points out that only one of Beethoven's piano sonatas was
performed in public during his lifetime[8] since solo piano music and
lieder were performed at home rather than in the concert hall. At the
end of the eighteenth century, the Leipzig periodical, *Allgemeine
Musikalische Zeitung* reported that there were more than three
hundred piano teachers in Vienna alone.[9] Voice teachers were also in

great demand. Luise Reichardt, an unmarried woman, took the bold step of moving to Hamburg in 1809 so that she could earn her living as a voice teacher. One of her friends, scholar Wilhelm Grimm, expressed his concern about this decision in a letter to Achim von Arnim: "I don't know whether she will be fortunate enough to get so many pupils right at the start." Within a few weeks after her arrival she had twenty-six pupils![10] Modern voice teachers would find it difficult to establish their studios so rapidly in any town. Most likely the Hamburg burghers were happy to entrust their lovely daughters to the care of a modest woman teacher.

During the nineteenth century, both song and solo piano music became major categories of composition. Robert Schumann might exhort his fellow composers to establish their reputations in traditionally accepted mediums such as the symphony, but his and their success was now often achieved in the more intimate genres such as song and piano solo literature. The refinement of the piano was a fortuitous circumstance for this new era, so committed to individual expression. While the development of the piano's capabilities only partly explains the change of status for these genres, it is, nevertheless, a significant factor. Schubert, Schumann, and Brahms each discovered his own "voice" in writing for the solo piano and translated mastery of the instrument into a brilliant partnership with the human voice. The great lieder composers of the nineteenth century used the piano as a full participant in their songs. Mozart and Haydn, although just as interested in keyboard writing, nevertheless chose not to use their mastery of the piano to tread outside the traditional boundaries of songwriting in their time.

Certainly, a growing sense of the individual's significance played a rôle in stimulating the development of a genre that encouraged self-expression. The American and French revolutions had focused society's awareness on the power and importance of each person's unique characteristics and rights. In the nineteenth-century musical world, this was translated into a glorification of the "artist," whether that meant the composer, the virtuoso performer, or the conductor. Beethoven had appreciated this change as he indicated in his letter to Bettina von Arnim (see Chapter 2, "Politics and Poetry"): "Princes can certainly create . . . titles . . . but they cannot create great men."

Schubert, who benefited little from this changing climate, was usually too poor to have a piano at home. He is said to have owned for a brief time a five-octave piano made by Konrad Graf (1783–1851),[11] one of the best known Viennese piano manufacturers of that time who was later admired by Chopin.[12] Graf placed one of his pianos at Beethoven's disposal in 1825, a piano with a six-and-one-half octave range whose dynamic level was magnified by placing four strings on each note so the deaf Beethoven might hear some sound. Both Schubert and Beethoven also played on pianos made by another famous Viennese firm, that of Nanette and Andreas Streicher.[13]

The Viennese piano had a shallow keyboard, required a light touch, and had an even tone quality from top to bottom. Its tone was beautiful but thin—interesting characteristics when one considers such accompaniments of Schubert's as the undulating figuration for the fish of "Die Forelle" (The Trout), the crystalline scales of "Seligkeit," and the shimmering sound of the Suleika lieder. Many of Schubert's accompaniments incorporated the effortless brilliance of sound that so characterized Mozart's piano writing (Example 3-4).

Example 3-4. Schubert, "Seligkeit" (Bliss), mm. 1–12.

Clarity, warmth, and beauty of tone are everything in this delicate yet exuberant style. Even the relatively simple accompaniment of "Seligkeit" is obviously designed for the piano rather than the harpsichord. The right-hand piano part must be shaped by dynamic gradations to achieve its full beauty. Subtle dynamic and harmonic contrasts were built in to Schubert's writing for the piano as illustrated in Schubert's harmonically bold "Dass sie hier gewesen" (That She Was Here) (Example 3-5).

Schumann points out that

> [Schubert] has something more to offer than others, in some ways, more even than Beethoven (however marvelously the latter, in his deafness, heard with his imagination). This superiority consists in his ability to write more idiomatically for

That the east wind fragrance

Example 3-5. Schubert, "Dass sie hier gewesen" (That She Was Here), mm. 1–4.

Holy night, you descend;

Example 3-6. Schubert, "Nacht und Träume" (Night and Dreams), mm. 1–7.

the piano, i.e. everything sounds as if drawn from the very depths of the instrument, while with Beethoven we must borrow for tone color, first from the oboe, then the horn. (1835)[14]

Schubert also availed himself of the tonal depth and rich sonorities that so characterized Beethoven's writing. Song repertory profited from the piano's ability to produce a warm web of sound out of which beautiful melody could emerge. The accompaniment to Schubert's "Nacht und Träume" (Night and Dreams), written entirely in the bass range of the piano, is a sea of undulating, dreamlike tone with a melodic line that must be defined dynamically to distinguish it from the thick texture of the accompaniment. The voice part is particularly effective as it floats well above the murmuring ripples of the accompaniment (Example 3-6).

The Viennese piano of Schubert's time produced a very clear sound in its bass range. Schubert took advantage of this clarity by frequently giving the bass line of the accompaniment melodic material. In "Fischerweise" (The Fisherman's Way), for example, a charming little melody moves back and forth from the bass line to the upper voices of the accompaniment. There are, of course, numerous songs such as "Die junge Nonne" (The Young Nun), "Der Atlas," and "Erlkönig" with dramatic bass lines that dominate the entire song (Example 3-7).

Example 3-7. Schubert, "Erlkönig" (The Erlking), mm. 2–5.

Schubert is famous for his ability to create a seemingly endless variety of piano figurations, many of them programmatically linked to the text. These figures can be properly termed "romantic" because they are so crucial to the establishment of atmosphere and mood. In "Die Stadt" (The Town), for example, Schubert instantly portrays mist, gloom, and a sense of foreboding; although we can observe that he does this with the assistance of the damper pedal in conjunction with a pedal point tremolo in the bass and the eerie repetition of a diminished seventh chord in the right hand of the piano part, it is still a feat that defies technical analysis (Example 3-8).

Example 3-8. Schubert, "Die Stadt" (The Town), mm. 1–4.

The piano's expanding capabilities in the nineteenth century coincided with the rise of great vituoso performers such as Franz Liszt, Friedrich Wilhelm Kalkbrenner, Marie Moke Pleyel, Sigismond Talberg, and Clara Wieck Schumann. Composers and performers, frequently one and the same, were participants in the development of the piano, for they were eager to let the builders of this new instrument know its limitations and its virtues. They expressed opinions about its responsiveness, tone quality, and durability, while piano manufacturers responded with constant changes and improvements to their instruments.

Piano makers questioned and experimented with every element that went into their pianos: the shape of the piano; how to build frames strong enough to withstand the tremendous tension of the strings; where to place the strings; the number and thickness of strings; where the hammer should strike the strings most efficiently for the most vibrant tone; what materials were best for soundboards, strings, and hammers; how to keep the hammer from rebounding and restriking the strings; how to transfer the vibrations of the strings to the soundboard. The considerations were endless!

Performers were perfectly aware of the different characteristics of English, French, and Viennese pianos and often carried on lively discussions among themselves about the merits and demerits of these instruments. Liszt, Felix Mendelssohn, and Verdi owned Érard pianos; Chopin is said to have preferred the pianos of Pleyel.[15] Fanny Mendelssohn Hensel longed to own an English (Broadwood) piano, while Clara Schumann was often subject to the advertising ploys of piano manufacturers. These manufacturers found it in their best interests to encourage performers and composers to use their particular instrument. Clara Schumann reveals the subtleties of this persuasion in several of her letters to Robert in 1839 during a concert tour in Paris.

> 14 February 1839 (Paris)
>   I have an Érard in my room, which is dreadfully stiff. I had lost all heart, but yesterday I played on a Pleyel and they are a little more manageable. . . . I could have three grand pianos in my room already—everyone wants me to take his. If only I knew how to begin playing on a Pleyel without offending Érard, who has shown me every possible kindness.[16]

> 25 February—I think possibly of playing at the Conservatoire on March 9th, and should I happen to succeed, of giving a concert in Érard's salon.[17]

> 28 February—Where am I to find a lady with whom I can trust myself to go to London, that huge city? I do not know what to do, and I will talk to Érard about it today.[18]

Pierre Érard (nephew and heir of Sébastian Érard who had invented the "double-escapement" action, which allowed for rapid repetition of notes) was the foremost manufacturer of French pianos at this time, and Pleyel was his major French competitor. Both had their own concert halls where they could display the virtues of their instruments. At the same time, they had well-known performers provide an indirect endorsement of their product since the performer was obviously obligated to use the piano of the hall's owner. A little friendship toward the performer was also profitable, as the above quote shows. Clara Wieck was particularly vulnerable to the kindnesses of Érard at this time. She had just lost her father's managerial talents because of their estrangement over her decision to marry Robert Schumann, and she had set off on this concert tour to prove that she was capable of directing her own career.

Clara was to have other difficulties in achieving pianistic independence from her father, whose opposition to her marriage to Robert became cruel and vindictive. In October of 1839, she went to Berlin to give several concerts, but her father wrote a letter to the city councilor, Behrens, and warned him not to let Clara use his piano. Wieck claimed that Clara was so used to playing on English pianos with their stiff action that she broke all other instruments! Fortunately, Herr Behrens kindly allowed Clara to use his piano for

her debut at the Berlin Opera House, a concert which was tumul-
tuously received.[19]

Robert Schumann's rôle as editor for the *Neue Zeitschrift für
Musik* obviously benefited him as a composer for the piano. He
reviewed a wealth of his contemporaries' piano works, methods, and
techniques and reflected on the nature of this wonderful instrument, so ideally suited to nineteenth-century romantic music.
Schumann had an intimate musical knowledge of the era's two most
innovative writers for the piano, Chopin and Liszt. Although Liszt's
virtuosic display in some of his writing was contrary to Schumann's
own aesthetic ideals, Schumann neverthless respected Liszt's creative exploration of the piano's potential. His unfolding of pianistic
effects was a revelation to all composers of the period, for Liszt had
an understanding of the dramatic potential of the piano that has
never been surpassed.

In his song "Die drei Zigeuner" (The Three Gypsies), Liszt
exploits a variety of pianistic devices that do not simply illustrate
Nikolaus Lenau's poem but occur for the sheer joy of bravura
(Example 3-9). Liszt discovered surprising textures and colors while
incorporating the piano's entire range, coupled with every possible
pianistic technique. He trills for the brilliance of the effect, rolls
chords for dramatic emphasis, repeats melodic figures at increasing
tempi to heighten excitement, arpeggiates chords over four octaves,
has the right and left hand in canon an octave apart and a sixteenth
rest apart to lend a virtuosic character to the accompaniment, and has

Example 3-9. Liszt, "Die drei Zigeuner" (The Three Gypsies),
mm. 3–6.

Figure 3-2. Franz Liszt, photograph ca. 1880. Courtesy of the Library of Congress.

an amazing understanding of how the grace note can increase the musical power of his figurations. He writes widespread chords and octave doublings for dramatic emphasis but magnifies even this writing with grace-note chords and sixteenth- and thirty-second-note rhythms (Example 3-10). He frequently shifts to the treble range of the piano as a color contrast to his weighty sonorities, and "even" to illustrate portions of the text, as for example, when he describes the gypsy who is playing his fiddle (mm. 29–32). With a depressed damper pedal and a rising melodic figure that dies away, he highlights the image of delicately rising wisps of smoke (Example 3-11). And he knows the power of silence after noisy bravura: each new section and change of figuration is anticipated with a rest. In the final segment of the song, the voice is in recitative, and a few sparse octaves punctuate the text of the vocal line, an effective contrast after all the previous fireworks.

Example 3-10. Liszt, "Die drei Zigeuner," mm. 61–62.

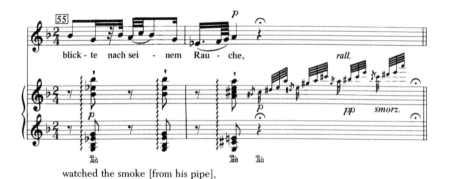

Example 3-11. Liszt, "Die drei Zigeuner," mm. 55–56.

In a review of Loewe's piano music, Schumann discussed those characteristics of the piano which he believed composers must understand if they were to write successfully.

Rich in that inward, deep melody, which characterises his ballads, he [Loewe] selects an instrument, which, to sound and to sing, needs a different treatment from, and produces another effect than, the human voice. Loewe plays truly enough with his fingers what he hears within him. A shabby little pianoforte melody, well sung, may sound pretty well; but a rich melody for the voice only makes half its proper effect on the pianoforte. The older I grow, the more convinced I am that the pianoforte is especially prominent in three leading qualities peculiar to it— fullness and variety in exemplification of harmony (made use of by Beethoven and Franz Schubert), pedal effect (as with Field), and volubility (Czerny, Herz, etc.). The large, broad player exhibits the first, the fantastic artist gives the second, a pearly touch displays the third quality. Many-sided, cultured composer-performers, like Hummel, Moscheles, and, finally, Chopin, combine all these . . . those writers and performers who neglect to study any of these fall into the background.[20]

Since the majority of Schumann's piano pieces were written before his lieder, he had already developed a highly individual pianistic language and knew this instrument's potential for colors and expressive range. In his songs, the piano often takes the lead in its partnership with the voice. Not only does the piano carry much of the musical information, through preludes, postludes, and interludes, but Schumann's writing for the piano is the epitomy of romanticism in music: he is a master at conveying indefinable feelings. The "wash" of sound he achieves with the depressed damper pedal on the unresolved seventh chords of "Im wunderschönen Monat Mai" (In the Beautiful Month of May) creates an atmosphere of unfulfilled longing (Example 3-12). The piano, with its ability to produce nebulous sounds—so unlike the clear, distinct tones of the harpsichord—acts to reinforce the poetic quality of the words.

The piano made it possible to easily control the background figurations in the accompaniments while highlighting melodic materials that moved rapidly from voice to voice in the piano.

Example 3-12. Schumann, "Im wunderschönen Monat Mai" (In the Beautiful Month of May), in *Dichterliebe* (Poet's Love), mm. 1–2.

Schumann's technique of allowing multiple melodies to emerge in the accompaniment reflected not just his understanding of the piano's dynamic capabilities but also a contrapuntal sense that was uniquely transplanted to the romantic piano's vocabulary (Example 3-13).

Example 3-13. Schumann, "Hör ich das Liedchen klingen" (When I Hear the Little Song), in *Dichterliebe*, mm. 19–25.

The ability of the piano with its sustaining pedal to produce both harmony and lyrical melody made it the ideal instrument for the romantic composer and the lied in particular. Historians point out that melody and harmony were becoming so integrated during this period that neither could be heard separately without losing its significance—the whole appears to have become greater than the sum of its parts! The independent, tuneful melodies of Schubert are no longer characteristic of the lied, even in Schumann's generation. Schumann's beautiful melodies are not only shared by piano and voice but are often so harmonically defined as to be less effective without their harmonic underpinnings. In "Mondnacht" from the *Liederkreis*, Op. 39, for example, the voice line sounds pale without its harmonic definition and the counter melody in the bass line

(Example 3-14). And how cleverly Schumann pits the rhythm of the
piano accompaniment against the square rhythmic pattern of the
voice.

Example 3-14. Schumann, "Mondnacht" (Moonlit Night), in
Liederkreis (Song Cycle), mm. 5–13.

The composers who followed Schumann and Liszt profited by
the technical achievements of both. Yet Hugo Wolf used the piano as
just one more significant tool in his arsenal for textual expression. In
his music, harmony and melody are totally integrated and both are
directed toward the most sophisticated exploration of poetic
meaning. His rich harmonic vocabulary is supplied by the piano, and
his vocal lines rarely have the power to stand alone. They only
become whole and illuminated in the presence of the text (see
Chapter 14 on Wolf).

While both Brahms and Strauss were capable of using the piano
with great delicacy and simplicity, they also wrote many songs in
which the piano is given such a mass of sound that its treatment
approaches the grandeur of an orchestra. Brahms's "Meine Liebe ist
grün" (My Love Is Green), with its rich harmonies and dense piano
texture, or Strauss's "Liebeshymnus" (Hymn of Love), exploiting a
five-octave range in the piano part with many octave doublings and
nine-note chords, require from performers careful balancing

between voice and piano, even when the voice part soars above the piano's sound. It is not surprising that their poetic choices are not particularly significant in their songs, for poetry often recedes into the background.

By 1880, major technical innovations in the piano's development were complete. All of the experiments with materials, double-escapement action, pedals, stringing, frames, and soundboards had resulted in the modern piano, capable of producing loud, brilliant sounds that could be heard above large orchestras. One hundred and eighty years of exploration had produced a technically complex musical instrument that could produce its own rich, unique sounds. The piano's great range, dynamic fullness and varied colors were now at the disposal of song. Ironically, composers at the end of the century such as Mahler and Strauss began to move from the piano to the orchestra as the accompanying medium for song.

CHAPTER FOUR

Composers, Performers, and Performances

Full many a flower is born to blush unseen,
And waste its sweetness on the desert air.
  —"Elegy written in a Country Churchyard," by Thomas Gray

It is wishful thinking to believe that all great ideas will eventually be recognized for their inherent worth. Bringing an important idea or creation to the attention of the public can be an insurmountable problem for its creator. The monumental play *Woyzeck*, by Georg Büchner (1813–1837), did not receive its first performance until 1913, seventy-six years after its creator's death. Fanny Mendelssohn Hensel, composer of nearly three hundred songs, has never achieved fame, despite the admiration of Robert Schumann, Charles Gounod, and her brother, Felix Mendelssohn. Even Franz Schubert, whose genius is now universally recognized, died in relative obscurity.

But Schubert's songs did eventually achieve the recognition they deserved. Some of the credit for bringing his wonderful music and the songs of other lieder composers to the attention of the public must be given to devoted performers who saw the merit of these works. The important rôle played by performers and performances in the story of the lied reveals much about the place of the lied in nineteenth-century society.

Segments of this chapter have appeared in *Music and Musicians, International* and in papers delivered to the College Music Society, Mid-Atlantic Chapter, and the American Musicological Society, Mid-Atlantic Chapter.

Figure 4-1. Caspar David Friedrich: *On the Sailing-boat,* 1818. Hermitage, St. Petersburg.

FROM HOME TO RECITAL STAGE

14 March 1840 (Berlin)

My best-beloved Robert,
    Thank you very much for the songs. They surprised me, and indeed they are quite unusual; they all require good singers who have intelligence enough to understand them.
    —Clara Wieck to her future husband, Robert Schumann[1]

In the early stages of its development, the lied was performed at home by amateurs. Composers such as Johann Friedrich Reichardt, Luise Reichardt, and Carl Zelter wrote songs with modest vocal ranges and simple piano accompaniments that were well within the capabilities of the talented amateur. But as the art song became more complex and sophisticated, lieder composers needed special performers with highly developed musical skills. They needed singers with beautiful tone, a subtle understanding of poetry, and the ability to convey delicate nuances of sound. When the performance of lieder moved from the home to the recital hall, composers were also given much greater freedom in writing for the piano, utilizing the growing technical flexibility of the instrument and the wizardry of a growing number of piano virtuosi. The rôle of the piano expanded in its partnership with the voice. The nineteenth-century art song seems to have created a special alliance between composers and performers as together they explored the parameters of this wonderful, new genre. Performers often became the champions of composers, acting as proselytizers for the lied.

The patronage of the arts was shifting from the aristocracy to the general public, and composers were no longer servants in the households of the rich who would provide their living and dictate the kind of music they wrote. Consequently, musicians were now placed in the precarious position of appealing to a nebulous mass of people whose tastes in music were often unformed or unknown. The rise of the virtuoso was a logical development at this point in the history of music since the public could be captured and entertained with astounding feats of showmanship. But whereas composers such as Louis Spohr and Franz Liszt possessed the personal magnetism and virtuosic skill to command an audience for their own works, other composers such as Franz Schubert and Robert Schumann, did not and were therefore dependent upon the interest and sympathy of well-known performers to bring their works to the general public.

One of the most poignant alliances between composer and singer occurred between Franz Schubert and the famous opera singer Johann Michael Vogl (1768–1840). Vogl, a well-educated, highly effective baritone known for his magnificent declamation, skeptically agreed to meet the little-known composer, Schubert. Vogl resisted this meeting by stating that he had often been told about young talents who turned out to be disappointments. As Schubert's friend Joseph von Spaun later recalled,

> At their first meeting, Schubert was not without shyness. He placed his setting of Mayrhofer's "Augenlied" in front of Vogl for his judgment. Vogl, immediately recognizing Schubert's talent in this song, examined with increasing interest the series of other songs which the overjoyed young composer presented to him. Already after a few weeks, Vogl was singing Schubert's "Erlkönig," "Ganymed," "Der Kampf," "Der Wanderer," etc. to a small but enthralled circle of friends, and the excitement with which this great artist performed these songs was the best proof of how much he was smitten by them. This glorious singer, however, had the greatest effect upon the young composer, who felt himself so fortunate to see his hesitant wishes fulfilled beyond all expectation. A bond between these two artists, which continued to grow until death ended it, was the result of this first meeting.[2]

Vogl was fifty-six years old when he met the twenty-year-old Schubert. What an interesting contrast this tall, distinguished singer must have made alongside the less-than-five-foot Schubert! In drawings by Schubert's friends that include both Vogl and Schubert—such as "Setting out to Fight and to Conquer," by Franz von Schober, and "Schubert and Vogl Performing a Song" or "A Schubert Evening at Josef von Spaun's," by Moritz von Schwind—Vogl is portrayed as something of a pompous poser. Schubert modestly deferred to Vogl who, according to Schubert's friend poet Eduard von Bauernfeld, "swaggered wherever he went. . . . Schubert was quite content to take a back seat."[3] In fact, Schubert was so unassuming that he allowed all the singers of his songs to reap the applause and gratitude of the audience while he remained in the background. Otto Deutsch, in his documentary biography of Schubert, states that Vogl, who also composed music, even made changes in Schubert's songs whenever it suited him![4] Schubert, on the other hand, must have taken the aging Vogl's vocal limitations into consideration when they performed together, for in his recollections of Schubert, Hüttenbrenner mentions that Schubert had to add several bars to "Erlking" in order to give Vogl more time to breathe. Vogl, for his part, spent the rest of his singing career as an advocate of Schubert's songs and has achieved lasting fame as their first major interpreter.

Another famous singer, Wilhelmine Schröder-Devrient (1804–1860), helped to reconcile the poet Goethe to the songs of Schubert. Goethe preferred the simple settings of his poetry by Carl Zelter and Johann Reichardt, perhaps because their songs never became more interesting than Goethe's poetry. When Schubert's friend von Spaun sent fourteen of Schubert's songs to Goethe in April of 1816, Goethe returned them without comment; there is no mention of these songs in his letters or diary. Schubert himself wrote to Goethe in 1825 to ask that Goethe accept the dedication of a volume of songs based on Goethe's poetry; again Goethe failed to respond, although this time he mentioned his receipt of the songs in his diary. Not until 1830, two years after Schubert's death, did Goethe admit any merit in Schubert's songs. This occurred when Wilhemine Schröder-Devrient sang "Erlkönig" for Goethe. "After the performance, Goethe kissed her forehead saying: 'I have heard this composition once before, when it did not appeal to me at all, but sung in this way, the whole shapes itself into a visible picture.' "[5] Otto Deutsch suggests that possibly, because it was the famous Schröder-Devrient who sang "Erlkönig," Goethe acknowledged it to be an uncommon achievement.[6]

Franz Liszt, virtuoso pianist and composer, was also Schubert's champion although they never met (see Chapter 6 on Schubert). He helped introduce Schubert's music to the rest of Europe, particularly through his piano transcriptions of Schubert's songs. Liszt was truly generous in his praise of his contemporaries' works and willingly performed their music. He admired such varied talents as Robert Schumann, Hector Berlioz, Robert Franz, and Richard Wagner and did not hesitate to promote their works.

Liszt introduced the famous French singer Adolphe Nourrit to the songs of Schubert. Nourrit, a widely read, intelligent singer, was the leading tenor at the Paris Opéra. Rossini, Auber, Halévy, and Meyerbeer had written rôles specifically for this gifted dramatic tenor. When Nourrit first heard Liszt play a piano transcription of "Erlkönig," Nourrit was seized with a desire to know more of Schubert's songs and then spent the rest of his life presenting Schubert's vocal masterpieces to the French world (see Chapter 6). Liszt describes Nourrit in his biography of Chopin:

Adolphe Nourrit, a noble artist, at once ascetic and passionate, was also there [Chopin's home]. He was a sincere, almost a devout Catholic, dreaming of the future with the fervor of the Middle Ages, who, during the latter part of his life, refused the assistance of his talent to any scene of merely superficial sentiment. He served Art with a high and enthusiastic respect; he considered it, in all its divers manifestations, only a holy tabernacle, "the Beauty of which formed the splendor of the True." Already undermined by a melancholy passion for the Beautiful, his brow seemed to be turning into stone under the dominion of this haunting feeling: a feeling always explained by the outbreak of despair, too late for remedy from man—man, alas! so eager to explore the secrets of the heart—so dull to divine them![7]

Liszt's description tells us perhaps as much about himself and romanticism as it does about Nourrit.

Hugo Wolf clearly recognized the advantages of engaging a famous performer to sing and promote his music. He tried to interest a number of well-known singers, including the renowned soprano Lilli Lehmann, in his work, but all his early efforts were singularly unsuccessful. He crassly pursued a relationship with the Dutch Wagnerian tenor Ernest van Dyck, stating that "if I should be successful in interesting Van Dyck seriously in my things I am ... made for life." Wolf cunningly noted that he must avoid revealing his purpose to Van Dyck, for "these confounded tenor-singing gentlemen are incalculable in their insane vanity, and, moreover, revengeful as Corsicans." Although he failed to lure Van Dyck into singing his songs, Wolf comforted himself, in typical sour-grape fashion, by noting that Van Dyck was not a lieder singer anyway.[8] Finally, when he did engage singers to perform his works, the temperamental Wolf sometimes castigated them on stage in the middle of a recital! Frank Walker, Wolf's biographer, offers this recreation of one of Wolf's concerts:

The real cause of ... [Wolf's] displeasure was that ... [Friederike Mayer] took liberties with his music which he had ... forbidden. ... During the performance of "In dem Schatten meiner Locken" he spoke angrily to her. The song was admirably suited to Frl Mayer's dark, velvety mezzo-soprano voice and the audience tried to obtain its repetition. This Wolf utterly refused to allow. In the artists' room he strode ill-humouredly up and down ... while the singer alone acknowledged the applause. He went out separately later to receive an ovation.[9]

The famous contralto Rosa Papier took an interest in Wolf and sang two of his early songs, "Morgentau" (Morning Dew) and "Zur Ruh', zur Ruh'" (To Rest, to Rest), at the Bösendorfersaal in March of 1888. Wolf was a friend of her husband, Hans Paumgartner, and had expressed admiration for her voice over and over again in his reviews for the *Salonblatt*.

Wolf's favorite singer must have been himself. There are numerous accounts of his performances as both singer and accompanist in the home of his friends. He would first read the poetry of the song aloud, and then, although he had a virtually "toneless" voice, he held his audience enthralled with the expressiveness of his singing.[10]

Actually, the composer as performer of his own music has been a common occurrence. Schubert often sang and accompanied himself in the intimate setting of his friends' homes, but unlike the "voiceless" Wolf, Schubert possessed a sweet, but somewhat weak, lyric-baritone voice. In his youth, he had been a boy mezzo-soprano in the chapel choir of the Emperor Franz II. Since many of Schubert's works were not performed during his lifetime, particularly works on a large scale such as his symphonies, song composition must have been particularly satisfying for him. He was able to hear performances of his songs either when he accompanied Vogl and other singers who participated in Schubertiads, or he could sing and accompany himself. Otto Deutsch identifies the following letter as emanating from the first Schubertiad, a social evening devoted to the music of Franz Schubert.

Josef Huber to his betrothed, Rosalie Kranzbichler

30 January 1821 (Vienna)
    Last Friday I had excellent entertainment. . . . Franz invited Schubert in the evening and fourteen of his close acquaintances. So a lot of splendid songs by Schubert were sung and played by himself, which lasted until after 10 o'clock in the evening. After that punch was drunk, offered by one of the party, and as it was very good and plentiful the party, in a happy mood anyhow, became even merrier; so it was 3 o'clock in the morning before we parted.[11]

Carl Loewe was another lieder composer who sang his own songs in public (see Chapter 11, "The Supporting Cast").

Johannes Brahms, a noted pianist during the early days of his career, frequently accompanied singers when they performed his songs. But there is also a touching account of Brahms as a singer. Dr. Ophüls, a young lawyer and friend, tells in his *Erinnerungen an Johannes Brahms* that he heard Brahms sing his *Vier ernste Gesänge* (Four Serious Songs) shortly·after the death of Clara Schumann in 1896.

> It was an intensified declamation of the Bible words that he gave us in his hoarse voice. . . . These songs, coming in this improvised way from their creator, affected me more powerfully then than they have done from any singer since. . . . It was exactly as though the prophet himself spoke to us. . . . [Brahms] was so deeply moved during the rendering of the third song, "O Tod, wie bitter bist du," that great tears rolled down his cheeks, and the pathetic ending (O Tod, wie wohl tust du) he almost murmured to himself in a voice choked with emotion. I shall never forget the tremendous effect of this song. It was characteristic of Brahms, who disguised a very tender heart with an armour of outward roughness, that after the last note had died away, obviously seeking to hide his emotion, he turned to me . . . and with a heavy slap on my leg said "Young man, this is not for you: you must not think of these things at all." [12]

Clara Schumann was very interested in the singers of her day and made many valuable observations about their gifts. She worshiped soprano Wilhelmine Schröder-Devrient and felt unworthy to call the great singer by the intimate "Du" after they became friends (1849): "For I thought I could never make up my mind to address as Du, the woman who had represented my artistic ideal ever since my earliest childhood." [13] It was to Schröder-Devrient that Robert Schumann dedicated his *Dichterliebe*.

Performers such as Schröder-Devrient have sometimes been credited with inspiring and focusing the talents of young composers. In his autobiography, *My Life*, Richard Wagner declared that the course of his musical career was determined when, as a sixteen-year-old boy, he heard the great German soprano, Wilhelmine Schröder-Devrient singing in Beethoven's *Fidelio*.

> After the opera was over I . . . [wrote] a short letter in which I told her succinctly that my life had henceforth found its meaning, and that if ever she should hear my name favorably mentioned in the world of art, she should remember that she had on this evening made of me that which I now vowed to become. . . . I wanted to write a work that would be worthy of Schröder-Devrient. [14]

Thirteen years later, when composer and singer finally met for the first time, Schröder-Devrient recited word for word to Wagner his boyish letter of dedication.[15] Wagner's apocalyptic conversion to art and a great singer's sympathetic response to an unknown, youthful admirer represent interesting facets in the complex story of relationships between composers and performers. As creators and purveyors of music, composers and performers have been essential to one another in the musical world, and while their relationships have not always been smooth, they have often collaborated intimately to the benefit of both.

Schröder-Devrient was also a good friend of Felix Mendelssohn, who related to his sister Fanny the details of an unusual concert with Madame Schröder-Devrient at the Leipzig Gewandhaus in 1841. The concert was to include a performance of Beethoven's song cycle, *An die ferne Geliebte* (To the Distant Love) with a singer named Mr. Schmidt.

> The other day... Herr Schmidt was suddenly taken ill, and could not sing to his "Ferne Geliebte" in the "Liederkreis." [i.e., Beethoven's cycle]. In the middle of the first part David said, "I see Madame Devrient." So during an interval I went up to her . . . and she agreed to sing "Adelaide." . . . Come she did, in a shabby travelling costume, and Leipzig bellowed and shouted without end. She took off her bonnet before the "publicum," and pointed to her black pelisse, as if to apologize for it. I believe they are still applauding! She sang beautifully . . . and the audience clapped their hands, till not a single bow of the shabby pelisse was any longer visible.[16]

This all-Beethoven concert was part of a series of "historical" concerts that Mendelssohn was presenting at the Gewandhaus. The program was unusual in that it was devoted to the works of one composer but was usual in its mix of symphonic, choral, and chamber music all on one program.

Leonore Overture No. 3
Kyrie and Gloria from the C Major Mass
Violin Concerto (M. Gulomy)
"Adelaide" (Madame Schröder-Devrient)
Ninth Symphony[17]

As the quote from Mendelssohn indicates, *An die ferne Geliebte* had been scheduled for this program. Not only were art songs becoming regular fare on concert programs by this time, but *An die ferne Geliebte*, a short song cycle, was being performed in a public setting. Liszt had accompanied Ludwig Titze in a performance of this cycle two years earlier (1839) at the hall of the Gesellschaft der Musikfreunde in Vienna.[18]

Recitals devoted exclusively to lieder did not occur until the second half of the nineteenth century. In fact, concerts in midcentury were generally a mixture of styles, instruments, and genres. A glance at one of Liszt's recital programs tells much about public concerts in the first half of the century. Until he retired from the stage in 1848, most of Liszt's concert appearances were not one-man shows but were shared appearances with other musicians. The following concert took place in Vienna in 1840 at the Hofburgtheater and is a prime example of a typical hodge-podge of musical offerings from this period.

Bellini/Liszt: Fantasy from the opera *Sonnambula*
Declamation, spoken by Miss Fichtner, Court Actress
Franz von Suppé: "Song by Helt," sung by Mr. Lutz, member
of the Royal Chapel Choir
Spohr: Concerto for Violin, performed by Mr. F. W. Bezdek
Declamation, spoken by Miss Rettich, Court Actress
Violoncello Solo, performed by Mr. Borzaga, member
of the Royal Chapel
Liszt: Fantasy and Variations on a Theme from the opera *Die Braut* (first performance), played by Liszt[19]

Liszt began to appear in public solo performances by the 1840s, shortly before his retirement, setting a precedent for other virtuoso pianists such as Carl Tausig and Sigismund Thalberg. Although some programs were devoted to the works of one composer, as was the case with Mendelssohn's all-Beethoven concert in 1841 and Tausig's all-Chopin recital at the Arnim'sche Hall (Berlin) in 1867,[20] consistent efforts to unify program content did not take place until the end of the century.[21]

Singers seem always to have struggled with the problem of knowing when to stop singing. By 1858, Schröder-Devrient's voice was noticeably failing. Clara confided to her diary:

Matinée at the theatre. Devrient sang some songs, and I endured perfect agonies of nervousness. She no longer has her voice under control, and naturally her execution suffers in consequence. . . . She has more than once offered to tour with me and sing at my concerts, but I would not have it for the world. I should daily have to witness the deterioration of the woman who was my highest ideal when I was young. What was not she to me? For what memories I have to thank her—indelible memories! And shall I allow this woman to sing at my concerts, expose her to the rough multitude, which will ask not what she was, but what she is?[22]

Schröder-Devrient did retire, but shortly thereafter considered returning to the stage. Clara wrote a very frank letter to her in which she advised Schröder-Devrient not to ruin the glory of her legend by performing, now that her voice was gone.

January 1859

Dear, admired Wilhelmine,
    I cannot tell you how dismayed I have been by the news that you intend to return to public life. Dearest Wilhelmine, if there is still time to change your mind, do so. Believe me, you are on the way towards sad experiences; and is this fitting for a great artist such as you? If you sang your heart out of your body they would not acknowledge it, because your voice no longer has its youthful freshness. . . . If you reply that in Dresden you are advised on all sides to do it, believe me that most of those . . . would be among the first to fall upon you as soon as you sang in public. Why will you not rather train girls of talent for the stage, and unlock the treasures of German song?[23]

Clara received no reply. Schröder-Devrient, in poor health at this time, died in January of the next year.

Clara Schumann also knew and admired the international star Jenny Lind, a singer of great modesty and sweetness. When the Schumanns went to Vienna in the winter of 1846 to present four concerts with Robert's works as the centerpiece, they were coolly received; ticket sales barely covered expenses. Jenny Lind, present at the third concert, offered to sing at the fourth and consequently lured a sellout crowd. The Schumanns were able to make enough money from this final concert to pay for their journey and make a profit.[24] Robert Schumann said of Jenny Lind,

The rehearsal of a number of my songs . . . I shall never forget. I have never before met so clear an understanding of music and text at first sight, and simple, natural perfection. . . . We parted with her as with an angel from heaven, she was so lovable and gentle.[25]

Figure 4-2. Jenny Lind, ca. 1851. Photograph of painting. Courtesy of the Library of Congress.

Robert dedicated his Op. 89 songs to her. Jenny Lind again offered to sing in a concert Clara was giving in Altona. Clara recalled in her diary that during the rehearsal for the concert

> she sang quite a number of Robert's songs; and how she sang them! What a pure, genuinely artistic soul! . . . These songs will sound for ever in my heart . . . and . . . I should like to say that I will never again hear them sung by anyone except her. I need scarcely say that Robert is no less enthusiastic about her than I am; it is a joy for any composer to hear his songs sung with such heart-felt feeling.[26]

When the concert took place,

> How she sang! How she sang Mendelssohn's "Rheinisches Volkslied," how Robert's "Sonnenschein"—no, it cannot be described! Robert said to her, "One really feels the sun on one's back. One wants to listen to freshness and child-like innocence and simplicity such as this, again and again"—and indeed the audience took care to make her repeat it.[27]

In her usual frank manner, Clara suggested to Jenny Lind that from now on she should devote herself to good music and stop singing Meyerbeer, Bellini, and Donizetti! Jenny Lind must certainly be considered one of the most famous singers of all times; over seventy books have been written about her life and career.

The Schumanns lived in Leipzig during the early years of their marriage and were in close contact with Felix Mendelssohn, who was at this time conductor of the Gewandhaus orchestra. Mendelssohn's admiration for Clara and his willingness to promote the compositions of Robert are reflected in the following program in which Clara and Liszt were soloists on 6 December 1841.

Schumann: Overture, Scherzo and Finale for Orchestra
Mendelssohn-Bartholdy: Capriccio for Piano and Orchestra,
played by Clara Schumann
Mozart: Aria, sung by Mr. Schmidt
Liszt: Fantasy on a Theme from *Lucia di Lammermoor,*
played by Clara Schumann
Schumann: Second Symphony
J. S. Bach: Prelude and Fugue
W. St. Bennett: Allegretto for four hands
Chopin: Etude (in C), played by Clara Schumann
Schumann: "Die beiden Grenadiere" by H. Heine,
sung by Mr. Pögnen

Liszt: Reminiscences on *Robert le Diable* (Meyerbeer)
for the piano, played by Franz Liszt[28]

Schumann's second symphony was premiered in the concert, but he and Clara were disappointed by the performance, partly because the audience of nine hundred people were so eager to hear Liszt play that they showed little interest in anything else.[29] Contemporary reports indicate that Liszt's performances and personality over-shadowed anyone who appeared with him.

Clara Schumann performed the music of both her husband and of their young protégé, Johannes Brahms. Brahms often called upon her for advice about his music (see Chapter 13 on Brahms).

24 April, 1877 (Vienna)

(Brahms to Clara:)
I want to publish my songs and should be so very much obliged if you could play them through beforehand and give me a word of advice about them. . . . If possible write me a short comment on each.[30]

In the quote that opens this chapter, Clara Wieck Schumann said that Schumann's songs required a good singer with the intelligence to understand them. The combination of voice and intelligence is a veritable "leitmotif" in the correspondence of nineteenth-century musicians. Theodor Billroth, a friend of Brahms for many years, expresses this thought in a letter to Brahms.

[Your songs] need a great deal of study, for both accompanist and singer. . . . I can see very clearly that these songs demand a dramatic disposition on the part of the singer. It has been recently said, and it fits the songs fully, "People are still entirely too stupid for such songs." . . . You have already done so much in this field that improvement is scarcely to be thought of. . . . With your music you have exerted a solemn blessing over the poetry. . . . All of them need a peculiarly beautiful voice which must express a very deep and sensitive emotional inner self and completely perfect declamation. . . . These songs can't be sung simply like any other. They must in the best of senses be beautifully—yes, completely beautifully—proclaimed. I can think of them then as being infinitely beautiful, but I'll scarcely ever hear them that way.[31]

Brahms often relied on the master lieder singer of the era, Julius Stockhausen (1826–1906), to interpret his songs, and he even dedicated his *Romanzen aus Ludwig Tiecks Magelone* to Stockhausen.

Eugenie Schumann, seventh child of Robert and Clara Schumann, described Stockhausen as having "made the Germans fully aware of the glorious treasure which they possessed in their songs. His singing of the *Müllerlieder, Dichterliebe* ... has never been equalled."[32] Stockhausen was the first singer to offer a complete public performance of Schubert's *Die schöne Müllerin* in 1856, and he performed Schumann's *Dichterliebe* with Brahms at the piano in Hamburg in 1861. But he sang *Dichterliebe* in two parts and had Brahms play sections of Schumann's *Kreisleriana* in between![33]

Critics were cautious in their reception of Stockhausen's efforts to present such lengthy complete song cycles. Eduard Hanslick (1825–1904), the most famous German music critic of the century, reviewed Stockhausen's first performance of *Die schöne Müllerin* and noted that Schubert's popularity in Vienna made it possible for the singer to present a song recital restricted to the works of one composer and unified in mood and material.[34] After Stockhausen performed a second recital of *Die schöne Müllerin* in 1860, Hanslick warned that the novelty of these concerts would soon lose their appeal to audiences.[35] Undeterred, Stockhausen continued to sing *Die schöne Müllerin* with great success. He even took the bold step of organizing a mass public concert for which he charged modest ticket fees. Over two thousand people came to hear his performance![36]

Purists should note that Stockhausen sang Schumann's *Frauenliebe und -leben*[37] (A Woman's Love and Life) and also saw nothing wrong in having female singers perform songs that represented a male's point of view. In 1873, he gave a concert with his student Johanna Schwartz in which she sang parts of Schubert's *Winterreise*.[38]

Clara Schumann, who sometimes acted as accompanist for Stockhausen, was surprised to learn that he was not very popular in England. She concluded that

> the English do not understand him; they cannot, since they do not understand German ... and therefore cannot appreciate ... his peculiar gift, which is the interpretation of German songs. But their judgment of singing is altogether different from ours; they demand voice, training, and aplomb, and they also like warmth; but in Germany ... with all that, we require interpretation, such as Stockhausen gives. If one is incapable of appreciating the way in which by tone and enunciation he gives each word its full meaning, one is incapable of appreciating him. But much as the English love music, this depth of feeling, this perfect, profound respect for the sacredness of art, is incomprehensible to them.[39]

There was at least one Englishman who fully appreciated Stockhausen. Sir George Grove offers a charming eyewitness account of a
Stockhausen concert:

> Stockhausen's singing in his best days must have been wonder-
> ful. Even to those who, like the writer, only heard him after he
> had passed his zenith, it is a thing never to be forgotten. Perhaps
> the maturity of the taste and expression made up for a little
> falling-off in the voice. His delivery of opera and oratorio
> music ... was superb in taste, feeling and execution; but it was
> the songs of Schubert, Schumann and, later on, Brahms that most
> peculiarly suited him, and these he delivered in a truly remark-
> able way. He exerted a strong formative influence on the style of
> Brahms's songs. ... It has been suggested that Stockhausen "was
> to Brahms's songs very much what Joseph Joachim was to his
> chamber music." The rich beauty of the voice, the nobility of the
> style, the perfect phrasing, the intimate sympathy, and, not least,
> the intelligible way in which the words were given—all com-
> bined to make his singing of songs an unforgettable experi-
> ence.[40]

Stockhausen's credentials as a singer were impressive. He was
the son of the German soprano Margarete Schmuck Stockhausen,
studied singing with the famous pedagogue Manuel Garcia, and even
wrote a treatise on singing: *Method of Singing* (1886–87). Hugo Wolf
was surprised and delighted when Stockhausen, a devotee of
Brahms, took an interest in Wolf's songs as well.[41] Stockhausen was
certainly one of the most important champions of the lied in the
nineteenth century.

Brahms had the support of several fine singers of his era.
Hermine Spies, a student of Stockhausen, established her reputation
as a singer of Brahms's songs. She was to be caught in the cross fire
between Brahms and Wolf after the critic Hanslick, a partisan of
Brahms and an enemy of Wagner, praised her for her "artistic cultivation and the freshest naturalness. The blend is as irresistible as it is
rare."[42] Wolf had praised Miss Spies four months earlier: "The young
lady rejoices in a sympathetic organ, darkly colored, and knows well
how to express the most varied moods in a highly dramatic manner"
[28 Nov. 1886].[43] Wolf now characterized her singing quite differently: "Fräulein Spies's accomplishments do not surpass the level
of good, modest mediocrity, and ... every unbiased listener must con-
fess that the paeans in her behalf sound far better than her singing"
[27 March 1887].[44]

The contralto Amalie Joachim, wife of the great violinist Joseph

Joachim, frequently sang Brahms's songs. Brahms's outspoken sympathy for her when she and Joachim divorced caused a major rift between the two men. Frau Joachim was particularly fond of Brahms's *Alto Rhapsody*, a work she sang many times. The *Alto Rhapsody* was performed by the well-known singer Pauline Viardot-Garcia as well, who also joined with Julius Stockhausen to perform duets by Brahms.

Sometimes composers and performers achieve more than artistic intimacy. Felix Mendelssohn and the Swedish nightingale, Jenny Lind, have been the subject of much romantic speculation. Mendelssohn expressed high admiration for her spectacular voice and wanted to write an opera that would display her talents. Not only was she a favorite guest artist in Mendelssohn's Gewandhaus concerts in Leipzig, but he also considered her the ideal voice for his demanding "Hear Ye, Israel" in the oratorio *Elijah*. There is no doubt that great personal warmth existed in their relationship, for after Mendelssohn's death, Jenny Lind established a music scholarship in his memory. Clara Schumann wrote in her diary that "I was enchanted by Jenny Lind's rendering of . . . Mendelssohn's 'Auf Flügeln des Gesanges' (On Wings of Song). I had never heard this song sung so well, but there was a double influence at work, for as I see from everything she says about Mendelssohn, she loves him no less as a man than as a composer."[45]

Hugo Wolf also fell in love with a singer. The unfortunate object of his affections was Frieda Zerny, a mezzo-soprano at the opera house in Mainz. Wolf first heard Zerny in a recital of his songs in Darmstadt and immediately developed a consuming passion for her. "She is young and beautiful . . . and sings my things with a devotion and an understanding such as one cannot conceive bettered even in a dream."[46] At first he thought of her as the perfect mate, for she was willing to give up the stage "in order to live entirely for the propagation of my songs."[47] Then, suddenly, Wolf's ardor for Frieda cooled, and the bewildered singer found herself repulsed by Wolf, who did all in his power to avoid her. Wolf's biographer, Frank Walker, thinks that Wolf sought inspiration in Frieda when his creative powers appeared to be gone. After he found that their relationship did nothing to rekindle those powers, Wolf dropped her.

Richard Strauss married the singer Pauline de Ahna and spent many years on tour as her accompanist in the performance of his songs. Especially during the 1890s, Pauline and Richard presented Liederabende that consisted solely of Strauss's songs. Strauss not only wrote numerous songs with his wife's high, lyric-soprano voice in mind, but his orchestration of song was another way for him to provide Pauline with the opportunity to appear with him when he conducted orchestras in Europe and the United States. The following program from one of their concerts in Zürich in 1898 included both orchestral lieder and songs for piano and voice:

"Wandrers Sturmlied" by Goethe for Chorus and Orchestra
Richard Strauss

Four Songs for Soprano with Orchestra
Richard Strauss
a. "Rosenband," by Klopstock
b. "Liebeshymnus," by Henckell
c. "Morgen," by Mackay
d. "Cäcilie," by Hart
Performed by Frau Strauss-de Ahna

Also sprach Zarathustra, tone poem, based freely on Friedr. Nietzsche, for large Orchestra
Richard Strauss

Three Songs with piano accompaniment
Richard Strauss
a. "Sehnsucht," by Liliencron
b. "Traum durch die Dämmerung," by Bierbaum
c. "Ständchen," by Graf Schack
Performed by Frau Strauss-de Ahna

Overture to the Opera *Der Freischütz*
Weber[48]

Strauss may have orchestrated some of his songs in response to efforts by musicians and critics at the end of the century to provide more consistency in programming. Composers orchestrated songs that had originally been written for piano and composed new orchestral lieder so that more unity of sound was possible in orchestra concerts.[49] Programs at the beginning of the twentieth century show a clearer division of mediums: an evening of Mahler's songs for orchestra and voice was designated "Ein Liederabend mit Orchester"; a concert that consisted of a string quartet, lieder for piano and voice, and a piano quintet was called "Ein Kammermusik-und Liederabend"; and a concert for the orchestra was called simply "Orchesterkonzert."[50]

Pauline de Ahna devoted herself to her husband's songs and performed many recitals that exclusively presented his lieder from the year of their marriage, 1894, to the end of her singing career in 1908.[51] After Pauline retired from singing, Strauss did not publish another song for several years. His most intense period of songwriting occurred between 1899 and 1901 when he and Pauline performed the greatest number of concerts together.[52] In his "Recollections of My Youth and Years of Apprenticeship," Strauss wrote, "she certainly did sing my Lieder with unrivalled expression and poetic fervour. Nobody even remotely approached her in the singing of 'Morgen,' 'Traum durch die Dämmerung,' or 'Jung Hexenlied.'"[53] Reviews of her performances note her poetic interpretations and subtle penetration of the text.[54] Strauss himself mentions a review of their performance in which one critic wrote, "Frau Strauss performed her husband's songs so vitally that one could believe she had composed them herself, while he sat somewhat over-bored at the piano."[55]

Strauss was quite critical of his own pianistic abilities and admitted that he enjoyed sight-reading but didn't like to practice.

> This is the reason why I never managed to become technically efficient (especially as far as my left hand is concerned). . . . On the other hand, I was a good accompanist of Lieder—in the free manner, never entirely faithful to the music.[56]

The free manner of his accompaniments was noted (see Chapter 15 on Mahler and Strauss) by the Viennese music historian Alfred Orel, who was asked to turn pages for Richard Strauss and the soprano Elisabeth Schumann in a concert during the 1920s.

> When I opened the music at the first song, Strauss whispered to me, "you mustn't follow the music, because I play it quite differently." . . . The printed notes were often admittedly no more than aids to the composer's memory. . . . Without becoming expressly "orchestral," he went far beyond the printed accompaniment and exploited all the possibilities at the piano. . . . Countless times Strauss doubled the bass line and enriched the chords. Yet he could also, in "Morgen" for instance, follow the written notes punctiliously. In "Cäcilie" . . . it was as though one was hearing the surge of a full orchestra.[57]

The "mythology" of the Strauss marriage is a fascinating chapter in the history of music. Strauss met Pauline in 1887 when she became his student. He coached her in operatic rôles and actively sought to advance her career by recommending her for singing engagements.

In a letter to his friend, Eugen Spitzweg, Strauss requested that Spitzweg mention Pauline's debut in the *Muenchner Theater-Anzeiger*.

> My pupil, Fräulein de Ahna, making her debut here as Pamina [in Mozart's *Magic Flute*] on 22 May, scored a great success (the wonderful voice, excellent technique, and the beautiful and assured dramatic talent aroused great, well-earned public interest).[58]

Pauline, while described in numerous reviews as an artistic interpreter of Strauss's songs, was also perfectly willing to focus attention on herself and away from her husband-accompanist by eliciting applause from the audience during his postludes.[59] In many ways she fits the stereotype of the temperamental singer. Alma Mahler recounts one dramatic scene between Pauline and Richard after their marriage:

> The door flew open and Strauss reeled in followed by Pauline.
> "You can go now," she shouted. "I am going to the hotel and I shall spend the evening alone."
> "Can't I take you there?" he begged.
> "Ten paces behind me—not otherwise." She went off, Strauss following at a respectful distance.
> We went on to the restaurant in silence. Soon Strauss joined us in a state of exhaustion, sat down beside me and said these very words: "My wife's a bit rough sometimes, but that's what I need, you know."[60]

A discussion about the relationship of composers and performers, often diverting and humorous, also reveals much about the period and conditions under which songs were written and performed. The alliance between performers and composers, even when tenuous and stormy, played an interesting and essential rôle in the development of nineteenth-century song.

CHAPTER FIVE

Ludwig van Beethoven

To measure Beethoven's influence is like measuring Shakespeare's. It is an influence either too vaguely universal to name or too profoundly artistic to analyse.

—Tovey[1]

Although the specific contribution made to the lied by Ludwig van Beethoven (1770–1827) is not easy to assess, his influence on all nineteenth-century music was profound. His titanic example was too staggering for many composers to emulate; they were left overwhelmed and voiceless. But for composers such as Brahms and Wagner, Beethoven was an inexhaustible well of inspiration.

The art song had not yet emerged as a distinctive genre during Beethoven's early life, and he himself did not display an inspired interest in song, despite the substantial number he wrote. There is little stylistic uniformity in his more than seventy songs, and his use of terminology—Lied, Gesänge, Ariette, or simply Gedicht von ——— in Musik gesetzt von L. van Beethoven (poetry of ——— in a musical setting by L. van Beethoven)—shows how undefined this medium was for him.

Beethoven is rightly credited with composing the first German song cycle, *An die ferne Geliebte* (1816), a wonderfully intriguing piece of music. Yet some of his other songs might not merit our attention if they had been written by a less illustrious composer. His song "Mollys Abschied" (Molly's Farewell), for example, is a pleasant, tuneful song but leaves the listener with nothing distinctive or memorable. The voice is accompanied by simple, broken-chord

Figure 5-1. Caspar David Friedrich: *Oak Tree in the Snow,* ca. 1829. Courtesy of the Staatliche Museen zu Berlin—Preussischer Kulturbesitz, Nationalgalerie. Photograph by Jörg P. Anders, Berlin.

figurations in the left-hand piano part while the right hand doubles the voice; the piano is given no introduction and only a brief postlude (Example 5-1). The inflexiblity of strophically setting five stanzas of poetry soon becomes apparent in phrases like "halb zum Mindesten im Schattenrisse" in stanza 3, where an unaccented syllable, "Mindesten," falls on a strong beat (mm. 4–6). Many of Beethoven's songs are strophic, although he sometimes avoids awkward text settings for second or third stanzas by writing out the melodic line for each stanza and then making modest rhythmic adjustments for each stanza of text.

1. Farewell, you man of desire and pain,
2. As a remembrance, I offer you, instead of gold
3. Of my face, which received your kisses,
4. Take, you sweet cajoler, a lock of my hair,
5. Take this little blue [wreath] as a memento of my eyes,

Example 5-1. Beethoven, "Mollys Abschied" (Molly's Farewell), mm. 1–2.

Beethoven's setting of Goethe's "Mailied" (May Song), the song that precedes "Mollys Abschied" in Op. 52, links poetry and music more successfully. The piano introduction anticipates the vocal melody and creates a mood that is compatible with the poetry in a relatively simple harmonic setting. The sprightly piano interludes contribute to the general good humor of the song. Although this song is strophically organized, Beethoven underlays each stanza of text so that minor adjustments allow for the slight variants in the poetry.

Not all of Beethoven's songs are so simple. His beautiful "Adelaide," worthy of performance on any recital program, eludes being categorized as an art song. One historian calls "Adelaide" a cantata[2] while another defines it as a traditional andante-allegro.[3] What it does represent is another facet of a genre that was not yet clearly defined. The poetry of "Adelaide," by the popular writer Friedrich von Matthison (1761–1831), is so freely treated by Beethoven that there is no unity of word and tone: he expands Matthison's four short stanzas into a dramatic concert aria. Waxing rhapsodically on the lovely Adelaide, Beethoven mentions her name fourteen times (Matthison's poem states her name only four times) and expands the last four lines of text into the lengthy allegro portion of the song.

Beethoven's "Adelaide" illustrates the indirect influence that Italian vocal writing exerted on most of the early song composers. Italian arias generally appeared on concert programs in the early part of the nineteenth century and were considered the ideal in vocal writing. Italian singing masters and composers were all over Europe, and both Beethoven and Schubert studied composition with the Italian composer Antonio Salieri (1750–1825), Kapellmeister to the Austrian court. His influence as well as the aesthetics of the period were sufficient to make each composer sensitive to the Italian lyric style of writing. Beethoven, Schubert, and other early song composers such as Luise Reichardt (see Chapter 8 on women composers) even set a number of Italian poems by Metastasio because there was such a demand for Italian music, and Beethoven is said to have consulted with Salieri as late as the first decade of the nineteenth century when setting Italian poetry. Ironically enough, Italian art songs were written primarily by foreigners such as Beethoven and Liszt, while the Italians themselves continued to be consumed by their worship of opera. An emphasis on beautiful melody is thus a feature of the early German song, for the whole art of vocal writing was dominated by Italian vocal tradition. As the century progressed, and poetry took on an increasingly dominant rôle in the lied, melodies were shaped to the demands of the German language. Composers such as Hugo Wolf are often accused of lacking talent for writing melodies, but tuneful melodic writing was not a goal in his quest for greater textual expression.

Most of Beethoven's song melodies are lyrically conceived, and none exhibit the notoriously impractical vocal demands that occur in some of his choral writing. Just as the style of his songs is highly varied, so is the range. Two of Beethoven's Gellert songs cover the range of an octave and a fifth, while his second setting of "Sehnsucht" (Longing), also known as "Nur wer die Sehnsucht kennt" (Only One Who Knows Longing), is confined to the range of a perfect fifth. "Sehnsucht," Beethoven's title for this poem, is taken from Goethe's novel *Wilhelm Meisters Lehrjahre*, a novel which provided song composers with a number of very beautiful poems spoken by the character Mignon and her mysterious father, the Harper.

Although Beethoven set at least six of Goethe's poems, he also set the works of many lesser poets whose writings are no longer remembered. His "Der Wachtelschlag" is based on the poetry of S. F. Sauter and is another song that exhibits a certain mixture of styles. Angular recitative, more suitable to opera than to song, suddenly erupts in the middle of this piece. Recitative occurs in the writing of most of the nineteenth-century lieder composers when composers wished more freedom in their setting of the text. "Der Wachtelschlag" illustrates Beethoven's repetitive use of a distinctive rhythmic motive (mm. 1–4), which he derived from the words "fürchte Gott!" (fear God!) and which is, in turn, an imitation of the quail's call (Example 5-2). This motive, which acts as a unifying device throughout the song, is written in an augmented notation in the final section to accommodate changes in meter and tempo that intensify the drama at the conclusion of the song. Beethoven's "Der Wachtelschlag" was published in 1804; eighteen years later Schubert set the same poem, also using the short rhythmic motive (dotted sixteenth- and thirty-second-note) of the quail's call throughout.

Fear God! fear God!

Example 5-2. Beethoven, "Der Wachtelschlag" (The Quail's Song), mm. 6–8.

Beethoven was sometimes inspired by the same poem more than once. He set "An die Hoffnung" (To Hope) from Tiedge's *Urania* on two different occasions but responded with strikingly different styles for each. His first version, Op. 32 (1804), is a simple, lyrical strophic setting that bears little resemblance to the dramatic recitative-and-aria-like version, Op. 94, of 1815. It seems strange that the same text could call forth a full-blown da capo aria with word-painting in his second version, whereas his first attempt, though pleasant, was slightly monotonous.

In 1808, Beethoven set Goethe's "Nur wer die Sehnsucht kennt" four times. (This poem inspired many other settings including one from Wolf, three from Schubert, one from Schumann, one from Loewe, two from Johann Reichardt, and the very famous setting by Tchaikovsky.) Although not as stylistically diverse as his "An die Hoffnung" settings, Beethoven's four versions do, nevertheless, employ a variety of meters (4/4, 3/4, 6/8) and keys (G minor, E-flat major). Since he published all four versions as a group called "Sehnsucht" (Longing) in 1810, he must have felt that each song was worthy of his name and a designated opus number. Yet some very awkward treatment of the text occurs in these settings. In the first three songs, for example, the rigid strophic division of the poem into two stanzas does not permit response to the drama of the words "Es schwindelt mir, es brennt mein Eingeweide" (I am dizzy, my insides burn). Each musical stanza is in ABA' form so that the final line of text, the return of "Nur wer die Sehnsucht kennt," does coincide with the return of the original music at the opening of the song. The piano part in all four versions is totally subordinate to the melodic line, with almost no material of its own. Nevertheless, versions one, two, and four in G minor do manage to capture some of the poignancy of Mignon's sadness and longing.

In the well-known "Der Kuss" (The Kiss), there is again little unity of word and tone. Beethoven calls this piece an ariette, which it certainly is: musical development takes precedence over the text. The poem presents a charming little scene in which the speaker asks Chloe if he can kiss her. She coyly replies that she will scream if he kisses her. He kisses her and she screams—much later. Beethoven bludgeons the punch line by repeating it over and over again,[4] but he compensates somewhat by creating an elaborate musical setting. The later song composers such as Hugo Wolf, whose goal was the faithful depiction of the poetry, rarely allow their musical ideas to obscure the intent of the poet. Here, however, Beethoven illustrates a basic quality of his genius—his magnificent gifts were grounded in his ability to think on a much grander stage than the lied provided; something as short, delicate, and ephemeral as song was not a natural medium for him.

Given his penchant for complex organization, it seems quite natural that Beethoven would ultimately decide to link a group of his songs into an intricate unit, the first song cycle. *An die ferne Geliebte* is based on the poetry of Beethoven's contemporary Aloys Jeitteles (1794–1858), a young doctor who had published some of his works in periodicals of the day. Each of the six sections, or songs, of the cycle is tied to the next with transitional material in the piano, which prepares for the changes of key and figuration that will be used in the next song. (Beethoven's use of connective music between songs was not imitated by the famous composers who followed him.) *An die ferne Geliebte* is also unified by continuity in the poetry—the meditations of a young man who is separated from his beloved by distance and by some undefined barrier. Beethoven completes the circle when he returns to the home key of E-flat in the final lied and brings back the music of the first song. The cycle ends with the same words that ended the first song: "und ein liebend Herz erreichet, was ein liebend Herz geweiht!" (and a loving heart achieves that to which a loving heart has consecrated itself), implying that the poet's love will ultimately triumph.

In the first song of the cycle, a strophic variation, the piano immediately takes an aggressive role: while each stanza of text is presented strophically with a simple, slightly altered vocal line, the piano part presents the variations (Example 5-3). Although the piano is not independent of the voice part, it nevertheless commands the listener's attention because of its creative vitality.

In the second song, a short piano introduction anticipates the vocal line, after which the melody occurs in the voice. In the middle of the song, however, the voice becomes a pedal point and is subordinate to the piano, which now has the melodic line. The technique provides an interesting musical variation and, at the same time, conveys a sense of the peaceful scene being described (Example 5-4). While it may not seem surprising that Beethoven allows the voice to function in such an instrumental manner, similar examples of the voice presenting a pedal point against the solo treatment of the piano can be found in the works of other composers as diverse as Fanny Mendelssohn Hensel and Richard Strauss.

The third song begins programmatically, with a rest after each note of the vocal line as the text describes clouds lightly floating in the heavens. The figure is so intriguing, however, that the listener becomes more aware of the music than the poem (Example 5-5).

The third and fourth songs are both strophic variations. The fifth song with its bird calls, running figuration in the right hand of the accompaniment, and square phrasing (mm. 7–10) must certainly have influenced Mahler in his *Lieder eines fahrenden Gesellen* (Songs of a Wayfarer).

Example 5-3. Beethoven, "Auf dem Hügel sitz ich spähend" (Looking out, I Sit on the Hill), in *An die ferne Geliebte* (To the Distant Love).

Ziemlich langsam und mit Ausdruck

Stanza 1, mm. 1–4.

Auf dem Hü - gel sitz' ich spä - hend in das blau-e Ne - bel -

Stanza 2, mm. 11–14.

Weit bin ich von dir ge-schie-den, tren-nend lie-gen Berg und

Stanza 3, mm. 21–24.

Ach, den Blick kannst du nicht se - hen, der zu dir so glü - hend

Stanza 4, mm. 31–34.

Will denn nichts mehr zu dir drin - gen, nichts der Lie - be Bo - te

Stanza 5, mm. 41–44.

1. I sit on a hill, looking out into the blue fogged [land]
2. I am far from you, separated by mountain and
3. Ah, you cannot see the gaze which so fervently for you
4. Will then nothing more penetrate through to you, nothing of love's message
5. For song banishes all space and all

There in the peaceful valley, pain and torment are silent.

Example 5-4. Beethoven, "Wo die Berge so blau" (Where the Mountains Are So Blue), in *An die ferne Geliebte*, mm. 20–23.

Lightly sailing in the heavens,

Example 5-5. Beethoven, "Leichte Segler in den Höhen" (Lightly Sailing on High), in *An die ferne Geliebte*, mm. 5–6.

In the sixth and final song of the cycle, Beethoven truly captures the reflective sweetness of the poetry. Again he has the piano anticipate the vocal line, but he organizes this song flexibly in an ABA' form: music from the first song in the cycle returns and is then modified in the final coda.

The songs of *An die ferne Geliebte* achieve their maximum effectiveness in their cyclical setting and are seldom performed as separate pieces. An inner momentum in the whole cycle lends strength to the individual songs, which seem pale when removed from this context. While their performance time is only thirteen to fourteen minutes, their uniformity of mood requires the partnership of two fine performers to do them justice. Although condensed versions of the cycle have been published, they have been unable to capture the spirit of the cycle as a complete entity.

Beethoven also wrote a group of six songs to the words of poet and theologian Christian Fürchtegott Gellert (1715–1769). Although these songs do not form a cycle, the texts are all religious. Beethoven was obviously attuned to their message, for they stimulated a high level of inspiration from him. The first five songs are just one page each, with a relatively simple but noble musical setting; each has just the first stanza of Gellert's lengthy multiple strophed poems. The vocal line is doubled by the piano part, which is frequently chordal and subordinate. The last song of the group, "Busslied" (Song of Penitence), is more musically complex, with its great length and elaborate music. It is divided into two sections, the first of which is a sinner's supplication to God for undeserved mercy, followed by his anticipation of mercy and the joy that will result. The sinner's pleading is expressively reflected in the music of the first section, with its minor key and mild dissonances on upper neighboring tones; the joyful second section, in the parallel major to the key of the first, is musically organized as a strophic variation, with the variations occurring in the accompaniment. Part of the voice's melody is anticipated by the piano in its introduction and is then stated fully by the voice when it enters, a common technique of Beethoven's. The musical excitement generated by the piano variations dominates the text and carries the listener on a buoyant wave of emotion.

Several of Beethoven's most charming songs are based on Goethe's poetry. "Aus Goethes Faust" (From Goethe's Faust) and "Neue Liebe, neues Leben" (New Love, New Life) are both taken from Beethoven's Op. 75, along with his setting of "Mignon" (or "Kennst du das Land"—Do You Know the Land), another poem spoken by the character Mignon in *Wilhelm Meisters Lehrjahre.* "Aus Goethes Faust," also known as Mephistopheles's "Song of the Flea," is an exuberant, humorous strophic song with a short choral coda in which Beethoven totally captures the vitality of Goethe's poem. Although the accompaniment is carefully subordinated to the voice, it not only echoes the vocal line at the end of every stanza in a jovial, mocking fashion but also has its own imitation of a jumping flea, which appears in the introduction and interludes (Example 5-6).

Example 5-6. Beethoven, "Aus Goethes Faust" (From Goethe's Faust), mm. 1–3.

In "Neue Liebe," Beethoven freely shapes Goethe's poem to accommodate a complex musical form, repeating the first two stanzas of the poem in their entirety before continuing with the third stanza. Music historians point to the use of sonata form to organize this song: the musical material in the vocal line presents the primary theme in the tonic (mm. 1–17), then modulates to the dominant in the first recitative. After the recitative, two more themes are presented, followed by a short development section in which the first line of text is repeated. The repetition of the first two stanzas of music and text constitutes the recapitulation in the tonic followed by the coda, which uses the third stanza of poetry.[5] The delightful, lilting music certainly captures the mood of the poetry. Stylistically, this song is difficult to categorize because of its unusual form and its additional incorporation of recitative and an operalike ending.

There should be no surprise in finding that Beethoven, the ingenious master of sonata form, should explore its possibilities in the lied. Other composers who were linked to the classical style of the eighteenth century also employed sonata form in their songwriting. Louis Spohr wrote "An Sie am Clavier" (To Her at the Piano), which he identified as a "Sonatine für Pianoforte." Spohr, however, used the piano part to realize the sonata form while maintaining formal independence in the voice part (see the section in Chapter 11 on Spohr's songs).

Beethoven represents a unique transitional figure in the development of the lied. His many simple strophic songs in which the voice line is doubled by a modest chordal accompaniment contrast with others, such as "Busslied," in which the voice floats upon a wave of exquisite variations. Although songs held only peripheral interest for him, Beethoven contributed a number of wonderful lieder to a fledgling genre and introduced important creative ideas that would have a major impact on those who followed. His original concept of the song cycle would be translated into the particular vocabularies of Schubert, Schumann, Brahms, and a number of other nineteenth-century composers.

CHAPTER SIX

Franz Schubert

"I can teach him nothing, he has learnt it from God himself."
—Court organist Ruzicka, engaged to give Schubert lessons
in thorough-bass.[1]

*Hearing "Der Leiermann" or "Der du von dem Himmel bist" we
kiss Schubert's hand, not only because these songs are close to
God: their simplicity and purity defeat us and hold us, eternally
hold us through our inability to explain why or how they are so
sublime.*
—Pianist Gerald Moore[2]

Franz Schubert (1797–1828) left a legacy of over six hundred
songs which exhaustively explore the possibilities of this genre. No
other major composer since Schubert has come close to matching
him for sheer numbers of beautiful songs: strophic songs, such as "Ave
Maria," whose wonderful melodies bear repeating with each new
stanza of text; modified strophic and strophic variations, such as "Im
Frühling" (In Spring), with delicate, subtle alterations that continue
to delight audiences; through-composed songs, such as "Erlkönig"
and "Der Zwerg" (The Dwarf), that are highly effective in telling
their dramatic stories. Nearly fifty of Schubert's lieder, not including
his two cycles, *Die schöne Müllerin* and *Winterreise*, are part of
today's active concert fare. Schubert elevated song to the status of a
major musical genre and made it possible for all the great lieder composers after him to accept the art song as being "worthy" of their
attention.

Figure 6-1. Franz Schubert. Lithograph, after painting by Wilhelm August Rieder. Courtesy of the Library of Congress.

Beautiful songs were written by composers before Schubert— song is, after all, one of the oldest forms of musical expression. Max Harrison in *The Lieder of Brahms* traces the lineage of the nineteenth-century art song, and J. W. Smeed in *The German Art Song and Its Poetry, 1740–1900* discusses the impressive outpouring of song by forgotten composers in the eighteenth and nineteenth centuries. Not until the last quarter of the eighteenth century, however, did composers begin to use the piano as the accompanying instrument for the voice in their songs. The piano in conjunction with the great flood of lyric poetry that had been written in the second half of the century provided new soil on which song could grow.

Johann Friedrich Reichardt, Johann Zumsteeg, and Carl Friedrich Zelter were among the better-known composers who wrote songs before Schubert, preparing the foundation for his contributions. Schubert studied and admired the songs of Zumsteeg (1760–1802) and even set some of the same poems to music. As was mentioned earlier, Haydn, Beethoven, and Mozart also wrote songs, but songwriting was not a primary interest for them and did not add much to their musical reputations.

Would song have become an important musical genre in the nineteenth century without Schubert? Schubert was the first major composer who devoted a generous amount of his musical attention to song. Some critics in his day chided him for writing songs that were not "true" German song; they considered his songs too artificial.[3] This criticism represents a tacit recognition that Schubert was doing something different in song from his predecessors and contemporaries.

Schubert elevated song to the rank of major genre primarily by writing with great artistry, artistry that demonstrated what a varied, challenging, sophisticated medium song could be. He was the first important composer who explored the vast possibilities of song composition, and it is significant that he presented a repertory of such bulk and variety to illustrate the limitless potential of a musical domain that had largely been taken for granted or ignored by other composers. Certainly, Johann Friedrich Reichardt, who wrote more than twice as many songs as Schubert, should also be credited with making an important contribution to the development of the lied, but most of his songs failed to venture beyond the modest level of home entertainment.

All significant nineteenth-century composers of the lied who followed Schubert took his songs as their point of departure.

Schumann, Brahms, and Wolf admired Schubert's songs and measured their own accomplishments with Schubert in mind. Schumann viewed Schubert's songs in something of an evolutionary sense, believing that his generation would move the lied to new heights as it pursued the linking of music and great poetry. Brahms also studied Schubert's songs and commented that his decision to minimize directions to singer and pianist was modeled on Schubert's approach. Hugo Wolf not only studied Schubert's songs but consciously avoided setting any poem that he felt Schubert had already successfully treated.

Schubert was not universally recognized during his life as the musical genius who single handedly put song "on the map." "Gretchen am Spinnrade," "Lachen und Weinen" (Laughing and Crying), "Du bist die Ruh" (You Are Peace), and "An die Musik" are heard and recognized more frequently by modern audiences than they were in Schubert's day. The *Allgemeine musikalische Zeitung*, an influential Leipzig periodical that reviewed the musical happenings of his time, illustrates Schubert's neglect. Its table of contents for the period covering Schubert's life and the twenty years following requires a total of less than one column for references to articles about his work. In 1835, seven years after Schubert's death, Schumann began a review of three Schubert piano sonatas in the *Neue Zeitschrift für Musik* with the statement, "most people, by far, hardly even know his name. . . . It would require whole books to show in detail what works of pure genius his compositions are. Perhaps there will be time for this some day." [4] Maurice Brown points out that since Schubert was neither a well-known performer nor a conductor, he had few ways to draw attention to himself outside of his composing. [5] Deutsch, in his documentary biography of Schubert, states that although 187 of Schubert's 600 songs were published during his life, none of his nine symphonies, neither of his quintets, none of his ten operas, and only one of nineteen string quartets, one of seven masses, and three of his twenty-one piano sonatas were published before his death. [6] The works of his contemporary Louis Spohr (1784–1859) were usually published and were quite popular during his lifetime because Spohr was a virtuoso violinist, festival director, and conductor. His name appears countless times in the press accounts of his day, and he had no difficulty in having his compositions heard throughout Europe because of his influence and fame.

Schubert was also a very modest man who did not compromise his artistic standards for the sake of money or popularity. In fact, his friend Josef von Spaun stated in Schubert's obituary that Schubert would frequently neglect to attend events that were sponsored by important patrons if he could spend that time with his friends or outside in the open air.[7] He loved music above all else and was totally lacking in jealousy. Von Spaun recounts that when Schubert's friends denigrated the songs of another composer, Konradin Kreutzer, Schubert quietly replied: "I wish I had written them."[8]

Music publishers sometimes told Schubert that the public found the accompaniments to his songs to be difficult to play and, for the sake of his popularity and finances, they suggested that he should keep this in mind. Schubert's reaction was uncompromising. He stated that "anyone who could not play his compositions should leave them alone."[9]

Composers such as the proud, opinionated Spohr considered song to be of secondary musical importance, a kind of home entertainment rather than a serious art form. He states in his autobiography that he wrote some of his songs for royal acquaintances simply because they were fond of singing, and he even allowed his patrons the choice of text to be set![10] His attitude, mirrored by many other composers, reflects how the lied had functioned in society up to this period. Since amateurs were initially the primary consumers of the lied, composers such as Spohr wrote with the amateur's more limited abilities in mind and rarely offered anything but songs with modest levels of difficulty. In 1781, when Johann Peter Schulz had published a collection of songs, *Lieder im Volkston bey dem Klavier zu singen*, he stated in the preface that "melodies should be composed that can be sung by everyone and are suited to folklike poetry."[11]

The resistance in Schubert's time to the idea that song should be anything other than a simple form of musical expression was an attitude that later existed in France where the *romance* would stand in the path of the developing *mélodie*. In 1839, for example, the French composer Henri Blanchard complained: "What is happening to the *romance*? . . . Will it be transformed into a *Lied*? Will it grow longer, acquire more modulations? Or will it remain simple, naïve, and as characteristic as it has always been of our native taste.[12]

Schubert successfully wrote many strophic songs of great simplicity such as "Seligkeit" and "Heidenröslein," but this simplicity is not calculated to serve a particular audience; it is simplicity that best expresses Schubert's artistic vision for the text he was setting. Simplicity in the hands of a great artist such as Schubert defies analysis, as Gerald Moore states in the opening quote of this chapter. As successful a composer as Franz Liszt was only occasionally able to muster such simplicity in the cause of profundity, as he did, for example, in "Es muss ein Wunderbares sein" (It Must Be Something Wonderful). And composers like Reichardt and Zelter, who wrote in a very simple style, could be simply boring. These two men adhered to a highly restrained, conservative style of songwriting that is sometimes called the Berlin School. Advocates for this "school" clung to the idea that strophic poetry should be set to strophic music, generally with syllabic treatment of text and little musical repetition to detract from the poet's work. The songs of composers Luise Reichardt, Fanny Mendelssohn Hensel, and Felix Mendelssohn can be traced to these ideals.

Schubert, influenced by the elaborate ballads of the south German Johann Zumsteeg, wrote numerous songs whose complexity challenges the technique of both singer and pianist. "Die Allmacht" (Omnipotence), "Erlkönig," and "Der Hirt auf dem Felsen" (The Shepherd on the Rock) are highly demanding for the singer just as "An·Schwager Kronos" (To the Coachman Kronos), "Die Forelle", and "Erlkönig" are for the pianist. In 1821, a reviewer in the Vienna *Allgemeine Musikalische Zeitung* commented that

> the triplet accompaniment [in "Erlkönig"] keeps the whole alive and gives it more unity, as it were; but one could wish that Herr Schubert had occasionally transferred it to the left hand and thus facilitated performance; for the ceaseless striking of one and the same note in triplets throughout whole bars tires the hand, if the piece is to be taken at the rapid pace demanded by Herr Schubert.[13]

Goethe's great ballad "Erlkönig," based on Herder's translation of the Danish folktale *Ellerkrone* (Elf Woman), fascinated the literary and musical worlds after its debut in Goethe's play *Die Fischerin* (The Fisher Maid) in 1782. The poem tells the eerie tale of a child who is riding with his father late at night through a dark, mysterious forest where he sees a spirit—the Erlking—who literally frightens the little boy to death (see translation in Chapter 2, "Politics and Poetry"). Over one hundred years after "Erlkönig's" first appearance, there were already twenty-eight different musical settings of this macabre poem,[14] and at least twenty-nine other versions have been discovered since then by music historians.[15]

The term *ballad*, as it applies to the German lied, refers to a narrative poem—a poem that tells a story in simple, dramatic language. In the early folk ballad, whose origins may go as far back as a thousand years, the poem was both sung and danced. By the time the poetic ballad was recaptured in the folk collections of Herder and others, it existed primarily as a poetic narrative. The story was usually told in dialogue, sometimes with the aid of an anonymous narrator. Throughout the romantic era, many poets, translators, and composers were attracted to the drama of the ballad: Heine's "Die beiden Grenadiere," Mörike's "Der Feuerreiter" (The Fire Rider), Collin's "Der Zwerg," and Uhland's "Das Lied vom Herrn von Falkenstein" (The Song of Lord Falkenstein) are just a few of the multitude of ballads that were set to music by song composers such as Schumann, Loewe, Wagner, Wolf, Liszt, Schubert, and Brahms.

The musical ballads of Johann Zumsteeg (1760–1802) were much admired and carefully studied by Franz Schubert. Many of Schubert's early, sprawling narratives reflect Zumsteeg's influence. The dramatic nature of the ballad brought excitement even to many of the simple, strophic settings of Schubert's predecessors Carl Zelter and Johann Friedrich Reichardt. For example, Zelter's repetitious setting of Goethe's "Der König in Thule" (The King in Thule) is never tiresome because of the poem's beautiful story and Zelter's sweetly haunting melody.

Reichardt's setting of "Erlkönig" is a fascinatingly creative use of strophic form. The narrator's introduction is presented in the first musical stanza, and each succeeding stanza of text conforms to these same harmonies and melody as the story unfolds. Although Reichardt does not differentiate the characters of father, son, and narrator, his melodic material has been created in such a way that the child's voice rises each time he asks a question, while the rhythms of his melodic line are adjusted to suit the textual flow. Reichardt differentiates the Erlking from the other characters but without deviating from his strophic material. The melody of the song appears in the voice and is doubled in the accompaniment in the first two stanzas. In the third stanza, when the Erlking speaks, Reichardt retains the melody in the accompaniment but has the Erlking sing his part in a monotone on D, a pitch that had acted as an internal pedal point in the piano part of each stanza. This Erlking has none of the allure of Schubert's seducing figure of death but represents the more traditional character of death as inescapable and inexorable. It is curious that Reichardt's choice of G minor for "Erlkönig" is the same as both Schubert's and Loewe's in their versions.

Reichardt's "Erlkönig" is instantly relegated to the position of historical curiosity when we hear the amazing tour de force written by the eighteen-year-old Schubert. Each character in the drama is musically differentiated: the narrator, the frightened boy, his worried father, the suave Erlking. The father's melody is written in a low vocal range and shows the father, who cannot see the Erlking, trying to calm his child; his responses are always short, square, and reassuring. The boy's voice is harmonically unstable, and each one of his entrances is a whole or half step higher than the previous as his hysteria grows; Schubert heightens the musical tension of the boy's part by creating a series of dissonant seconds between the vocal line and the right hand of the accompaniment. The overall key of "Erlkönig" is G minor, and the song is unified by the driving triplet figure of repeated notes. This figure changes only when the Erlking speaks and in the final three measures. The Erlking is given a longer, more lyrical vocal part than the other characters, and his accompaniment consists of a seductive triplet figuration in G major. In this song as in many others, Schubert exploits the expressive potential of parallel major and minor keys. He brilliantly uses the natural colorations of the human voice, differentiating father and child by range. The child's continual move to the upper part of the voice allows the interpreter the possibility of using a thin, shrill tone to convey the illusion of a child screaming with fear. (Some singers, choosing to avoid an "ugly" sound at the climax of the child's part, opt for a beautiful, rich tone—maintaining, perhaps, their vocal reputations but denying the dramatic implications of the song.)

Schubert himself participated in a "quartet" performance of "Erlkönig," singing the part of the father; Josefine von Koller, the young daughter of a friend, sang the part of the little boy; the retired opera singer and famous interpreter of Schubert's songs Johann Michael Vogl sang the part of the Erlking; and Schubert's friend Albert Stadler played the piano.[16]

Schubert's setting of this poem, while not quite crossing into the realm of opera, is certainly grand in scale, and its recitative-like ending, although reversing the usual order of recitative and aria in opera, completes a drama that is "larger than life." This song was later dedicated to Schubert's friend Count Moritz von Dietrichstein who was, appropriately enough, director of the Court Opera.

All of the great romantic art song composers of the nineteenth century were interested in writing opera, yet their operas were singularly unsuccessful. Perhaps their gifts for intimacy and subtle understatement could not coexist with the grand scale that opera demanded. Although Schubert, Schumann, and Wolf each wrote operas, none of these achieved lasting recognition. Both Schumann and Wolf spent years trying to find a libretto with which they could work, and Brahms, although always on the lookout for an appropriate libretto, finally abandoned all plans for an opera. It was not until the end of the century, in the post-Wagnerian era, that song composers began to achieve success in both song and opera, but by then song itself had changed.

Schubert not only unifies the music of "Erlkönig" but drives it forward with a programmatic accompaniment that imitates the pounding hooves of the horse. Since he did not wish to play "Erlkönig's" difficult accompaniment in performance, Schubert wrote a simplified version in 1816 that he used when accompanying singers. Benedikt Randhartinger, successor to Schubert as boy soprano in the Court Chapel and later its musical director, claimed in 1888 that it was he and not Vogl who had premiered "Erlkönig," in a performance at the Stadtkonvikt of Vienna that was so inspired the audience demanded its repetition. During this repetition, Schubert supposedly omitted the triplets with eighth-notes because, he said, "they are too difficult for me; a virtuoso may play them."[17]

And many virtuosi have played them! Felix Mendelssohn was commended by a critic for his forceful accompanying of Karl Adam Bader, a tenor at the Berlin Opera. The reviewer, however, lamented that Schubert's "Erlkönig" could not match either Reichardt's or Zelter's setting of the poem![18] Clara Schumann, one of the great pianists of the nineteenth century, played Liszt's transcription for piano of "Erlkönig" in her recitals. Franz Liszt made two transcriptions of the song—one for piano (1837–38) and another for orchestra (1863). The repeated triplets of "Erlkönig" presented no difficulties for the spectacular pianist, Liszt, who even played the dramatic melodic figure of the left hand in octaves (Example 6-1)!

Example 6-1. Schubert/Liszt, "Erlkönig," mm. 1–4.

Liszt's rôle as a champion of Schubert's music cannot be overestimated. When Schubert died in 1828, few musicians outside the intimate circle of his friends knew his music. Not only did Liszt transcribe over fifty-seven of Schubert's songs for the piano, but since he performed and traveled constantly, he was able to introduce Schubert's music throughout Europe. In France, for example, when the famous French singer Adolphe Nourrit heard Franz Liszt play a piano transcription of "Erlkönig," Schubert's music gained a new champion.

> [Liszt] was at the piano playing "Erlkönig" when Nourrit entered.... As he became aware of this dramatic music, he showed deep emotion and his face lit up. When the piece ended, he requested that it be played again, but Liszt replied that it would be better if he sang it. Nourrit excused himself on the grounds that he did not know German. When Liszt explained the text to him, the singer agreed to merely vocalize the melody, which he did with the expressiveness of an inspired interpreter.... From that day on he was taken with an intense passion for those songs; at his request a certain number were translated and he became their indefatigable propagator.[19]

By 1850, more than 360 of Schubert's songs had been published in France. Hector Berlioz, who commented that he prized Schubert's music because it "contains nothing of what certain people call melody—quite fortunately!"[!],[20] made a powerful orchestral arrangement of "Erlkönig" for tenor and orchestra in 1860. Frits Noske suggests that Schubert's songs helped to precipitate a musical "revolution" in French song that later resulted in the emergence of the mélodie.[21]

"Erlkönig" was also the vehicle that introduced Schubert to England, for in 1831, the famous soprano Wilhelmina Schröder-Devrient sang "Erlkönig" in its first London performance. Unfortunately English audiences failed to respond to Schubert's music with anything resembling the enthusiasm which they later showered upon the music of their favorite, Felix Mendelssohn.[22]

Schubert achieved only modest recognition during his pathetically short life of 31 years and was unable to find a publisher for "Erlkönig" when it was written. Finally, in 1821, three of his friends published it at their own expense, and "Erlkönig" began to draw attention to the music of this great master. Throughout the nineteenth century, "Erlkönig" remained Schubert's most popular song, and its accessibility led listeners to examine more of his impressive repertory of instrumental and vocal music. Schubert's popularity continued to grow after his death so that by 1857 the Austrian music critic Eduard Hanslick would state that Schubert had an ardent group of supporters in Vienna.[23] Schubert's growing popularity was important for other composers of the lied. By 1876 the Viennese opera singer Gustav Walter was giving annual Liederabende that were devoted solely to Schubert's songs. Walter then branched out into evenings of Beethoven, Schumann, and Brahms, and other singers followed suit.[24]

Schubert wrote with a brilliant understanding of the human voice. In his famous "Gretchen am Spinnrade," he pushes the singer throughout the song to mirror the agitation of the distraught Margaret as she repeats in her refrain that she will never again find peace now that she loves Faust. In her final statement of longing, "Oh could I but hold him and kiss him as I would wish, and expire under his kisses," the vocal phrases become short and breathless, and the voice rises to a frantic pitch. The famous accompanist and vocal coach Paul Ulanowsky would tell his students that the singer should be exhausted when she reaches the final refrain of the song, "Meine Ruh ist hin, mein Herz ist schwer" (My rest is over, my heart is heavy).

Schubert often sang and played his own songs in the homes of his friends and admirers. In *Schubert: A Documentary Biography*, Otto Deutsch includes a letter from one Josef Huber to his fiancée, Rosalie Kranzbichler, in which Huber describes the first known "Schubertiad," "a kind of evening party among friends and their families at which music by Schubert alone was to be heard"[25] (see Chapter 4 for the complete quote).

Among his many musical gifts, Schubert possessed a pleasing singing voice as a child. His musical education included violin, piano, and singing lessons with Liechtenthal parish organist Michael Holzer.

> Whenever I wished to teach him anything new, I found that he had already mastered it. Consequently, I cannot be said to have given him any lessons at all; I merely amused myself, and regarded him with dumb astonishment.[26]

By the time Schubert had reached the age of eleven, he was a soprano in the Liechtenthal church. His brother Ferdinand observed that Schubert was wonderfully expressive and always seemed to understand the music.[27] Also at the age of eleven, Schubert became a choirboy in Vienna's Imperial Chapel Choir. As an adult, he pleased his friends and acquaintances with his light baritone voice when he presented them with his latest vocal compositions. "At Schober's . . .

we spent an evening too, where Schubert sang quite beautifully."[28]
"When all these afternoon guests had gone, the old cosiness
returned, and Schubert sang splendidly."[29] This vocal gift influenced
and infused his compositional style with a melodic brilliance that has
never been surpassed. The sheer "tunefulness" of his songs has been
a primary factor in his secure position as a beloved composer of song.
The fact that Schubert sang his own songs would also account for the
skillful vocal writing they exhibit. What voice teacher has not felt safe
in assigning "Lachen und Weinen" or "Die Forelle" to young voice
students? In a lengthy obituary notice written in 1829, Josef von
Spaun, lifelong friend to Schubert, tells this apocryphal story:
because he chose to display his melodic gifts in German song,
Schubert lost the support and guidance of his famous teacher Salieri,
who was not sympathetic to either German poetry or German song
and tried to convince Schubert to save his talents for Italian opera.[30]

Schubert represents a culmination of the many great Viennese
composers' love of melody. Haydn and Mozart reveled in the power
of melody, and each brought his individual talents to bear on this fundamental musical element. Schubert seems to have possessed a limitless fund of beautiful melodies—a uniquely long-breathed type—
which he used to enrich his instrumental works as well as his songs.
One of Schubert's friends, Leopold von Sonnleithner, discusses this
melodic gift and its realization in performance.

> The beauty of his melodies . . . is also an independent, purely
> musical one . . . entirely independent of the words, even though
> it follows these closely in every respect and always interprets the
> poet's feeling profoundly. . . . Schubert, therefore, demanded
> above all that his songs should not so much be declaimed as sung
> flowingly . . . to the complete exclusion of the unmusical
> speaking voice, and that by this means the musical idea should
> be displayed in its purity. . . . Schubert always indicated exactly
> where he wanted or permitted a ritardando, an accelerando, or
> any kind of freer delivery. But where he did not indicate this, he
> would not tolerate the slightest arbitrariness or the least devia-
> tion in tempo. (1860)[31]

Although he was not a virtuoso pianist, Schubert's performances
of his songs were highly moving. The well-known conductor, composer, and teacher Ferdinand Hiller recounts a performance of
Schubert's songs in the home of Katharina Buchwieser when
Schubert accompanied the aging baritone Johann Michael Vogl.

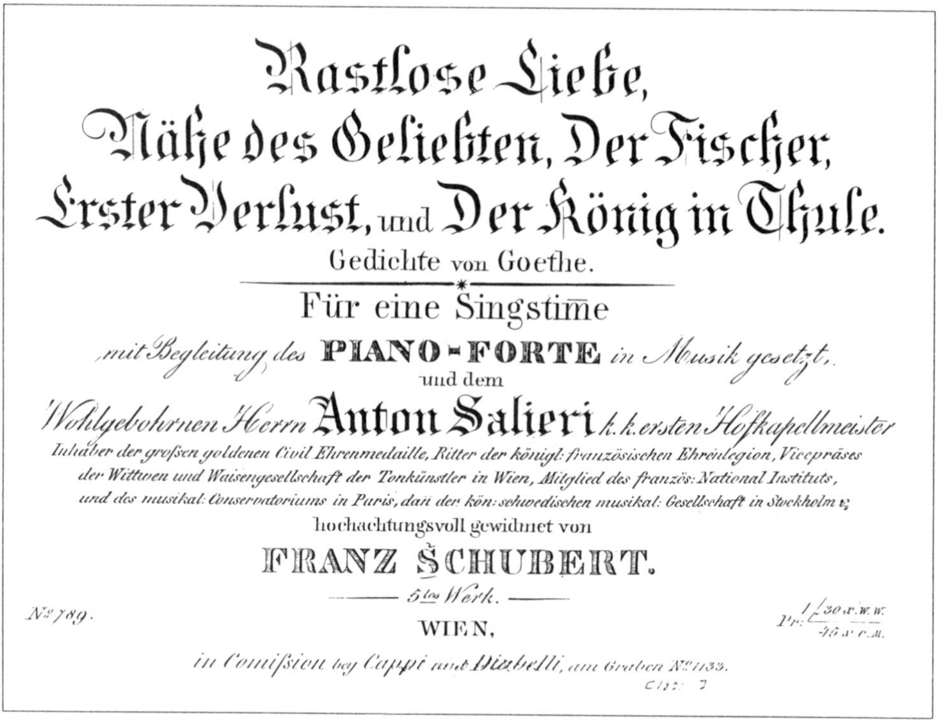
Rastlose Liebe,
Nähe des Geliebten, Der Fischer,
Erster Verlust, und Der König in Thule.
Gedichte von Goethe.
Für eine Singstim̄e
mit Begleitung des PIANO-FORTE in Musik gesetzt,
und dem
Wohlgebohrnen Herrn Anton Salieri k. k. ersten Hofkapellmeister
Inhaber der großen goldenen Civil Ehrenmedaille, Ritter der königl: französischen Ehrenlegion, Vicepräses
der Wittwen und Waisengesellschaft der Tonkünstler in Wien, Mitglied des französ: National Instituts,
und des musikal: Conservatoriums in Paris, dan̄ der kön: schwedischen musikal: Gesellschaft in Stockholm &c.
hochachtungsvoll gewidmet von
FRANZ SCHUBERT.
5tes Werk.
No. 789.
WIEN,
Pr: 1 f 30 x. W. W. / 45 x. C. M.
in Comission bey Cappi und Diabelli, am Graben No. 1133.

Figure 6-2. Title page to Franz Schubert's Op. 5, dedicated to his former teacher Antonio Salieri and published 9 July 1821 by Cappi and Diabelli.

In early 1827, I traveled to Vienna with my teacher [Johann Nepomuk Hummel] where I was supposed to see and speak to Beethoven a few weeks before his death; we had never heard of Schubert. A young friend of Hummel's, the former singer Katharina Buchwieser, . . . raved about him and his songs. It was in her house that Schubert was introduced to the famous conductor [Hummel]. We ate there several times in the company of the quiet young man and his companion, the tenor [*sic*], Vogl. The latter, already old but full of fire and life, had very little voice left—and the piano playing of Schubert, in spite of considerable skill, was far from masterly. And yet, I have never again heard Schubert songs as at that time! Vogl knew how to make one forget his vocal shortcomings by using the most intimate, striking expressions, and Schubert accompanied as he had to accompany. One piece followed another—we were insatiable—the performers tireless. I can still see my stout, true-hearted master as he sat in the great salon, sideways to the piano on a comfortable easy chair. He said little, but glistening tears ran down his cheeks. . . . It was a revelation. On one of the days that followed, I visited Schubert in his shabby room. . . . "You compose so much," I said to the young master. "I write every morning for a few hours," he replied in a most modest voice, "and when I have finished a piece, I begin another." [Hiller then quotes Schubert's friend, the painter Schwind who describes Schubert's artistic life as follows:] "No happier existence could there be. . . . Every morning he composed something beautiful, and every evening he found enthusiastic admirers."[32]

Schubert's ability to capture in music the essence and mood of a poem is magical: the frightened, breathless girl who faces calm, inexorable Death in "Der. Tod und das Mädchen," the sense of nostalgia and regret in "Im Frühling," the light-hearted joie de vivre of the poet in "Der Musensohn" (Son of the Muses), the eerie, mysterious atmosphere of "Die Krähe" (The Crow), the feeling of hope for the future in "Frühlingsglaube" (Belief in Spring).

"Der Tod und das Mädchen" is only one page in length, yet two characters clearly emerge from the music. The panic-stricken girl is portrayed through a short, choppy, breathless vocal line; her fear is also mirrored, at first, in the rising melodic line and the rapidly repeated figuration in the accompaniment (Example 6-2). Death, on the other hand, whose music is anticipated in the piano introduction, moves with slow deliberation. He speaks at a slower tempo than the girl, his range is lower, and the long note values and dirgelike rhythm tell the girl who he is (Example 6-3). Text and music paint Death as a comforting friend who offers rest—peaceful, eternal sleep. Unlike the wiley, evil Erlking, this figure of Death is almost loving in his offer of release from life. The music conveys the sense of death's inevitability, and yet the sheer calm steadiness of the musical rhythm

Pass by, ah, pass by; go, savage skeleton! I

Example 6-2. Schubert, "Der Tod und das Mädchen" (Death and the Maiden), mm. 9–12.

Give me your hand, you lovely, sweet thing, I am your friend and

Example 6-3. Schubert, "Der Tod und das Mädchen," mm. 22–26.

removes his fearfulness. Death speaks in a monotone, chanting most of his words on two basic pitches, D and F, much like some of the monotonous declamations of the Commendatore in Mozart's *Don Giovanni* or the oracle in Gluck's *Alceste*. Death was a familiar theme for Schubert, who lived in an age when death was a frequent visitor: he lost his mother when he was fifteen and was himself one of only five children who survived childhood in a family of fourteen. Nearly fifty of his songs deal directly or indirectly with death.

Schubert also wrote many dramatic songs, conceiving them on a grand scale. These include "Gruppe aus dem Tartarus," "Prometheus," "An Schwager Kronos," "Dem Unendlichen," "Die junge Nonne," "Die Allmacht," "Aufenthalt" (Abode), "Der Atlas," and "Rastlose Liebe" (Restless Love). Most of these songs are through-composed, allowing Schubert considerable flexibility in responding to the text.

"Die junge Nonne," a modified strophic song, exemplifies many essential features of his dramatic songs. Poetry and music reflect a young woman's inner turmoil as she decides whether to become the bride of Christ. A thunderstorm outside, paralleling her inner struggle, is presented by Schubert in a dramatic piano part: the right hand plays an agitated sixteenth-note figure against the left hand's bold octaves, which anticipate the voice's opening melody (Example 6-4). Many of Schubert's dramatic songs, such as "Erlkönig" and "Der Atlas," use this device of a rapid, often tremolo-like figuration in the right hand against a melodically and rhythmically aggressive bass line (see Chapter 3, "The Piano"). Melodic material moves back and forth between voice and piano throughout the song. The young nun's indecision and struggle are mirrored in the melodically irregular vocal line, which sweeps dramatically over an octave and a fifth. The tumult is rhythmically enhanced in both the voice and the piano parts

Example 6-4. Schubert, "Die junge Nonne" (The Young Nun),
mm. 1–4.

with an eighth-note upbeat figure, particularly effective when it outlines a minor third or diminished fifth in the piano part (mm. 43–46).
Schubert often controls the "dramatic" dynamics of his songs by
shifting melody and harmony upward to increase tension or downward to decrease tension. With the conclusion of the first stanza, for
example, he subdues the previous musical tempest by moving the
vocal phrase from repeated Ds to repeated D-flats to repeated C-
naturals, while harmonically shifting downward from a diminished
chord on G-sharp to a diminished chord on G and resolving to an F-
minor chord. He heightens the emotional conclusion of the song by
transposing an entire melodic figure from C to D and finally to F. Two
dotted quarter-notes are repeated throughout the song to imitate the
ringing of a church bell, an image that becomes clear only at the
conclusion of the song when the young woman's struggle is over and
she has dedicated her life to God (Example 6-5). The "rightness" of
her decision is confirmed when the music becomes harmonically
stable. Schubert moves to F major to indicate the positive resolution
of the nun's struggle and allows the music to become melodically and
rhythmically steady. The bass line now becomes more regular and
moves more slowly as the imitation of church bells resounds back and
forth between the treble and bass of the piano. The rhythmic motion
of the vocal line also slows down and becomes regular.

Example 6-5. Schubert, "Die junge Nonne," mm. 84–87.

Some of Schubert's through-composed songs are very loosely organized, depending almost entirely on the poem for organization. In "Ganymed," for example, Schubert changes the music with every poetic nuance of Goethe's poem. This results in a song with seven different figurations in the accompaniment, three key signature changes (A-flat major, E major, F major), enharmonic key shifts, and a conclusion that is a minor third away from the key in which he began! He whimsically word-paints throughout the song, stretching out words like "unendliche" (endless) for nine beats and using a long trill to depict the wind. Despite the sectional nature of this piece and its lack of formal cohesiveness, it is somehow still a pleasing song.

Another song that is even more sprawling, less organized, and less effective than "Ganymed" is "Der Sänger" (The Singer), based on a poem by Goethe and set by Schubert twice. More a scene than a song, "Der Sänger" consists of long sections of recitative alternating with arioso. "Der Sänger" begins in D major with a fairly conventional piano introduction in common time and then launches into recitative. There are a total of six key signature changes, six time signature changes, and eight sections of recitative and arioso in the song; Schubert ends the piece in B-flat major, a major third lower than his starting point of D major. Although seldom performed today, "Der Sänger" owes much to the style of writing found in Zumsteeg's ballads such as his "Ritter Toggenburg" (Knight Toggenburg) (1800), based on a poem by Schiller. Zumsteeg changes figurations more than sixteen times in this fifteen-page, highly sectional song and often moves to distant keys (from A-flat major to G major, for example) without any preparation. Nevertheless, Zumsteeg's writing was a wonderful example of stylistic freedom for Schubert, who could profit from studying these long, rambling forms in the process of discovering his own musical language. Zumsteeg's writing, unlike the music of the so-called Berlin School, was not restricted by a preference for strophic form. Although most of his figurations in the accompaniment are relatively thin textured and conventionally shaped chords, scales, Alberti basses, and so on, his bold lack of restraint was a positive example for the young Schubert.

Schubert's fascinating facility for word-painting unfolds naturally and unaffectedly in most of his songs. His amazing skill in creating water images, as in "Auf dem Wasser zu singen" (To Sing on the Water), "Die Forelle," or "Wohin?" (Where To?), has certainly never been matched (Example 6-6). But he also creates a great variety of other images, such as the hopping rhythms and calling of a bird in

Example 6-6. Schubert, "Auf dem Wasser zu singen" (To Sing on the Water), mm. 1–4.

Example 6-7. Schubert, "Gretchen am Spinnrade" (Gretchen at the Spinning Wheel), mm. 1–4.

"An die Nachtigall" (To the Nightingale), the strumming of the lyre in "An die Leier" (To the Lyre), the sound of a spinning wheel in "Gretchen am Spinnrade," a galloping horse in "Erlkönig," and the plucking of the guitar in "Ständchen" (Serenade), among many others (Example 6-7).

Yet his word-painting is not an end in itself and cannot be viewed as a distraction from the song's overall expression. The spinning-wheel figuration in "Gretchen am Spinnrade" heightens the song's mood of agitation; its complex levels of rhythmic activity push the dramatic tension forward. Schubert's effortless fluency in manipulating graphic figurations is truly astounding. He captures the hesitant motion of restarting the spinning wheel after Margarete's distracted thoughts of Faust have allowed it to stop (mm. 65–73). He seems to have possessed a limitless supply of unique figurations for the piano, which he used with amazing ease to create and enhance the meaning of the text. In songs such as "Der Jüngling an der Quelle" (The Youth at the Spring), the piano establishes the mood with a placid sixteenth-note figure in the right hand against an eighth-note figure in the left, which moves in contrary motion to the right hand over a pedal point.

Whether the accompaniment is depicting a rippling brook or the whispering of the breeze is less significant than the lyric beauty of this wonderful song.

In "Seligkeit," Schubert matches the charming mood of the poet Hölty's cheerful little poem with a Viennese-like waltz. Hölty describes the wonders of heavenly bliss, and then says that he would rather remain on earth with the delightful Laura. Schubert matches this playful poem with a waltz accompaniment—the left hand supplies the chordal structure and the right hand plays a rippling scale that is altered slightly with each appearance so the harmony is never static. When the voice enters with its own melody, the piano part becomes pure accompaniment, supplying support chords for the voice. This joyful strophic song with just three stanzas of text seems far too short, as music and poetry are artlessly united. But "Seligkeit" represents only one side of this multifaceted composer who also wrote the Wagner-like, harmonically bold "Dass sie hier gewesen" and the horrifying "Der Doppelgänger."

Schubert often found the spirit of a poem without extramusical suggestion. "Der Doppelgänger," written in the last year of his life, is a strangely morose song. Heinrich Heine's poem takes us to an eerie, silent street in the middle of the night; a man, passing the house of his former love, sees a mysterious figure in front of her window and discovers, to his horror, that the figure is himself. Schubert enhances the nightmarish atmosphere of the poem with a four-bar ground-bass figure combined with a pedal point on F-sharp; the accompaniment is plodding, rhythmically static, circular in shape yet moving steadily and relentlessly. The vocal line, recitative-like and melodically monotonous, conveys a trancelike state as the speaker observes and moves toward the discovery of his other self; the vocal phrases are short, chopped, and laborious (Example 6-8). The accompaniment echoes the voice like footfalls in a silent street; each echo seems to mock the speaker, just as Schumann would later mock his rejected lover in "Ich hab' im Traum geweinet" (I Cried in My Dream). When the protagonist realizes who the mysterious figure is, Schubert intensifies this primary climax with a triple-forte dissonance on "*Gestalt*" (figure); then, as the speaker addresses his double, the music pulls back dynamically and begins another buildup, this time with a tempo acceleration, to a secondary climax on "manche Nacht" (many a night). There is resignation at the end of the song as the fourth chord of the ground is altered in its last appearance and the third of the final chord is raised. Richard Capell, a biographer of Schubert, calls "Der

Still ist die Nacht, es ru-hen die Gas-sen,

in die - sem_ Hau-se wohn - te mein_ Schatz;

The night is still, the streets are asleep,
in this house my sweetheart used to live;

Example 6-8. Schubert, "Der Doppelgänger" (The Double), mm. 1–14.

Doppelgänger" "the finest of all achievements in matching of music and verse. . . . The vocal writing represents the culmination of Schubert's art."[33]

Schubert's eclectic taste in poetry for his songs ranged from excellent to banal. While he set to music fifty-five poems by Goethe, a few of them several times, his friendships with numerous obscure poets of his day account for many of the lesser poems he chose. His close friend, Franz von Schober, for example, was the poet for the famous "An die Musik." Schubert responded to many second-rate poems with a flood of great song. His monumental cycle *Winterreise* would certainly fall into this category, as would some of his most beautiful songs such as "Im Frühling." Schubert set poetry with great individuality, seeking the essential meaning of each poem.

"Im Frühling" is another example of a minor poem from which an inspired song results. It works, in this case, because the musical ideas dominate, communicating the mood of the poem without drawing the listener's attention to the weaknesses of the text. Schubert uses two separate melodies, one in the accompaniment, the other in the voice. The vocal line incorporates modest variants from stanza to stanza, while the piano executes variations that include both melodies. After a very simple statement of each melody in the piano part and the voice, the variations unfold so delicately that the listener becomes increasingly absorbed in the beauties of the music. Whereas in "Wanderers Nachtlied" II, poetry and music seem to stride along together as equal partners, the poetic structure of "Im Frühling" recedes into the background. We are so captivated by the musical development that we accept simple virtues of the poem—its story of a young man who looks at nature's beauties as he recalls his love and its dissolution.

Schubert unites many musical qualities of his predecessors within his own style. His melodies have the balance, clarity, and purity of sound that are reminiscent of Mozart or Haydn, yet their long-breathed quality incorporates and is supported by surprising harmonic novelties that point to the new era. His frequent reliance on clearly delineated forms in many of his songs also ties him to his predecessors. Yet even his use of free form in songs like "Der Zwerg" has precedents with classical composers such as Mozart in "Das Veilchen." In the lengthy "Der Zwerg," the musical structure is quite nebulous, responsive primarily to changes in the text. The song is unified only by its continuous piano figuration. The growing dependence of the romantics on words was to mirror itself in program music: instrumental music provided with printed texts.

While his harmonies are often couched in the slower harmonic rhythms of the classical period (Example 6-9), his bold harmonic vocabulary exhibits the romantic love of experimentation with colorful, unconventional harmonic progressions. Schubert's rich harmonies and surprising key shifts are important underpinnings of his lieder.

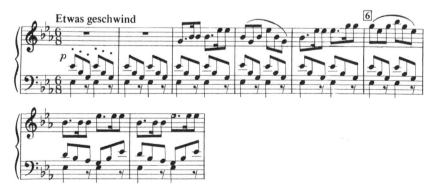

Example 6-9. Schubert, "Die Post" (The Mail), in *Winterreise* (Winter Journey), mm. 1–8.

THE SONG CYCLES[34]

Schubert's song cycles, *Die schöne Müllerin* (The Pretty Miller-Maid) and *Winterreise* (Winter Journey) illustrate the final measure of his greatness. Each of these cycles is based on the poems of the popular writer Wilhelm Müller, and each holds a highly individual place in the history of the song cycle. Unlike Beethoven's *An die ferne Geliebte*, which is compact and obviously cyclic in form, Schubert's cycles are sprawling in length and tenuously linked by key; they employ only the slightest motivic unity and, in the case of *Winterreise*, have almost no story at all.

Both of Schubert's cycles have heroes (or "anti-heroes") who travel, and consequently Schubert establishes a kind of walking pace in many of the songs, a pace that changes to reflect the changing mood of the wanderer[35] (Examples 6-10a and 6-10b). The protagonist of *Winterreise* starts his journey steadily and with determined resolution; the hero of *Die schöne Müllerin* begins with cheerful optimism.

Example 6-10a. Schubert, "Gute Nacht" (Good Night), in *Winterreise*, mm. 1–6.

Example 6-10b. Schubert, "Das Wandern" (Wandering), in *Die schöne Müllerin* (The Pretty Miller-Maid), mm. 1–4.

Nature, a favorite romantic theme, predominates in both cycles, particularly in *Winterreise* where it serves as a reflection of the main character's mental state. Each cycle highlights other common romantic themes: unrequited love and the artist as an outcast from society, a stranger, a wanderer without a home. Although Müller's characters are or become disillusioned, they are also vulnerable, possessing an insufficient store of the cynicism and self-mockery that so predominate in the poetry of Heinrich Heine. There are no surprises in Müller's heroes. Heine is said to have admired Müller, and each drew generously from a common store of romantic images such as sobbing angels, lilies and other flowers, and stars looking down on poor mortals.

Müller's *Die schöne Müllerin* poetry, consisting of twenty-three poems along with a prologue and an epilogue, was published in 1821 as part of a collection entitled "Seventy-seven Poems from the Posthumous Papers of a Travelling Horn-player." Schubert used twenty of these poems, omitting the prologue and epilogue in his musical version of 1824, which appeared in five volumes as his Op. 25.

In *Die schöne Müllerin*, the poet, like Goethe's hero Werther, finds the ultimate romantic solution to his problems—suicide. The story of this cycle is brief: a young miller goes out into the world to find adventure by following the course of a bubbling millstream. The millstream becomes a living thing for him, personified as a friend and confidant that is addressed as the miller proceeds on his way. The stream leads the young man to a mill where he seeks employment, and it is here that he sees and immediately falls in love with the beautiful daughter of the miller. Although the girl shows little sign that she returns his love, the miller convinces himself that she does. He learns that he is sadly mistaken when a hunter appears and becomes the obvious recipient of her admiring glances. The young miller seeks release and peace from his misery by drowning himself in the millstream.

The characters of this drama are the young miller, the beautiful girl, the hunter, and the all-pervading brook, which is graphically represented by a variety of musical figures throughout the cycle. In "Der Müller und der Bach" (The Miller and the Brook), for example, a dialogue between the miller and the brook, the figuration of the accompaniment changes to a rippling arpeggio when the brook begins to speak (mm. 24–35). The brook is the only character who actually speaks to the miller during the twenty songs of this cycle, reinforcing the hero's relationship with nature and his isolation from other human beings. In *Winterreise*, the protagonist's isolation from society is carried to the extreme until the final song when the hero makes contact with another alienated human being, the organ grinder.

Schubert uses many pictorial musical figures to enhance the presence of characters and ideas in *Die schöne Müllerin*. The sound of hunting horns is used to represent the hunter (Example 6-11); in addition to the water figure in "Der Müller und der Bach," several other water figures appear in *Die schöne Müllerin* (e.g., "Wohin").

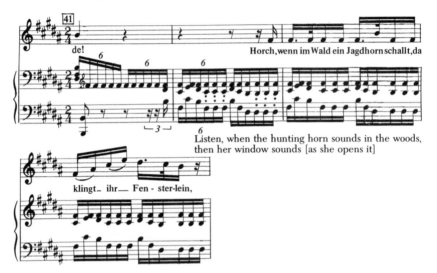

Listen, when the hunting horn sounds in the woods, then her window sounds [as she opens it]

Example 6-11. Schubert, "Die böse Farbe" (The Hateful Color), in *Die schöne Müllerin*, mm. 41–44.

Much of the unity of this cycle is provided by the text itself as the listener follows the progress of the miller's adventure. The poetry has additional links that pull the drama together. The color green, for example, is the favorite color of the miller's daughter; it is the symbol of the forest and the hunter who claims the love of the girl; green also symbolizes Spring and new love but ultimately becomes the "böse Farbe" (the hateful color). The ever-present brook also unifies the cycle. This confidant and constant companion of the miller perceives more clearly and realistically the actual state of affairs than the love-blinded miller. In "Der Neugierige" (The Curious One), for example, the miller asks the brook if he is deceiving himself about the maid, and the millstream is strangely silent. Unfortunately the miller ignores the implication of this silence. The color blue is another unifying image: it is the color of the brook and of the beloved's eyes, and the color of the flowers for the miller's grave.

The range of emotions in the music and the text of *Die schöne Müllerin* makes this cycle a highly appealing work. The tremendous energy and cheerfulness in the music at the beginning of the cycle provide both performer and audience with buoyant hopes; then the music shifts to reflectiveness, anger, hopelessness, and finally peace. Almost half of the songs are strophic, with mostly syllabic text settings, which allows the story to unfold with great clarity and simplicity, although there is certainly nothing simple about the musical setting of the poems.

Many of the melodies in *Die schöne Müllerin* are folklike with their robust rhythms, strophic organization, and regular phrasing (e.g., "Das Wandern"). But Schubert couples this with a rhythmic energy and supple rhythmic variety that many of his contemporaries, such as Louis Spohr, could not match. And, of course, there is a profusion of beautiful melodies, as in "Der Müller und der Bach," which haunt and enchant, possessing an independent life that can exist without harmonic support (Example 6-12). Here Schubert's melodic gift is unrivaled. The triple meter that controls this melody lends it the character of a slow, ritualistic dance, which could easily be performed with a simple waltz accompaniment. Schubert chose instead to begin with a halting, thin, hollow accompaniment that emphasizes the poignancy and pathos of the miller. Like

the full moon must go into the clouds,
so that men will not see its tears;

Example 6-12. Schubert, "Der Müller und der Bach" (The Miller and the Brook), in *Die schöne Müllerin*, mm. 8–16.

"Einsamkeit" (Isolation) and "Der Leiermann" (The Hurdy-Gurdy Man) of *Die Winterreise*, these empty fifths plod beneath the melody, heightening a sense of the protagonist's sorrow and suffering.

Some of Schubert's most profound works were written in the last two years of his life: *Winterreise*, "Der Doppelgänger," the String Quintet in C major (D. 956), the "Great" C Major Symphony (D. 944). He was dying when he wrote *Winterreise*. Schubert had contracted syphillis sometime early in 1823 and had experienced several severe bouts of illness when he discovered a set of twelve poems by the poet Wilhelm Müller in the almanac *Urania*. He immediately seized upon these poems and began composing. They were dark, unhappy poems that must have echoed some of the misery and desperation that Schubert was feeling. Later, he learned that Müller had actually written twenty-four poems in this group, but Schubert's twelve songs were already in the process of being published and had been considered a complete cycle. In fact, in Schubert's first draft of the cycle, song No. 12, was written in the key of D minor, the key of the opening song. Schubert decided to add the additional poems to his first group and used the buoyant music of "Die Post" (The Mail) to lift the curtain on the second act of the cycle. Although Müller had inserted the twelve new poems between others in the original group, Schubert placed the new poems at the end of the twelve that were already set to music, rearranging the order of two of the new poems to maintain the dramatic unity of his work. In step with romantic sensibilities, some of Schubert's friends believed that the composing of *Winterreise* caused his early death.[36] Schubert himself was highly affected and disturbed by these songs, according to his friend Josef von Spaun.

> Schubert, for a time, appeared gloomy and strained. When I asked him what was the matter, he only said, "You will soon hear about it and understand!" One day in October of 1827, he said to me, "Come to Schober's today. I will sing a cycle of some hair-raising songs for you. I am eager to see what you will say about the songs. They have touched me more than all of my other songs." He sang through the entire *Winterreise* for us with an emotional voice. We were bewildered by the gloomy atmosphere of these songs, and Schober said that only one song, "Der Lindenbaum," had pleased him. Schubert said, "These songs please me more than all [of my other songs] and they will also soon please you!" And he was right: soon we were enthusiastic about the appeal of these melancholy songs which Vogl performed brilliantly. There are no more beautiful lieder

than these, and they were his actual swan song. From then on, he was strained, although his condition didn't cause any alarm.[37]

Winterreise was conceived in the grand style of symphonic litera- ture, exhibiting a pathos and profundity that had not previously been explored in song. The depth of musical expression that occurs in *Winterreise* does not simply entertain us; it requires our total atten- tion and intellect. Like the great tragedies of Shakespeare, these songs are difficult and provoking. For an English-speaking audience, there is the additional problem of language if the songs are experi- enced through translations. *Winterreise* is also difficult because the topic is one of loss, misery, and insanity—a relentless winter journey into the darkness of life without relief or even the release of death. Schubert is portraying a bleak landscape that explores the protagonist's isolation from other human beings, an isolation that Schubert universalizes to include all of us. We, like the protagonist of *Winterreise*, come into the world strangers and alone, and must face our end alone.

Predictably, *Winterreise* was not received by everyone with equal enthusiasm. The critic for the *Allgemeine Musik-Zeitung* found the songs monotonous as a group (this was only the first twelve songs!) and suggested that

> German song ... should be but an overflowing of a full and deeply moved heart and ... exclude all that is didactic, historical, or reflective. ... We do not on the whole approve of song cycles. Only in the first, fairest days of life's blossoming does true song thrive, and so it should unfold itself only in single flowers. To wind it into wreaths is infinitely difficult.[38]

Nature and the "hero" are moving in tandem throughout the cycle. Nature, in *Winterreise*, is one with the protagonist and mirrors his state of mind as well as the reality of his situation. The winter ice is matched by his frozen tears; the earth is frozen, stiff, and dead like his sweetheart's love; a dead leaf hanging from a tree represents his last hope.

We are given most of the story elements in the first song. The poet reveals that he is leaving the town where he was rejected by his sweetheart. He caustically observes that he came to this town as a stranger and leaves as one. Some of the images of this first poem are later repeated in the cycle—wandering, snow, dogs barking. Schubert provides a steady, walking rhythm for this first song, thereby beginning the poet's winter journey from the first note of the cycle. The protagonist's pace in the music reflects his state of mind: a swift leave-taking in the first song, "Gute Nacht" (Good-Night), plodding in "Auf dem Flusse" (On the Stream), brisk and defiant in "Mut" (Courage).

Schubert's use of rhythm throughout the cycle is calculated to enhance the strangeness of the story. In "Gefrorne Tränen" (Frozen Tears), his shift of rhythmic emphasis lends an unbalanced quality to the song, while at the same time figuratively painting a frozen tear on the cheek of the hero. Not only does Schubert alter the natural accent of the meter (accents on the first and third beats of the measure) by accenting the second beat, but he further dislocates the natural rhythm of the introduction in the third measure; he transposes the bass line's previous upbeat leap of a fourth so that what had been an accent on the first beat of the measure in the bass becomes an accent on the weak fourth (Example 6-13). He obscures the rhythmic pulse and tonality (diminished seventh chords) at the beginning of "Letzte Hoffnung" (Last Hope, No. 16), immediately revealing to the listener that rather than a last hope, there is no hope. At first the vocal line wavers back and forth like the trembling leaf and trails behind the figuration of the accompaniment (Example 6-14). "Letzte Hoffnung," like so many other songs in *Winterreise*, illustrates Schubert's reduction of his musical vocabulary to bare bones. The accompaniments are skeletal in texture, sometimes offering nothing more than minimal chordal support. Only a great master could use so little to create such overwhelming beauty (Example 6-15). In "Der greise Kopf" (The Gray Hair, No. 14), the accompaniment is not only limited to simple chords, but these chords sound even more subdued and restricted because the tonic of C minor is used as a pedal point for ten bars at the beginning of the song, supporting a melodic line that outlines a diminished seventh chord in its second half.

Despite the amazing starkness of the piano textures, Schubert captures the elemental character of his subject, using the colors of the piano to assist him. Much of the grayness of mood is captured by his exploitation of the piano's middle range. When he does move away from this range of the piano, the effect is that much greater. In "Die Krähe," for example, he enhances the eerie picture of a crow circling above the protagonist by writing much of the piano part in the treble clef. In "Die Nebensonnen" (The Mock Suns), the hallucinating lover's vocal line is supported primarily by an accompaniment written in the bass clef, with close harmonies that sound like a German Männerchor.

Example 6-13. Schubert, "Gefrorne Thränen" (Frozen Tears), in *Winterreise*, mm. 1–4.

Here and there, many colored leaves can be seen on the trees,

Example 6-14. Schubert, "Letzte Hoffnung" (Last Hope), in *Winterreise*, mm. 1–8.

Example 6-15. Schubert, "Auf dem Flusse" (On the Stream), in *Winterreise*, mm. 1–4.

The music of *Winterreise* often graphically illustrates the text. "Im Dorfe" (In the Village, No. 17), for example, mimics the sound of dogs rattling their chains (Example 6-16). The wavering of the weather vane is musically depicted in "Die Wetterfahne" (The Weather Vane, mm. 1–5). And one hears the drone of the medieval hurdy-gurdy in "Der Leiermann" (Example 6-17).

Example 6-16. Schubert, "Im Dorfe" (In the Village), in *Winterreise*, mm. 1–2.

Example 6-17. Schubert, "Der Leiermann" (The Hurdy-Gurdy Man), in *Winterreise*, mm. 1–5.

Schubert is even sparing in his use of beautiful melodies in *Winterreise*. When the lover remembers the past, as in "Der Lindenbaum" (No. 5), or dreams of happiness as in "Frühlingstraum" (Dream of Spring, No. 11), Schubert grants us one of his great melodies. The barren melodic line of "Letzte Hoffnung" and "Der Doppelgänger," written in this same period, is a new Schubert. An underlying abstract starkness emanates from beneath the music, a cold futility that defies description. Rarely has any composer been able to sustain such profound despair and anguish on so monumental a scale. Not until the end of the nineteenth century did other composers again attempt such dark probing of the psyche.

The outward events of Schubert's short life seem so pathetic— poverty, obscurity, ill health. Yet Schubert's life might be considered one of great success—he lived a life of the mind and of inspiration. He was surrounded by devoted friends and admirers, poets and intellectuals; he composed every day from 9 o'clock in the morning until 2 o'clock in the afternoon and then devoted the rest of his day to his friends and the performance of music.[39] He seems never to have lacked inspiration; in fact he appears to have rushed to get his music on paper.

The shortness of his life and his lack of material success led many of Schubert's friends and later biographers to conclude that he died before he was able to achieve the full measure of his greatness. Failing to grasp what he had accomplished, they inscribed on his grave: "The art of music buried here a rich possession, but even far greater hopes." Schubert's genius was unlocked in his sixteenth year and was sustained at white heat for the next fifteen. Not only did he create great symphonies, piano music, and chamber music, but he brought the lied to fruition. How can we fail to recognize his greatness?

Figure 7-1. Robert Schumann. Color halftone reproduction of lithograph by Prang & Co. Courtesy of the Library of Congress Music Division.

Robert Schumann

February 1840

My dear Clara,

I am sending you a little song, to comfort you; sing it to your-self softly, simply, like yourself.... During the last few days I have finished a great cycle of Heine songs. Besides these another ballad, "Belsazar," a volume from Goethe's *West-Oestlicher Divan*; a volume of R. Burns (an Englishman whose works have as yet been little set).... With the cycle, that makes seven volumes. There! is that not good of me?... I cannot tell you how easily all this has come to me, and how much I enjoyed doing it. As a rule I compose them standing or walking, not at the piano. It is quite a different sort of music, which does not come first through the fingers—much more direct and melodious.

—Robert Schumann to Clara Wieck[1]

Robert Schumann (1810–1856), the next major composer after Schubert to turn his creative talents to songwriting, was at first reluctant to recognize the lied as worthy of his attention. As late as June of 1839, the year before he "burst into song," Schumann wrote in a letter to the composer Hermann Hirschbach, "All my life I have considered vocal composition inferior to instrumental music—I have never regarded it as great art. But don't tell anyone about it!"[2] Although his earliest, unpublished works had been songs, Schumann devoted the first ten years of his compositional life to writing for the piano. In his reviews as critic for the *Neue Zeitschrift für Musik*, he continually admonished young composers to cultivate the large instrumental forms such as the symphony if they were to follow in the footsteps of Beethoven. Most musicians of the period believed that they had to measure themselves against the figure of Beethoven, a view that prevailed even to the end of the century. The famous physician Theodor Billroth, for example, urged his friend Johannes Brahms to "continue to write symphonies, cantatas, chamber music, 'but not such little jokes on the piano.'"[3]

Yet, in his role as critic, Schumann reflected on the musical developments of his era and admitted that important changes had taken place in the genre of song since Beethoven.[4] Perhaps this realization was part of the reason that Schumann began to compose lieder.

There has been much speculation about what finally ignited the spark that caused Schumann to write songs. Some historians believe his songs were a manifestation of his love for Clara and his anticipation of their marriage after the prolonged struggle and court battle with her father for permission to marry. Schumann fuels this argument in a letter to Clara when he writes,

> The songs [Op. 24] are the first I have printed, so do not criticize them too severely. When I was composing them, I was rapt in the thought of you. Your eyes haunt me, you romantic girl, and I often think that without such a betrothed, one could not write such music.[5]

Schumann seems, in retrospect, ideally suited to the task of songwriting, for he possessed prodigious literary and musical talents, which he initially explored both as a music critic and as a composer of a unique body of piano music. He expressed his desire to combine his literary and musical abilities when he said, "If only my talent for music and poetry would converge into a single point, the light would not be so scattered, and I could attempt a great deal."[6] Actually, his literary bent asserted itself even in his piano music, particularly in the literary allusions of his titles such as "Pierrot," "Arlequin," "Eusebius," and "Florestan" of *Carnaval*. Even his use of musical ciphers links his literary and musical interests. (Eric Sams has written extensively on the hidden messages and word games in Schumann's music. Some of Schumann's not-so-secret messages are spelled out in the titles of his works such as Op. 1, *Theme on the name of "Abegg" with variations*, Abegg being the last name of a female acquaintance of Schumann; and the movement from *Carnaval* titled "A.S.C.H.-S.C.H.A.," spelling out the name of the town Asch where his sweetheart, Ernestine von Fricken lived.)

Schumann's associate, Carl Banck, wrote most of the early song reviews for the *Neue Zeitschrift für Musik*, while Schumann dealt with instrumental music—particularly piano literature. His passing references to Schubert's songs give scant information about how much of that repertory Schumann knew, but his studies of Schubert's music began as early as 1828. His friend Emil Flechsig recounted that "when Schubert died . . . [Schumann] got into such a state at the first report of his death that I heard him sob the whole night long."[7] Schumann, the spiritual heir to Schubert, did more than any other musician of his generation to bring Schubert's instrumental music to the public. He frequently coupled Schubert's name with Beethoven's and not only had a number of Schubert's instrumental pieces published in the *Neue Zeitschrift für Musik* but also reviewed at least twelve of Schubert's works. In 1839, during a visit to Vienna in which Schumann visited Schubert's brother Ferdinand, Schumann "discovered" Schubert's C Major Symphony ("the great"), which he sent to Felix Mendelssohn for its premier performance in Leipzig. This symphony was for Schumann the final evidence of Schubert's musical genius.

> He who doesn't know this symphony knows little of Schubert. . . . He gives us something . . . very originally formed. . . . The brilliance and novelty of the instrumentation, the breadth and expanse of the form . . . there is always the feeling that the composer knew exactly what he wanted to say and how to say it.[8]

It is possible that this confirmation of Franz Schubert as a worthy successor to Beethoven also elevated the lied in Schumann's eyes, for Schubert had devoted so much of his musical life to the composition of songs.

In the year 1840, Schumann suddenly began to write songs— over 140 of the finest lieder of the century poured from his pen in that year alone. He and Clara viewed this unexpected change of course with a charming astonishment.

> [Clara in her diary] He showed me a number of his songs, today—I had not expected anything like them! My admiration for him increases with my love. Amongst those now living there is not one so musically gifted as he.[9]

> [Robert to Clara] It is quite a different sort of music, which does not come first through the fingers.[10]

Reflecting his literary heritage as the son of a bookdealer, publisher, and translator, Schumann chose works of such great poets as Eichendorff, Goethe, Robert Burns, and Heinrich Heine. His often quoted statement, "Why select mediocre poetry that is certain to mirror itself in the music?"[11] was the credo of his art. Unlike Schubert, who was willing to set the modest poetic offerings of his friends as well as the great poetry of his age, Schumann was usually quite selective in his poetic choices and paid verbal homage to the importance of word/tone unity. In a review of several songs by W. H. Veit, Schumann compliments Veit for giving "a true reflection of the words in musical expression; and this is the highest praise that can be bestowed."[12] Whether he was more successful than Schubert in the quest toward perfect unity with the text has been debated at length by scholars. Each composer wrote many beautiful songs that seem perfectly united with the text as well as many other fine songs in which music dominates the text.

Although Schubert was born just thirteen years earlier than Schumann, his use of form, melodic structure, and harmonic rhythm seems more in the tradition of Beethoven than that of the romantic Schumann. Schumann discusses changes that had occurred in song composition since Schubert's time in an 1843 review of songs by Robert Franz.

> The songs of Robert Franz's . . . are intimately connected with the whole development of our art in the last decade. . . . Franz Schubert had laid the groundwork for the lied, but principally after the manner of Beethoven; the work of the north Germans, on the other hand, showed more of the effect of Bach's spirit. The emergence of a new school of German poetry also speeded this development. Rückert and Eichendorff, though they had flourished earlier, became better known to musicians; but more than any others, the verses of Uhland and Heine were set to music. Thus there arose a more artistic and more profound kind of lied of which the earlier composers could have no inkling— for it was but a reflection in music of the new poetic spirit.[13]

Certainly Schumann's own poetic choices would influence the nature of the songs he wrote. His most successful songs were those that elicited his most subjective responses. Rarely did he choose those highly realistic poems that Hugo Wolf would treat so successfully. In this sense, Schumann is the embodiment of the romantic spirit. He is inspired by unrequited love, by the mystery of the past, by longing. His review of Franz continues:

> The Lieder of Robert Franz belong to this nobler new category. The kind of wholesale song fabrication that rejoices equally in a clumsy jingle and a poem by Rückert is beginning to be recognized for what it is. . . . In fact, the Lied may well be the only form in which important progress has been made since Beethoven.

> Compare, for instance, the industry that has gone into encompassing the content of a poem right down to the individual word in these songs of Franz with the indolence of the older procedure where the poem was, at best, of secondary concern. . . . He seeks to recreate the poem in all its vital depth.[14]

Most of Robert Franz's songs have been forgotten. Ironically, it was Schumann himself who represented the next generation of lieder composers. If Schumann's observations about developments within the art song genre were supposed to mean that song had evolved into a "higher state" from Schubert to Franz, history has proved him wrong. It is always tempting to seek "progress" in the arts, a concept more relevant to the world of technology. Musical styles change and composers bring the artistic vision of their time to composition—but a genuine work of art remains valid long after techniques have altered the approach of subsequent generations. Mozart did not invalidate or "update" the works of J. S. Bach, nor did Robert Franz or even Schumann, for that matter, "improve" upon the songs of Schubert, whose songs are still loved today. Comparisons are often made among the songs of Schubert, Schumann, and Wolf, with some writers stating that Wolf's songs represent the culmination of the art song. Although his songs are quite wonderful, they still constitute his particular vision of song and the musical vocabulary of his era. They do not diminish the works of his predecessors.

Even the comparison of songs in which the same poetic text has been set by different composers, while interesting, usually fails to focus on the essence of each composer's work. Goethe's Mignon poems, for example, were set by Schubert, Schumann, and Wolf (along with many other composers), and scholars who compare these songs often end by declaring Wolf to be the winner. Can these songs be compared? If we discuss each composer's setting of "Nur wer die Sehnsucht kennt," are we comparing the best as well as the most representative work of each composer? Were all three composers equally inspired by this poem when they read it? Schubert set this poem six times between 1815 and 1826; the original poem in *Wilhelm Meister* was a duet between Mignon and the harper, but Schumann and Wolf set it as a solo song, and only one of Schubert's songs was written as a duet. Was Schubert dissatisfied with each of his six versions or was he so inspired by this poem that he could not stop setting it? Which of these settings do we compare to Wolf's? What are our criteria for determining which setting is best? Some critics prefer Schubert's 1826 version because its simplicity appears to suit

Mignon's character. But others like the more complex, chromatic setting by Wolf. Another prefers Schumann's setting but later concludes
that the *Wilhelm Meister* poems are just too complex to be translated
successfully into music.[15]

Some critics judge success on how closely a composer remains
faithful to the poetic text, while others admire the ability of the composer to stretch the poetry to fit a brilliant musical setting. Often comparisons are exercises in personal preference or become observations about who violated poetic accents, who had the most unusual
harmonic setting (which has as much to do with when the song
appeared in the century as with what is good or bad), what kind of
accompaniment figurations were used, how varied was the rhythmic
vocabulary.

During the early part of his musical career, Schumann's interests
were focused on the piano—as a performer, critic, and composer.
Although his family had hoped that he would find a career in law, his
great desire to become a virtuoso pianist led him to study with the
well-known teacher, Friedrich Wieck, father and teacher of his
future wife, child prodigy Clara Wieck. Friedrich Wieck assured
Schumann that, if he applied himself, he would be ready to begin a
career as a piano virtuoso within three years. During this period, in
December of 1831, Schumann published in the *Allgemeine
musikalische Zeitung* his first review of a piano piece, Chopin's *Variations on Là ci darem la mano*. He was at the same time engaged in
composing music for the piano, including his now famous *Papillons*.
In 1832, Schumann permanently injured the third finger of his right
hand with a mechanical device he had invented to strenghten his
fingers. He then had to give up the idea of becoming a piano virtuoso
and began to devote more of his energies to the composition of music
for the piano. By the time he started to write songs in 1840,
Schumann had already written most of his major piano works.

Obviously his imposing, multifaceted background in piano
criticism, performance, and composition influenced Schumann's
approach to songwriting. He wrote lengthy postludes at the end of
the great song cycles *Dichterliebe* (Poet's Love) and *Frauenliebe und
-leben* (A Woman's Love and Life), postludes which are almost as
long as some of the songs in the cycles. Schumann has been credited
with elevating the piano to an equal status with the voice in the lied.
He definitely expanded the piano's rôle in the lied—through melodic
material that often migrates between voice and piano and is shared
by both, through harmonic material controlled by the piano that

And misty forms rise up from the earth

Example 7-1. Schumann, " Aus alten Märchen winkt es" (Old Fairy Tales), in *Dichterliebe*, mm. 41–44.

leaves the voice part incomplete without it, and through the ways the voice sometimes seems to accompany the piano (Example 7-1).

Martin Cooper suggests that Schumann's use of pianistic figures in his vocal lines is more prominent in the 1840 songs than in his later lieder because he is coming to song fresh from his period of writing exclusively for the piano. These pianistic figures are exemplified in his use of turns in the vocal lines of "Er, der Herrlichste von allen" (He, the Most Noble of All) and "Helft mir, ihr Schwestern" (Help Me, Sisters) from the *Frauenliebe und -leben*. (Clara Schumann, primarily a pianist, also uses turns in her vocal lines.) On the other hand, Cooper postulates, it might be explained as an unconscious imitation of operatic style.[16]

Schumann was fully aware that a good song represented a partnership between voice and piano, not simply a doubling of the vocal line by the piano, as he indicated in a review of songs by Hubert Kufferath:

> Almost throughout, these lieder show the peculiarity that the piano accompaniment doubles the melody, so that it could even stand by itself without the vocal part. This is certainly nothing to be admired in lied composition; it is especially limiting for the singer. But we always see this in the lieder of the younger composers who have formerly been preoccupied with instrumental composition. (1842)[17]

Schumann sometimes failed to observe his own advice and doubles the voice line in the piano part of his songs as in "Wehmut" (Melancholy) from *Liederkreis*, Op. 39. Generally, however, his knowledge of the piano is used to produce highly expressive settings for the voice. He exploits the ability of the piano to produce rich, full sounds—(see "Aus alten Märchen" [Out of Old Fairy Tales] from *Dichterliebe*)—without overpowering the voice; but he does not "limit" himself to thick-textured writing. In "Zwielicht" (Twilight) from the Eichendorff *Liederkreis*, for example, he begins with an unaccompanied melodic line for the piano; in "Ich hab' im Traum geweinet" from *Dichterliebe*, the voice is unaccompanied when it begins.

Schumann also produces constant harmonic novelty in the piano part. In the postlude of "Hör ich das Liedchen klingen" (When I Hear the Little Song) from *Dichterliebe*, he writes an arpeggiated figuration with multiple suspensions to express graphically and uniquely "the intolerable grief" of the poet (see Chapter 3, "The Piano"). The counterpoint of the emerging melodic lines and shifting rhythmic schemes reflects Schumann's brilliant idiomatic use of the piano.

Schumann often writes repeated chord figurations such as those of "Mein schöner Stern" (My Beautiful Star), here a particularly effective technique because of the multiple accented suspensions and dissonances that result in the right-hand piano part (Example 7-2). The repeated octaves of "Sonntags am Rhein" (Sunday on the Rhine), perhaps reflecting inspiration from Chopin's Prelude in D-flat Major, No. 15, incorporate dissonances and melodic imitations between piano and voice that are sufficiently interesting to override the somewhat monotonous symmetry of phrasing and rhythmic simplicity.

While many sections of Schumann's songs are diatonic, he also uses chromaticism as both a linear and a harmonic feature of his music. "Stille Liebe" (Silent Love) from the Kerner lieder, for example, exhibits a typical example for Schumann of descending

My beautiful star! I entreat you

Example 7-2. Schumann, "Mein schöner Stern" (My Beautiful Star), mm. 1–4.

chromatic chords in the postlude (Example 7-3). Chromaticism results from the passing tones of the descending bass line of "Das verlass'ne Mägdelein" (Example 7-4). (See also mm. 24–25 of Example 3-13, from "Hör ich das Liedchen klingen," where a rising chromatic scale occurs in an inner voice of the accompaniment.) In the very linear accompaniments such as "Einsamkeit" (Solitude) and "Aus den hebräischen Gesängen" (From the Hebrew Songs) in *Myrten*, the writing is quite chromatic. Schumann's harmonic rhythm is generally more rapid than that which characterizes either Beethoven's or Schubert's songs, a feature that distinguishes romantic from classical music.

Example 7-3. Schumann, "Stille Liebe" (Silent Love), mm. 43–46.

I stare at them, absorbed in sorrow.

Example 7-4. Schumann, "Das verlass'ne Mägdelein" (The Forsaken Girl), mm. 14–18.

Schumann possessed a melodic gift that is not always fully recognized, perhaps because his melodies are often not presented as a whole by the voice but are divided between voice and piano. In Schumann's famous "Der Nussbaum" (The Nut Tree), piano and voice share the melodic material as interest shifts back and forth between the two (Example 7-5). Schumann's particular knowledge of the piano allows him to write lyrically for an instrument that is not always considered lyrical. Hans Joachim Moser states that the piano functions here to express the inexpressible, to voice a meaning that the words of the poet can only suggest.[18] (Philip Miller, in the *Ring of*

A nut tree stands green in front of the house,

Example 7-5. Schumann, "Der Nussbaum" (The Nut Tree), mm. 3–6.

Words, even suggests that perhaps the poem is shortchanged in this setting of "Nussbaum.")[19]

At times, when Schumann's melodies are divided between the voice and piano, the piano part may be more interesting than the voice part. The vocal line given earlier in Example 7-1 would function well as a bass line in the accompaniment. At other times, for example in "Ein Jüngling liebt ein Mädchen" (A Boy Loves a Girl), the piano plays a separate melody from the voice with its own rhythmic character and moving in the opposite direction from the voice part.

Nevertheless, Schumann also writes many songs where the voice carries the melodic line while the piano is pure accompaniment (e.g., "Helft mir, ihr Schwestern," mm. 27–34). In "Du bist wie eine Blume" (You Are As Lovely As a Flower) or "Widmung" (Dedication), only in the postlude does he allow the piano to step forward. In "Helft mir, ihr Schwestern," the piano acts as a subordinate partner for the main body of the song, and not until the postlude does it offer material that programmatically comments on the text preceding it. In the song, the bride-to-be, speaking to her friends, reflects on her hopes and fears for her new life. After the voice concludes, the piano continues the "conversation" by playing a wedding march, which affirms the bride's confident resolution of her apprehensions (Example 7-6).

Example 7-6. Schumann, "Helft mir, ihr Schwestern" (Help Me, Sisters), in *Frauenliebe und -leben* (A Woman's Love and Life), mm. 47–49.

Schumann organized the majority of his songs into groups and cycles. Just as his piano music was poetically focused—*Children's Scenes*, *Fantasy Pieces*, or *Album for the Young*—so too is his vocal music presented in units. He wrote not only the monumental cycle *Dichterliebe* and the intimate cycle *Frauenliebe und -leben* but also a number of miniature cycles such as "Der arme Peter" (Poor Peter) and "Tragödie" (Tragedy), using several short poems by Heine. Even the *Liederkreis*, Op. 39, although loosely ordered, is musically arranged according to key progression and based on the works of a single poet, Joseph von Eichendorff.

An examination of Schumann's entire repertory of song reveals his frequent grouping by poet, subject, mood, or key relationships. Many of the songs of 1840 begin with the poet as the basis for organizing the collection: in addition to the just mentioned Eichendorff *Liederkreis*, Op. 39, Schumann wrote another group of songs which he also called *Liederkreis*, his Op. 24, using the poetry of Heinrich Heine. Other examples are Op. 30, *Drei Gedichte*, three poems by Emanuel von Geibel; Op. 35, *Zwölf Gedichte*, twelve poems by Justinus Kerner; Op. 36, *Sechs Gedichte*, six poems by Robert Reinick; and Op. 37, *Zwölf Gedichte aus Friedrich Rückert's "Liebesfrühling"* (Twelve Poems from Friedrich Rückert's Love's Spring), poems which he and Clara set together.

Later in the century, Hugo Wolf would also focus on the writings of individual poets; he, however, was not seeking to create a single unit or cycle in these settings, and in fact he explored a great variety of moods as he searched for the heart of each poem. Wolf's musical style subtly changes for each poet in his effort to express the individual character of the poetry, so the listener is unlikely to confuse his Goethe settings with his Mörike lieder. Schumann, on the other hand, writes with more uniformity of style from poet to poet; he is often expressing his own inner thoughts rather than seeking the poet's individual voice. Of course, all the great art song composers revealed themselves in their choices of poets and poetry, selecting poetry that touched their spirit and inspired musical kinship with the poet. Heine's words of intense love and abject misery struck a sympathetic response from Schumann, who had struggled for years to win Clara, just as Eichendorff's dreams and longing evoked a reply from the inner sanctum of Schumann's soul.

Schumann's last vocal work (1852) is also a cycle, the seldom performed *Gedichte der Königin Maria Stuart* (Poems of Queen Mary Stuart). Mary Stuart has captured the imagination of musicians and

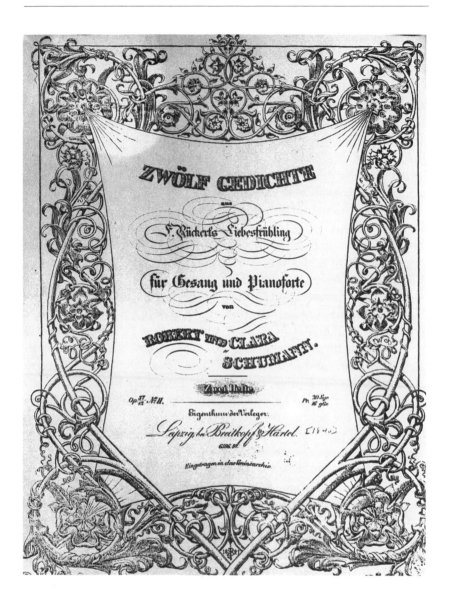

Figure 7-2. Decorative frontispiece to song edition by Robert and Clara Schumann, 1841.

writers for centuries. Wagner set to music the words of Pierre Jean de Béranger (1780–1857) in his "Adieux de Maria Stuart," and in our own time, Thea Musgrave has written an opera, *Mary, Queen of Scots* (1977). Schumann set five poems by Mary, Queen of Scots, which briefly describe her melancholy departure from France, her reflections on the birth of her son, her care-filled letter from prison to Queen Elizabeth, her farewell to the world, and a prayer for salvation. It is easy to see why these poems appealed to Schumann in this stage of his life, a man on the verge of insanity. Organized by subject matter, key (A minor and E minor), poet, and mood, this cycle is haunting, somber, and resigned—a touchingly appropriate monument to Schumann himself. Although the songs rely on the relatively simple piano figurations of Schumann's late, spare style and are harmonically conservative compared to many of his earlier works, still the Maria Stuart songs are highly effective in performance and appropriate to the mood of the poems on which they are based. Although not vocally difficult, they require a sensitive, intelligent interpretation.

A much earlier miniature cycle, "Der arme Peter," consists of three short charming songs written in Schumann's Liederjahr— 1840. These songs have much in common stylistically with the Maria Stuart lieder because of the simplicity of their music. Heine's poetry tells the story of poor Peter, who, biting his nails and wearing his work clothes, commands our sympathy as he stands off to the side, watching the wedding dance of his sweetheart, Grete, with her new husband, Hans. The simple harmonies and key relationships (G major, E minor, E minor), and unaffected figurations in the accompaniment of "Der arme Peter" complement Heine's modest story. These songs, however, are not folk songs, a style of writing that would have been foreign to Schumann. Although he was often attracted to folk poetry, his writing in lieder such as "Im Walde" (In the Woods) from *Liederkreis*. Op. 39, "Erstes Grün" (The First Green), or "Volksliedchen" (Little Folk Song) reveals an artifice and sophistication that clearly remove them from the realm of folk music. Schumann captures the poetry's informality at the beginning of "Der arme Peter" with two dronelike chords (perhaps imitating bagpipes or a hurdy-gurdy), which then move into a tinkly, music-box-like waltz; he conjures up a delicate picture of little wooden figures swaying to the music of the dance (Example 7-7). Peter has none of the bitterness and anger of the rejected lover portrayed in the discordant dance of Schumann's "Das ist ein Flöten und Geigen" from

Hans and Grete dance around,

Example 7-7. Schumann, "Der Hans und die Grete tanzen" (Hans and Grete Dance), in *Der arme Peter* (Poor Peter), mm. 1–6.

and sleep until Judgement Day.

Example 7-8. Schumann, "Der arme Peter wankt vorbei" (Poor Peter Totters by), in *Der arme Peter*, mm. 23–25.

Dichterliebe. Peter will simply weep and pine away. Schumann uses the piano to comment on the text in the dirgelike third song when the piano imitates Gabriel's trumpets on judgment day (Example 7-8). Word-painting is often less obvious in Schumann's songs than it is in Schubert's. Schumann creates moods that do not rely on using onomatopoetic sounds, although as the previous example shows, there are instances of pure sound imitation. Usually, however, when he chooses to suggest the meaning of a word as, for example, by using a long note on the word "längst" (long) in "Ich grolle nicht" (I Bear No Resentment) of *Dichterliebe*, or in the tearlike descending figuration of "Hör ich das Liedchen klingen," the result is more subliminal for the listener than conscious. He even passes up an opportunity to word-paint in the second song of "Der arme Peter" when he writes a descending musical line on the phrase "Ich steig' hinauf des Berges Höh." (I climb up to the top of the mountain).

Schumann often repeats melodic phrases, either at the same pitch level or as a sequence, a technique evident throughout "Der arme Peter." Examples 7-9a and 7-9b illustrate both techniques. The slight harmonic change in the accompaniment at bar 12 adds variety to the melodic repetition. In the musically complex Eichendorff *Liederkreis*, however, the harmonic changes in the accompaniment of "In der Fremde" (In a Foreign Land, No. 1), are much more elaborate, and even the repetition of the melodic line is varied.

Der ar - me Pe - ter die Nä - gel_ kaut und_steht im Wer-kel-tags - klei - de.

Der_ Pe - ter spricht lei - se vor sich_ her und schau-et be - trü-bet auf Bei - de:

Poor Peter bites his nails and wears his work clothes.
Peter speaks softly to himself and looks sadly at the couple:

Example 7-9a. Schumann, "Der Hans und die Grete tanzen," in *Der arme Peter*, mm. 27–42.

Es treibt mich nach der Lieb - sten Näh', als könnt's die Gre - te hei - len; doch

wenn ich Der in's Au - ge seh', muss ich von hin - nen ei - len.

It [my pain] drives me to be near my love, as if Grete could cure it;
but when I look into her eyes, then I must hurry away.

Example 7-9b. Schumann, "In meiner Brust" (In My Breast), in *Der arme Peter*, mm. 11–18.

Schumann wrote several song cycles in 1840, but the two major cycles—*Liederkreis*, Op. 39, and *Dichterliebe*—confirmed him as one of the century's finest composers. Surely Schumann is closest to pure ecstacy in the twelve songs of *Liederkreis*. Eichendorff's poetry incorporates a wealth of romantic images: the transience and mystery of life, the wanderer, the beauty of night, moonlight, nature, and the wonder of love. Schumann also chooses dark poems of suspicion, isolation, spiritual evil, and anxiety—feelings that would ultimately engulf him. *Liederkreis* is a wreath of moods, reflections, and images, with no story. It is, however, tonally unified: the songs shift from relative minor to major, to dominant keys, parallel keys, or the favorite romantic move to a key a third away. "Auf einer Burg" (In a Castle) is most closely linked to the song that follows: it ends on the dominant of A minor, suspending the listener until the key is resolved in the next song, "In der Fremde" (No. 8), which begins in A minor. "Auf einer Burg" also ends with a question that not only emphasizes the mystery of the weeping bride but also leads inevitably to the next song. The piano is given fewer lengthy preludes, interludes, and postludes in this cycle than in *Dichterliebe*; in fact, there is no piano prelude or postlude in "Auf einer Burg," no prelude to "Die Stille" (Tranquillity), and no postlude to "Im Walde," since these songs follow or lead directly to another song. Schumann called this group of songs a cycle, but there is no obvious recurrent musical or textual material to tie the parts into a whole. The cycle does begin in F-sharp minor and concludes in the parallel major, F-sharp, but there is no concluding postlude at the end of the final song, "Frühlingsnacht" (Spring Night), to tie the group together, as in *Dichterliebe* or *Frauenliebe und -leben*.

The first edition of *Liederkreis*, Op. 39, began with "Der frohe Wandersmann," which Schumann replaced in 1850 with "In der Fremde." Since the eighth song of the cycle was already titled "In der Fremde," some confusion is inevitable even though each song uses a different poem.

"In der Fremde" (No. 1) begins with an arpeggiated figuration in the piano that is dependent on the blend of sound created by the depressed damper pedal. Schumann also writes an arpeggiated figure for the first song of *Dichterliebe*, "Im wunderschönen Monat Mai" (see Example 3-12), yet how different are the moods communicated in these two songs: "Im wunderschönen Monat Mai" is the essence of longing while "In der Fremde" is all sadness and nostalgia. Like many of the songs in *Liederkreis*, "In der Fremde" is short and has only one piano figuration. The transitoriness of life lies at the heart of this song's melancholy atmosphere.

Next, "Intermezzo," a song with a modest vocal line, is musically extraordinary because of the piano's countermelody and syncopated chordal figuration. Forty-four years later, Brahms would write in a similar syncopated style in "Sapphische Ode" (Sapphic Ode), a strange coincidence, since the figure is an unusual way to begin a song; many inattentive singers have stumbled over their entrances in each of these musically treacherous songs. Although hemiola is a rhythmic technique that listeners associate with Brahms's music, many examples also occur in Schumann's: in the final two bars of the voice part of "Intermezzo" and in the last vocal phrase of "Mondnacht," for example.

In 1853, when he met the young Brahms (1833–1897), Schumann hailed him as "called to give ideal form to the highest expression of his times."[20] Brahms would exhibit Schumann's influence in subtle ways. The meandering, chromatic, arpeggiated accompaniment in "O wüsst ich doch den Weg zurück" (Oh, If I Knew the Way Back), written in 1874, has much in common with Schumann's "Zwielicht" of *Liederkreis*, Op. 39, and "Aus den hebräischen Gesängen" from the collection *Myrten*, Op. 25, Schumann's wedding present for Clara. There are other examples of Schumann's influence on Brahms's style: Brahms's Intermezzi for the piano contain arpeggiated figures that outline multiple melodies like those appearing prominently in Schumann's music—in "Am leuchtenden Sommermorgen (On a Bright Summer Morning)," *Dichterliebe*), for example; even Brahms's *Liebeslieder Walzes* have precedents in Schumann's piano duet accompaniments to his *Spanische Liebeslieder*.

Certainly many of these similar musical characteristics resulted from both composers' interest in writing for the piano. Brahms is often described as treating the voice in an instrumental manner because so many of his vocal lines have large skips and long lines. While Schumann's vocal lines are not as disjunct as those of Brahms, they are often just as expansive and require careful monitoring of the breath by the singer (e.g., "Sonntags am Rhein," mm. 42–50).

The third song of *Liederkreis*, "Waldesgespräch" (Conversation in the Woods), is one of the longest, loudest, and boldest of the cycle. It is the story of a man who is riding through the forest when he comes upon the beautiful but deadly Loreley. The prelude introduces a musical imitation of hunting horns, which recurs as a primary unifying feature when the male character speaks and later returns in the postlude. The Loreley, like Schubert's Erlking, has her own enticing music—a flowing arpeggio figuration. Both characters also use recitative when they need to speak aggressively.

"Die Stille," in contrast to "Waldesgespräch," is a short, simple song sung quietly and in a parlando style. It is followed by one of the sublime moments in song, "Mondnacht." To be sung sweetly, secretly, this song represents the ecstatic high point of the cycle. The material from the prelude, interludes, and postlude remains separate from the accompaniment of the vocal line until the voice part, which is repeated four times in eight-measure phrases, expands to include new melodic material that mirrors the words "and my soul spreads wide its wings." Then the accompaniment incorporates the material from the introduction along with the repeated-note figure that had, until then, supported the voice. It was mentioned earlier that Schumann frequently uses repeated notes in the accompaniments of his songs. But there is a uniqueness in each of these figures because of their bold harmonic characteristics and Schuman's exploitation of the piano's range and color. In "Ich grolle nicht," for example, from *Dichterliebe*, the accompaniment is aggressively conceived, with octave doublings in the bass and chords that encompass more than four octaves. A certain amount of noble bluster is conveyed here. A similarly expansive use of the piano occurs in "Mein schöner Stern." In "Mondnacht," Schumann achieves an entirely different result: he creates an ethereal atmosphere, utterly uniting music with text, using chords that expand and contract from repeated sixteenth-notes focused around the pitch B; the chords expand outward from a tight figuration in the middle range of the piano (see Example 3-14). As the voice and bass line of the piano proceed in contrary motion, dissonances result from cross-relationships between them as well as from other linear alignments; the result is inexplicably one of deli-cate, intense intimacy. The cross-relationship of E-sharp in the melody against E-natural in the accompaniment makes the melodic line anything but commonplace. Schumann generates a sense of rhythmic dislocation in several sections of "Mondnacht" by using syncopation in the introduction material and in the vocal line; while the voice phrase begins on an upbeat, the piano part starts solidly on the beat (mm. 10–13). Voice and piano finally move in tandem when they reach the expansive phrase "weit ihre Flügel aus" (spread wide their wings). The piano postlude, rife with multiple melodic frag-ments that interweave to generate a variety of rhythmic schemes (much like the postlude of "Er, der Herrlichste von allen" from *Frauenliebe und—leben*), finally presents a resolution of tonality, which until this point had been intentionally nebulous.

The poem for "Schöne Fremde" (A Beautiful Foreign Land) incorporates many of the recurring images of the cycle: the forest, night, anticipation, the past, spirits, love. Schumann writes a brief, ecstatic response: the figuration of the accompaniment, which despite its agitated syncopated inner voices, is stabilized by its outer voices and the slower moving vocal line; the brief prelude of only three beats introduces a motive in the right hand that is continued by the entering voice part; during each brief piano interlude the melodic fragment reappears, sometimes answering the voice line but fluctuating between a fourth and a fifth, then finally expanding to a sixth. The figuration for the rapturous postlude of seven measures anticipates Brahms's "Meine Liebe ist grün" by nearly thirty-four years.

"Auf einer Burg," No. 7 of *Liederkreis*, shares a number of similarities with "Im Rhein, im heiligen Strome," No. 6 of *Dichterliebe*. Both occur in a similar position in each cycle, the accompaniment of each is relatively thin-textured, contrapuntal, and stately. Eichendorff's "Auf einer Burg" has a cryptic textual conclusion that might even have surprised Heine. Both songs provide marvelous contrast in texture, tempo, style, and mood to the songs that surround them. "Stirb, Lieb' und Freud'!" (Die, Love, and Happiness!) from the Kerner lieder is also similar in character to these two songs. Schumann shows the influence of his Bach studies in all three of these songs with the linear writing in their accompaniments.

"In der Fremde" (No. 8) begins with two separate figures in the accompaniment, which are presented in the first two bars and constitute the only musical material for the accompaniment. The image of life's transitoriness returns: "meine Liebste auf mich warten, und ist doch so lange tot" ([it seems as if] my love must be waiting for me, but she is long since dead).

"Wehmut" returns to the topic of melancholy—a secret sadness in the midst of others' happiness. The poem is given a stately, hymn-like setting, which doubles the voice throughout and is followed by a highly chromatic postlude.

The accompaniment of "Zwielicht" like that of "Auf einer Burg," presents a total contrast of texture and mood to the songs around it. Schumann communicates the suspicion and secrecy of this text, a text that must have had intense meaning for him in his delicate mental state. The piano part begins with a single line, which contrapuntally wanders along, anticipating the vocal melody and gradually adding voices, until it changes to recitative at the end of each stanza. The wandering pattern is varied for each of the first three stanzas, and then in the fourth stanza it changes to repeated chords. Schumann captures the paranoia behind the words "hüte dich, sei wach und munter!" (be careful, be awake and vigilant!) in the final vocal recitative by moving the voice part to a low muted A-sharp below middle C. Throughout "Zwielicht," Schumann writes a monotonous voice part, using many repeated notes within the modest range of a ninth to enhance the eeriness and achromatic quality of twilight. The augmented fourths and diminished fourths in the melody, along with with diminished seventh chords in the accompaniment, bolster a strange atmosphere of mistrust and confusion.

"Im Walde" brings back the images of the wedding procession, a singing bird, hunting horns, night, the forest, and the poet's cryptic, uncertain state: "und mich schauert's im Herzensgrunde" (and my heart trembles within me). The music isolates each verbal image, just as the poet presents himself as a solitary figure. Piano and voice, confined by pedal points—particularly the pedal point on E, which lasts for thirteen bars at the beginning—are restrained, their figurations moving outward, then pulling back.

The final song of the group, "Frühlingsnacht," is the most rapturous of the cycle. This poem was set to music by more than forty composers[21] many of whom, such as Fanny Mendelssohn Hensel as well as Schumann, translate the elation of the words into brilliant musical energy. The short postlude that concludes Schumann's song does not bring back material from the rest of the cycle but concludes the "wreath of song" with a flourish of bravura in F-sharp major, the parallel key to the opening song in F-sharp minor.

Schumann's *Dichterliebe* is probably the most famous of all song cycles. Using sixteen poems from Heinrich Heine's collection of sixty-five in the *Lyrisches Intermezzo*, Schumann melded these poems of unrequited love, pain, and bitterness into an intimate symphony for the voice. The poet's longing, wonder, and exuberance of love are destroyed when he finally realizes that his love is not returned. Schumann's seventh song, the monumental "Ich grolle nicht," is the pivotal song of the cycle, for the poet, angry and sour, now knows that his love is hopeless. From this point to the end of the cycle, the songs express the myriad emotions of loss: resentment, anger, self-pity, false hope, nostalgia, and misery. Schumann uses a battery of musical techniques to convey each of these moods, and he finds with Heine the bite and pungency that make these songs so compelling.

Every musical element in *Dichterliebe* is tightly integrated within each song. In "Allnächtlich im Traume," for example, the short, three-note figure of the voice is closely tied to an accompaniment, which defines the voice motive, extends it, and gives it direction. Schumann's various rhythmic figures are often locked into a harmonic figuration, as in "Hör ich das Liedchen klingen," for example; here, the accompaniment anticipates the melody of the voice by outlining it in its harmonies. The melody, however, does not fall on the beat because of its position in the piano figure, and the result is a delicate syncopation. Brahms uses a similar figuration in "Die Mainacht," but the resulting sound is quite different from "Hör ich das Liedchen klingen" because he places the melody in the middle range of the piano. Notice the word-painting in each song: Schumann's falling piano figuration symbolizes drops of tears while Brahms's rising melodic line reflects the rising moon mentioned in the text[22] (Examples 7-10a and 7-10b; mm. 1–4). In the postlude of Schumann's song, the multiple melodies emerge on various parts of the beat, thereby creating multiple rhythmic schemes (see Example 3-13).

When I hear the little song that my love once sang.

Example 7-10a. Schumann, "Hör' ich das Liedchen klingen," in *Dichterliebe*, mm. 1–8.

Example 7-10b. Brahms, "Die Mainacht" (May Night), mm. 1–4.

Although the cycle ends in a different key from the one in which it begins, the songs are linked to one another through progressions of keys a fifth or a third apart.[23] The poems are by one poet, Heinrich Heine, and are placed in an order that implies a story of lost love. One of the strongest linking devices in the cycle is Schumann's use of music from song No. 12 in the postlude of the final song, No. 16.

Schumann's postludes not only complete the musical ideas of the song in which they occur, but they also provide important psychological and musical links to the songs that follow. In "Und wüssten's die Blumen, die kleinen," for example, the sudden violence of the piano part at the song's conclusion illustrates the breaking of the poet's heart, but it also prepares the listener for the bitter wedding music that follows.

Schumann relies on an impressive variety of musical figurations in the piano throughout the cycle, although individual songs, with a few notable exceptions, are usually based on only one accompanimental figure. In songs 1, 5, 10, 12, and the postlude to 16, for example, Schumann has melodies emerging from a mass of arpeggiated harmonies to depict sensual desire, feelings of yearning, nostalgia, and inner suffering. The accompaniment of "Das ist ein Flöten und Geigen" is completely independent of the voice. A dissonant, disturbing dance rhythm in the left hand clashes with an incessant sixteenth-note melody in the right hand, bitterly communicating the poet's misery and suffering at the wedding dance of his love.

The accompaniment of "Ich hab' im Traum geweinet," is eloquent in its silence. The voice begins alone, chanting in a hypnotic, trancelike manner, as the poet recounts his dream; when the voice stops, there is an "eloquent" silence; then, the accompaniment answers with a brief, staccato set of chords that seem to mock

Example 7-11. Schumann, "Ich hab' im Traum geweinet" (I Cried in My Dream), in *Dichterliebe*, mm. 1–4.

the words (Example 7-11), much like the chords which echo the speaker in Schubert's "Der Doppelgänger." The chordal interlude that leads to the third and final stanza of text takes up the monotonous motive of the voice, then moves chromatically upward as the voice chants on a pedal point D-flat against the shifting dissonances of the piano part. After the voice stops, the piano completes the melodic line; then, following a dramatic silence of nine beats, it repeats the motive that appeared throughout the first two stanzas. Ten more beats of silence precede the tail of the motive (mm. 28–38). The starkness of this song contributes some of the most compelling moments in the entire cycle. Schumann has presented us with a dreamworld of intense misery. This dream is followed by another, "Allnächtlich im Traume," a dream of strange images and forgetfulness. Heine's poems and Schumann's music are artistic harbingers of Freud's exploration of dreams.

Another song, "Ein Jüngling liebt ein Mädchen," has a uniquely syncopated accompaniment, which runs counter to a fairly simple, conventional vocal part that relates a tale of mismatched love. Schumann's use of accent marks coupled with the added weight of chordal emphasis on the second half of the first beat in each measure lends this song a harsh, off-center character. (Singers sometimes treat this song as a cheerful ditty, failing to observe Heine's bitter text and Schumann's subtle, ironic interpretation).

Schumann, despite his respect for great poetry, was never a slave to the poet: he did not hesitate to put his own title on this cycle, changing Heine's words and repeating poetic phrases when musical demands warranted it. In "Das ist ein Flöten und Geigen," for example, the original poem reads: "Da tanzt den Hochzeitreigen," but Schumann's music requires an extra syllable, which results in "Da tanzt wohl den Hochzeitreigen." The most notable alteration of text,

however, occurs in "Ich grolle nicht." Schumann completely alters
the form of Heine's poem by not observing the poet's organization of
stanzas and by constantly repeating the phrase "Ich grolle nicht." The
poem has become the servant of the music.

Schumann's vocal lines vary stylistically from song to song,
closely united to the textual rhythms and moods. "Aus meinen Tränen
spriessen" (From My Tears Spring Up) and "Ich hab' im Traum
geweinet," are chantlike for the most part, with the voice line often
focusing on one pitch; "Wenn ich in deine Augen seh' " is recitative,
as the voice, supported by chords, moves with the inflections of the
text; there are many lovely, lyrical melodies for the voice—"Im
wunderschönen Monat Mai," "Ich will meine Seele tauchen" (I Will
Immerse My Soul), "Hör ich das Liedchen klingen," and "Am
leuchtenden Sommermorgen." And the voice part of "Das ist ein
Flöten und Geigen," is appropriately angular, almost like an accompaniment to the piano, and expressive of the blaring dance music at
the wedding of the lost love.

Frauenliebe und -leben was another song cycle of 1840. Unified
by key, subject, and poet, it is truly a cycle since the postlude of the
final song brings back material from the first song, allowing the music
to travel full circle; in fact, this is Schumann's only song cycle in
which he returns to the beginning for his final material. The songs
flow from one to the next, several having no piano introductions to
separate them from the previous song; the key scheme moves from B-
flat major to E-flat major to C minor to E-flat major to B-flat major to
G major to D major to D minor, with the postlude returning to the B-
flat major of the first song. Schumann continually emphasizes the
intimacy of these songs with numerous soft dynamic markings (the
first song varies from piano to pianissimo) and expressive indications
such as *innig, mit innigem Ausdruck* (intimate, with intimate expression), even tempering the *fröhlich* (cheerful) of "An meinem
Herzen" with another *innig*.

Based on eight poems by the popular poet Adalbert von
Chamisso (1781–1838), the *Frauenliebe und -leben* is a highly
romantic nineteenth-century view of a young woman's love.
Schumann was obviously attracted to the sentiments expressed in
these poems as he anticipated his own happiness. The poems relate
the story of a young girl who meets and falls in love with a man whom
she considers to be far too wonderful to notice her. "Only the most
worthy of all should be your choice, and I will bless her thousands of
times." Suddenly she realizes that he loves her. As she meditates on

the ring he gives her, she discovers that life now has meaning. She promises "to serve him, live for him, yield to him, and find her reason for existing in his bright light." They marry and have a child, which causes her to discover that her previous happiness does not compare with the happiness she is experiencing as a mother. She expresses pity for men because they can never be mothers. Then, without warning, her husband dies. The starkness of the recitative in the last song of the cycle, "Nun hast du mir den ersten Schmerz getan" (Now, for the First Time, You Have Given Me Pain), conveys the sudden shock that death brings to a love without shadows. (In 1856, Clara would also find herself a widow with seven children to support). Schumann omitted Chamisso's final poem, which reflects the thoughts of the woman, now old, as she shares her memories of love with her young granddaughter. This verbal denouement was unnecessary to Schumann's cycle, for his twenty-one-measure musical conclusion causes the listener to look back over the musical portrait he has painted.

Frauenliebe und -leben presents problems for modern performers. Martin Cooper points out that "to a modern taste there is something supremely unattractive in the poet making his bride speak of herself as a 'nied're Magd' (lowly maiden) who only asks to gaze on her husband in all humility." [24] Even in the nineteenth century, this picture of the submissive woman was not universally admired. "As early as 1874, Theodor Storm wrote to Paul Heyse about these poems: 'Mörike once told me how distasteful all this was to him, and those are exactly my sentiments.' " [25]

Can a modern woman convincingly sing songs that present such a highly subservient view of women? Can *Frauenliebe und -leben* be sung by a man? As a matter of fact, the famous nineteenth-century lieder singer Julius Stockhausen did have these songs in his repertoire. [26] The poems of the *Frauenliebe*, representing the most private thoughts of a woman, were actually written by a man. Is this a male's perspective on how he would like to think a woman felt? Might it then be more appropriate for a man to sing these songs than a woman? Or are men and women so foreign to one another that they cannot empathize or identify with each others' humanity? Nietzsche would answer yes! [27] The rest of us might respond differently. Singers are often given stock answers to questions about what is appropriate for them to perform; some vocal coaches categorically state that songs from a man's point of view should be sung only by men, while other songs can be appropriately sung only by women. Yet conventional responses to complex problems of performance are often meaningless and certainly not artistically adventurous. Most of us accept that an actor can play an alcoholic without being an alcoholic. And audiences are called upon to suspend disbelief whenever they walk into the theater. Sometimes this suspension is stretched to include women disguised as men in Shakespeare's plays or women who are singing male rôles in opera, the so-called trouser rôles. Richard Strauss opens *Rosenkavalier* with two women making love, while the audience must pretend that one of them is really a man. If there were convenient answers to these questions, the questions would not be asked. The answers lie with the individual performer, who must decide if he or she has the resources to bring particular songs to life and whether the artistic content of the work merits making compromises.

Even the question of whether to sing a song in the key in which it was written (ignoring the whole question of standard pitch) ultimately rests with the performer. It must be granted that a song such as Wolf's "Wie glänzt der helle Mond" (How Brilliantly Shines the Moon) from *Sechs Gedichte von Keller*, has a limited tolerance for transposition because Wolf has so carefully used the soprano range of the piano to create an ethereal atmosphere. Also, some composers have expressed strong feelings about the colors of certain keys. Schumann himself stated that

> [it must be granted] that through transposition from the original key into another a composition will achieve a different effect, and that this would seem to indicate a fundamental difference between one key and another! ... The composer hits upon the correct key immediately, much as the painter chooses his colour, and without giving much thought to it. [But Schumann went on to say that:] "there have been arguments for and against; the truth, as always, lies in the middle."[28]

Great artists, such as Dietrich Fischer-Dieskau in his monumental recordings of German lieder or Lotte Lehmann in her recording of *Dichterliebe*, have gone against conventions of both key and rôle gender. They have thrilled their listeners with their artistic talents and insights and should cause us to question easy answers to artistic questions.

Schumann's bouts with mental illness have caused many observers to dismiss his later songs as the product of failing powers and a deranged mind. But after 1840 and his marriage to Clara, Schumann turned away from his intense involvement with song composition and began to explore larger musical forms. He wrote his first symphony in 1841, completed the oratorio *Das Paradies und die Peri* in 1843, and began working on his opera *Genoveva* in 1847. When he again turned his attention to song composition in 1847, his style of writing had become leaner, less directed to the lyrical elements and passion that had characterized his earlier song style. Fischer-Dieskau suggests that Schumann was "working toward a new stylistic goal that he was not allowed to reach; during this period of experimentation his efforts consisted largely of condensing and paring."[29]

One of his 1847 songs was the delicate "Das verlass'ne Mägdelein," which was to inspire and influence Hugo Wolf's fine setting of this Mörike poem. Schumann's dispirited music mirrors the mood of a heavy-hearted girl who has been deserted by her sweetheart. As she wearily begins her day, she suddenly remembers that she has dreamed of her lover and is overcome with misery. Schumann responds to the despondent girl's plight with the plodding, steady rhythmic movement of voice and piano and a descending melodic line in the opening phrase of both parts; the bass line of the piano continues its chromatic descent for over two octaves. He doubles the vocal line in an unpretentious three-part contrapuntal accompaniment and includes five measures of pedal point in the third section of the song to contribute to the static, spiritless character of the music. The distilled contrapuntal style of this song shows the result of Schumann's continuing studies of J. S. Bach, whose influence, although present even in some of Schumann's early songs, became more prominent in the late songs—as, for example, in his *Gedichte der Königin Maria Stuart* songs.

Schumann wrote a number of fine songs in 1849 as part of the *Liederalbum für die Jugend*, based on texts by a variety of poets. Much like the piano collection *Album für die Jugend* of 1848, the first seven of which were presented to his little daughter Marie as a birthday present, these songs were written as Hausmusik. He told his publisher, "I composed poems suitable for young people, chosen from only the best writers, proceeding from the easy to the more difficult. Mignon provides the conclusion, providing insights into a more complex soul."[30] Three of the most popular from this group—"Der Sandmann (The Sandman)," "Marienwürmchen" (Ladybird), and "Schneeglöckchen" (Snow Bells)—are wonderful for the young singer because they are not vocally taxing and are artistically rewarding. "Schneeglöckchen," for example, is a delicate miniature with melodic fragments that emerge from the piano and voice to suggest a delicate winter scene. Although the poem fits somewhat awkwardly into its strophic setting, the mood of the music is so wistful and lovely that the listener finds the musical repetition pleasing. The music suggests a world of quiet wonder and anticipation, perhaps reflecting something of Schumann's own strange inner world. He became more silent as time passed and would sit with acquaintances in total silence, living entirely within himself.

"Mein schöner Stern!" composed in 1849 on a poem by Friedrich Rückert, has the accessibility of Schumann's best 1840 lieder. While avoiding the tonic key at the beginning of the song, Schumann uses continuously shifting harmonies of voluptuous tenderness to support long melodic phrases. He enhances the tonal warmth of the song by keeping the accompaniment in the lower register of the piano, anchored with rich octave doublings in the left hand. Beginning in the third measure, the melodic line of the voice is answered by the piano and provides motivic material for the accompaniment throughout the song. The result is a song of richness and lyric beauty (Example 7-2).

In 1850, Schumann set six poems by the poet Nikolaus von Lenau, concluding the group with an anonymous poem (translated from Latin and possibly a paraphrase of a poem by Heloise on the death of Abelard) called "Requiem" in memory of Lenau, who Schumann thought was dead. Lenau actually died shortly after the songs were written. "Meine Rose" (My Rose), is a beautiful, compelling song, which is sometimes dismissed by historians as an example of Schumann's waning musical powers. There is an interesting rhythmic imbalance throughout the song, sometimes enhanced by shifting harmonies on unexpected beats of the measure and by the piano's sudden changes of figuration to chordal support of the voice. Schumann's haunting, hypnotic melodies weave together against an interesting rhythmic background as he plays upon various rhythmic divisions of 6/8 while also writing duplets in the voice line when he wishes to articulate extra syllables of text. These duplets draw attention to the parallel images of stanzas one and two, "der Rose, meiner Freude" and "Du Rose meines Herzens." The vocal line is quite segmented, but melody is continuous since it is divided between voice and piano. The form of the song, AA'A, is treated with a favorite romantic device of third relationships: the two outer sections are in B-flat major while the middle section is in G-flat major. The A' section consists primarily of material that appears in the two outer portions but differs because of key, text, and slight motivic development. At the end of the song, the melody stops and is followed by a series of chords in irregular rhythms, which seem to be stumbling back to the home key of B-flat. Schumann takes the musical "license" of repeating the A section of text and music at the end of the song, a repetition that does not occur in Lenau's poem; with this repetition, Schumann answered "no" to the poet's unanswered question, "can this love be revived?"

The voice line of "Kommen und Scheiden" (Arriving and Parting) is shaped into short, meditative statements that wait for the piano to respond; each part is meaningless without the other. In "Der schwere Abend" (The Oppressive Evening), the vocal line also rises and falls with the thoughts of the speaker and is presented in short, thoughtful phrases. Because the piano part is so similar to "Ich hab' im Traum geweinet" from *Dichterliebe*, the listener must hear this new song without reference to the earlier setting to appreciate Schumann's brilliance in juxtaposing the strong rhythmic accompaniment and the free-flowing vocal line. Both "Kommen und Scheiden" and "Der schwere Abend" show Schumann now writing for the voice with a recitative-like expressiveness that shares the musical direction being taken by Wagner and Liszt.

"Requiem," the final song of the group, is overflowing with passion—long melodies divided between piano and voice, surging forward over a churning, arpeggiated accompaniment. The melody is generally in the top line of the accompaniment or in the vocal line and is anchored over a strong bass, often enriched with octave doublings.

Scholars love to ask, "What if . . . ?" What if Schubert and Mozart had lived longer? What if Beethoven had not become deaf? What if Schumann had not become insane? Schumann's insanity is blamed for what is often considered the waning of his talents in his last years.

But didn't the fanciful Schumann—the romantic Schumann— find inspiration in his unique inner world, an inner world that appears always to have been tinged with insanity? Would a sane man have so wholeheartedly embraced Jean Paul or entertained Florestan, Eusebius, and Raro? Perhaps his creativity and insanity were interwoven, inseparable. Perhaps these are the wrong questions. And perhaps romanticism is tinged with insanity.

We are surprised that Schumann suddenly started to write songs in 1840 and then surprised that he did not continue to write songs at the same superhuman pace in later years. In 1840, he was a young man anticipating happiness. The excitement of the unrealized was, perhaps, greater than the goal—certainly the epitomy of romanticism was unfulfilled longing. Many romantic poets, if they managed to live to old age, lost the spark that had defined their particular type of creativity. Robert married Clara in 1840 and settled into a world of children and responsibility. Schumann, the romantic, may have said most of what he had to say in his songs of 1840 and been ready to explore other facets of his talent. Yet he did periodically return to songwriting, almost as if songwriting were a luxury.

Schumann's desire to move *forward* meant for him writing large-scale music. While he was composing music for the piano, he looked to the day when he would be able to write symphonies. In fact, his definition of musical success required that he had to write symphonies; at the same time, he was also looking for the right opera libretto. It was inevitable that he would move from song and solo piano music to oratorios, operas, and symphonies.

Although scholars fail to agree about his success or failure with these larger genres, his reputation in song and piano literature is secure. He was one of the most original composers of all times, and we are grateful that he was inevitably led to song.

CHAPTER EIGHT

Women Musicians in Nineteenth-Century Society

In 1762, Jean Jacques Rousseau, the ultimate romantic who would place his stamp upon the century that followed, published his *Émile*, or *Education*, in which he stated his multifaceted, if crippling, view of women:

> The man should be strong and active; the woman should be weak and passive. . . . Woman is specially made for man's delight. If man in his turn ought to be pleasing in her eyes, the necessity is less urgent. . . . He pleases because he is strong. . . . She ought to make herself pleasing in his eyes and not provoke him to anger. . . . (322)

> Little girls always dislike learning to read and write, but they are always ready to learn to sew. . . . (331)

> She should early learn to submit to injustice and to suffer the wrongs inflicted on her by her husband without complaint. . . . Obstinacy only multiplies the sufferings of the wife and the misdeeds of the husband. . . . (333)

> As a woman's conduct is controlled by public opinion, so is her religion ruled by authority. . . . Unable to judge for themselves they should accept the judgment of father and husband as that of the church. . . . It is more important to show her plainly what to believe than to explain the reasons for belief. . . . (340)

> Sophy has natural gifts . . . but never having had a chance of much training she is content to use her pretty voice to sing tastefully and truly. . . . She has had no singing master but her father, no dancing mistress but her mother; a neighbouring organist has given her a few lessons in playing accompaniments on the

169

spinet, and she has improved herself by practice.... She discovered that the thin clear tone of the spinet made her voice sound sweeter; little by little she recognized the charms of harmony.... But she has taste rather than talent; she cannot read a simple air from notes. Needlework is what Sophy likes best.... (357)[1]

The nineteenth century was an era that provided many conflicting views about women and their status. Although not all women were relegated to home and family, few were free or educated enough to pursue independent careers. Most, like Alma Mahler, a promising composer who became the young wife of Gustav Mahler at the beginning of this century, quickly learned that it was their job "to hold the stirrup" for others. Singers such as Wilhelmine Schröder-Devrient, Pauline Viardot, and Jenny Lind were certainly recognized artists of their day. Marie Moke Pleyel (1811–1875)—briefly engaged to Hector Berlioz and later married to Camille Pleyel, head of the Paris piano manufacturing firm—attained international fame with her vivacious personality and pianistic gifts. Nannette Stein Streicher, student of Mozart and friend of Beethoven, was taught how to build pianos by her father, piano maker Johann Andreas Stein. She was a fine pianist who took her father's business to Vienna in 1793 after his death and established a successful piano manufacturing company there.

As part of the expanding middle class, nineteenth-century German women began to cultivate their talents and tastes as amateur musicians. They had leisure to practice the piano and sing, and they began to provide an important market for music publishing companies, composers, and piano makers. They bought songs and piano pieces that composers such as Louis Spohr, Franz Schubert, and Johannes Brahms often arranged for voice and guitar or piano four-hands. In cities such as Leipzig, they could attend subscription concerts of the Gewandhaus orchestra and hear the most recent compositions of Mendelssohn or performances by popular artists of the day such as Franz Liszt, Sigismond Thalberg, Jenny Lind, or Clara Schumann. Women were, in fact, becoming an important segment of a public that was replacing the nobility as prime patron of the arts. Sara Itzig Levy, great aunt of the Mendelssohn children, studied keyboard with Wilhelm Friedemann Bach and was a patron of Carl Philipp Emanuel Bach. She owned many manuscripts by J. S. Bach, which she donated to Carl Zelter, head of the Berlin Singakademie and teacher of Fanny and Felix Mendelssohn.

Figure 8-1. Caspar David Friedrich: *Woman at the Window,* 1822. Courtesy of the Staatliche Museen zu Berlin—Preußischer Kulturbesitz, Nationalgalerie. Photograph by Jörg P. Anders, Berlin.

The homes of middle-class women became the setting for evening concerts, either of their own amateur music-making or as a gathering place for professional musicians and amateurs. In the beginning of the nineteenth century, it was in the intimate setting of the middle-class home that the lied was performed. Schubert spent his evenings playing the piano and singing at the homes of his friends and acquaintances, while the Mendelssohn family held concerts every Sunday in their mansion on Leipziger Strasse in Berlin. Fanny Mendelssohn Hensel (see Chapter 9 for a discussion of her music) continued the family tradition of Sunday concerts after the death of her parents, and through her efforts, many works of Bach, Handel, and Gluck were heard in Berlin for the first time in the nineteenth century. She attracted many important people to her home as the following letter attests.

> Last Sunday we had the most brilliant Sunday-music that ever was, both as regards the music and the audience. When I tell you that we had twenty-two carriages in the court, and Liszt and eight princesses in the room, you will dispense with my describing the splendours of my dwelling. . . .[2]

Often the women who achieved the greatest musical sophistication were members of musical families: Clara Wieck Schumann's mother was a pianist and her father, a piano teacher; the mother of Felix and Fanny Mendelssohn was a pianist; song composer, pianist, teacher, and singer Emilie Zumsteeg (1796–1857) was the youngest child of composer Johann Zumsteeg; composer and conductor Luise Reichardt was the daughter of two composers.

Coming from a musical family, however, did not guarantee women a musical education, and most of the women mentioned in this chapter were "self-taught" composers. Luise Reichardt received no musical instruction from her parents, despite the fact that her father was well known for his educational theories. On the other hand, composer, singer, and actress Corona Schröter (1751–1802) might have been better off without her father's assistance. Her father, a court oboist, recognized his daughter's exceptional musical talent and gave her singing lessons. Unfortunately, he permanently damaged his young daughter's voice. She eventually received instruction in singing from Johann Adam Hiller and achieved some success as both a singer and a composer, although she appears to have had no training in either composition or music theory.[3]

Hiller was an advocate of teaching young women to sing and founded a singing school in 1771 that included both men and women.

Until now, only boys have been instructed in singing. But why should girls be excluded from singing? Are not the best voices often found among persons of the opposite sex, who, moreover, are not subject to the male change of voice? *Allgemeine musikalische Zeitung*, 1800.[4]

Schröter was such an expressive performer that she was able to please her audiences despite her vocal imperfections. She attained success as both a singer and an actress and was appointed Chamber Singer at the Weimar court in 1776 where she remained for twenty-five years. This was the brilliant court of Anna Amalie and her son, Karl August. Their intellectual circle included not only Herder and Wieland but also Goethe and Schiller, with whom Schröter became friends. She acted in plays with Goethe and was the first composer to set his famous poem "Erlkönig." She also composed other music for his play *Die Fischerin*, which was first performed in 1782.[5]

Schröter published two collections of very simple songs: *Fünf und zwanzig Lieder mit Musik gesetzt* in 1786 and *Gesänge mit Begleitung des Fortepiano* in 1794. The titles of these collections reflect the changing status of the accompanying instrument, from an unspecified category in the 1786 collection to the specific inclusion of the piano in 1794. The musical notation of each group of songs also reflects the lied's changing style: her first collection is written on two staves with the right-hand piano part doubling the voice; in her second collection, the voice is given a separate staff, and the piano part shows a little more musical independence.[6]

LUISE REICHARDT

Composer, singer, and conductor Luise Reichardt (1779–1825) was the daughter of Juliane Benda Reichardt and Johann Friedrich Reichardt (1752–1814), Kapellmeister to the court of Frederick the Great. Both parents were song composers, and Juliane Benda has the distinction of being one of the earliest women musicians to publish her lieder.[7] Although Benda died when her daughter was only four years old, and Luise's father showed little interest in her education, Luise Reichardt still managed to develop some of her musical talent. She is said to have had a beautiful soprano voice,[8]which probably contributed to the lyric quality of her songwriting. Largely self-taught, she supported her family by teaching voice after her father lost his job because of his political views. She was one of the founders of the Hamburg Gesangverein and actively trained its soloists and chorus for performances of Handel's *Messiah, Saul, Samson,* and *Israel in Egypt.* She also translated some of Hasse's and Graun's texts from Latin into German.

Luise Reichardt was at the center of early German romanticism, acquainted with a circle of influential, innovative artists, thinkers, and musicians. This is reflected in the poetry she set to music— Goethe, Novalis, Tieck, Achim von Arnim, and Clemens Brentano— each of whom visited the Reichardt family estate. She also set poems from Arnim and Brentano's famous collection of folk poems, *Des Knaben Wunderhorn.* Her songs were particularly pleasing to Arnim and Brentano, who found her simple, lyrical style complementary to the folk character of the text.[9]

Reichardt wrote over ninety songs and choruses.[10] Most of her songs are harmonically simple, with one or two unassuming piano figurations that are subordinate to the vocal line. Yet there is a wonderful charm and energy in her music that is reflected in songs such as "Betteley der Vögel" with its bird imitations in the piano introduction and its genial good humor (Example 8-1). In "Hier liegt ein Spielmann begraben" (A Player Lies Buried Here), another poem from *Des Knaben Wunderhorn,* Reichardt captures the character of the folk idiom with her square phrasing and buoyant rhythm (Example 8-2). Simplicity was cultivated by the so-called Berlin School of songwriters of which her father and Carl Zelter were prominent members. They were interested in providing a musical setting that would not draw attention to itself but would highlight the text. Strophic form was the preferred means of organization, and the first stanza of text was often the only one that was underlaid to the music, with additional stanzas printed at the end of the song.

Luise Reichardt's melodies are the most important feature of her songs. Sweetly lyrical and flowing, they are carefully constructed to convey the meaning of the text. In songs such as "Unruhiger Schlaf" (Restless Sleep), there are two examples of large intervallic leaps downward to illustrate the phrases "Die Blüthe sinkt" (The flower falls) and "Auch sinkt der Mond" (Also the moon sets) (Example 8-3).

When word-painting occurs in the vocal line of a strophic song, the device can generally be linked only to the first stanza of text; words in subsequent stanzas may find themselves inappropriately matched with devices that no longer apply. In her "Betteley der Vögel," Reichardt avoids any possible mismatching of words and

Example 8-1. Luise Reichardt, "Betteley der Vögel" (The Begging Birds), mm. 1–4.

1. Good morning, player man, why are you so slow? Then
2. the women came with sickles and shovels and

Example 8-2. Luise Reichardt, "Hier liegt ein Spielmann begraben" (A Player Lies Buried Here), mm. 1–4.

Die Blü - the sinkt   Auch sinkt der Mond
The flower falls   Also the moon sets

Example 8-3. Luise Reichardt, "Unruhiger Schlaf" (Restless Sleep), mm.5–6; mm. 9–10.

music by allowing the piano rather than the voice to carryout a word-painting figuration, one that is meant to suggest birds, the subject of the entire poem. In her "Vaters Klage" (A Father's Lament), she captures the melancholy character of the text without relying on graphic musical figures (Example 8-4).

Not all of her songs are strophic nor are they all written in a folk-song style. In the through-composed "Das Mädchen am Ufer" (The Girl on the Shore), she highlights the word "süssen," referring to the sweet song of the bird, with an ornamental figure (Example 8-5). The use of more flexible form and of melismatic flourish was not uncommon among the later Berlin composers. (Also see Chapter 9 on Fanny Mendelssohn Hensel). Zelter himself sometimes used melismas that are unrelated to text expression and are sheer vocalizations for their own sake (Example 8-6). (Zelter's elaborate setting of Goethe's delicate little poem "Gleich und gleich" [Like and Like] is more in the style of an Italian aria with astoundingly elaborate, complex scale passages, one thirteen measures long. These vocal fireworks seem hardly appropriate to Goethe's charming little poem and must have sparked an interesting conversation between Zelter and Goethe!)

Reichardt's exploration of a more abstract vocalization of the melody is perhaps related to her interest in Italian song. Her melisma on "piante" (wept—Example 8-7) in "Ombre amene" (Pleasant Shade; this song is also called "Canzone") can be explained as word-painting, but the vocal flourish in the song's final phrase is pure vocal display.

Italian musicians and music played such a dominant rôle in European culture during this period that German composers were often compelled to write music in the Italian style and language. Luise's father wrote Italian operas for the Prussian court, and Luise herself wrote Italian songs as a means of earning money since they were in great demand with the public, particularly with young women. She set to music the poetry of the famous Italian poet and librettist Metastasio (1698–1782), and her Italian songs exhibit the typical Italian vocal conventions of her time with their tuneful melodies and simple accompaniment. But Italian conventions also appeared in unlikely places in her German songs, as Example 8-5 illustrates. Although she does not use the great mixture of styles that so often characterized Beethoven's songs, she does occasionally employ Italian vocal techniques in her songs, particularly in those that are not easily characterized as folk song. Both her Italian and German songs would have been ideal for her young lady students since the music is tuneful and written in a modest vocal range within the capabilities of an amateur performer.

In 1800, four of her songs appeared in a published collection of her father's songs. During the next twenty-six years, she published twelve other groups of solo and choral pieces; one of her songs, "Heimweh" (Nostalgia), is still printed in vocal collections today, generally under the title "Wenn die Rosen blühen" (When the Roses Bloom).

Reichardt's work is representative of a pre-Schubertian style of writing in which simplicity was valued. Her songs, with their engaging melodies and charming, unpretentious sincerity, deserve to be included in any study of the early lied.

Zu Ber - koch an der Kir - che, Da ist ein neu - ge - mach - tes Grab.
Ich muss, so lang' ich le - be, Ums Weg - ge - trag' - ne kla - gen.

In Berkoch by the church, there is a fresh grave.
So long as I live, I must mourn the one who was carried away.

Example 8-4. Luise Reichardt, "Vaters Klage" (A Father's Lament), mm. 5–8.

Das Vög-lein hat sich ge-schwung-en schon, durch wir-belnd die Luft mit dem süs-sen Ton,

The little bird rocks back and forth, warbling through the air with its sweet tone,

Example 8-5. Luise Reichardt, "Das Mädchen am Ufer" (The Girl on the Shore), mm. 27–30.

in al-len Wip - feln spü - rest du kaum ei - nen Hauch,

in all the treetops you can scarcely notice a breeze,

Example 8-6. Zelter, "Wandrers Nachtlied" (Wanderer's Night Song), mm. 7–9.

pian - te

wept

Example 8-7. Luise Reichardt, "Ombre amene" (Pleasant Shade), m. 8.

JOSEFINE LANG

She has the gift of composing lieder and singing them as I have never heard before; it is the most complete musical joy I have ever experienced.

—Felix Mendelssohn[11]

Strong words from the brother of Fanny Mendelssohn Hensel!

Many musical careers were launched in the nineteenth century through the endorsement of prominent composers and musicians. Robert Schumann's recognition of Brahms, Chopin, and Robert Franz in the *Neue Zeitschrift für Musik* was important in bringing their names before the musical public. Felix Mendelssohn's praise of Josefine Lang (1815–1880) appeared in a letter to his sisters but has been repeated since in every biographical description of Josefine Lang. Although his endorsement may be the primary reason that she has not been forgotten, an examination of her music should secure her a respectable place in the history of the art song.

Lang, like Luise Reichardt, was largely self-taught, although she too was the product of a musical family: her grandmother, mother, and three of her aunts were all singers, and her father was a musician at the Court in Munich.[12] In 1830, at the age of fifteen, she sang for Mendelssohn and received his enthusiastic endorsement. Mendelssohn gave her some lessons in counterpoint and composition and impressed upon her his views about song composition.

Over half of her 150 songs were written between 1830 and 1840 when she was between the ages of fifteen and twenty-five. In 1840, she was named court singer in Munich, but gave up this post two years later when she married Christian Reinhold Köstlin, a lawyer, professor, and amateur poet whose works appeared under the name Christian Reinhold.[13] Some of Köstlin's poetry was set by a number of musicians of the time including Brahms in his Op. 97, Nos. 1 & 2, and Op. 106, Nos. 2 & 5. Josefine Lang herself set over forty of her husband's works. After her marriage, Lang had little time to compose, particularly with her growing family of six children. When her husband died in 1856, she returned to composing with the hope of earning a living for her family and asked Ferdinand Hiller's help in having her music published. Hiller later wrote an account of her life which appeared in his collection of articles and essays *Aus dem Tonleben unserer Zeit* (From the Musical Life of Our Time), Vol. 2 (Leipzig, 1867). Her son, Heinrich Adolph Köstlin also wrote a biography of his mother.[14]

Formal clarity and subordination of the accompaniment to the voice are basic qualities of Lang's songs. Most are strophic, strophic variations, or ternary (ABA) in form. One of her early strophic songs, "Fee'n-Reigen" (Fairy Round Dance) is a graceful little picture of swarming, dancing fairies, the rapid fluttering of their wings symbolized with the interval of a minor second that appears first in the introduction, then in the voice and interspersed throughout the song. She uses the treble range of the piano at the beginning with a repeated diminished seventh chord to create a mood of airiness and mystery. This delightfully energetic song must have appealed to Felix Mendelssohn, who was also a master of fairy music in his *Midsummer Night's Dream* (Example 8-8).

Example 8-8. Lang, "Fee'n-Reigen" (Fairy Round Dance), mm. 1–4.

Material from the piano introduction is often repeated in the postlude as a unifying feature, a device that is especially important in her through-composed songs such as "Scheideblick" (Parting Glance) and in the longer songs where several figurations appear in the accompaniment. In "Scheideblick," when Lang repeats the introductory material in the postlude, she reverses the bottom notes of the first triplet; thus the lowered seventh note of the scale, which was treated as a lower neighboring tone in the prelude, is now a member of the chord because it falls on the strong part of the beat (Example 8-9). Interesting harmonic dissonances in both prelude and postlude result from chromatic linear movement: a diminished fourth in the bass line is emphasized through repetition and as part of the linear movement of the bass in parallel with the melody of the right-hand piano line. The linear movement of the right-hand piano part also progresses from a subdominant chord on beat three of the first full measure, through a diminished seventh chord, to resolve to a tonic chord in measure two; Brahms would use a similar harmonic gesture in "Minnelied" (Love Song—1877). Her piano figuration for the main body of the song is a simple arpeggiation of the harmonies— pleasant and flowing, but rhythmically bland and thin-textured, characteristics present throughout her songs.

Example 8-9. Lang, "Scheideblick" (Parting Glance), mm. 1–3, mm. 20–21.

The rhythms of her melodies, which are closely linked to poetic rhythms, usually provide the primary distinctive rhythmic interest. In her least successful songs, Lang's use of non-functional melodic chromaticism sounds banal to modern ears because of its senti-mental character. It is in the lyric nature of her melodies, however, and in their relationship to harmonic changes in the accompani-ment, that they gain their power. Lang's harmonic vocabulary is often fresh and unique: in her best songs, she generates harmonic sur-prises. For example, in "Wie glänzt so hell dein Auge" (How Brightly Shine Your Eyes), she begins with a German sixth chord over a pedal point, which temporarily resolves to a tonic six-four chord, then returns to the German sixth before moving to a dominant-seventh and resolving to the tonic (Example 8-10). This highly expressive music is akin to Liszt (see his "Freudvoll und leidvoll"—Joyful and Sorrowful). Lang is using these harmonies to symbolize the brilliance of the beloved's eyes, but she also word-paints in the voice line when the melody rises for "Himmel" (heaven) and descends at "tiefes

Example 8-10. Lang, "Wie glänzt so hell dein Auge" (How Brightly Shine Your Eyes), mm. 1–7.

Meer" (deep sea). In "Wie glänzt so hell dein Auge," as in "Scheideblick," the piano prelude is repeated as the postlude.

Although a large number of her songs are written in major keys, Lang's songs exude intimacy and even melancholy. This is the result of her choice of texts coupled with her use of chromaticism, her shifts to minor keys, and her manner of resolving dissonance. In general, the rate of harmonic change in her songs is relatively slow, more classical than romantic in style.

The texts of her songs, however, display a typical array of romantic subject matter: love, longing, nature, home. She even wrote a humorous song about a philosophical cat, "Lied des Katers 'Hiddigeigei' " (Song of the Cat "Hiddigeigei"), and ends each stanza onomatopoetically with a "Miau."

Few of the poems she set were popular with other composers of her day. Although she did occasionally use the works of famous poets such as Heine, Goethe, Lenau, and Byron, she seldom adopted their more popular poems.[15] Not only were a quarter of her songs based on poems by her husband but a large percentage of her works were settings of forgotten poets such as Scheffel, Tiede, and Carl Stieler. A number of her songs are based on biblical texts, and one of her most beautiful songs, "Arie" (no opus number), uses a poem by Thomas Aquinas. In "Arie" she creates an organlike richness of sound with octave doublings in both the treble and bass of the accompaniment (Example 8-11); she has the vocal line drop a diminished fifth in stanzas 1 and 2 to express the words "Noth" (misery) and "Streit" (strife) (Example 8-12); and she alters the second stanza of the song so she can use a long note on the word, "Ruhe" (peace) (Example 8-13).

The range of subject matter and emotion in Lang's songs, while mostly restricted to topics that evoke a lyrical style of writing, compares favorably with the works of her contemporary Robert Franz, who also avoided the extremes of drama and passion. They each worked within a relatively narrow emotional range to produce

Example 8-11. Lang, "Arie" (Aria), mm. 6–9.

pleasing songs of taste and charm. Yet in a few of her songs, such as "Wie glänzt so hell dein Auge" and "Arie," Lang transcends conventional boundaries and surprises us, challenging our ears and our expectations.

Example 8-12. Lang, "Arie," mm. 24–27.

Example 8-13. Lang, "Arie," mm. 32–35.

CLARA SCHUMANN

Brahms called her "The Greatest Singer," a tribute to her exquisite pianistic tone and wonderful legato playing.[16] Pianist and composer Clara Schumann (1819–1896) achieved international fame, first as a child prodigy and later as a mature artist. She was groomed by her ambitious father, Friedrich Wieck, to be the most famous woman pianist of her day and, at the same time, an advertisement for Wieck's teaching methods. He nurtured her talents, often at the expense of his other children, and benefited enormously from the income her playing generated. His vicious efforts to prevent her marriage to Robert Schumann could most certainly have been grounded in economic self-interest.

Franz Liszt, who heard Clara when she was nineteen years old, had the highest opinion of her playing:

> I was fortunate enough to make the acquaintance of the young and most interesting pianist Clara Wieck, who during the past winter has deservedly made an extraordinary sensation here. Her talent delighted me; she has perfect mastery of technique, depth and sincerity of feeling, and is specially remarkable for her thoroughly noble bearing. Her extraordinary and remarkably fine rendering of the famous Beethoven sonata in F minor inspired the celebrated dramatic poet Grillparzer to write a poem in which he honours the charming artist.   (Quoted in the *Neue Zeitschrift für Musik*, Oct. 1838)[17]

The magnificence of Clara's musical understanding, technique, and tone has been confirmed by many great musicians of her age besides Liszt: Robert Schumann, Johannes Brahms, Felix Mendelssohn, to name a few. The musical respect she commanded allowed her to become the "spokesperson" for her husband's compositions and a champion for the works of Brahms as well. In her *Memoirs*, Eugenie Schumann, seventh child of Robert and Clara, describes her mother's playing. "Her technique was made entirely subservient to the musical thought and feeling. As a means to an end her technique was perfect and infallible. It sounds almost incredible, and yet it is true that I have never known my mother to fail in the most difficult passages."[!][18]

Clara's career as a pianist was curtailed after her marriage to Robert Schumann. Not only did she give birth to eight children during their fourteen years together, but Robert was reluctant to share her with the rest of the world and also did not wish to live in her artistic shadow. Her technical facility at the piano probably suffered temporarily during her marriage because she was weighed down with household duties and was not allowed to practice while Robert composed.[19] After Robert's insanity and death, she resumed a strenuous performance career to become one of the most distinguished pianists of the century.

Most concert pianists in the first half of the nineteenth century would include at least one of their own compositions on a program, a work usually designed to show off their technical virtuosity. From childhood, Clara had been encouraged by her father to compose (one thing in his favor!); she wrote a number of beautiful songs, piano pieces, cadenzas, romances for violin and piano, a trio, and one piano concerto. Yet she lacked confidence in her abilities as a composer. "I once thought that I possessed creative talent, but I have given up this idea; a woman must not desire to compose—not one has been able to do it, and why should I expect to? It would be arrogance, though indeed, my Father led me into it in earlier days."[20] Clara's words reflect the prevailing attitude of her day, a debilitating attitude that crushed more robust spirits than hers. Robert was to record in his "Book of Projects" that "children, and a husband . . . do not go well with composition. [Clara] cannot work at it regularly, and I am often disturbed to think how many tender ideas are lost because she cannot work them out."[21]

When Clara presented him with several songs on their first Christmas together, Robert decided that they should publish a volume of lieder together. This collection, *Zwölf Gedichte aus Friedrich Rückert's "Liebesfrühling" für Gesang und Pianoforte von Robert und Clara Schumann*, Op. 12 (1841), contained three songs by Clara—Nos. 2, 4, and 11. She published a total of eighteen songs and is known to have composed at least ten others, several of which have been lost.[22] In 1843, six of her songs on poetry by Heine, Geibel, and Rückert appeared, and another collection of songs based on poems of Hermann Rollet was published ten years later—her last appearance in print. This coincided with the death of her husband and her return to the concert world as a full-time performing artist.

Clara Schumann's songs are sophisticated and challenging, illustrating not only her talent but the quality of her musical education. She possessed a rich and varied harmonic vocabulary, and her piano figurations are pianistically well conceived.

One of her most dramatic pieces is "Er ist gekommen" (He Has Come), the second song of the Schumanns' Op. 12 collection. It begins with four measures of sweeping arpeggios in the introduction, which are repeated when the voice enters *forte* with the words "Er ist gekommen in Sturm und Regen" (He came to me in storm and rain). Although many of Clara Schumann's piano accompaniments are only moderately difficult, this particular one requires a highly skilled pianist (Example 8-14). "Er ist gekommen" is divided into two sections, the first of which is repeated with new text; the second section begins with music from the first, then continues with a lengthy C section (AB|AB|AC). The rising short melodic phrases of the voice part in the A sections (in F minor) capture the excitement of the words "Er ist gekommen." Robert's influence may be present here, for Clara uses the same kind of parallel phrasing that occurs so often in his writing. For example, mm. 5 and 6 of "Er ist gekommen" are

Example 8-14. Clara Schumann, "Er ist gekommen" (He Has Come), mm. 1–4.

melodically identical as are the melodies of mm. 11 and 12. (Compare this to Robert Schumann's "Im wunderschönen Monat Mai" from *Dichterliebe*. Here the melodic line of the voice can be designated AABB′ with the A phrase repeated on the same pitch and the B′ repeated sequentially a fourth above its first appearance.)

The voice line itself is frequently doubled in the accompaniment, but it is both melodically beautiful and highly expressive. The dramatic nature of "Er ist gekommen" required Clara to use a high tessitura for the voice (A-flat² is sung four times) and a more expansive vocal range (an octave and a fourth) than she uses in most of her other songs, which usually fall within the range of a ninth. The descending vocal line and simple block chords in the final section of the song, coupled with the words "Nun ist gekommen des Frühlings Segen" (Now the blessing of Spring has come), defuse the tension of the previous music; the postlude follows with a dramatic arpeggiation of the final harmonies that recall the earlier passionate mood.

In "Liebst du um Schönheit" (If You Love for Beauty), of the Schumanns' Rückert lieder, Clara captures the poetry's mystic character with her circular, static piano part, which hovers around the tonic of D-flat major; the first measure of the accompaniment is repeated over and over (Example 8-15). For each of the four lines of poetry that expectantly begins with the words, "Liebst du um . . ." (If you love for . . .), Clara Schumann reflects the text repetition by repeating the music in both piano and voice. She also preserves the intimacy of the text by restricting the vocal line to a major seventh.

Example 8-15. Clara Schumann, "Liebst du um Schönheit" (If You Love for Beauty), mm. 1–4.

The ecstatic conclusion, "Liebst du um Lieb, o ja mich liebe! Liebe mich immer, dich lieb ich immerdar!" (If you love for love, oh, love me! Love me always, I will always love you!), is reflected in the shift from quarter-notes to eighth-notes in the voice line and a quickening of the tempo. The postlude, very much like the conclusion to Robert Schumann's "Er, der Herrlichste von allen," consists of interweaving melodic lines, perhaps symbolizing the uniting of the lovers.

Heinrich Heine's "Ich stand in dunklen Träumen" (I Stood in Dark Dreams) was set by Clara Schumann as well as by Franz Schubert in his so-called *Schwanengesang*. Less stark and morose than Schubert's version, Clara's through-composed setting focuses on the melancholy of the poem with a slow tempo and linear melody. Although the music seems to trap the poem in its ¾ meter, the overall mood of the song conveys the delicacy and fragility of the poem. The descending melody of the voice as the speaker's tears flow down his cheeks and the chromaticism of the melody and harmony contribute to the song's nostalgic character.

Clara Schumann used discreet word-painting techniques for the most part, such as a rising vocal line on the words "Die stille Lotosblume steigt aus dem blauen See" (The silent lotus flower rises out of the blue pond) in "Die stille Lotosblume," (Example 8-16). She ends the song in both the voice line and the accompaniment on a dominant seventh chord when the poem asks the question, "Kannst du das Lied versteh'n?" (Can you understand this song?)—a question that the music had already asked in the brief piano introduction (Example 8-17). She structures "Die stille Lotosblume" as a modified bar form (AA'B) and moves through a delicate array of keys at the beginning of the second stanza (A') by lowering the third of several chords, moving from A-flat major through D-flat major to C-flat major with a

The silent lotus-flower rises out of the blue pond,

Example 8-16. Clara Schumann, "Die stille Lotosblume" (The Silent Lotus Flower), mm. 1–6.

Can you understand this song?

Example 8-17. Clara Schumann, "Die stille Lotosblume," mm. 42–47.

relatively static voice line, as the swan circles the lotus flower (Example 8-18). "Die stille Lotosblume" exudes a unique air of pensive intimacy. Its subject, the night-blooming lotus flower, an exotic Oriental blossom, was popular not only with the poet of this song, Emanuel Geibel (1815–1884), but with other romantics of the nineteenth century (c.f., Heine's "Die Lotosblume").

Heine's poem "Sie liebten sich beide" (They Loved One Another) from *Die Heimkehr* (The Homecoming) tells the sad story of two people who would never admit their love for each other. Clara Schumann's strophic setting captures the longing of the text with a short rising motive in G minor coupled with gentle dissonances that result from pedal points on the tonic and dominant, suspension chords, and diminished seventh chords. The irregular phrase lengths of the voice part—short phrases punctuated by rests that extend as the speaker's thoughts gather momentum—effectively communicate the narrative character of the poem. She also uses no text repetition and thereby keeps the story moving forward.

The swan, it sings so sweetly, so softly, and gazes at the flower.
The swan, it sings so sweetly, so softly, and wants to expire in the singing.

Example 8-18. Clara Schumann, "Die stille Lotosblume, mm. 25–33.

"Das ist ein Tag" (That Is a Day) reveals a surprisingly lighthearted facet of Clara Schumann's personality, for it is a delightful, rollicking song of spring with birdcalls and hunters' horns in the accompaniment. She uses a pedal point from a to a^2 in the piano introduction to give a folklike quality to the music. The melody of the prelude, presented in clipped two-note installments, is lyrically taken up by the voice on its entrance and then repeated in the alto voice of the accompaniment in mm. 6–9 and again in the next piano interlude at mm. 18–21, not shown in the musical example (Example 8-19). Only the final phrase of text is repeated at the climax of the song as the voice rises to a^2 (in fact, she is generally moderate in the amount of text repetition she uses in all her songs). As cheerful and as captivating as Wolf's "Er ist's" (It Is He), the through-composed "Das ist ein Tag" is unified by its exuberant mood and accompaniment figuration.

During a trip with Robert to Berlin, Clara met the pianist and composer Fanny Mendelssohn Hensel. "I have taken a great fancy to Madame Hensel and feel especially attracted to her in regard to music." This musical kinship was so strong that the Schumanns

Example 8-19. Clara Schumann, "Das ist ein Tag" (That Is a Day), mm. 1–9.

actually considered moving to Berlin, plans that never materialized because of Hensel's untimely death. "I was very much upset by this news [of Hensel's death] for I had a great respect for this remarkable woman."[23] The only fault Clara could find in Fanny was that she was a woman. "Women always betray themselves in their compositions, and this is true of myself as well as of others."[24] This self-deprecating remark actually applies to neither woman. As will be seen in the next chapter, some of Fanny Mendelssohn Hensel's songs were published under her brother's name, and reviewers failed to detect that they were not by Felix. In fact, they were frequently cited as being the best songs in his collections! Clara's writing was also "genderless" despite her protests to the contrary. She wrote with skill and flair that are entirely worthy of the nineteenth-century lied.

Figure 9-1. Fanny Mendelssohn Hensel. Drawing by her husband, Wilhelm Hensel in 1832. Berlin: Staatsbibliothek Preußischer Kulturbesitz, Musikabteilung.

CHAPTER NINE

Fanny Mendelssohn Hensel

Poor, poor Fanny! It makes one's heart beat with indignant pity to think of her wasted genius; and it is almost intolerable to look beyond her and to become aware how many gifted souls enclosed in female bodies have suffered in like manner. Poor women! And poor world, which has wasted so much of its all too rare genius on wiping dust off furniture and rubbing soup through sieves! And poor, poor fools of to-day, who chuckle over the waste, as though it were a thing to delight in, when it is, indeed, one to most bitterly regret!

—"A Genius Wasted" by Florence Fenwick Miller (1892)[1]

Fanny Mendelssohn Hensel (1805–1847), a gifted composer of approximately three hundred songs, accepted obscurity as the rightful condition of her sex. She has never been totally forgotten, primarily because of her intense relationship with her famous brother Felix Mendelssohn (1809–1847). While she willingly acted as his musical advisor and guide, her own talents provided a challenge for her younger brother.

When Fanny Mendelssohn was born in November of 1805, her pianist mother, Leah, observed that her little daughter had "Bach-fugue fingers."[2] Fanny's wealthy parents nurtured her talents as carefully as those of her younger brother, Felix, and much was expected of the precocious Mendelssohn children who arose at five o'clock every morning (except Sunday) to begin their studies. Both children

Part of this chapter appeared in "Fanny Mendelssohn and her Songs," *NATS Journal*, Vol. 42, 1986, 6–11.

displayed extraordinary musical memories: at the age of thirteen, Fanny astonished her father by playing all the preludes from Book One of Bach's *Well-tempered Klavier* from memory; Felix would later conduct massive musical works such as the *St. Matthew Passion* from memory. Fanny's talents as a composer and pianist were also impressive—her first extant composition was a song "Ihr Töne, schwingt euch freundlich" (Oh, You Tones Vibrate Cheerfully), written for her father's birthday when she was fourteen.[3] Her gifts as a pianist were said to be at least as great as those of her brother. Singer Eduard Devrient commented that Felix's "technical command of the pianoforte, and musicianly way of playing, struck me then as surprising, but still inferior to that of his elder sister Fanny."[4] In 1831, Carl Zelter would write to Goethe that Fanny played "as well as any man."[5]

Fanny, three years older than her brother, not only acted as his musical mentor but even kept a childhood diary of Felix's progress as well as a catalogue of his early works. Felix depended on Fanny's musical judgment throughout most of his early career and especially admired the lovely songs she composed. When he was eleven years old, he was taken by his teacher, Zelter, to visit Goethe, who was charmed by the talented young boy. During his two-week stay, Felix gave the young Frau von Goethe some of Fanny's songs so that she could sing them for the great poet. Goethe was impressed and, in turn, composed a poem for Fanny, asking Zelter to "take that to the dear child."[6] Although Fanny did not set this particular poem to music, she used more than twenty other poems by Goethe for songs during her musical career; in fact, she set more poems by Goethe than by any other poet. When Felix visited Goethe a second time, Fanny went with him. Their mother recalled that [Fanny] "had to play a good deal of Bach to him, and he was extremely pleased with those of his poems which she had set to music."[7] After the children returned home, Goethe wrote a letter to Felix that ended: "Remember me to your good parents, your equally gifted sister, and your excellent master [Zelter]."[8]

In his young adulthood, Felix extolled the virtues of Fanny's songs: "[They] are more beautiful than anyone can say. Indeed I speak as a cool critic, and declare them very pretty... the quintessence, the soul, of music.... I know no better!"[9] When his own works began to be published, Felix thought so highly of Fanny's songs that he included three in his Op. 8 (one of the three was a duet, "Suleika und Hatem"—Suleika and Hatem) and three in Op. 9—but with no attribution to Fanny. There has been much speculation on whether to blame Felix or his parents for this omission. Fanny herself was silent about the matter, at least in her correspondence, but she was evidently actively involved in the actual choice of music that appeared in both collections. In a letter to his father in 1829, Felix declared that "Fanny . . . should select from her works or mine just as she pleases."[10]

Both collections received favorable reviews after their publication, and critics usually cited Fanny's songs as being particularly lovely. Only the reviewer for *The Harmonicon*, however, was aware of Fanny's authorship: "Three of the best . . . are by his sister, a young lady of great talents and accomplishments. . . . Her songs are distinguished by tenderness, warmth, and originality."[11]

Her early solo songs already show many of the qualities that characterize all of Fanny's writing. They are clearly structured, usually as strophic songs, with an accompaniment subordinate to the vocal line. "Verlust" (Loss), No. 10 of Felix's Op. 9, is a setting of the popular poem "Und wüssten's die Blumen" taken from Heine's *Lyrisches Intermezzo* (this poem was set by ninety other composers including Robert Schumann in his *Dichterliebe*).[12] Two stanzas of text are delegated to each stanza of the music, but each musical stanza is written out separately in order to accommodate slight alterations in the vocal line. Although only two pages long, "Verlust" is quite dramatic, with its sudden shifts from minor to major (a frequent occurrence in Fanny's music), its chromatic chord alterations, and its melismatic phrases, first on the word "erquickenden" (refreshing) at the conclusion of the first stanza and then on "zerrissen" (torn) at the end of the final stanza. Since the poem begins in mid thought, "Und wüssten's die Blumen, die kleinen, wie tief verwundet mein Herz" (And if the little flowers knew how deeply wounded my heart is), Fanny responded musically by beginning the song with a tonic six-fou chord in D minor and then immediately moving to the dominant. This progression is repeated in the final three measures of the postlude, thereby ending the song on a dominant chord, a subtle means of backing away from Heine's brutal conclusion that "er hat ja selbst zerrissen, zerrissen mir das Herz" (he has torn, torn my heart) and enhancing the wishful thinking of the poem (Example 9-1).

"Die Nonne" (The Nun), No. 12 in Felix's Op. 9, is another dramatic song, based on a poem by Uhland that tells the surprising story of a nun whose sweetheart has just died; the young nun ironically states that she can now show her love for her sweetheart

- ris - sen, zer-ris - sen mir das Herz.

has broken my heart.

Example 9-1. Hensel, "Verlust" (Loss), mm. 35–39.

since he has become an angel. The voice line surges forward with an octave leap in the opening phrase over an arpeggiated figuration of driving sixteenth-notes in the accompaniment. The chromatic alteration of the fourth scale step (in A minor) and its frequent use as a lower neighboring tone in the vocal line contribute to a general atmosphere of unrest. When the young nun finally expires and her misery ends, the agitation of the sixteenth-notes in the right hand of the accompaniment is countered with a pedal point of dotted quarters and eighths on G and D in the left; final calm is musically achieved as the sixteenth-notes of the right hand shift to eighths and then to dotted quarters. "Die Nonne" is the only one of the five solo songs in these early collections with both a prelude and postlude.

These early songs later proved to be a source of discomfort to Felix, as he indicated in a letter to his mother. In 1842, Felix met Queen Victoria and Prince Albert for the first time while he was performing in England.

> The Queen asked if I had written any new songs, and said she was very fond of singing my published ones. "You should sing one to him," said Prince Albert; and after a little begging she said she would try. . . . I rummaged about among the music, and soon discovered my first set of songs. . . . And which did she choose?—"Schöner und schöner schmückt sich"—sang it quite charmingly, in strict time and tune, and with very good execution. . . . It was really charming, and the last long G I have never heard better or purer or more natural from any amateur. Then I was obliged to confess that Fanny had written the song (which I found very hard, but pride must have a fall).[13]

This was Fanny's song "Italien" (Italy), published years earlier (1827) as Felix's Op. 8, No. 3.

The relationship of Felix and Fanny appears to have been one of love and pride in each other's accomplishments. Their three-year age difference stimulated Felix to imitate his older sister, yet at the same time it gave her an obvious advantage in childhood competition, even over the precocious Felix. That some sibling rivalry existed between them is shown in a letter from Felix to Alfred Novello in 1838:

> It is altogether impossible for me to do anything in the way of prize composition; I cannot do it, if I would force myself to it; and when I was compelled to do so, when a boy, in competition with my sister and fellow-scholars, my works were always wonders of stupidity—not the tenth part of what I could do otherwise.[14]

The Mendelssohn family sponsored concerts every Sunday, for which father Abraham Mendelssohn often engaged a small orchestra to accompany his brilliant children. Many distinguished visitors, such as Franz Liszt, Paganini, the philosopher Hegel, and the poet Heine, were entertained by the Mendelssohns. (Fanny, who disliked Heine, nevertheless called him "a true poet! . . . What feeling he has for nature" and used a number of his poems in her songs).[15] Fanny and Felix often premiered their own compositions for this kind of audience or performed works they were studying. Since most of Fanny's works were written to be performed in her home, chamber music and song resulted naturally.

Lea Salomon Mendelssohn was Fanny's and Felix's first piano teacher.

> How far she was herself a pianoforte-player we are not told. . . . For some time [she] taught the two eldest children music, beginning with lessons five minutes long and gradually increasing the time until they went through a regular course of instruction. For many years Felix and Fanny never practised or played without the mother sitting by them, knitting in hand.[16]

Abraham Mendelssohn, son of the great Jewish philosopher, Moses Mendelssohn, was a dominant force in the lives of his children, and it was he who shaped the goals of Fanny's future life. In a letter on 16 July 1820, Abraham pointed out Fanny's "womanly" obligations, which he believed must supersede any obligations to her talents.

> Music will perhaps become his profession [Felix's] while for you it can and must only be an ornament, never the root of your being and doing. We may therefore pardon him some ambition and desire to be acknowledged in a pursuit which appears very important to him, because he feels a vocation for it, while it does

you credit that you have always shown yourself good and sensible in these matters; and your very joy at the praise he earns proves that you might, in his place, have merited equal approval. Remain true to these sentiments and to this line of conduct; they are feminine, and only what is truly feminine is an ornament to your sex.[17]

Abraham continued the theme of feminine responsibility in a letter to Fanny on her twenty-third birthday.

You must become more steady and collected, and prepare more earnestly and eagerly for your real calling, the only calling of a young woman—I mean the state of a housewife. . . . Women have a difficult task: the constant occupation with apparent trifles . . . the unremitting attention to every detail.[18]

Although Abraham Mendelssohn fostered his daughter's talents, he also provided the major stumbling block to her future as a professional musician. Fanny would later write to Felix that all her life she was intimidated by the opinions of both her father and Felix.[19]

Fanny married the Prussian court painter, Wilhelm Hensel, in 1829. One of the happiest periods in her life began when she and her husband decided to take an extended trip to Italy where they both became part of the artistic community that included the young composer Charles Gounod. Later Gounod described Fanny in his autobiography.

Madam Hensel was a first-rate musician—a very clever pianist, physically small and delicate, but her deep eyes and eager glance betrayed an active mind and restless energy. She had rare powers of composition, and many of the "Songs without Words," published among the works and under the name of her brother, were hers. . . . She would sit at the piano with the readiness and simplicity of one who played because she loved it. Thanks to her great gifts and wonderful memory I made the acquaintance of various masterpieces of German music which I had never heard before, among them a number of the works of Sebastian Bach . . . and many of Mendelssohn's compositions, which were like a glimpse of a new world to me.[20]

Despite her extraordinary talents and the respect she commanded among other musicians, Fanny failed to venture outside the performance world of her home. Her only public appearance as a pianist occurred in the winter of 1837–38 when she played for a charity concert, an acceptable outlet for her sex and social standing. She was prisoner to her upbringing and was not encouraged to change that view by the one person who could, her brother Felix, who shared his father's view of her obligations to home and family and actively discouraged her from public performance or publication of her works. Her husband, Wilhelm Hensel, tried to convince Fanny that she should publish her music, but she modestly refused.

Finally, in 1837, Fanny agreed to publish one of her songs in a collection by A. M. Schlesinger, and the song became very popular. Felix wrote the following letter to Fanny in March of 1837:

> I must write to you about your song yesterday. How beautiful it was! You know what my opinion of it always has been, but I was curious to see whether my old favorite, which I had only heard hitherto sung by Rebecca [their younger sister] to your accompaniment in the gray room with the engravings, would have the same effect here in the crowded hall, with the glare of the lamps, and after listening to noisy orchestral music. I felt so strange when I began, your soft, pretty symphony imitating the waves, with all the people listening in perfect silence; but never did the song please me better. The people understood it, too, for there was a hum of approbation each time the refrain returned with the long E, and much applause when it was over. . . . I thank you in the name of the public of Leipzig and elsewhere for publishing it against my wish.[21]

The song in question, "Die Schiffende" (The Woman on the Boat), paints the graceful picture of a young woman in a boat who is being observed by an admirer. Fanny's lyrical music, akin to Schubert's delicate "Der Jüngling an der Quelle" or his "Schlummerlied" (Lullaby), captures the image of a boat, gently swaying in the shimmer of moonlight on a pond surrounded by hanging branches and shrubs. The slow harmonic rhythm of the accompaniment and the sustained, slow-moving vocal line eliminate all sense of urgency from the sixteenth-note figuration in the right-hand piano part and, at the same time, subtly mask the boldness of her harmonic vocabulary; she moves easily from A major in the song's first section to B major (secondary dominant) in the next section and outlines a series of diminished seventh chords with the arpeggiated accompaniment—all within the context of irregular phrase lengths that lend a unique character to her music. Felix's description of this song—"your soft, pretty symphony imitating the waves"—indicates the programmatic fashion in which he and Fanny must have viewed this music. Not only did her sixteenth-notes imitate the gently swaying boat on the waves, but she used other word-painting devices such as "helle" (bright) on a high note, an octave leap for "erwachen" (awaken) (Examle 9-2), and a more rapidly moving, melismatic treat-

awakens from sleep.
you alders do not hide her.

Example 9-2. Hensel, "Die Schiffende" (The Woman on the Boat), mm. 14–16.

ment of the vocal line when the word "Well" (wave) occurs. (These word-painting devices apply only to the first stanza of text.) Later, when his mother asked Felix to persuade Fanny to publish more of her works, he refused. This is his explanation to his mother in a letter of 2 June 1837:

> You write to me about Fanny's new compositions, and say that I ought to persuade her to publish them. . . . I need not say that, if she does resolve to publish anything, I will do all in my power to obtain every facility for her, and to relieve her, so far as I can, from all trouble which can possibly be spared her. But to persuade her to publish anything I cannot, because this is contrary to my views and to my convictions. . . . I consider the publication of a work as a serious matter (at least it ought to be so), for I maintain that no one should publish unless they are resolved to appear as an author for the rest of their life. . . . Nothing but annoyance is to be looked for from publishing, where one or two works alone are in question . . . and from my knowledge of Fanny I should say she has neither inclination nor vocation for authorship. She is too much all that a woman ought to be for this. She regulates her house, and neither thinks of the public nor of the musical world, nor even of music at all, *until her first duties are fulfilled* (emphasis added). Publishing would only disturb her in these, and I cannot say that I approve of it. I will not, therefore, persuade her to this step. . . . If she resolves to publish, either from her own impulse or to please Hensel, I am, as I said before, quite ready to assist her so far as I can; but to encourage her in what I do not consider right, is what I cannot do.[22]

Without the approval of Felix, Fanny declined to publish her music for nearly ten years. Finally in 1846, the year before her death, she agreed to publish a few of her best works. By this time, her musical reputation had become so great in Berlin that she could publish as much as she desired. She had offers from two publishers, Bote und Bock and Schlesinger, for whom she selected six songs, twenty piano solos, and six part-songs, which appeared between 1846 and 1847 as Opera 1 through 6; her Op. 1 was a collection of six songs. (During her life and in the three years following her death, a total of thirty-one of her songs were published.)

Nature and love are the primary topics of Fanny's first song collection, with poetry by Heine, Goethe, Eichendorff, and an anonymous poet. "Schwanenlied" (Swansong), which opens the group, is a haunting, nostalgic lied of lyric delicacy. In 6/8 meter, as are many of Fanny's more lyrical songs (e.g., "Die Schiffende" and "Gondellied"), "Schwanenlied" has an arpeggiated accompaniment which slowly unveils a variety of harmonic changes that support and enhance the dominant vocal line. Each of the song's two stanzas concludes with a lengthy melisma, a device she occasionally used in an operatic fashion, drawing attention to the voice as an instrument capable of beautiful sound and minimizing its rôle as a conveyer of text. One can often make a case for word-painting in these vocalizations—as in the melismatic treatment of "Wonne" (bliss) in "Die Ersehnte" (The Desired One)—but melismata and long sustained notes at the ends of stanzas are also basic to her vocal writing. Her repetition of the final line of text at the end of each musical strophe in "Schwanenlied" is also a common feature of her style and one that often occurs in Brahms's songs as well. She creates a moment of absolute stillness and beauty in the second stanza of the song when the voice sings a sustained d^2 on the word "Fluthengrab" (water grave) and is followed by silence in both voice and piano; the voice then reenters with the words "Es ist so still und dunkel" (It is so quiet and dark).

For her Op. 1, Fanny chose songs of varied moods, tempi, keys, and meter. "Mayenlied" (May Song) bubbles with brilliant vitality; its piano prelude begins with the stretch of a tenth in the right-hand piano part, perhaps indicating that Fanny had more than "Bach-fugue fingers." "Morgenständchen" (Morning Serenade) is a dramatic tour de force with pulsing sixteenth-notes in both hands of the accompaniment and a syllabic, wordy-sounding vocal line that negotiates an octave scale up to G-sharp^2 and then back down to G-sharp^1 within the first two measures. The final song of the collection, "Gondellied," is a beautiful example of the gondola songs that were so popular with composers of the nineteenth century.

Fanny gratefully accepted words of approval from Felix after her Op. 1 was published.

> At last Felix has written, and given me his professional blessing in the kindest manner. I know that he is not quite satisfied in his heart of hearts, but I am glad he has said a kind word to me about it.[23]

There is much tragedy in Fanny's timid beginnings. She obviously did not feel confident in the encouragements of her non-musician husband and depended on a brother whose discouragements were not rationally offered. He claimed that "nothing but annoyance is to be looked for from publishing, where one or two works alone are in question." Yet, when she died at the relatively young age of forty-one, Fanny had already written between four and five hundred works. Felix also argued that "she regulates her house, and neither thinks of the public nor of the musical world, nor even of music at all, until her first duties as a housewife are fulfilled." But Fanny was obviously consumed by music, even while she performed her duties as a housewife. Her letters are the letters of a musician, always directed toward performances she was sponsoring in her home, musicians she had met, music she had heard.

It seems ironic that Felix was able to recognize his sister's talent yet was willing to accept her obscurity. Sir George Grove, a friend of Felix Mendelssohn, stated that "Felix's letters show how much he loved her, and the value which he placed on her judgment and her musical ability.... Mendelssohn used to say that at one time she played better than he."[24]

Perhaps Felix was not really comfortable with his rôle in Fanny's musical obscurity. After she died, he began to prepare an edition of her music for publication, which he was unable to complete because of his own death.[25] A volume of her lieder, Op. 7, with six songs, was issued by Fanny's family shortly after her death, and two additional song collections appeared two years later as Op. 9, with six songs, and Op. 10, with five songs. (Op. 8 consisted of four "Lieder ohne Worte," and Op. 11 was a Trio for piano, violin, and 'cello.) Although Fanny seems to have accepted her modest status as a home-musician, she did suffer from an extended period of discouragement. In July of 1836, she wrote to one of her German friends, Klingemann, who was living in London.

> I must add that it is a pleasure to me to find a public for my little pieces in London, for here I have none at all. Once a year, per-

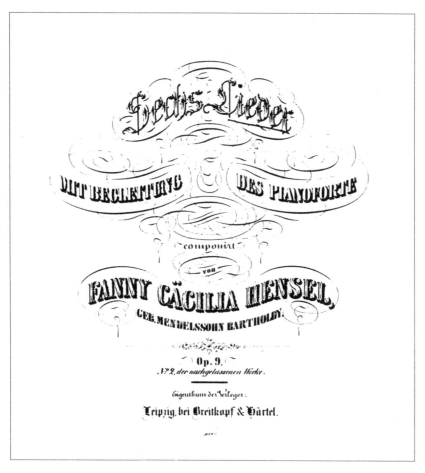

Figure 9-2. Decorative frontispiece to song edition of Fanny Mendelssohn Hensel's Op. 9.

haps, someone will copy a piece of mine, or ask me to play something special—certainly not oftener; and now that Rebecca [her sister] has left off singing, my songs lie unheeded and unknown. If nobody ever offers an opinion, or takes the slightest interest in one's productions, one loses in time not only all pleasure in them, but all power of judging of their value. *Felix, who is alone a sufficient public for me* (emphasis added), is so seldom here that he cannot help me much, and thus I am thrown back entirely on myself. But my own delight in music and Hensel's sympathy keep me awake still, and I cannot help considering it a sign of talent that I do not give it up, though I can get nobody to take an interest in my efforts.[26]

Fanny did not have the benefit of outside encouragement, respect, criticism, and general give-and-take with other composers during most of her adult life. Felix had been her most important colleague at the beginning of her career as a composer, and she developed a stifling dependency on his opinions and his support.

By the spring of 1838, she was experiencing writer's block.

> Dear Felix, I have not composed a single note this winter, although for that reason, perhaps, I have played more than ever; but I scarcely remember what it feels like to be writing a song. Will it ever come back?[27]

During this same time she was also disillusioned with her pianistic ability.

> With all my talk of buying an English grand piano, I shall probably neither get that nor any other, and I need it less than I did, for my playing seems to me quite antiquated after hearing these modern wizards and acrobats, and I shrink back more and more into my nothingness.[28]

Fanny Mendelssohn's fate was interwoven with her brother's to the very end. On 14 May 1847, while conducting a rehearsal of Felix's *Walpurgisnacht*, Fanny, only forty-one years old, fell ill and died by eleven o'clock that evening. Her unexpected death proved to be a hard blow to her ailing brother. Felix died six months later.

A great number of Fanny's works are still in existence, many of them in the Mendelssohn Archive in Berlin (Staatsbibliothek Preussischer Kulturbesitz), the Bodleian Library at Oxford University, the Goethe Museum and the Heinrich Heine Institut in Düsseldorf, and private collections. A growing awareness of her music among scholars bodes well for her future reputation. An exact account of her works has not been given at this time because some of her music in private collections has not been available to scholars. Since she often made copies of her music as gifts for friends, some of the pieces in private hands may be duplicates of music already known. Scholars estimate that of her four to five hundred works, approximately three hundred are songs. She has been called the most important woman composer of the nineteenth century, and some music historians are suggesting that she, rather than her brother Felix, first conceived the well-known piano genre "Songs without Words."[29]

Fanny's music was written for home performance, and we know that her sister, Rebecca, often sang these songs. Fanny's Op. 7, in fact, was dedicated to her sister, Frau Rebecca Lejeune Dirichlet. The vocal range of her songs generally extends from an octave to an octave and a sixth, and frequently lies within a tessitura most suitable for soprano or tenor voice. Piano accompaniments in Fanny's songs vary from very simple to quite difficult. In "Die frühen Gräber," for example, the sparse but strangely atmospheric accompaniment, which is set entirely in bass clef, is simple enough to be played by most amateur pianists. Yet "Frühling," written in the key of F-sharp major and expressing the exuberance of Spring with a basic figuration of sixteenth-notes to be played allegro molto, is a challenge to the most competent player; the arrangement of sixteenth-notes in both hands often results in double trills that imitate the singing of birds (Example 9-3). Since Fanny was a virtuoso pianist, one may wonder why her song accompaniments are not consistently demanding. It is important to remember, however, that she had been a pupil of Carl Zelter, a composer who believed that musical settings should not infringe on the sense and dominance of the poetry.

Example 9-3. Hensel, "Frühling" (Spring), mm. 1–3.

Fanny's accompaniments are often simply chordal—sometimes doubling the vocal line—or are arpeggiations of chords, figurations that commonly appear in Felix's songs as well. How much both reflected Zelter's aesthetic ideals is revealed in Felix's letter of 1829 concerning the publication of his Op. 8 and Op. 9, which included the six early songs of Fanny. He declared that Fanny should choose songs with simple accompaniment and include at least one "cheerful piece in quick tempo."[30]

The voice parts are often chromatic and sometimes surprisingly sweeping in nature (Example 9-4). She used chromaticism, either to embellish the melodic line or as a function of the harmonic scheme. In the following illustration from one of her later songs, "Dein ist

1. I wander sadly from bush to bush.
2. and a solitary tear falls.

Example 9-4. Hensel, "Die Mainacht" (May Night), mm. 15–17.

mein Herz" (My Heart Is Yours), Op. 7, her music seems surprisingly
progressive (Example 9-5).

Her vocal lines are lyrical and generally pleasing. They may alter-
nate between an outline of the song's harmonic scheme and simple
linear movement (Example 9-6). The octave leap that occurs in the
melody of "Schwanenlied" is quite common in Fanny's songs ("Die
Nonne," Die Schiffende," "Mayenlied," "Bergeslust," "Morgenständchen"). As was mentioned earlier, her vocal lines often incorporate
melismatic features at the ends of stanzas, which can enhance the
poetic text or simply complete a musical idea (see Examples 9-1 and
9-4). These melismatic phrases are usually longer than the phrases
that precede them, allowing the stanza or entire song to conclude
with a broad flourish. Since she often used melismata in strophic
songs, she could expect to word-paint only with text from the first
stanza of the poem. In "Die Ersehnte," she was able to word-paint in
both the first and third stanzas with a melismatic vocal line that soars
up to high A-flat on the word "Wonne" (bliss) in the first stanza and
"komm" (come) in the third stanza. But in the second stanza, the
melisma falls on the syllables "abend" (evening), part of the word
"Frühlingsabend" and serves no graphic function; also, the resulting
textual phrase is quite long and beyond the breath capacity of some
singers. Nevertheless, "Die Ersehnte," like Schubert's "Nähe des
Geliebten" (The Nearness of the Beloved), is a song of sublime
beauty.

The vocal line becomes an important harmonic device in her
songs, as can be seen in Example 9-7 where the singer provides a
pedal point to the shifting harmonies of the accompaniment.

It is to me a word which gives you joy, a silent glance, a silent glance which [touches] you

Example 9-5. Hensel, "Dein ist mein Herz" (My Heart Is Yours), mm. 28–31.

A star fell
from its brilliant heights, the star of

Example 9-6. Hensel, "Schwanenlied" (Swan Song), mm. 1–6.

1. why are you killing me?
2. who then might think of me, who?
3. and that I must wander.

Example 9-7. Hensel, "Ferne" (From Afar), mm. 19–23.

Fanny was multilingual and composed a few songs in French, Italian, and even English. She wrote several interesting songs on texts by Lord Byron as well as a short cycle of three songs based on English translations of Heine's poetry by Mary Alexander.

All of her published songs and the majority of her unpublished songs are in German. She set poetic text carefully, using the metric scheme of the music to enhance poetic accents. On a few occasions, her music takes on a recitative-like character, as in the B section of "Dein ist mein Herz," but her usual writing is generally more melodic than this. In the strophic songs she published, she sometimes provided a separate text underlay in the second or third stanza, with slight melodic alterations either to accomodate extra syllables in the poetry or to provide some variety and drama in the song's conclusion. In many of her unpublished songs, however, the text for the second and third stanzas is not underlaid but is simply written at the end of the song.[31] She, like Schubert, was successful in her use of the strophic form because so many of her lovely melodies bear repeating, but she also used less restricted structures with great skill. "Frühling" and "Dein ist mein Herz," for example, are both ABA' in shape and are two of her most beautiful songs.

"Nachtwanderer" (Night Wanderer), Op. 7, another excellent song, is through-composed with a thick chordal accompaniment and motivic treatment of the melodic line that exemplify Beethoven's influence on her style. Both accompaniment and voice part share and exchange melodic material throughout the song, with the piano prelude, interludes, and postlude tightly integrated into the structure of the song (Example 9-8). Thematic material introduced in the prelude is completed by the entering voice part; the opening voice line is repeated sequentially in the second phrase, returns in the

And back and forth in the valley, [awakens]

Example 9-8. Hensel, "Nachtwanderer" (Night Wanderer), mm. 9–12.

piano interlude in mm. 17–18, and appears in various guises throughout.

Fanny met many poets of her era and set to music the works of famous poets such as Goethe, Heine, Eichendorff, Byron, Tieck, Uhland, Hölty, and Rückert as well as poems of lesser-known writers and acquaintances such as Gerstenberg, Droysen, and Luise Hensel. The subject of nature played a dominant rôle throughout her works, as we can see in her settings of the popular texts "Frühling," "Bergeslust," and "Die Mainacht."

"Die Mainacht" (May Night), using a poem by Hölty (familiar to most lovers of art song through Brahms's famous setting in a slightly altered version of the text), begins with a melody in the piano prelude that anticipates the voice line. The irregular phrase lengths occurring throughout the song are characteristic of Fanny's style and are a unique feature of her music. Each stanza concludes with a sweeping melismatic phrase, longer than the phrases that precede it and covering an octave and a fifth, much in the style of a grand vocalise (see Example 9-4). It is interesting that Brahms responded to the poetry in a similar fashion, also including two majestic melismatic flourishes at the ends of his last two stanzas. (Both Fanny and Brahms omit the second stanza of Hölty's poem, but Brahms includes a fourth stanza that Fanny does not.)

Her last song, published posthumously by her family in Op. 10, was "Bergeslust"—a song that exuberantly extols the joy of wandering through the mountains. The piano has its own cheerful melody, which first appears in the tenor part of the piano introduction, reappears in interludes, and is finally taken up by the voice in the coda (Example 9-9).

Fanny Mendelssohn Hensel wrote songs of surprising richness and beauty. Her unique voice deserves to be heard, for she has justly earned a place among the respected lieder composers of the nineteenth century.

Example 9-9. Hensel, "Bergeslust" (Mountain Joy), mm. 1–4.

Figure 10-1. Felix Mendelssohn. Reproduction of painting by Eugene A. Perry, Perry Pictures. Courtesy of the Library of Congress.

Felix Mendelssohn

You want me to devote myself to operas.... I respond: give me a really good text, and in a few months it shall be composed; every day I long anew to write an opera. I know I could produce something bright and fresh, but I have no words.
—Letter of Felix Mendelssohn to Eduard Devrient (1832)

But as you say, above all things, I should write an opera; sometimes I long for it exceedingly.... It appears that I do not possess the talent to arrange a plot into scenes ... the ground plan! There's the rub! It should be German, and noble, and cheerful.
—Letter of Felix Mendelssohn to Eduard Devrient (1845)[1]

Felix Mendelssohn (1809–1847) was admired and revered by many of the great musicians of his day. Clara Wieck, commenting on his pianistic talents, stated unequivocally: "He is the pianist whom I love best of all."[2] Robert Schumann called Mendelssohn "the Mozart of the nineteenth century ... who most clearly sees through the contradictions of the age, and reconciles them."[3] Jenny Lind performed Mendelssohn's works with loving devotion, and Franz Liszt made piano transcriptions of seven of Mendelssohn's songs.

A virtuoso pianist and an innovative, brilliant conductor with a phenomenal memory, he was a source of wonder to those who knew him. He was probably the most well-educated and well-rounded musician of the century, qualities that would have been ideal for a composer of song. But while his knowledge of literature and languages, his understanding of the piano, and his ability to write lyrical melodies would have provided him with a unique arsenal of tools, the lied was only of incidental interest for Mendelssohn. Nevertheless, he still managed to write more than seventy songs, lavishing his melodic gifts on many of them.

As the opening quotes indicate, Mendelssohn was eager to write operas. Despite this fervent desire, however, he was never able to find a libretto that suited his demands. His friends Eduard Devrient and Jenny Lind continued to hope that he would venture into this field, and although Mendelssohn promised to write a work for Lind, he did not complete the task. He did make two youthful excursions into the field with *Die Hochzeit des Camacho* (The Marriage of Camacho), 1825, and *Die Heimkehr aus der Fremde* (The Home-coming from a Foreign Land), 1829, written for his parents' anniversary, but these immature efforts have been largely forgotten.

The poetry in Mendelssohn's songs reflects the literary preferences of the period; more than one-third of the poems he set were by famous poets: Heine (six), Uhland (three), Goethe (four), Lenau (four), Eichendorff (five), and Byron (two). His four songs on Goethe's poetry were not written until after Goethe's death— probably a wise decision, given Goethe's opinionated view of the lied and Mendelssohn's acquaintance with Goethe.[4] Felix, fluent in English (as well as in French, Italian, and Greek), chose Byron's English words for some of his songs as had his sister Fanny. Like so many other song composers, Mendelssohn sometimes used undistinguished poems by his contemporaries, including eight poems by his close friend Carl Klingemann, attaché to the Hanover consulate in London. Fanny and Felix also chose a number poems written by their Berlin acquaintances Johann Gustav Droysen and the renowned beauty Friederike Robert, both of whom are mentioned in Mendelssohn family letters. Felix set several folk poems, including two from *Des Knaben Wunderhorn*. Although Mendelssohn wrote no song cycles, over half of his songs appeared in collections of six, as was customary at that time.

Generally Mendelssohn adhered to the Berlin School's ideal of simple style and strophic form. For his heartfelt "Volkslied" (Folk Song), he composed an accompaniment in the shape of a four-part chorale with the top line doubling the voice. Many of his early songs are purely strophic, but he soon began to vary some of his material. In "Entsagung" (Resignation), "Auf Flügeln des Gesanges," and "Frühlingslied" (Spring Song), for example, he uses the same music for the first two stanzas of poetry and then varies his music for the third stanza of text (AAA'). Sometimes Mendelssohn even gave entirely new music to the third stanza of a poem, resulting in a bar form (AAB), but more often he mixed new music with his A material as in "Das erste Veilchen" (The First Violet) and "Neue Liebe." His "Herbstlied" (Autumn Song), for example, consists of two A strophes divided into two sections (A minor to A major and two separate figurations); this is followed by a third stanza (B) which introduces new music for the first half of the stanza and then repeats the second half of the original A. The text in this final section is repeated over and over.

Mendelssohn treated poetry with noticeable casualness. He, like Brahms, focused musical attention on the melodies of his songs, and when his melodies took on a life of their own, they overrode the structure and shape of the poem being set—it was the melody that "won." He freely repeated words and phrases when his musical ideas had not yet run their course but the poem had been "used up." In songs such as "Suleika" and "Frühlingslied," for example, the final section of each song is constructed around one repeated textual phrase, much in the way that Beethoven filled out his musical structures with repeated words ("Adelaide," "Der Kuss").

Mendelssohn's beautiful melodies are the most important and successful feature of his songs. The shape and direction of the melodic phrase dominate as he focuses all attention on the vocal line, subordinating the accompaniment as well as the setting of text to this single quality. His most popular song today, "Auf Flügeln des Gesanges," exhibits a graceful melody that audiences prize for its "singing" character. In fact, the best of Mendelssohn's songs depend upon charming tunes, a characteristic usually considered basic to song but one that lost some importance as harmonic elements received more emphasis from composers during the later part of the nineteenth century. "Venetianisches Gondellied" (Venetian Gondola Song), "Suleika," "Die Liebende schreibt" (The Beloved Writes), "Allnächtlich im Traume," and "Schilflied" (The Reed's Song) each have melodies of true beauty.

Mendelssohn's lyrical style carried over into his piano music. He was the world's most famous proponent of the genre, *Lieder ohne Worte* (Songs Without Words), a concept not too far removed from the early lied in which the voice part was doubled in the piano, allowing the song to be performed as a piano solo if a singer was not available. Mendelssohn's Songs Without Words consisted of a melody with an accompaniment subordinate to the melodic line, a style of piano writing that was also popular with his sister Fanny Hensel.

The accompaniments for some of his best-known songs, such as "Auf Flügeln des Gesanges" and "Suleika," are simple arpeggiations of the harmonies (Example 10-1). This combination of flowing figurations in the accompaniment and very lyrical, tuneful vocal lines results in many lovely songs. But often his songs simply lack variety and operate within a limited range of expression, an observation that can be applied to his sister's songs as well.

Example 10-1. Mendelssohn, "Auf Flügeln des Gesanges" (On Wings of Song), mm. 1–5.

His setting of "Suleika,"—"Ach, um deine feuchten Schwingen" (Ah, of Your Damp Wings)—a poem that was popular with many musicians including his sister Fanny Hensel and Franz Schubert, is a beautiful example of Mendelssohn's lyrical style, despite noticeable conflicts between musical and textual accents (e.g., measure 25, "Freudiges"). Organized as a strophic variation (AAA'), the first two A sections of music each combine two stanzas of poetry so that only one stanza of the poem is left for the final section; this results in considerable word repetition in the A'. Mendelssohn begins in E minor, capturing the longing of the poetess for her beloved (Marianne von Willemer's poem to Goethe published in the *West-östlicher Divan*). The arpeggiation of the harmonies is reduced to simple block chords at the end of each A section, focusing attention on the graceful, melismatic vocal line. The final section of the song moves to the parallel A major, reflecting the joyous love of the poet for her sweetheart. Here, too, Mendelssohn incorporates a melismatic conclusion to the stanza, much in the style that Fanny Hensel used in her songs (Example 10-2).

One of Mendelssohn's most compelling songs, "Neue Liebe," on a text by Heine, is highly varied in both piano and voice part. With music reminiscent of his *Midsummer Night's Dream* music, this hyperactive lied, marked *presto*, brilliantly conveys an exciting

sei - ne   Nä - - - - - - he, sei - ne   Nä - he ge - ben,

his nearness gives [to me].

Example 10-2. Mendelssohn, "Suleika," mm. 30–33.

atmosphere of elves and wild swans flying through the mysterious forest. The piano prelude presents two distinctive motives. (Examples 10-3 and 10-4). The light, elfin rhythm of the first motive permeates the entire song, first reappearing when the voice enters. The second motive also occurs throughout the song, appearing in augmentation in mm. 103–105. The vocal line, with a range of an octave and a sixth, frequent octave skips, and dotted eighth- and sixteenth-note rhythms, contributes to the energy and vitality of the music (Example 10-5). Both Fanny and Felix relied on octave leaps in their vocal lines to add some excitement (as in "Neue Liebe"), high-light important words (as in "Die Liebende schreibt"), or simply to begin a song (as in "Hirtenlied"—Pastoral Song). With both com-posers, the piano plays a subordinate rôle to the voice. The piano's doubling of the voice part in "Neue Liebe" gives a lilting quality to the music, enhancing its elfin character. The protagonist of the poem, who has been describing a night scene of elves riding on fantastic

Example 10-3. Mendelssohn, "Neue Liebe" (New Love), mm. 1–4.

Example 10-4. Mendelssohn, "Neue Liebe," mm. 5–9.

I hear the ringing of their bugles,
I hear the sounding of their bells

Example 10–5. Mendelssohn, "Neue Liebe," mm. 27–34.

horses with golden antlers, suddenly becomes a part of the drama as
the elf queen nods at him, a nod that may imply either new love or
sudden death. The music for this surprising turn of events is reduced
to recitative before concluding with the frantic piano music from the
introduction and interludes (Example 10-6).

"And'res Maienlied" (Another May Song), also known as "Hexenlied" (Witches' Song), was one of Mendelssohn's successful forays
into the world of the spirits. The dramatic piano introduction and
postlude, wide vocal range of an octave and a sixth, wild allegro
vivace tempo, and bold text make this an exciting song. (See the
chorus, "Kommt! Mit Zacken und mit Gabeln" from his cantata
Walpurgisnacht for an additional example of Mendelssohn's ability to
capture the mysterious, exotic world of the supernatural.)

"Die Liebende schreibt," based on a sonnet by Goethe, was set by
a number of composers including Schubert and Brahms. Surely one
of Mendelssohn's most beautiful songs (despite some awkward text
setting—"die einzige" in measure 18 and "Zeichen" in measure 42),
it has a three-part form that is freely shaped to the music. The song is
unified by quotes from portions of the opening music in mm. 14–15
and in the final section of the song, where the opening material is

Example 10-6. Mendelssohn, "Neue Liebe," mm. 103–122.

developed in a new manner. Mendelssohn constructed a Beethoven-like piano part, which effectively uses the lower range of the piano and, while never dominating the vocal line, is harmonically more interesting than many of Mendelssohn's other accompaniments. At the end of the first section, as the lover begins to weep, Mendelssohn modulates to the mediant key and changes the piano figuration from eighth-note motion to sixteenth-notes. This quickening of the pace continues through the B section and the returning A material, acting as a subtle unifying device. (Mendelssohn frequently uses more than one figuration in his song accompaniments.) There is pleasing asymmetry in the vocal line, as its short phrases in the middle of the first section push the music forward until it broadens with long notes at the conclusion of this section. This stretching of the voice part overlaps with the increased agitation of the accompaniment. The piano is given its own melodic material in its interludes and postlude.

Repeated notes on the tonic and mediant of the piano part in the lengthy A section subtly enhance the image of longing that nags at the lover who has not received a letter from her sweetheart.

In "Schilflied" Mendelssohn captures the delicate imagery of Lenau's poem. Almost Brahmsian in flavor, Mendelssohn's music establishes a melancholy tone with its minor key and the right-hand piano part's arpeggiated figuration against the left hand's repetition of the tonic in the low, dark register of the piano. Mendelssohn anticipates the poet's sadness, a sadness not revealed in the text until the final stanza. Here Mendelssohn moves to the parallel major of the tonic key with music that reflects a prayerful homage to the beloved.

Mendelssohn rarely used highly graphic onomatopoetic devices in his music but generally suggested and enhanced the mood of the poetry. The accompaniment to "Bei der Wiege" (By the Cradle), for example, is calm and charming, providing a serene setting for the text. Its triple meter and swaying piano part support the image of a child dreaming in the cradle. His music is more obviously programmatic in "Venetianisches Gondellied," where the accompaniment creates the feeling of a gently rocking boat (Example 10-7).

Example 10-7. Mendelssohn, "Venetianisches Gondellied" (Venetian Gondola Song), mm. 1–2.

Mendelssohn had no difficulty in finding famous performers such as Jenny Lind to sing his songs, nor did he experience difficulty in having them published. His tremendous popularity and his rôle as a well-respected conductor even provided an audience for anything he wrote. But he showed only a modest interest in his songwriting. His training and background linked him to the traditional compositional techniques and styles. His teacher, Carl Zelter, a prolific songwriter, chose to exploit a simple, cautious vocal style, an approach encouraged by the musically opinionated but conservative Goethe, and although some of Mendelssohn's songs reflect the influence of Zelter and Spohr, his talent was far superior to theirs. Mendelssohn lived his relatively brief life of thirty-eight years during the vibrant

Spring of the art song but seldom devoted his complete attention to this genre. He may well have considered songwriting to be the province of his sister Fanny. Inspired examples of his art such as "Neue Liebe," "Suleika" ("Ach, um deine"), and "Die Liebende schreibt" contrast sharply with his pleasant but dull "Pilgerspruch" (Pilgrim's Message) or "Maienlied" (May Song), in which he failed to penetrate the subtleties of the poetry and was content merely to mirror its general mood.

Yet Mendelssohn, like Liszt and Wagner, is a central figure of the era. Not only did he affect standards and taste as the conductor of Leipzig's Gewandhaus Orchestra, but his highly respected music influenced the styles of many of his contemporaries, an influence seen by some historians in Robert Schumann's later music.[5]

Mendelssohn also provides us with valuable information about his times. He and his highly educated family knew many artists, writers, actors, and musicians of the period. He grew up in a home that was a cultural hub in Berlin, and the wealth of the Mendelssohn family was devoted to the acquisition of important cultural artifacts that reveal the family's sophisticated interests. As presents for his wife Cécile, for example, Felix compiled albums that included poems in the hand of Goethe, Lenau, Rückert, Victor Hugo, Uhland, and the Schlegels; letters and signatures of Frederick the Great (in French, naturally), Jean Paul, Carl Maria von Weber, Wieland, Klopstock; original musical manuscripts by Chopin, Beethoven, and Haydn; verses from *Faust* by Goethe and from Schiller's translation of Racine's *Phedre*.

Amateur attainments were prized, reaching high levels of artistic proficiency in the social circle of the Mendelssohns. Felix and his friend singer and actor Eduard Devrient, for example, were fine amateur landscape artists who gave their paintings as gifts to those close to them. Cécile Jeanrenaud, Mendelssohn's wife, was a very talented painter as was Luise Hensel, Fanny's sister-in-law. Beauty was valued in functional things: a calendar might be hand-decorated with an exquisite drawing. When gifts were exchanged, they were gifts of art, poetry, and music. Josefine Lang, a friend of Mendelssohn's family, composed lullabies for Felix's grandchildren and copied them onto beautifully decorated manuscript paper. Fanny Hensel also copied her songs for friends, after which her husband, Prussian court painter Wilhelm Hensel, would illustrate them. In 1829, Fanny and her sister Rebecca gave their brother Felix a copy of Jean Paul's admired *Flegeljahre* with a sketch by Hensel of the two sisters on the inside front cover. Their lives were *Gesamtkunstwerke*.

Felix Mendelssohn and Eduard Devrient are rightly credited with bringing the music of Johann Sebastian Bach to the attention of musicians and the musical public through the historic performance of the *St. Matthew Passion* in Leipzig on 11 March 1829. This single performance, which focused the attention of the musical world on Bach's music, represents a watershed in the study of Bach. After this event, no serious musician's education was considered complete without a knowledge of Bach's counterpoint and harmonization. Robert and Clara Schumann, for example, undertook a systematic study of important composers in the second week of their marriage and began with Bach's *Well-tempered Clavier*. Brahms also carefully studied Bach's works and incorporated many baroque techniques into his own writing style.

Mendelssohn's revival of the Bach *Passion* was just one manifestation of his deep sense of history. He conducted what he considered to be historical concerts at the Gewandhaus, that is, chronologically ordered concerts "of the great masters from one hundred years ago to the present time."[6] These concerts included works of Bach, Handel, Mozart, and Beethoven. He also championed the works of Schubert, premiering his C Major Symphony.

Schumann said of Mendelssohn that "he was like the magic picture, always some inches higher than one felt oneself to be."[7] His contributions to the music of his age go well beyond his own compositions.

Other than the popular "Auf Flügeln des Gesanges," few of Mendelssohn's songs are performed today, despite their many beauties. Yet Mendelssohn's songs are well written for the voice, and his lovely melodies are always pleasing to audiences. Singers need to remind themselves of this neglected resource.

CHAPTER ELEVEN

The Supporting Cast

LOUIS SPOHR

An era often reveals much of itself in those composers who achieve success in their lifetime but are forgotten by succeeding generations. The long life of Louis Spohr (1784–1859) spanned the creative eras of Beethoven, Schubert, Schumann, and early Wagner, and he himself participated in and contributed to many of the ideals and genres of romanticism. He knew and heard the great music and musicians of his age and, in fact, gives a most interesting account of the period in his autobiography. He was a well-known conductor and universally acknowledged violin virtuoso in an age of virtuosity, which provided him with an entrée for his musical compositions into the concert hall, an entrée unavailable to Schubert who was neither a performing virtuoso nor a conductor. Yet the music of Spohr has fallen into oblivion because it failed to venture beyond a conformity with the music of his time. He wrote symphonies, concerti, operas, and songs that display many innovative, original ideas, but lack that intangible quality—genius.

Spohr published about eighty songs during his lifetime, songs that were generally well received in Germany and were reviewed at the time of publication. Again we think of Schubert, whose works were virtually ignored and who saw few of his works in print. Schubert's wonderful "Gretchen am Spinnrade," written in 1814, was not published until 1821 and then only at the instigation of his friends

---

Some of the material in this chapter appeared in "The Songs of Louis Spohr," *The Music Review*, 39:31–38.

through private subscription! The conservative journal *Allgemeine musikalische Zeitung* in Leipzig, which devoted little space to Schubert's music even in the twenty years following his death when he began to achieve fame, reviewed many of Spohr's song collections, including several of the popular guitar arrangements that Spohr made of his songs. The songs in his Op. 41 were praised as being "among the finest Lieder compositions available."[2] The *Allgemeine musikalische Zeitung* honored Spohr by printing his picture on the frontispiece of its volume for 1832, a gesture that Schumann imitated three years later in his *Neue Zeitschrift für Musik*.

In the Berlin music periodical *Iris im Gebiete der Tonkunst*, the contentious critic Rellstab perceptively discussed two of Spohr's collections, Op. 103 (six songs for clarinet, piano, and voice) and Op. 105 (six songs for piano and voice).

> It is not difficult to find the weaknesses of the Spohr songs. . . . The master repeats himself. . . . He remains true to . . . certain forms and phrases . . . to the point of boredom. But it would be better if one looked for the many beauties of the lieder. . . . Among them we count the coherent direction within the longer songs, the natural grace of the melody in the shorter, the warm, ardent expression which almost always confers its fullest due to the thought or word of the poem; finally, the confident, fully developed hand which advances us in the most intricate harmonic movements, in the complicated accompaniment, never by means of violent jerking or clumsy patching; rather, he reveals the steadiness of the thoroughly trained musician.[3]

Nine of Spohr's song collections consist of six songs each. (Collections of six songs were quite common in the first half of the century.)[4] Spohr's attitude toward the lied represents an interesting musical link between the eighteenth and nineteenth centuries. He, like Beethoven, lavished most of his attention on his larger works and was only secondarily interested in song. Between 1800 and 1830 most songs were written for home consumption rather than the concert hall, and Spohr's autobiography shows the casual manner in which he approached his songwriting. "As the members of the prince's family were very fond of singing, this was inducement sufficient to me to write two small books of songs the text of which was furnished by the sister of the princess from her large collection of poetical pieces."[5] There seems to have been little poetic inspiration involved in Spohr's choice of text! He placed musical considerations above the demands of poetry and reprimanded another composer who, he felt, "sacrificed both form, rhythm, and melody to the right

Figure 11-1. Caspar David Friedrich: *Winter Landscape with Church,*
1811. Courtesy of the National Gallery, London.

declamation."[6] Spohr believed that poetry was the handmaiden of
music. At the same time, however, he was too much of a craftsman to
violate the mechanics and spirit of the poetry he set. He often used
poems that were popular with composers of his day or were written
by people he knew, and he showed little preference for any particular poet. Although he did set six poems by Goethe, including
"Erlkönig" and "Gretchen am Spinnrade," these poems were all
romantic favorites rather than clear indications of his personal
preference.

He focused the primary interest of his songs on the vocal line,
which was generally melodically pleasing and rhythmically sympathetic to the metrical demands of the text. But he also weakened
some of his most beautiful melodies with excessive chromaticism,
lending a saccharine sentimentality to his songs. His accompaniments, like those of Zelter and Reichardt, seldom had unusual figurations and were completely subordinated to the vocal line. Spohr
generally doubled the voice in the piano part and used bland figurations such as arpeggiated harmonies throughout the song.

Formal clarity was a significant feature of Spohr's songs.

Although he clearly favored strophic and modified strophic forms for most of his songs, he nevertheless wrote a number of through-composed pieces that reveal a surprisingly subtle understanding of the poetry. Goethe objected to Spohr's setting of Goethe's "Kennst du das Land?" (Do You Know the Land?) because the setting obscured the strophic construction of the text, yet this setting demonstrates a perceptive enhancement of the poem's peculiarities. Each stanza of the poem begins with "Kennst du . . ." and includes a refrain that also begins "Kennst du . . .". Spohr emphasizes each "Kennst" rhythmically with long notes but differentiates between the "Kennst" that begins each stanza and the "Kennst" of the refrain by changing the meter and by placing each on a different beat of the measure (Example 11-1).

1. Do you know the land? where the lemon trees
   Do you know it well? There! there
2. Do you know the house?
   Do you know it well? There! there
3. Do you know the mountain and its cloudy path?
   Do you know it well? There! there

Example 11-1. Spohr, "Lied der Mignon" (Song of Mignon).

His most interesting formal organization of a song occurs in Op. 138, "An Sie am Clavier, Sonatine für Pianoforte mit Gesang." Published in 1848, the piano part of this song is, in effect, a sonatina. Spohr prefaces the song with a recitative in B-flat minor (3/4 meter) and then launches into the main body of the song with a change of meter (to 3/2) in the key of B-flat major. The second section of the song moves to the dominant F major and includes a short development section, then returns to the tonic key with rhythmic and melodic variations in the melody. There is no repetition of text up to this point. When the B section material returns in the accompaniment, however, with a reworking of rhythmic and melodic material followed by a coda, Spohr then repeats some of the poetry that was presented in the original B section, but now with a new melodic line for the voice.

Spohr possessed a rich harmonic vocabulary, which he often used to enhance the meaning and mood of the text. He, like Schubert, frequently fluctuated between major and minor tonalities, shifted suddenly to unexpected keys, and relied on the diminished seventh chord for dramatic moments. Some historians believe that Spohr, whose music was well known throughout the German-speaking world, played a significant rôle in influencing harmonic conventions of the period. "Undoubtedly Spohr's music contains certain expressive elements which may have by now become commonplace through Wagner's and Liszt's methodical use of them, but which acted as a powerful stimulant in their day."[7]

A few of Spohr's works are still performed, partly because of the originality of his instrumentation. His Op. 31, a nonet in F, and Op. 32, an octet in E, are sufficiently novel to remain in the performing repertory of today, as is his Op. 103, songs for voice, clarinet, and piano; his violin concerto, No. 8 in A minor, "in modo d'una scena cantante" (Gesangsszene), is also occasionally presented. Spohr can be a vital key to the period that revered his name. Prolific, influential, honored, famous—these adjectives describe the kind of image he projected to his contemporaries. He examined and experimented with the trends of his day and thus reveals those currents that represent the rule—just as the great composers often reveal the exception.

CARL LOEWE

Carl Loewe (1796–1869) wrote oratorios, operas, symphonies, string quartets, and hundreds of songs, most of which, except for a handful of his ballads, have been forgotten. His setting of Goethe's "Erlkönig" has been most responsible for keeping Loewe's name alive and has caused numerous comparisons between his version and Schubert's. Many scholars like to point to Loewe's close adherence to Goethe's poetic rhythm, which captures the hoof beats of the horse rushing through the forest. Richard Wagner is also often quoted in an apocryphal statement as having preferred Loewe's setting to Schubert's.[8] When the arguments degenerate to subjective statements based on personal bias, however, there can be no winners— both versions are dramatically brilliant.

Loewe wrote many exciting ballads that deserve to be a part of today's active vocal repertory. His great ballad "Edward," based on Herder's translation of a grim Scottish tale of patricide,[9] is a feat of virtuosic writing. Loewe selected many of Herder's poetic versions of ancient tales, but Herder's translations also inspired other poets to create their own ballads. Goethe, as was mentioned earlier, wrote the "Erlkönig" as an incidental offering for one of his plays, *Die Fischerin*.

The intensity and excitement of Goethe's "Erlkönig" is heightened by Loewe in his dissonant, driving music. He immediately establishes a mood of agitation with a tremolo-like figure in the right hand of the piano against the octave pedal point on the tonic in the left hand, which doubles the vocal line as soon as it enters. The tinkly right hand of the accompaniment creates a fairy-tale world of evil elves and witches, a world that Loewe excelled in depicting. "Der Nöck" (The Merman), "Elvershöh," "Herr Oluf," and "Tom der Reimer" all have supernatural topics with good and evil fairies. In fact, Loewe was a committed romantic in his choice of topics for ballads: "Archibald Douglas" centers on love of homeland; "Der Mohrenfürst" paints an exotic, noble picture of a distant land and a Moorish prince; the Scottish poem "Edward" displays the romantic interest in folk literature.

The characters of father and son are not so clearly differentiated in Loewe's "Erlkönig" music as they are in Schubert's version; they depend on the singer's acting abilities for definition. Since Loewe was himself a singer and the primary interpreter of his songs during his lifetime, he must have taken such dramatic reponsibilies for granted. He directs the singer to use an alluring, mysterious, whispering quality for the Erlking. He does, however, set the Erlking off from the other characters by shifting from minor to major while statically retaining the same chord in the accompaniment when the Erlking speaks. He often doubles the vocal line of the father and the Erlking in the bass of the piano, whereas the child's vocal line is doubled in the treble of the piano (Example 11-2). The Erlking's part is very square, beginning each time with the leap of a fourth and then a mere outlining of the tonic chord. Only when the Erlking reveals his evil intentions does his music shift to the parallel minor key. The intensity of the song continues forward as the terrified child screams the highest notes of the song. Loewe uses a galloplike figure in the middle of the song which, while not exclusively associated with the Erlking's daughter, enhances her image as a dancing, singing young woman (Example 11-3).

"Father, my father, do you not see there
the Erlking's daugther in that
shadowy place?" "My son, my son, I see it now,
the old willows look very gray,

Example 11-2. Loewe, "Erlkönig," mm. 59–66.

und wie-gen und tan-zen und sin-gen dich ein."

and rock and dance and sing you to sleep.

Example 11-3. Loewe, "Erlkönig," mm. 56–58.

Although the song is through-composed, Loewe achieves unity with his continuous use of tremolo figuration in the accompaniment and frequent repetition of vocal material; on his first entrance, for example, the father sings a continuation of the opening vocal line of the narrator; father and son repeat their music in their second and third conversations. The real unifier is the Erlking who uses the same music for each speech until he seizes the little boy.

Loewe often writes irregular phrase lengths in his songs, which contribute to their unique sound. He first introduces the Erlking in 6/8 meter and then extends his phrases by keeping the Erlking's statements in 9/8 during his two remaining entrances. The young boy also uses 6/8 in his final cries as his dying words are shrieked in short, breathless phrases. Loewe maintains the folk character of "Erlkönig" by squarely repeating the last line of many of the poem's stanzas.

The ballad "Edward" is one of Loewe's greatest musical achievements. "Edward," the powerful Scottish poem that Herder had translated into German (1773) from Thomas Percy's *Reliques of Ancient English Poetry* (1765), captured the imagination of numerous composers: Schubert wrote two versions of the song, one of which is a dialogue for two voices; Brahms set the poem for two voices (contralto and tenor) and also wrote a piano Ballade in D minor, Op. 10, called "Edward."

The story unfolds in a conversation between a mother and her son, and Loewe's song immediately reflects a great tension between them. With no introduction, the mother is first to speak, agitato, her vocal line climbing as she interrogates her son. Her questions and her son's answers are repeated in the third line of every stanza; each time the mother repeats her question, Loewe intensifies the sense of her urgency by moving to a higher pitch. He conveys a variety of dramatic feelings with the repeated words: "O", "Edward," and "Mutter."

Here, as in "Erlkönig," Loewe heightens musical intensity with irregular phrasing. The mother's first three stanzas are in 6/8, as though she is dancing about her son, trying to appear innocent of events that she has precipitated, yet panting to hear a desired answer to her questions. Her questions are pressing, supported by a series of diminished seventh chords; her son's answers, set off from his mother's dialogue with duple meter and a slower tempo, are evasive and filled with misery. His music is rhythmically square and, coupled with the jarringly persistent repeated notes in the right hand of the accompaniment, at first makes him seem oafish. His confession that he has killed his father, the first shock of the poem, is harmonically stagnant compared with the building suspense that has preceded it. Here Loewe repeats a G minor tremolo chord for five measures, all, however, in duple meter—a dramatic break from the 6/8 meter of the mother's part. Loewe often resorted to tremolo in the piano at dramatic moments (mm.51–66), as did most of the nineteenth-century composers at one time or another. Tremolo figures in Schubert's music, however, are more skillfully managed, usually coupled with other musical devices such as an independent dramatic melodic figure in the bass ("Der Zwerg"). Loewe obviously felt that here the text would carry forward the drama. He interrupts the rocking motion of the 6/8 meter with recitative in order to highlight the son's confession. Following the son's horrifying admission are eleven measures of pedal point on D, introduced with dissonant fervor—an E-flat major chord over the D—then gradually fading into hopeless quiet. Loewe evokes brilliant dramatic silence here and in several other crucial moments in the song.

The mother's music continues to be urgent as she presses her son to find out what will happen now. Loewe gives her new figurations in the piano that mark the beginning of the song's second section and drive to the final climax. Although her part is now in 4/4, the urgency of her music is heightened by piano figures with scales on the weak beats of the measure to push the music forward (m. 69).

The son's responses fluctuate between bitterness and restless energy as his rising melodic line reveals that he will never find peace again (Example 11-4). Loewe now begins to paint the son with a broad brush, giving him a nearly two-octave range and highly graphic music. When Edward states that his house can sink and fall, his melodic line descends over an octave (mm. 93–102). Edward's part

My foot will not rest on this earth! Mother, mother! My foot will not rest on this earth!

Example 11-4. Loewe, "Edward," mm. 76–80.

also requires the expressive freedom of recitative; as he describes the cruel future of his wife and child, Edward's weariness and despair are brilliantly mirrored in his music (Example 11-5).

Loewe then writes short, breathless, chromatically ascending phrases punctuated by rests for the mother as she suddenly realizes that she is in trouble herself (Example 11-6). In the song's second climax and dramatic conclusion, the son stentoriously curses his mother as the music resolves to an E-flat minor arpeggiated chord repeated twenty times! The voice part again breaks into recitative at the conclusion with a diminished seventh followed by a bold dominant nine-seven chord resolving to the tonic as the son reveals that his mother "made him do it." Throughout the song, each stanza of text ends with the word, "O," which Loewe intensifies with his music, concluding the song with a final "O" of hatred, rage, and despair.[8]

"Archibald Douglas," another ballad by Loewe, illustrates Loewe's use of musical motives to organize a very long, through-composed song. By means of a dialogue between the aging Lord Archibald Douglas and King James, this song recounts the tale of Lord Douglas's exile from his land because of his family's enmity to King James. Douglas, who had never participated in the feud and had

Example 11-5. Loewe, "Edward," mm. 119–126.

"And what should your mother do, Edward? Edward? And
what should your mother do, my son, my son, tell me? Oh! Oh!

Example 11-6. Loewe, "Edward," mm. 127–135.

looked after the king in his childhood, begs the king to forgive him
and let him return home. At first the king is unmoved. He finally
accepts the sincerity of Douglas's plea and reinstates Douglas to the
king's service. The song sprawls over seventeen pages, beginning
starkly with a three-note motive that is later reduced to a half-step

motive in the king's first speech and when he forgives Douglas
(Example 11-7). A second, more lyrical motive is also introduced in
the first stanza and recurs throughout the song. This motive is
particularly effective when a nostalgic mood is necessary (Example
11-8). As Douglas is pleading his cause with the king, he uses this
same melodic phrase seven times. Later, when King James leaps onto
his horse and tries to ride away from Douglas, Loewe sequentially
transposes the riding music five times for five stanzas of text; at first,
the shifting upward increases the song's intensity, but after the third
move up, the gesture loses its effect. Loewe redeems this section of
the music with a touching, lyrical conclusion to the final repetition.
Several other motives act as unifying devices, although there is no
Wagnerian attempt to link motives with characters or ideas.

Example 11-7. Loewe, "Archibald Douglas," m. 1.

wo im - mer die Welt am schön-sten war, da war sie öd und leer.
where the world has been most beautiful, there it was barren and empty for me.

Example 11-8. Loewe, "Archibald Douglas," mm. 9–12.

In "Herr Oluf" (subtitled Whoever Danced with the Elves
Would Feel Such Joy That He Would Not Stop Dancing Until He Fell
Dead), Loewe does relate specific themes to characters and events.
This ballad by Herder tells the story of Oluf, who meets the Erlking's
daughter late at night while he is out inviting friends to his wedding.
She asks him to dance, and when he refuses, she wounds him
mortally. He staggers home, and his bride finds him dead the next
day. The story is told by a narrator and through dialogue between
Oluf, the Erlking's daughter, Oluf's mother, and his sweetheart.

The eleven-measure introduction presents the ominous riding
music of Herr Oluf as well as the graceful, alluring fairy music that
will be associated with the Erlking's daughter (mm. 1–4 and 6–7).
There is no space between the speeches of the Erlking's daughter
and Oluf, but their accompaniments and vocal lines are differentiated. The Erlking's daughter has an exotic melodic line, which she

statically repeats over and over (Example 11-9). Her music changes as she warns Oluf that she is going to hurt him. When she strikes him in the heart, the music rises to its highest pitch.

"Come closer, Herr Oluf, come, dance with me, a

Example 11-9. Loewe, "Herr Oluf," mm. 37–38.

After Oluf is struck by the Erlking's daughter, Loewe modifies the riding music of the piano part to include an ominous chromatic figure on the second and fourth beats of the measure. This chromatic figure changes in the following section, suggesting a crawling motion as Oluf drags himself home (Example 11-10). Loewe then introduces another motive which is Oluf's death music (mm. 94–97).

Example 11-10. Loewe, "Herr Oluf," mm. 89–90.

Loewe's songs require a talented storyteller and are most successfully presented by a charismatic singer—which Loewe was. His songs are written for baritone—which he was. He obviously tailored his songs to the advantage of the singer, for the accompaniments never dominate the voice and always provide adequate support. (See Robert Schumann's comments on Loewe's ability to write for the piano in Chapter 3, "The Piano"). The page-long piano introduction to "Tom der Reimer" is a rarity in his music, as is the song's long piano conclusion. Attention is usually focused on the voice, and the vocal line is eminently singable. Loewe, like Liszt, sometimes used the bass range of the piano to double the voice line for a weightier sound.

Loewe's skill in setting text was significant in the natural flow that underlies his storytelling. But his success was limited to one facet of the lied. Without the dramatic impetus of a story, his other songs are generally not individual enough to be remembered today. His "Wandrers Nachtlied" II (Wanderer's Night Song), a beautiful setting of Goethe's poem, effectively captures the reflective character of the poetry, but like the settings of this poem by Hiller, Medtner, and many others, it has been forgotten. In contrast, Hugo Wolf, who was also meticulous in his choice and setting of words, was able through his great versatility and musical sophistication to interpret the broadest variety of poetry and mood in a memorable manner. In "Fussreise" (Hiking), for example, he managed to convey the joy of walking in the woods without relying on a plot to hold the listener's interest. Schubert, too, could take a relatively insipid poem with no plot, such as "An die Musik," and create a remarkable song that has been sung for 150 years. But Loewe is remembered today only for his ballads. Although he sometimes relied on stock harmonic gestures, he possessed a genuine talent for realizing the theatrical. A superb storyteller, he capitalized on the dramatic content of the ballad in such a compelling fashion that the listener is totally drawn into the tale he tells.

ROBERT FRANZ

Robert Franz (1815–1892) achieved recognition for his songs from some of the most important composers of his generation—Felix Mendelssohn, Robert Schumann, and Franz Liszt all welcomed his first books of songs. Liszt even published a biography of Franz in 1872. Yet Franz failed to fulfill the expectations of his illustrious contemporaries, and although his songs are written with skill and exhibit careful workmanship, most of them have been forgotten. He wrote many songs of lyric beauty, a few of which still appear on recital programs—"Widmung," "Aus meinen grossen Schmerzen" (Out of My Great Pain), "Gute Nacht!," "Bitte" (Supplication). But there is a sameness and lack of passion in most of his songs that has relegated them to a secondary rôle in the history of the nineteenth-century lied.

In 1843 Franz sent some of his songs to Robert Schumann for his opinion, and Schumann was so impressed that he sent them to a publisher. When the songs appeared in print—much to the surprise of Franz—Schumann greeted them with a laudatory review in the *Neue Zeitschrift für Musik* (see Chapter 7 on Robert Schumann for the text of the review). This review brought Franz to the attention of the music-loving public and was highly important in furthering his musical career. It is strange today to read Schumann's lavish praise of Franz's work—almost at the expense of Schubert's—but Franz's careful text settings and choice of poets were obviously appealing to the literary Schumann.

Franz set over sixty of Heine's poems as well as works by Robert Burns, Eichendorff, Goethe, Lenau, Mörike, Rückert, and Hoffmann von Fallersleben. But he did not limit himself to the great poets, as is demonstrated by his songs with poems by Osterwald, Petöfy, and Mirza-Schaffy. In fact, Wilhelm Osterwald, a friend of Franz, seems to have been another favorite poet, since Franz set fifty-one of his poems to music.

Between 1843 and 1884, about 280 of Franz's songs appeared in print. Stylistically, there is little change between the early and the later works, and Franz admitted,

> I can give no accurate account of the chronology of my compositions.... I never possessed vanity enough to ... date ... my songs. Some ... in my very last publications really date from between 1840 and 1845.... Op. 1 in my opinion is neither better nor worse than Op. 52.[10]

His loss of hearing, which began in 1848 and resulted in total deafness by 1867, may have contributed to his conservative approach to song.

Many of his songs are truly beautiful but have more in common with the *Hausmusik* of composers such as Louis Spohr than with the innovative songs of Schumann and Schubert. Like the songs of Louis Spohr, Franz's are most suited to the amateur. The range of these songs is relatively modest, and the voice part is frequently doubled in the accompaniment. This doubling is not always in the top voice of the piano part: the well-known "Aus meinen grossen Schmerzen" has the vocal line doubled in an inner voice while in "Ja, du bist elend" (Yes, You Are Miserable), the doubling occurs primarily in the bass line (Example 11-11).

Strophic form is the foundation for many of Franz's songs. Each stanza of music is sometimes slightly varied harmonically to relieve the monotony of repetition or to respond to obvious changes in the mood of the text. In the lovely "Mädchen mit dem roten Mündchen" (Girl with the Red Lips), for example, he varies the third stanza to reflect the poet's (Heine's) sudden revelation that the love he has treasured is flawed.

Yes, you are miserable and I bear no grudge; my

Example 11-11. Franz, "Ja, du bist elend" (Yes, You Are Miserable), mm. 1–3.

Franz is sometimes considered the last representative of the so-called Berlin School, with its emphasis on strophic form and clear presentation of the words.[11] Although strophic form allowed him to follow the poet's stanzas, it also increased the potential for musical boredom. Because he also preferred slow tempi and introspective poetry, there is little variety in his overall production.

Franz used melodic repetition to structure many of his songs. Even in a very short, through-composed song such as "Bitte," which consists of only four musical phrases, three phrases share the same melodic material (AA'BA''). Franz varied the accompaniment slightly for lines two and four and varied both melody and harmony in the second half of line two. In his still-performed song "Für Musik" (For Music), Franz again used the same melody in three out of four phrases of the strophe, starting the melody on different pitches each time it appears (AAAB) (Example 11-12). The melodic repetition, however, becomes slightly tedious in a strophic setting consisting of so many stanzas, despite the energy of the moving eighth-notes in the accompaniment. There is an absence of passion in these examples as well as a lack of rhythmic variety.

Now the shadows darken, star upon star awakens:
what a breath of longing swells through the night. Through the sea the

Example 11-12. Franz, "Für Musik" (For Music), mm. 1–9.

His accompaniments are within the capabilities of an accomplished amateur. They often consist of four-part hymnlike writing, reflecting his close ties with the Protestant chorale and his rôle as organist. In his well-loved "Widmung," Franz captured a mood of quiet dignity and beauty (Example 11-13). He used octave doublings in the accompaniment to increase the richness of the sonority in this short gem.

Oh, do not thank [me] for these songs,

Example 11-13. Franz, "Widmung" (Dedication), mm. 1–3.

Word-painting, while not completely absent from his style, is not a significant feature, in either the accompaniment or the vocal line. The piano is subordinate to the vocal line and is frequently given no prelude or postlude material. In "Gute Nacht," this subordination is carried to the extreme; the piano part consists solely of one rhythmic figure—a quarter-note eighth–note pattern in 6/8, which gives a dirgelike feel to the song. Yet rhythmic variety occurs in the voice part, which is allied to the rhythms of the text, and the melodic material of the vocal line is more varied than in many of his other songs, contributing to the effectiveness of this pretty song.

Some contrapuntal techniques appear in Franz's music, which historians credit to his editing of the music of Bach and Handel. Although counterpoint is not a dominant feature, it does enrich some of his better songs, as in "Kommt Feinsliebchen heut?" (Is My Fine Love Coming Today?). In the opening phrases, the contrary motion of vocal and bass-lines, together with the piano's answer to the voice in the right hand, creates one of the most musically satisfying moments in his works. The haunting melody that permeates both the vocal and the piano part is also highly effective (Example 11-14).

Franz had an interesting harmonic vocabulary but was sparing in its use. His musical conservatism was intentional, and although he

in the morning I get up and ask, "does my fine little love come today?"

Example 11-14. Franz, "Kommt Feinsliebchen heut?" (Is My Fine Love Coming Today?), mm. 1–4.

sometimes used terms like *appassionato, con brio,* and *allegro molto agitato* for expression indications, his music rarely lives up to their meaning.

Franz's songs are excellent teaching material for young singers: the voice part is usually linear, the range is modest, and many of the songs are quite pleasing. "Mutter, o sing mich zur Ruh!" (Mother, Oh, Sing Me to Rest) and "O, säh ich auf der Heide dort" (Oh, If I Could Look on the Heath), for example, are very pretty songs; "Widmung," with its range of a seventh and descending melodic lines, is pedagogically sound material for the singer who is beginning a study of German song. Franz's careful setting of text and his moderate interpretive demands are also important considerations for students in their early studies. But even the mature artist can find value in occasionally programming Franz's songs, as points of vocal and emotional calm.

PETER CORNELIUS

In his brief autobiography, Peter Cornelius (1824–1874) stated that he wanted to "capture the moment when . . . those two heavenly forces—music and language—are finally joined into a delightful union in my mind." Poet and composer Cornelius joined the ranks of Walter von der Vogelweide, Machaut, and Richard Wagner in writing the words for his music. Although Cornelius set the poetry of Tieck, Heyse, Eichendorff, and Hölty, more than half of his eighty-one songs are based on his own poems. His poetry and the libretti for three operas (the third opera was completed after his death) were well respected by his contemporaries and add a unique dimension to the discussion of formal unity in his works. Liszt selected two of Cornelius's poems to set to music.

Overshadowed by his friends Liszt and Wagner, Cornelius nevertheless represents an interesting, creative voice in the mid nineteenth century. Liszt acted as mentor to the young Cornelius and produced his first opera at Weimar in 1858, a comedy called *Der Barbier von Bagdad*. Unfortunately, the production became the center of a battle between progressive and conservative musical factions in Weimar and caused Liszt to resign his position there. Cornelius linked his life to Wagner's after 1861, became salaried by Ludwig II, and through Wagner's intercession, was appointed to a position at the Munich Royal School of Music in 1867. Although he often acted as an apologist for Wagner and his ideas, Cornelius developed his own compositional style.

His novel song, "Ein Ton" (A Note), which consists entirely of a B-natural pedal point for the voice against a constantly varied piano part, is included in a number of song anthologies today. "Ein Ton" is the third song of *Trauer und Trost* (Sorrow and Consolation), a song cycle about the death of a loved one. The meditation of the poet on his beloved and the eventual acceptance of his loss act to unify the cycle, along with a number of interesting musical devices. For example a rhythmic figure—dotted eighth-, sixteenth-, quarter-note—recurs in Nos. 1, 2, 4, 5, and 6; the B-natural pedal point in the voice part of No. 3 ("Ein Ton") is taken over by the accompaniment in No. 4 (An den Traum—To Dream), while the voice now offers musical variations, weaving a web around the pedal point of the accompaniment.

Cornelius wrote a number of song cycles, including *Weihnachtslieder* (Christmas Songs) and *Trauer und Trost*, each based on his own poetry. *Weihnachtslieder*, harmonically the more conservative of the two cycles but also the more famous, presents the composer's warm, sincere faith as well as his vivid picture of the Christmas story and German family life at Christmas. Cornelius unifies the cycle with the Christmas theme and with closely related key progressions linking one song to the next. Although the piano accompaniment is relatively simple throughout, this simplicity acts to heighten the clarity of text declamation; in "Christus der Kinderfreund" (Christ, the Friend of Children), for example, the voice begins with and returns to a chantlike line against an unobtrusive, thin-textured piano part, which echoes some of the voice line (Example 11-15). In "Die Hirten, IIa" (The Shepherds), the texture is

Mich a-ber mahnt die Weih-nachts-zeit an Träu-me   der Ver-gan-gen-heit. __

But Christmas time reminds me of dreams of the past.

Example 11-15. Cornelius, "Christus der Kinderfreund" (Christ, Friend of Children), in *Weihnachtslieder* (Christmas Songs), mm. 21–24.

reduced to two contrapuntal lines in the piano refrain, which suggests the image of two shepherds playing pipes while they watch their sheep in the silent fields. When the voice enters, the piano part still remains simple, alternating between three and four parts and doubling the voice line. The pastoral nature of the sweet, tender music is enhanced by triple meters (9/8 and 6/8) as well as by the drone of pedal point in mm. 6–9. Cornelius charmingly incorporates the opening phrase of Franz Gruber's "Stille Nacht" (Silent Night) at the end of each stanza. In "Die Könige, IIIb" (The Kings), Cornelius uses the Christmas chorale, "Wie schön leuchtet der Morgenstern" (How Beautifully Shines the Morning Star), in the accompaniment while the voice presents its own countermelody. The old man Simeon tells the story of how he identified the eight-day-old baby Jesus as savior of the world when the infant was brought to the temple. Cornelius has a walking figure in the accompaniment with a descending scale that extends over three and a half octaves in the song's middle section when Simeon speaks. The joyous wonder of Jesus' parents is contrasted with a brief segment of the melody of "O Haupt voll Blut und Wunden" (Oh Sacred Head Now Wounded). This cycle has remained a part of the vocal repertoire for over one hundred years because of its seasonal usefulness and its heartfelt message.

Cornelius's *Brautlieder* (Bride's Songs), another cycle based on his own poetry, also remains in today's concert repertory. Like Schumann's *Frauenliebe und -leben*, *Brautlieder* is meant to represent a woman's point of view about love and life; the woman in this cycle sees her love as the wonderful ending to her own fairy tale.

The *Brautlieder*, more than any other group of Cornelius's songs, shows the influence of Schumann, possibly because it was inspired by Schumann's *Frauenliebe und -leben*. The dramatic nobility of "Aus dem hohen Lied" (From the Song of Songs), with bold melodies in the accompaniment and exchange of material with the voice, is highly reminiscent of "Er der Herrlichste von allen" (He, the Most Noble of All) (mm. 1–14). "Vorabend" (The Night Before) has the thin-textured accompaniment and semi-recitative opening of "Süsser Freund" (Sweet Friend). "Erwachen" (Awakening) emulates the contemplative quality of "Der Ring" (The Ring), while the accompaniment of "Der Liebe Lohn" (Love's Reward) is arpeggiated, with melodic material emerging from the arpeggios somewhat in the fashion of "Der Nussbaum" from Schumann's collection *Myrten*, Op. 25.

It is easy to see the advantage for the composer of using one's own poetry in a musical setting. Debussy, another composer who tried his hand at setting his own poetry to song, wrote the *Proses Lyriques* as a vehicle for his musical and verbal visions. In "De Rêve" (A Dream), for example, he creates a web of mystical word images surrounded by a mirage of sound that evoke the illogic of the dreamworld. A composer can choose images, meter, sounds, and even subject matter that is inspiring to him. Love, home, family, and religion are dominant themes in Cornelius's songs and poetry. His cycle *An Bertha*, for example, was written in honor of his wife, Bertha; although touchingly sincere, it is one of his least interesting works.

The poet-composer can repeat poetic lines without complaint from the poet and structure the poetry to fit his melodic ideas. In "Der Liebe Lohn" from *Brautlieder*, for example, Cornelius began the first three lines of stanza one with the word, "süss" (sweet), of stanza two with "schön" (beautiful), and so on. This extramusical structuring allowed Cornelius to provide a musical variation for the words. He also used poetic repetition as a unifying device in "Komm, wir wandeln zusammen" (Come, We Wander Together), a song that stylistically anticipates the songs of Richard Strauss. Here Cornelius repeated the words of the title at the beginning of each new musical section and also at the end of the song. The song is based on two melodies, the first of which appears in the piano introduction and the second with the entrance of the voice (Example 11-16). He establishes further unity in the third section by writing a sequence in the piano using melodic material that appears in the first two sections of the voice part on the words "Komm, wir wandeln zusammen." A

Come, we will wander together in the moonlight. So magically glows

Example 11-16. Cornelius, "Komm, wir wandeln zusammen" (Come, We Wander Together), mm. 1–7.

melody used in canon in the piano prelude (see Example 11-16) occurs again at the end of the song, where it is doubled by the vocal line (mm. 42–44).

Cornelius's religious beliefs were often at the root of his creative inspiration, as can be seen in the *Weihnachtslieder* and his cycle *Vater unser* (The Lord's Prayer). The structural basis for the entire *Vater unser* collection is provided by a series of meditations based on plainsong melodies for the Lord's Prayer. "Erlöse uns vom Übel" (Deliver Us from Evil), for example, has the plainsong "Sed libera nos a malo" repeated throughout the song in the top line of the piano part (Example 11-17).

Holy love, flaming heart, would penetrate the entire world

Example 11-17. Cornelius, "Erlöse uns vom Übel" (Deliver Us from Evil), in *Vater unser* (The Lord's Prayer), mm. 1–8.

These songs are very simple, almost stark, as Cornelius provides a musical background for his poetic elaboration of each phrase from the Lord's Prayer. The melodic line of the plainsong "Et ne nos inducas in tentationem" (And Lead Us Not into Temptation) accompanies the following words by Cornelius.

Als Du auf Erden, Herr, geweilt	When you, Father, stayed on earth
hast alle Kranken Du geheilt,	You healed all the sick,
von jedem Weh Erlösung fand,	Relieved from every sorrow
wen Du berührt mit deiner Hand,	Whomever you touched with your
gestreift mit deines Kleides Rand.	hand,
Der Blinde sehend vor Dir stund,	Whomever you brushed with the hem
der Stumme tat's dem Tauben kund,	of your garment.
Du heiltest alles, was da wund;	The blind were granted sight by you,
und zu dem Toten sprach dein Mund:	The deaf and dumb were made whole.
"Steh' auf und wandle!"	You healed all, every wound.
Herr! Herr! meine Seele liegt im Staub,	And to the dead you spoke:
ist krank und blind und stumm und	"Stand up and walk."
taub;	Father, Father, my soul lies in dust,
spriesst auch ein Quell, der Heilung	Is sick and blind and dumb and deaf.
schafft,	Even if a spring spewed forth,
ihn zu erreichen fehlt's an Kraft:	producing health,
O, wär' ich frei aus Sündenhaft,	I would not have enough strength to
O, dürft' ich schau'n dein Angesicht,	reach it.
darum das goldne Himmelslicht	O, were I only free of sin,
viel strahlenhelle Glorien flicht,	O, if I could look into your face,
und hören wie dein Mund mir spricht:	Which causes the golden light of
"Steh auf, und wandle!"	heaven
	To flicker with the brilliant beams of
	Glory,
	And hear your voice say to me,
	"Stand up and walk."

The uniqueness of Cornelius's contribution to the art song has allowed him to retain a modest foothold in the concert repertory long after his death. His sincere voice is still heard today.

All the composers in this chapter were prominent in the nineteenth century and, as such, influenced the direction of the lied. But many of their songs hold more for us than historical interest; Spohr, Loewe, Franz, and Cornelius have also bequeathed music of lasting value to this genre. Singers who seek novelty in programming and enjoy exploring unfamiliar repertoire will find among their works many songs of true beauty.

CHAPTER TWELVE

Franz Liszt and Richard Wagner

We have been hearing Liszt.... He cannot be compared to any other player—he stands alone. He arouses terror and amazement, and is a very attractive person. His appearance at the piano, is indescribable—he is an original—he is absorbed by the piano.... His passion knows no bounds, not infrequently he jars on one's sense of beauty by tearing melodies to pieces, he uses the pedal too much, thus making his works incomprehensible if not to professionals at least to amateurs. He has a great intellect, one can say of him that "his art is his life."... And where are pianos to be had which will respond to half what he can do?
—Diary of Friedrich Wieck and his daughter Clara, 1838

Clara to Robert (1840)
In his last concert... Liszt, with one chord, drove three hammers out of place and besides this broke 4 strings—so he must be well again.
—Clara Wieck

Clara to Robert (1840)
When I heard Liszt for the first time in Vienna, I hardly knew how to bear it, I sobbed aloud ... it over-came me so.
—Clara Wieck[1]

To gain some understanding of nineteenth-century music, one must look at the life and works of Franz Liszt (1811–1886)—a keystone of the century. He knew most of the great composers of his day, played in all the major European musical capitals, was a virtuoso pianist par excellence, championed the new music of his contemporaries, composed in almost every musical genre, and played a major rôle in the development of several musical forms including the

243

art song. Not only did he compose over seventy fine songs of his own, but his travels introduced German song to the rest of Europe. From England to Russia he played his piano transcriptions of songs written by Schubert, Schumann, Franz, Beethoven, and Mendelssohn, acquainting audiences with the works of these composers and fertilizing the development of song throughout Europe.

His firsthand knowledge of the German lied influenced his own compositional efforts.

> His songs to words of Victor Hugo, Musset, or Alexandre Dumas reveal no essentially French traits, just as his pieces set to Petrarch's sonnets show none that are typically Italian. The point of departure for Liszt was the German Lied; his best vocal works follow in the tradition of Beethoven, Schubert, and Schumann, whose songs he had long known.[2]

Although Liszt was not a German, his unique contribution to the lied deserves to be included in any discussion of nineteenth-century vocal music.

His love of music and generosity of spirit were continually exhibited in his praise and encouragement of other musicians: he thought so highly of his contemporaries Frédéric Chopin and Robert Franz that he wrote biographies praising each man. He was a friend and mentor of Peter Cornelius and did much to encourage the younger composer, even setting some of Cornelius's poetry to music. During the thirteen years that Liszt resided in Weimar as Kapellmeister, he produced forgotten musical works or premiered new works that ranged from Schumann's opera *Genoveva* to Gluck's *Orpheus*.

His talents as a virtuoso pianist not only astounded his contemporaries but stimulated other pianists to higher levels of technical achievement. Touring performers were expected to amaze their audience with a technical display of fireworks. Famous pianists Kalkbrenner, Thalberg, and Clara Schumann not only successfully engaged in such display but, like all touring virtuosi, were expected to present their own compositions, tailored to showcase their talents. Most of these compositions were filled with superficialities and were therefore doomed to obscurity.

The bravura of Liszt's piano playing naturally carried over into his writing for that instrument, whether for solo works or for the accompaniment of songs such as "Die drei Zigeuner" (The Three Gypsies). His virtuosity on the keyboard, like Paganini's on the violin,

evoked legends that time has scarcely dimmed. But Liszt's phenomenal pianistic facility was also at the root of much criticism that is still
leveled against him—a justifiable criticism that his facility often
masked shallow, trivial musical ideas. As a result, our century has
tended to overlook many of his great compositions because we could
not forget his many slight works.

Liszt also epitomized much of the romantic spirit, a spirit that
seems completely antithetical to our own. Today's listener is often
embarrassed by the sentimentality and emotionalism of his music.
But is this a valid aesthetic judgment or a matter of fashion?

Fashion in music is something of a curiosity. For example, the
excellent reputation of the French songwriter Henri Duparc is based
on a mere sixteen songs, only twelve of which are readily available.
Duparc, afflicted with a form of mental illness that caused him to
destroy most of his music, is nevertheless highly revered by our age
for his few existing works. Liszt, on the other hand, who has not been
generally in fashion, composed a wealth of interesting, beautiful
music, not the least of which are his songs. Many are of the finest
quality and deserve to be in the repertory of all serious singers of the
art song.

Liszt wrote approximately seventy-eight songs using German,
French, Italian, and English poetry. Since his travels as a virtuoso
pianist provided him with an intimate knowlege of the European
song literature of the day, his is a particularly interesting voice in the
discussion of song. Since, as Noske states, "his point of departure is
the German Lied," even Liszt's non-German songs exhibit characteristics of the lied. He also serves as a link between the songs of
Schubert and those of Mahler and Strauss at the end of the century.
His bold harmonic vocabulary contributed almost as much as
Wagner's to the growing dissolution of tonality. And he created his
own unique style, a style that was certainly influenced by the German
lied, yet was unlike the songs of any other lieder composer. His background as a virtuoso and dramatic personality are mirrored in songs
like "Die Loreley" and "Die drei Zigeuner," songs that challenge the
abilities of both singer and pianist. At the same time, he wrote one of
the most sensuous, intimate songs that came out of the nineteenth
century: "Es muss ein Wunderbares sein."

The accompaniment of "Es muss ein Wunderbares sein" is a
starkly skeletal set of simple chords in the right hand of the piano part
which shift and change for the first ten bars above a pedal point in the
left hand; little technical facility is demanded from the pianist—

hardly a style associated with the virtuoso Liszt. These chords interact unobtrusively with Liszt's sweetly sensuous melody, resulting in a song of great delicacy. Such simplicity occurs in other Liszt songs—"Du bist wie eine Blume" and "Ich liebe dich" (I Love You), for example. Even the dramatic "Mignons Lied" uses little independent solo material for the piano and relies on voice and piano to operate as a unit. In "Ihr Glocken von Marling" (You Bells of Marling), a late song written in 1874, he uses the repetition of chords to imitate the steady, sonorous pealing of bells: melodic phrases in the left hand-piano part are highlighted against the constant repetition of eighth-note chords, written entirely in treble clef. The linear, often chromatic movement of the chords, the sound of the upper range of the piano, and the soft dynamic markings used throughout much of the song contribute to an ethereal, religious atmosphere. Melodic material often echoes between voice and piano, and Liszt sometimes uses melodic figures in the voice line, and also the piano, to imitate the sound of pealing bells.

The piano figures prominently in "Der Fischerknabe" (The Fisher Boy), which like "Die drei Zigeuner," opens with a long solo for the piano, establishing mood and anticipating the vocal line (see Chapter 3, "The Piano"). The dramatic accompaniment to "Die drei Zigeuner" is more in the style of pianistic writing generally associated with Liszt. Its piano introduction covers a five-octave range of the piano, exploring sonorities of the keyboard with octaves in the bass, full chords of eight to ten notes, and virtuosic demands on finger flexiblity high in the treble. Liszt elicits uniquely colorful sounds from the piano that suggest the meaning of the text without overpowering the voice (Example 12-1). He adds further flair by introducing a Hungarian national dance, the Czardas, in his description of the second gypsy, then brings back the Czardas in the last section to formally tie the song together.

Example 12-1. Liszt, "Die drei Zigeuner," mm. 69–72.

Liszt, like Brahms, frequently relied on arpeggiated chords as the basis for many of his piano accompaniments. His idiomatic writing for the piano often exploited the range and color possibilities of the piano more successfully than Brahms's, creating the illusion of pianistic virtuosity, as in the passage from "Der König von Thule" shown in Example 12-2. Ironically, Liszt's song accompaniments are often less difficult to play than those of Brahms. Of course, many of Liszt's songs, such as "Die drei Zigeuner," do demand virtuosity from the pianist, but he skillfully balanced the force of the piano so that it did not overshadow the voice.

Example 12-2. Liszt, "Der König von Thule" (The King of Thule), mm. 71–73.

Liszt wrote lyrical yet unconventional melodies that are often structured around wide intervallic leaps rather than linear progressions. "Freudvoll und leidvoll" and "Du bist wie eine Blume," for example, each begin with the leap of a major sixth (Example 12-3). Both Liszt and Richard Strauss approached the voice in their lieder in a more operatic manner than did most of the other song composers. Unlike Strauss, however, Liszt was not an opera composer. After one youthful operatic venture, he did not approach that genre again.

To be joyful and sorrowful, thoughtful,

Example 12-3. Liszt, "Freudvoll und leidvoll" (Joyful and Sorrowful), mm. 5–8.

The range of "Die drei Zigeuner," an octave and a sixth, reflects the dramatic nature of his music. The full extent of this range is not called into play until the song's conclusion when the "philosophical" significance of the three gypsies is summarized. Many of Liszt's melodic phrases are sweeping in nature, covering a dramatic portion of the singer's range. "Die Loreley" couples word-painting with a brilliant passage for the voice on the word "Abendsonnenschein" (Example 12-4). In "O! Quand je dors" (Oh, While I Sleep), the singer is given a cadenza of an octave and a fifth to illustrate the word *rayonnera* (radiant) (mm. 53–55).

in the evening sunshine

Example 12-4. Liszt, "Die Loreley," mm. 46–48.

"Kling' leise, mein Lied" (Sound Lightly, My Song), another beautiful song by Liszt, anticipates the sublime atmosphere in several of Strauss's later songs. A major sixth and an octave leap figure prominently in the melody throughout. Liszt also relies on an octave leap as a means of character differentiation in his magnificent song "Comment, disaient-ils" (How? They Said). Each time the female characters answer the young men, their melody leaps an octave. The accompaniment to the males' musical refrain is of the utmost delicacy, a refrain that Liszt ingeniously combines with the contrasting figuration of the young women's music in the final portion of the song.

Liszt sometimes wrote optional embellishments for the vocal line within the song, as in "Élégie" (Elegy). "Die drei Zigeuner" has an optional coda that allows the singer to choose between a reflective ending and one that is dramatic. The vocal line of his songs demands excellent breath control, an extensive range, and the ability to negotiate large skips with grace.

Liszt's melodies are carefully structured around the text but occasionally violate natural word accents, as in "Der du von dem Himmel bist" (You Who Are from Heaven) and "Du bist wie eine Blume." He did not refrain from word repetition when it suited the musical structure of his song, a technique that works successfully in "O! Quand je dors" but less effectively in "Ich scheide" (I Am Leaving), and he did not always observe the stanza structure of the poem but preferred to superimpose his own musical form.

Throughout "Die drei Zigeuner" the vocal line slips from melody into recitative, a technique that Schubert used at times, and one that later occurred often in the French mélodie. For Liszt, the dramatic potential of the recitative is essential to the character of his song and the story he is telling. Dramatic songs that tell a story such as "Die Loreley" and "Der König von Thule" inevitably break into recitative.

Some historians suggest that the art song thrived when poet and composer knew and inspired one another. Liszt was a contemporary of many of the poets whose work he set to music—Victor Hugo (1802–1885), Ludwig Rellstab (1799–1869), Heinrich Heine (1799–1856), Ludwig Uhland (1787–1862). He set at least eight of Heine's poems to music, and in his biography of Chopin, Liszt admiringly describes Heine:

> Several men, of brilliant renown, were grouped in the luminous zone immediately around the piano: Heine, the saddest of humorists, listened with the interest of a fellow countryman to the narrations made him by Chopin of the mysterious country which haunted his ethereal fancy also, and of which he too had explored the beautiful shores. At a glance, a word, a tone, Chopin and Heine understood each other.[3]

About half of Liszt's songs are based on first-rate poetry, but he was also willing to set the works of lesser-known poets, such as the poems of his friend, composer Peter Cornelius.

A few of Liszt's songs, such as "S'il est un charmant gazon" (If There Is a Pleasing Lawn), are strophically organized or, like "Wieder möcht' ich dir begegnen" (I Would Like to Meet You Again) and "Das Veilchen," are strophic variations. But Liszt obviously preferred elastic organization for his songs as can be seen in his free ABA' structuring of "Kling leise, mein Lied." Many of his songs are loosely constructed around a motive, possibly suggested by the poetry, that permeates the entire structure. A three-note motive is used throughout the voice part and in the final phrase of the accompaniment in the through-composed, "Es muss ein Wunderbares sein." In "Der König von Thule," Liszt also uses a three-note motive that consists of a dotted eighth-, a sixteenth- and a quarter-note scale. This motive is presented in the piano introduction beginning on various pitches, is reversed in the left hand, and then reappears with the entrance of the voice (Example 12-5). The figure is sometimes used only as a rhythmic motive (e.g., m. 15), as a melodic motive (e.g., m. 66), or in its reversed form (e.g., m. 70), but more frequently it is used as a rhythmic-melodic whole. The motive is also often harmonically linked with a diminished seventh chord and is most dramatically coupled in mm. 54–60 at the height of his description of the king's ancestral castle. Liszt briefly pulls back from the dramatic excitement as he again prepares for the king to hurl the goblet into the sea; then Lisztian fireworks break loose. The piano chromatically rushes up the scale, much like Schubert's piano part in "Gruppe aus dem Tartarus," then rushes down the scale, incorporating the primary motive in a four-octave descent. The voice is also given a programmatic descent of an octave and a fourth as the goblet sinks into the sea. A subdued voice part returns to describe the death of the king in the melody with the unifying motive that opened the song, but this time a diminished fourth lower. Both voice and piano again descend, and then the song concludes with a postlude in which the unifying motive continues to be heard to the end.

Example 12-5. Liszt, "Es war ein König in Thule," mm. 1–9.

There are other examples of Liszt's programmatic use of piano and voice: he graphically depicts Alpine horns and the cuckoo in "Der Hirt" (The Shepherd); he contrasts happiness and sorrow with a major and minor sixth in the melody of "Freudvoll und leidvoll" (see Example 12-3); he uses rolling arpeggios to suggest the flowing river in "Im Rhein, im schönen Strome"; and he uses an ascending arpeggio in the voice to suggest the tall mountain in "Die Loreley" (mm. 43–44).

Liszt used his rich harmonic vocabulary to create mood and drama within his songs. The bold arpeggiation of the diminished seventh, the Hungarian minor scale, altered chords coupled with dramatic rhythmic motives, lend excitement to "Die drei Zigeuner." In "Der König von Thule," Liszt's frequent use of the diminished seventh gives him great freedom to move into distant keys. Through sequences, chromaticism, enharmonic spellings of notes and chords, and sudden shifts into keys that are a third away from the home key, he achieved amazing tonal freedom. Liszt certainly uses key shifts and colorful harmonies to highlight changes of section or important words, but he sometimes seems simply to delight in his own harmonic virtuosity.

In "Freudvoll und leidvoll" he toys with the possible chord colors that begin on E. In the introduction, he arpeggiates an E major chord, then an E minor chord, then a diminished chord on E, and finally a dominant seventh on E before the voice enters. As soon as the text begins, however, we realize how important chord coloration is with the words "joyful" and "sorrowful," "pensive," "hopeful," "fearful." He uses the interval of a sixth throughout the song in voice and piano as a unifying motive. The reflective, fragile inwardness of this song within Liszt's extravagant harmonic vocabulary is an astounding achievement.

Some of Liszt's songs, such as the extremely long "Die Macht der Musik" (The Power of Music with poetry by Helene von Orléans), will probably remain a historical curiosity and rarely be performed in public. But the fertility of Liszt's creativity offers performers a uniquely varied repertory with great programming possibilities. Why not a joint piano and voice recital that includes Liszt's *Tre sonetti di Petrarca* (Three Sonnets of Petrarach) for voice and "O! quand je dors," which refers to Petrarch, along with his *Tre sonetti del Petrarca* for piano? Or why not a group of Liszt songs with Goethe texts? The singer could present a group of Liszt songs with texts in German, French, Italian, and English. His transcriptions of songs by other composers such as Schubert, Schumann, and Franz could be included on a program with the original songs. Liszt is awaiting discovery by a concert world that is bogged down in old favorites.

RICHARD WAGNER

Song held little interest for Richard Wagner (1813–1883); it was a medium too narrow and intimate for his grandiose style. Of the twenty-one songs that are included in his complete works, only seven can be classified as German art songs, and even these seven do not resemble the songs of most of his contemporaries.

Between the years of 1839 and 1840, Wagner wrote six songs for voice and piano with French texts while he was living in France. At this time, Schubert's songs were becoming quite popular in France, and Wagner saw the potential of tapping into this new market. He was in desperate need of money, but unfortunately his songs failed to capture a French audience. His most interesting foray into French song was his setting of Heine's "Die Grenadiere," entitled "Les deux grenadiers." Wagner, like Schumann in his "Die beiden Grenadiere," included "La Marseillaise" at the climax of the song, although Wagner placed the French national anthem in the piano, not the voice. When Wagner learned that Schumann had written a setting of Heine's "Grenadiers," he wrote a letter to Schumann stating that he would rededicate his song to Schumann privately, although it was already publicly dedicated to Heine. "Likewise, I inform you that I accept the private dedication of your "Grenadiers" and await the dedication copy."[4]

Most of his *Sieben Kompositionen zu Goethe's "Faust"* (1832) also cannot be categorized as German art song. The collection consists of two songs for four voices, three songs for bass and chorus, a spoken melodrama, and only one lied for piano and voice set to the text "Meine Ruh' ist hin" (My Peace Is Over). Although this song is performed today only as a historical curiosity, it exhibits Wagner's close observance of Goethe's text: unlike Schubert who repeats the refrain, "Meine Ruh ist hin," Wagner ends with Goethe's final climactic phrase, "An seinen Küssen vergehen sollt'!" (see Chapter 1, "Poetry and Music").

The songs that have gained Wagner a place in a discussion of the nineteenth-century lied are his so-called Wesendonk lieder or *Fünf Gedichte für eine Frauenstimme von Mathilde Wesendonk*, songs

Figure 12-1. Richard Wagner. Lithograph by K.I.B., published by Franz Hanfstaengl, Munich. Courtesy of the Library of Congress.

written on the poetry of Wagner's lover of that time, Mathilde Wesendonk (1857–58). The grand style of these five songs and their dramatic range of an octave and a sixth point ahead, like the songs of Liszt, to the lieder of Richard Strauss.

Two of these songs, "Träume" (Dreams) and "Im Treibhaus" (In the Greenhouse), were subtitled as "studies to *Tristan und Isolde*," an opera composed during the years of 1857–59. The accompaniment of "Träume," which reappears as part of the love duet in the second act of *Tristan und Isolde*, is built around a two-note motive that is first presented in the song's long introduction. This motive permeates both the piano and vocal lines of the entire song and is associated with the word "Träume" (Example 12-6). The slow harmonic rhythm of the introduction, along with the constant repetition of chords, creates a sense of dreamlike ecstasy appropriate to the text. Wagner maintains his tonal reference to the key of A-flat major throughout the introduction with a pedal point on A-flat, allowing the tension of the pedal point against shifting harmonies to build until it is resolved when A-flat becomes the tonic of the A-flat major chord in preparation for the entrance of the voice.

Example 12-6. Wagner, "Träume" (Dreams), mm. 5–6.

As one would expect from a composer as verbal as Wagner, his setting of Mathilde Wesendonk's words is highly skillful. He occasionally word-paints in these five songs: for example, in "Träume" the melody falls on the word "sinken" (sink); in "Im Treibhaus" the melodic line drops on the word "Tropfen" (drops), while a dissonant second occurs in the accompaniment to imitate the sound of raindrops (Example 12-7).

Music from "Im Treibhaus" appears at the beginning of the third act in *Tristan und Isolde*. "Im Treibhaus," like "Träume," is motivically structured, this time around a four-note motive that occurs primarily in the accompaniment and only incidentally in the vocal line. Both the vocal line and the accompaniment are highly chromatic.

While Wagner and Liszt exploited an exceptionally rich

I see drops suspended on the edge of the green leaves.

Example 12-7. Wagner, "Im Treibhaus" (In the Greenhouse), mm. 56–59.

harmonic vocabulary in their songs, Wagner did not share Liszt's understanding of the color potential of the piano. The piano for Wagner was primarily a purveyor of harmonies, and his figurations in the accompaniment, such as those of "Stehe still!" (Stand Still!), are not pianistically conceived. The long-held chords in the final section die away much too soon to support the slow-moving, rising vocal line, which would benefit from a solid swelling of sound in the accompaniment (Example 12-8). Richard Strauss faced a similar problem in his song "Ruhe, meine Seele." (Peace, My Soul) (Example 12-9). Both

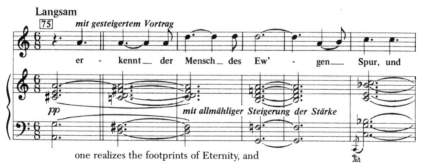

one realizes the footprints of Eternity, and

Example 12-8. Wagner, "Stehe still!" (Stand Still!), mm. 75–80.

Rest, rest, my soul,

Example 12-9. Strauss, "Ruhe, meine Seele" (Peace, My Soul), mm. 31–33.

songs are highly effective when orchestrated. Whereas the chords in these examples die when played on the piano, they can be colored and manipulated by those instruments of the orchestra, such as strings and winds, that sustain sound and are dynamically mobile. In fact, all five of Wagner's Wesendonk songs are more successful in their orchestrated form, for their slow tempi and motivic organization cannot be as effectively realized on the piano. Not only does the orchestra provide the grand setting that is inherent in the conception of these songs, but its great range of color is essential for the definition of their motivic structure. Although Wagner orchestrated only the fifth song, "Träume," the five are now most often heard in an orchestrated version that was completed by a disciple of Wagner, Felix Mottl. Orchestrated or not, the most effective realization of these songs demands singers with exceptional breath control.

The Wesendonk text itself contains a mixture of philosophical ideas: life is equated with the ephemeral character of blissful dreams; death and pain are necessary for life and happiness; nature mirrors human existence; love and eroticism define being.

Wenn Auge in Auge wonnig trinken,	When eye blissfully drinks in eye,
Seele ganz in Seele versinken;	Soul sinks completely into soul;
Wesen in Wesen sich wiederfindet,	Being finds itself again in being,
Und alles Hoffens Ende sich kündet,	And the goal of all hope is made
Die Lippe verstummt in staunendem	known,
Schweigen,	The lips are still in astonished silence,
Keinen Wunsch mehr will das Innre	The inner self desires nothing more:
zeugen:	One realizes the footprints of Eternity
Erkennt der Mensch des Ew'gen Spur	And solves your riddle, holy Nature!
Und löst dein Rätsel, heil'ge Natur!	

("Stehe still!" from *Fünf Gedichte von Mathilde Wesendonk für eine Frauenstimme und Klavier*)

Mathilde Wesendonk's poetry was also set to music by another of Wagner's disciples, the Hungarian composer Ödön Mihalovich.

Wagner's ideas dominated the musical world at the end of the nineteenth century. His effect on the art song occurred, not specifically through his songs, but through his theories about setting text and his, as well as Liszt's, expansion of harmonic vocabulary. Hugo Wolf would apply these ideas to song in his own unique manner and discover the outer limits of the intimate romantic lied.

CHAPTER THIRTEEN

Johannes Brahms

This is a chosen one.
—Robert Schumann on Brahms in
Neue Zeitschrift für Musik, 1853.[1]

Johannes Brahms (1833–1897) was a private man. He carefully destroyed any letters that revealed too much about him and about his personal life; he also destroyed his music when he believed it failed to meet his high standards. In her family memoirs, Eugenie Schumann, daughter of Robert and Clara Schumann, wrote in a chapter on Brahms: "While I was writing this chapter the thought, 'What would Brahms say if he read it?' came to me again and again. He who hated to be talked or written about."[2] This need to place a protective cocoon about himself makes Brahms unique among the many effusive personalities of the nineteenth century. Louis Spohr, Hector Berlioz, Carl Loewe, Eduard Devrient, and Richard Wagner are just a few of the men who left extensive autobiographical justifications of their lives and deeds. Even the more modest composers of the period have indirectly revealed many intimate details about themselves to the curious public. There was, for example, an aura that grew up around Schubert because of his poverty, brief life, sweetness of disposition, and circle of devoted friends, all of which has endeared him to subsequent generations; Schumann's struggles to marry Clara as well as his unsuccessful battle with insanity command sympathy and interest; even the outrageous, spiteful, and ultimately insane Hugo Wolf elicits curiosity and grudging admiration. But Brahms has hidden behind a façade that is difficult to penetrate, successfully concealing much about himself from the probing eyes of outsiders; his gruff, often abrasive personality concealed a tender heart. Of course, the absence of self-revelation has never deterred historians from speculating on the exact nature of his relationship with Clara Schumann or of his love life in general. But Brahms has ultimately triumphed. He has forced us to judge him on the basis of his music when many would have preferred the assistance of a personality cult. Ironically, this lack of personal information has stimulated much conjecture about Brahms's personal life, most of it unjust if we can trust Eugenie Schumann's account:

> [Brahms was] the finest type of a true German, who never wanted to appear other than he was. The few faults he had were very much in evidence; he took no trouble to draw aside the slight veil they formed, and left it to others to lift it from the heart of pure gold which was hidden beneath.[3]

While he concealed a highly vulnerable nature as well as his great generosity, he appears to have cultivated a kind of personal bruskness in his relationships with friends and acquaintances. The famous surgeon Theodor Billroth, who maintained a thirty-year friendship with Brahms, wrote to his daughter of Brahms: "He really makes it very difficult for one to keep on loving him."[4] Over the years, Brahms offended Clara Schumann many times yet did not hesitate to provide her with friendship, advice, and financial support throughout their lives. He was the anonymous benefactor to many musicians yet chose to live on a modest scale even after he became successful and prosperous.

Brahms also holds a unique place in the history of the nineteenth-century art song because he presents the listener with so many contradictions. While his inspiration for songwriting began with poetry, the poetry itself became a secondary feature of his composition. Although by working most of his adult life to overcome his inadequate childhood education he became a well-read man, he never actually developed a discriminating taste for great poetry in his songs. And finally, though one of the most skillful technicians of the century, he considered the simple folk song superior to other types of song. Of all the great composers of lieder, Brahms was most sympathetic to the folk-song movement, perhaps because his own humble origins caused him to identify with the "common man." He considered himself to be "of the people" and often used *Plattdeutsch* (Low German) expressions in his letters. And he valued the

Figure 13-1. Johannes Brahms. Reproduction of photograph. Courtesy of the Library of Congress.

opinion of the "Volk," as his letter to his friend Widmann indicates: "I wish you could witnesss, as I do, what it means to be loved in Vienna.... Others don't wear their hearts so openly... as they do here, and I mean the best of them; I mean the real people, those occupying the cheapest seats in the theater."[5]

Brahms composed over two hundred art songs (including his solo version of the "Zigeuner" vocal quartet) and also arranged nearly one hundred folk and children's songs. Even among the two hundred art songs, many are settings of folk poetry or poetry written in imitation of folk style. The charming "Der Jäger" (The Hunter), for example, is composed on the folklike poem of Friedrich Halm; and Brahms's very popular "Vergebliches Ständchen" was based on a poem taken from the *Deutsche Volkslieder*, a collection compiled and edited by August Wilhelm von Zuccalmaglio.[6] About half of Brahms's songs are harmonized folk melodies, songs based on folk poetry, or modern poetry written in folk style. While folk songs can be found among the works of Schumann, Mendelssohn, and Robert Franz, this medium did not represent such an important part of their song composition. Gustav Mahler was the only other prominent nineteenth-century composer who showed such a fundamental interest in folk song.

The scientific study of music history was in its infancy during the first half of the nineteenth century, and musicians were unaware that many of the sources they used for folk music contained corrupt versions of folk songs or songs that were not folk music at all. One of Brahms's favorite sources for folk tunes and poetry was Zuccalmaglio's *Deutsche Volkslieder*. Brahms did not realize that Zuccalmaglio had actually written some of these melodies and texts himself or had freely altered the folk music and poetry. Zuccalmaglio, capitalizing on the nineteenth-century appetite for folk literature, could find a larger audience by masquerading his works as genuine folk art. He would enhance his representations by using terms like "Old German" at the beginning of songs, although he may have composed the poem and the melody himself. Even the poem for Brahms's "Vergebliches Ständchen," which Zuccalmaglio had labeled a "Niederrheinisches Volkslied" (folk song from the lower Rhine), was Zuccalmaglio's own poem, loosely based on a genuine folk-song theme.[7] When Brahms eventually learned that many of these tunes were recently composed, he responded in a letter to Philipp Spitta: "Not really folk-music? Well, then we have one good composer the more."[8]

Zuccalmaglio and Andreas Kretzschmer had included in the

Deutsche Volkslieder thirty songs earlier issued as a parody by Friedrich Nicolai (1733–1811), a satirist who looked skeptically on the folk-song movement. Nicolai had published his collection in 1777 under the title of *Eyn feyner, kleyner Almanach vol schönerr echterr liblicherr Volckslieder, Berlynn vnnd Stettyn* (A Fine, Small Almanac of Beautiful, Pure, Lovely Folk Songs). Of Nicolai's sixty melodies, only twenty-seven were genuine; eleven had been composed by Nicolai himself and the other twenty-two had been composed by Johann Friedrich Reichardt.[9] Ironically, one of the few legitimate studies of folk music during the nineteenth century, by the German Ludwig Erk, was totally repudiated by Brahms, who considered the music so boring that it could not possibly be authentic.[10]

Modern historians need not berate Brahms for his lack of historical sensitivity; his interest in folk music inspired some of the most beautiful lieder in song literature—and his historical attitudes were not out of step with his time. He often consulted Clara Schumann about his work and in 1858 sent her a group of folk songs that he had harmonized.

25 June 1858

Dearest Clara,
    Do not look upon my folk-songs as more than the most casual studies, or you will be very dissatisfied. But perhaps in one or two of them you may see some gleam of better things. You should improve the accompaniment; try to make it freer.
    With love
                                                    Your Johannes

1 July 1858

[Clara to Brahms]
    How much I have been enjoying your folk-songs, dear Johannes—if only I dare say all that my heart feels about them! . . . I am often greatly struck by the richness of your genius, that you always seem to me one on whom heaven has poured out its best gifts.

8 July 1858

My dear Johannes
    One need only ask what are the songs without accompaniments, and what with yours? . . . Such accompaniments, such interpretation, such grasp of the characteristics of each song, such imaginative combination of melody and harmony, often so fine and delicate that the two have become inseparable, could only be the work of genius, of a mind that is all poetry and music, as you are, and as you know that you are.[11]

Clara Schumann correctly recognized that Brahms had molded the folk songs into his own compositions. While most are strophic or strophic variations[12] and have accompaniments that are often less complex than those of his other songs, they are, nevertheless, stamped with his unmistakable harmonic settings and great musical flexibility, contradicting the simplicity and squareness of phrase and musical conception that is associated with most folk music. He was no more a purist than his sources. His marvelous ingenuity with preexistent material is illustrated in his famous "Wiegenlied" (Lullaby). Setting Arnim and Brentano's *Des Knaben Wunderhorn* version of a fifteenth-century text, Brahms incorporated a Viennese waltz song into the accompaniment and, with a few significant rhythmic shifts and a new melody superimposed over the piano part, created a new song.[13]

Brahms was quite strict, however, about retaining the keys that were used in his folk-music sources, even when these keys were obviously unsuited for the intended performer.[14] In his folk songs for children, fourteen *Volks-Kinderlieder* dedicated to the seven children of Robert and Clara Schumann, several of the songs such as "Heidenröslein" are actually too high for most children's voices. Brahms was apparently more flexible about key choices in his art songs: on several occasions, after he had sent a song to his publisher Simrock, he then decided that the key might be too difficult for the performer to read or not completely comfortable. In "Wie bist du, meine Königin" (How [delightful] You Are, My Queen), for example, Brahms lowered the song from E major to E-flat major at the request of his friend Joseph Gänsbacher, a Viennese singing master and 'cellist.[15]

The *Volks-Kinderlieder* stand as a testament to the intimate relationship that Brahms shared with every member of the Schumann family. He exhibited concern for the Schumann children throughout his life and often advised Clara on decisions that dealt with their future. Eugenie Schumann writes:

> We children all liked Brahms, but we treated him as one who had always been there. . . . We took for granted that he was one of the family, and did not take much notice of him. As a composer we thought very highly of him, and emulated his warmest admirers in love for his compositions. . . . But it would never have occurred to us . . . to show these feelings before him.[16]

In the *Volks-Kinderlieder*, the accompaniments are rhythmically and harmonically simple, often duplicating the voice part at strategic places. In fact, the rhythmic squareness in most of these songs enhances their hymnlike or folk character. The tune for "Sandmännchen" (The Sandman), originally a hymn melody from the *Geistlicher Psalter* (Strassburg, 1697), is still popular today as the German Christmas carol "Zu Bethlehem geboren." Although Brahms doubled the melody of the voice in the left hand of the accompaniment, he provided a somewhat elaborate piano part for the right hand, possibly assuming that the tune was so familiar to children that they would not be mislead by the embellished accompaniment. Goethe's famous poem "Heidenröslein" also appears in the *Volks-Kinderlieder*. Zuccalmaglio had taken the melody for this poem from the *Liederbuch für deutsche Künstler*, published in 1833, a melody that the editors had adapted from a musical setting by Johann Friedrich Reichardt. The melodies for "Weihnachten" (Christmas) and "Marienwürmchen" were most likely composed by Zuccalmaglio.[17] "Marienwürmchen," from Arnim and Brentano's *Des Knaben Wunderhorn*, was also beautifully set to music by Robert Schumann in his *Lieder-Album für die Jugend*.

Brahms's forty-nine *Deutsche Volkslieder* cover a much wider vocal range than the children's songs; because Brahms retained the keys of the "original" sources, they too are sometimes written in a range too high for the average folksinger—"Es reit ein Herr und auch sein Knecht" (A Nobleman and Also His Servant Rode), for example. Here, again, Brahms is more composer than historian; the accompaniments illustrate his variation skills and rich harmonic vocabulary as he embroiders the strophic melodies. The haunting "Schwesterlein" (Little Sister), for example, is a dialogue between a brother and sister at a dance. Brahms suggests dance music with triple meter and differentiates between the two characters by having the brother speak in the key of A minor and the sister in C major. He strengthens the folklike quality of the music by using a slow harmonic rhythm throughout the song; at the same time, he conveys the agitation of the protagonists with a syncopated figuration in the first three stanzas and nonharmonic tones on weak beats in stanzas four and five.

Twenty-eight of Brahms's folk songs were published posthumously in 1926, the same songs that were discussed earlier in the letters between Brahms and Clara Schumann. Brahms must have considered these songs unfinished since they do not bear his signature or the date of composition. Although he identified the source for each song, many of the songs were incomplete, having only the first stanza of text written out. Consequently, all of these songs exist as purely strophic settings; the remaining stanzas of text have been added by an unknown person.[18] Brahms set sixteen of these same melodies and poems again in his *Deutsche Volkslieder* of 1894. Many of the earlier, uncompleted songs are, nevertheless, quite beautiful, with simple accompaniments that double the voice part while providing chordal support. Their simplicity brings them as close to the "feel" of genuine folk music as Brahms ever came. The haunting melody of "Der Reiter" (The Horseman), No. 6, which shifts from minor to major, is more touching than the later, slightly more elaborate setting of 1894, No. 23. The charming story of "Gunhilde" (No. 10 in 1858, No.7 in 1894), however, told with ten stanzas of poetry, fares better in the 1894 version; such a lengthy poem benefits from the variety provided by four variations in the accompaniment of the later setting. In fact, the 1894 settings are all much more complex and sophisticated than the uncompleted folk songs. Brahms wrote a subtle, distilled accompaniment for the poignant "Guten Abend" (Good-Evening) in his 1894 version (No. 4) that far surpasses the 1858 setting (No. 16).

The names of many great poets are represented in Brahms's two hundred art songs—Heine, Tieck, Goethe, Rückert, Eichendorff, Mörike, Uhland—but Brahms set only a few of their poems. Fifteen poems by Ludwig Tieck, the largest group of well-known poetry used by Brahms, make up his only song cycle, the *Romanzen aus Ludwig Tiecks Magelone Lieder*.

Works of secondary poets provide well over half his chosen text: Groth, Daumer, Frey, Kugler, Lemcke, and Wenzig, to name a few. Most of the poems he chose either were folklike or were works written by contemporary poets and acquaintances. When Clara Schumann asked Brahms for his honest opinion about a number of poems her son Felix had written, Brahms surprised her with musical settings of three of them. One of these, "Meine Liebe ist grün," has achieved great popularity among lovers of the lied. Brahms's admiration for the works of Georg Friedrich Daumer (he set nineteen of Daumer's poems) caused him to visit Daumer in 1872. Brahms was amused to learn that Daumer had never heard of him or his music.[19]

One scholar, in discussing Brahms's subordination of poetry to music, cites a number of examples of Brahms's faulty declamation and concludes that Brahms chose second-rate poetry because he couldn't hurt it in his musical settings.[20] Brahms, however, was too serious about music and literature to seek second-rate poetry, and he is known to have used poetry as a source of inspiration and also to have discussed the importance of careful text declamation. He even kept a notebook in which he copied out poems he thought would work well in songs.[21] When his poetic settings are less than ideal, as in "Wie bist du, meine Königin," it is generally because his musical concepts are dominating the poetry. Often, the lack of correspondence between poetic and musical accents is the result of the way Brahms coordinates the musical meter with the metrical accents of the poetry at the beginning of a song without adjusting for the irregularities that often occur later in the poetic line.

Brahms sometimes used poetry that had been altered from the poet's version by other composers or poets. For example, he set several poems by Ludwig Hölty (1748–1776), such as "An die Nachtigall," that had been drastically altered by the poet-translator Johann Voss (1751–1826) in his editions of Hölty's poems. Hölty died at the age of twenty-eight, and his works were not published during his life. A complete edition of Hölty's works, edited by Karl Halm and based on original manuscripts, did not appear until 1870. Brahms's version of "Die Mainacht," ca. 1868, was probably based on Schubert's 1816 setting of this poem since both omit the second stanza and change several of the same words. Brahms's version of "In der Fremde" by Eichendorff duplicates the text changes that Robert Schumann had made for his setting in the Liederkreis. Although these text changes seem to be irrelevant to Brahms's musical concepts, he may have accepted Schumann's version of the poem at face value. During his life, Brahms, who loved books, developed a wonderful library that included the poetry of Eichendorff. Perhaps he failed to consult an edition of Eichendorff's poems because he knew Schumann's song so well and preferred his changes, or perhaps, as Friedländer believed, the young Brahms may have been competing with Schumann.[22]

All of the "high" romantic themes are present in Brahms's songs: love—particularly lost love; an appreciation of nature for its own sake and as symbol of the poet's state of mind; reverence for the past and a nostagia for childhood, as in "Mit vierzig Jahren" (At Forty), "O wüsst ich doch den Weg zurück," and the fairy-tale theme of the Magelone lieder; classical subjects such as "Die Schale der Vergessenheit" (The Cup of Forgetfulness); exotic themes and poetic forms such as "Der Strom, der neben mir verrauschte," which is a ghasel, the poetic form mentioned earlier that originated in Arabia and was brought to Germany by way of Persia.

While Schubert, Schumann, and Wolf each had at least one year in which they produced as many as one hundred songs, Brahms's song production was steady, moderate, and extended throughout his adult life as a composer. His solo piano music and his songs flowed naturally and continuously from his pen, and historians like to point to the stylistic parallels between them. There is also some crossover in specific musical material between the piano and vocal works—the Scottish ballad "Edward" inspired both Brahms's 1854 "Ballad" for piano, Op. 10, No. 1, and his 1878 duet for contralto and tenor, "Edward," Op. 75, No. 1. (Liszt carried out a similar exercise in his Petrarch sonnets.)

The voice part and the bass line of the accompaniment provide the framework upon which the song is constructed, with the accompaniment acting as a subtle support system to highlight the melodic line of the voice. The sweep and grandeur of Brahms's melodies give them a life and vitality that often act to de-emphasize the text. In "Meine Liebe ist grün," the text is stretched and repeated to accommodate a soaring melody that floats over a pulsating, dramatic accompaniment (Example 13-1). Brahms's melodies often cover a wide

and fills it with fragrance and with delight,
and fills it with fragrance and with delight.

Example 13-1. Brahms, "Meine Liebe ist grün" (My Love Is Green), mm. 11–16.

range and are disjunct in character. In "Des Liebsten Schwur" (The Beloved's Promise), for example, the singer must negotiate an eleventh in the opening phrase (mm. 8–12). In "Sapphische Ode," the triadic melody, integrally locked into the harmonic support system of the accompaniment, is so disjunct that one can hardly call it melodic (mm. 1–4). It depends more on the harmonic conception than on its linkage to the nuances of the text, which contributes to its instrumental character.

While Brahms is focusing attention on the voice, he is also creating a complex web of interaction between piano and voice. He did not often write the kind of lengthy piano introductions, postludes, and interludes that are distinguishing features in the songs of Robert Schumann (Example 13-2). In fact, Brahms's song cycle, the Magelone lieder, does not have a single bar of postlude at the conclusion of fourteen very lengthy songs! Piano and voice are part of a musical whole that does not include the prominent musical meditations that Schumann so often delegated to the piano.

Example 13-2. Brahms, "Meine Liebe ist grün," mm. 1–2.

Although Brahms's piano parts sound as though they are subordinate to the voice, they are musically difficult and very challenging. They, like the vocal melody, are often based on triadic figurations, a technique that Brahms also used in his solo piano music. Notice in Example 13-2 that the left hand of the piano part outlines the harmonies of the music. In "Der Gang zum Liebchen" (The Way to My Love), both melody and accompaniment are harmonic figurations of the song's underlying chord structures (Example 13-3). In "Wie bist du meine Königin," Brahms arpeggiates the harmonies in each of the song's four stanzas but alters the third and fourth stanzas with changes in the harmonic structure, melody, and accompaniment.

The moon shines down. I should [go] again to

Example 13-3. Brahms, "Der Gang zum Liebchen" (The Way to My Love), mm. 1–4.

Coherent formal organization is basic to Brahms's songs, just as it is characteristic of his writing in general. Although he constantly sought to create variety in his songs, Brahms channeled this variety into recognizable forms, particularly the strophic variation and ABA forms. Brahms does not express the nuance of every word in his settings, and therefore fewer of his songs are through-composed than are those of his contemporary Hugo Wolf. Yet poetry does impose formal control over the whole in that his music is sectionally organized around the poetic strophe. Since he rarely said the same thing in the same way twice, Brahms relied on some form of variation within a song, either strophically varying the music or varying the return of the A material in ternary form. In his popular "Vergebliches Ständchen," a strophic variation, the primary variations occur in the piano part with the voice only slightly altered in stanzas 3 and 4 to accommodate the minor key of stanza 3 and textual variants. For "Wie Melodien zieht es mir" (Like Melodies, It Gently Runs Through My Mind), he uses harmonic and melodic variants at the end of each stanza while maintaining an arpeggiated figuration in the accompaniment. In the lovely "O kühler Wald" (Oh, Cool Woods), the vocal melody, the harmony, and the accompaniment's figuration are varied in the second stanza.

He also often used ternary (ABA) form, particularly in some of his most sophisticated songs such as "Die Mainacht" and "Ständchen." His use of ABA is never rigid, for the returning A segment of his songs is rarely an exact repetition of the initial A section, and even the B section may exhibit interesting modifications. In "Von waldbekränzter Höhe" (From the Forest-adorned Hill—ABB'A'), for example, he allows the A section to return exactly as it first appeared for eight measures before harmonically and melodically shifting to a freely composed, dramatic conclusion. In "Die Mainacht," Brahms not only changes the figuration from duplets to triplets in the returning A of the arpeggiated accompaniment, but he then inserts the final phrase of the B section and expands it in the dramatic conclusion of the song.

The melody in the B sections of many Brahms songs, such as "Die Mainacht," offers little contrast to the melody of the A sections and, by stretching a point, could sometimes be considered a variation of the A melody—not only because their melodic contours are similar but also because the same or similar rhythms occur in each melody. Brahms avoids any potential monotony inherent in this procedure by altering the piano's figuration as well as its rhythmic and harmonic content. Consequently, the melody of the B section may actually act as a unifying device. In the exceptional "Nicht mehr zu dir zu gehen" ([I decided] Not to Go to You Any More), the B melody of this ternary song bears a striking resemblance to the A melody: the B melody begins with a descending scale, and the A melody starts with an ascending scale with the same rhythmic motion that appears in the B (Example 13-4). The flavor of this song is Russian, with its dark, passionate text and declamatory musical style. The weighty octaves of

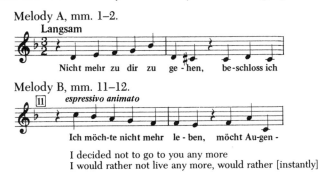

I decided not to go to you any more
I would rather not live any more, would rather [instantly]

Example 13-4. Brahms, "Nicht mehr zu dir zu gehen" ([I Decided] Not to Go to You Anymore).

the accompaniment double the voice in the beginning, while the melody hesitates with a kind of morose reflectiveness. Brahms expands the end of the opening melodic line into a three-note motive that permeates the entire song, echoing between voice and piano or between voices in the accompaniment (Example 13-5).

Brahms handled traditional song forms with enormous inventiveness and freedom. In "Mädchenlied" (The Girl's Song), for example,

I decided and swore not to go to you any more,

Example 13-5. Brahms, "Nicht mehr zu dir zu gehen," mm. 1–3.

1. At night in the spinning-room, there maidens sing, there
2. Everyone spins for her dowry, to please her beloved. Not

Example 13-6a. Brahms, "Mädchenlied" (The Girl's Song), mm. 1–4.

No man who is kind to me will inquire of me; how

Example 13-6b. Brahms, "Mädchenlied," mm. 13–16.

he further unifies the outward structure (AAA'B) by using the first
three notes of the melody as a motive from which he sequentially
structures the remainder of the melody and which he also allows to
permeate the entire song, echoing between voice and piano or
between voices in the accompaniment (Example 13-6a and 13-6b).
Notice that the motive of the accompaniment answers the voice in

line 3, but its rhythmic emphasis has now changed by beginning on beat 1, a strong beat, rather than on an upbeat; this pattern continues in the accompaniment but also includes the motive in reverse motion.

Brahms studied and collected scores and manuscripts of many earlier composers, often incorporating features of their styles into his own. His library included theoretical treatises as well as the works of Palestrina, Handel, Frescobaldi, Cesti, Bach, Caldara, and many others, and he was in contact with eminent music historians of the time such as the great Bach scholar Phillip Spitta. Brahms had a scholarly curiosity about many things but was not always a "purist" in his historical judgments, as we saw in his treatment of the folk song. This perhaps reflects the youthful state of historical studies at that time, but it also reveals some of the cultural decisions that were made by many musicians of the era. Mendelssohn, after all, adapted his performance of Bach's *St. Matthew Passion* to conform to what he thought were nineteenth-century expectations and taste. But Brahms, on the other hand, constantly compared the modern editions of older composers' works with the original editions at his disposal and made corrections in his scores. He also appears to have been very exacting in his editing of music—he edited Couperin's piano music [24] (for Handel scholar Friedrich Chrysander's *Denkmäler der Tonkunst*, Vol. 4), assisted Clara Schumann in editing Robert Schumann's music, and edited Handel's Chamber Duets and Trios, as well as two sonatas for piano and violin and two piano concerti by Philip Emanuel Bach, Mozart's *Requiem*, and music of Schubert and Chopin.

Baroque techniques such as pedal point, counterpoint, and augmentation are fundamentals in Brahms's songs. "Die Trauernde" (The Sad Girl) and "Ich schell mein Horn ins Jammertal" (I Play My Horn in the Valley of Woe) illustrate his attempt to recreate the sound of an earlier era. He achieves a Renaissance-like quality by using very simple chord progressions and avoiding seventh chords.

By the time Brahms began to compose, the music world was awakening to the works of Bach, Handel, Scarlatti, and other baroque composers. Brahms generally integrated contrapuntal techniques into his music and modified them to suit his nineteenth-century vocabulary (see Example 13-6). In his first published song, "Liebestreu" (True Love), the bass line and voice imitate each other (Example 13-7). In his comic "Unüberwindlich" (Invincible), he uses Domenico Scarlatti's harpsichord sonata in D major, No. 214, as the

"Oh, sink, oh sink your grief, my child, in the

Example 13-7. Brahms, "Liebestreu" (True Love), mm. 1–3.

Example 13-8a. D. Scarlatti, "Sonata in D major," mm. 1–4.

I have sworn a thousand times not to trust this flask,

Example 13-8b. Brahms, "Unüberwindlich" (Invincible), mm. 1–8.

basis for this drinking/love song's thematic material (Example 13-8a). The theme is first stated, vivace, by the piano in octave doublings and then repeated an octave lower in the bass of the piano before the voice enters with the theme a fifth higher, presenting the final third of the theme in augmentation (Example 13-8b). Brahms then playfully dissects the theme, allowing it to appear in various guises. He augments and alters the motive to enhance the pompous, tipsy rantings of the drunken singer as he restates part of his first statement, "I have sworn thousands of times not to trust this *flask*." Here he changes flask (Flasche) to false one (Falschen), and we now learn that he cannot resist women any more than he can resist the bottle.

Pedal point, another baroque technique, appears frequently in Brahms's songs and often becomes an important dramatic device. In "Denn es gehet dem Menschen wie dem Vieh" (For That Which Happens to Men) from the *Vier ernste Gesänge*, for example, pedals on the dominant and tonic occur throughout (Example 13-9). The plodding repetition of the inverted and internal pedal, the minor key, and the dismal outlook of the text combine to overwhelm the listener with a sense of hopelessness. Brahms creates an entirely different effect with a syncopated pedal point in "Minnelied" (Love Song). Here the pedal emphasizes the lover's melancholy as he contemplates what life would be like without his beloved (mm. 27–30).

For that which happens to men as to the

Example 13-9. Brahms, "Denn es gehet dem Menschen" (For That Which Happens to Men), in *Vier ernste Gesänge* (Four Serious Songs), mm. 1–4.

"His music often takes us by stealth rather than through immediate impact."[25] This statement is repeatedly born out when one examines the subtle rhythmic characteristics of the songs, many of which the listener may only vaguely perceive. Often several rhythmic and melodic lines are used simultaneously. The popular

"Wiegenlied," with its tuneful vocal line and straightforward triple meter, becomes a treacherous exercise for the singer when the rocking motion of the syncopated accompaniment is added, although the overall effect is one of charm and calm. Syncopation and hemiola, stock devices in Brahms's rhythmic vocabulary, always sound fresh and expressive in his songs. The obscured rhythmic pattern in the opening of "Sapphische Ode" has also frustrated many inexperienced singers. The syncopated figuration of the right-hand piano part of "Der Tod, das ist die kühle Nacht" (Death Is the Cool Night) conveys a mood of calm acceptance of death whereas in "Der Jäger" (mm. 12–13) syncopation becomes a device to further the mood of lively good humor.

In "Liebestreu," the imitation between the bass of the accompaniment and the voice sets in motion a highly complex set of rhythmic and harmonic results (see Example 13-7). Both the bass and the voice parts are in duplets against the triplets of the right-hand piano part, yet they are in conflict with one another rhythmically because the anacrusis of the bass begins on a strong beat while the answering voice, an octave and a third higher, begins on a weak beat. Brahms uses this agitated music to portray the anxious mother exhorting her daughter to forget her love. As the daughter dreamily tells of her sorrow and affirms the solidity of her love, her resolve is mirrored by her steady melodic line, which is partly doubled in the middle register of the piano (mm. 6–7). In the seemingly simple opening of "Ich wandte mich" (So I Returned), from the *Vier ernste Gesänge*, Brahms makes use of a great deal of subtle rhythmic activity. In the short introduction that anticipates the vocal line, the echo effect of the delayed right-hand part drags the melody back; when a new figuration follows in the accompaniment, the bass line, voice, and right hand of the piano all have their own gently contrasting rhythmic lines (Example 13-10). "Von ewiger Liebe" (Of Eternal Love) has several melodic lines moving in separate rhythmic patterns: the figuration of the accompaniment changes, and the beat pattern of the 6/8 meter shifts from emphasis on beats one and four to emphasis on beats one, three, and five, while the voice line continues to emphasize beats one and four. The resulting hemiola between voice and piano broadens the conclusion and builds in a ritard (Example 13-11).

Brahms takes full advantage of the romantic era's bold harmonic vocabulary yet keeps his music within the larger boundaries of tonality. He uses his rich harmonic palate with such subtlety that the

Ich wand - te mich,

So I returned,

Example 13-10. Brahms, "Ich wandte mich" (So I Returned), in *Vier ernste Gesänge*, mm. 1–4.

un - se - re Lie - be, un - se - re Lie - be muss

our love, our love must

Example 13-11. Brahms, "Von ewiger Liebe" (Of Eternal Love), mm. 111–114.

listener may be unaware Brahms has explored unusual territory. In "Die Mainacht," for example, he moves from E-flat major in the A section to the distant key of B major in the B section by treating E-flat as an enharmonic D-sharp. The thin, modest piano figurations that present this startling change obscure its boldness.

His famous "Immer leiser wird mein Schlummer" (My Sleep Grows Ever Lighter) is also harmonically dramatic, beginning in the key of C-sharp minor and ending in the enharmonically related key of D-flat major. At the end of the first stanza, as the speaker describes a dream that symbolizes her helpless isolation from her sweetheart, Brahms writes a three-note pattern that descends sequentially from G-sharp to F-sharp to E, while the supporting six-four chords in the piano also descend. Brahms concludes the second stanza with the same three-note pattern, this time ascending as the girl begs her love to see her once more before she dies. Each entrance of the motive is a minor third higher than the last until the voice has outlined a diminished seventh, mirroring her question, "Will you come to see me one more time [before I die]? Oh, come quickly!" The entire section is harmonically unstable until the final phrase. Then the harmonic resolution to D-flat major shows the resignation of the girl.

Even in his folk songs, Brahms could not resist unusual harmonic relationships. In "Vor dem Fenster" (Outside the Window), which he calls a folk song, there is little harmonic simplicity in his swift move from G minor to A minor.

Brahms's use of harmonic rhythm is highly varied as well. In "Feldeinsamkeit" (Solitude in the Field), he establishes a sense of repose with a very slow harmonic rhythm in the opening of the song, lingering on the tonic chord of F major for three measures. The harmonic rhythm of "Regenlied" (Rain Song, 1873) is more rapid and varied, reflecting the nostalgia and passion of the text. This same music occurs again in the song that follows, "Nachklang" (Reminiscence), and in the violin sonata in G major, Op. 78, of 1878, sometimes called the "Regenlied" Sonata.

Brahms successfully establishes moods that express the meaning of the poetry, but he usually avoids creating excessively graphic figurations. The arpeggios in the accompaniment of "Minnelied" are not specifically descriptive, yet they provide an atmosphere that is appropriate for the text. The 6/8 rocking motion of "Meerfahrt" (Sea Journey) moves closer to word-painting, but it is suggestive of the text rather than intrusively graphic.

But word-painting, while not a dominant characteristic of Brahms's songs, was a device that he could and did subtly employ on a surprising number of occasions. In "Minnelied," for example, he has the vocal line descend to the word "tot" (dead), and in his famous "Der Schmied" (The Blacksmith), he imitates the blows of the anvil and hammer (Example 13-12). Even in this seemingly simple folk song, the voice and each line of the piano has a separate rhythmic pattern.

In his "Nachtigallen schwingen" (Nightingales Merrily Flap their Wings), he mimics the twittering of birds. Like every other song composer of the century, when he wrote a serenade, Brahms could not resist the urge to imitate a guitar. In Examples 13-13a and 13-13b from two serenades, he finds two quite different figurations to portray plucking. The second of these examples is a delightful song that should be better known than it is.

In fact, only a small number of Brahms's songs are known to the musical public. Many of his rarely performed songs exhibit sur-

1. I hear my beloved, he swings the hammer,
2. By the black forge, there my love sits,

Example 13-12. Brahms, "Der Schmied" (The Blacksmith), mm. 1–4.

Example 13-13a. Brahms, "Ständchen" (Serenade), mm. 1–4.

Softly, around you

Example 13-13b. Brahms, "Serenade" (Serenade), mm. 1–3.

prising characteristics that are not usually associated with the stereotypical view of his work. "An eine Aeolsharfe" (To an Aeolian Harp), for example, shows the influence of both Schubert and Liszt (see Schubert's "An die Leier" and Liszt's "Ihr Glocken von Marling") but is transformed into something entirely new. His exquisite "Lerchengesang" (Lark's Song), with its delicate piano introduction, interlude, and postlude of identical musical material, is one of Brahms's few Schumann-like works. This is surely one of

Brahms's most beautiful songs, yet it is rarely performed. "Dämm-rung senkte sich von oben," (Twilight Has Fallen from Above) is a highly atmospheric, sensitive setting of Goethe's wonderful poem and is one of the finest songs of the nineteenth century.

Brahms used relatively few expression marks in the voice part. He is quoted by his friend Max Friedländer as saying,

> I learnt that from your Schubert, who was so extraordinarily chary of directions for the singer, in contrast with Robert Franz, for example, who could never put too great a variety of *p, mf, dim.*, even in . . . the same bar. I have given the singer an indica-tion, exactly as Schubert did, by inserting a tempo direction in the piano part. [Brahms also stated that he did not like great ritenuti].[26]

This sparseness of direction allows the singer considerable freedom in interpretation. "Vergebliches Ständchen," for example, from a collection of songs called *Romanzen und Lieder für eine oder zwei Stimmen* (in other words, songs that could be sung by two voices in dialogue) is a case in point. Brahms stated that he preferred the singer to show the haughtiness of the girl—yet he does not indicate this in the score. Therefore, singers are not restricted to his view, and those singers who see the girl as playful and teasing are free to pursue their own vision. Incidentally, some of Brahms's most cheerful music can be found among his folk-oriented songs, such as "Vergebliches Ständchen," "Der Jäger," and "Der Schmied."

It is often stated that Brahms preferred low voices, but he does not actually designate any of his songs for low voice until Op. 86, pub-lished in 1882. He wrote many beautiful songs for high voice, such as "Meine Liebe ist grün," "Ständchen," and "Wir wandelten" (We Wandered), and he even designated his first two published collec-tions of songs specifically for high voice. But certainly some of his most memorable music is written for low voice (the *Vier ernste Gesänge*, the two songs for alto voice with viola obbligato, Op. 91, and the *Rhapsodie* for contralto, male chorus, and orchestra, Op. 53), and he cultivated a number of personal relationships with women who had either mezzo or alto ranges (alto Rosa Paumgartner-Papier and mezzos Amalie Joachim, Hermine Spies, Alice Barbi, and Agathe von Siebold).

The serious moods in the songs for low voice reinforce his reputa-tion as a songwriter who preferred topics of sadness and melancholy. The five songs of his opus 105, for example, illustrate his penchant for nostalgia and sorrow. "Immer leiser wird mein Schlummer" presents wisps of the dreams and reflections of a dying girl who knows her sweetheart will love another after she is dead. "Klage" (Lament) is the story of a brokenhearted girl—"Ich werde nimmer froh" (I will never be happy)—and "Verrat," (Betrayal) is the tale of a man who murders his sweetheart's lover. But melancholy texts are not restricted to songs for low voice. The beautiful "Mädchenlied," in the style of Brahms's late piano music such as the A major Intermezzo, Op. 118, gives voice to the reflectiveness and unnamed sorrows in Brahms's instrumental music. Although the words of the song do not define the sorrow of the young woman, we sense her sadness and know only that she is weaving wedding clothes but has no lover.

Brahms's loving treatment of low, dark voices and melancholy topics finds its culmination in the *Vier ernste Gesänge*, published the year before he died. Brahms, like Schubert at the end of his life, meditated on the somberness, alienation, and despair of human life and death. He chose three anti-religious scriptures from Ecclesiastes as well as the famous but not specifically Christian text on love from 1 Corinthians, Chapter 13, for his final vocal statement to humanity. The dirgelike opening of "Denn es gehet dem Menschen wie dem Vieh" (see Example 13-9) and the somber "Ich wandte mich" harmonically and melodically recall his Requiem (1868). The "upbeat" mood of the final song, "Wenn ich mit Menschen- und mit Engelszungen redete" (Though I Speak with the Tongues of Men and of Angels), seems almost out of character with the rest of the group, like forced cheerfulness, artificially placed at the end to inject a more positive "note." The text's dark musings, "O Tod, o Tod, wie bitter bist du" (Oh death, oh death, how bitter you are), are matched by Brahms's disjunct vocal line, which bursts into a wail of misery and despair. The sparse chordal repetition of the voice part at the interval of a fifth in the accompaniment heightens the sense of death's starkness (Example 13-14). Although all of the texts for the *Vier ernste Gesänge* are taken from the Bible, and the songs are usually presented together as a group, they are not considered a cycle.

Brahms's only song cycle is the seldom performed *Romanzen aus Ludwig Tiecks Magelone*. The great length of this cycle and its sketchy, obscure story line are two of many reasons why these songs have not endeared themselves to the general public. Brahms extracted the poetry for this cycle from Tieck's *Wunderschöne Liebesgeschichte der schönen Magelone und des Grafen Peter aus der Provence* (The Wonderful Love Story of the Beautiful Magelone and Count Peter of Provence). The saga, written in 1797, describes the

Oh death, oh death, how bitter you are,

Example 13-14. Brahms, "O Tod, wie bitter bist du" (Oh Death, How Bitter You Are), in *Vier ernste Gesänge*, mm. 1–5.

love and trials of the beautiful Magelone and her sweetheart, Peter. There are four characters in the story: a wandering minstrel who acts as narrator, Peter, Magelone, and Sulima—a temporary romantic distraction for Peter. Unfortunately, the story is often obscured by Brahms's omission of important text; it is also not always clear which character is speaking. Plot is important in the Magelone cycle because this is a real adventure, a fairy tale where the story is a significant part of the concept. Although every song in this cycle is beautifully conceived and written, the lengthiness of each song and the lack of variety in the music, particularly in the figurations of the accompaniment, are problems. Most audiences are also unaccustomed to such a sustained narrative approach to storytelling, except perhaps in Wagner's music where the tradition of length has always been accepted as fundamental to his aesthetic concept. Furthermore, there is an absence of memorable tunes in the Magelone lieder, and given the length of the cycle, a dangerous monotony results.

The Magelone lieder do not fit neatly into any musical category, and the listener must discard traditional labels in order to appreciate this work. It does not fulfill our expectations for a song recital because it is so musically abstract: the vocal lines are extremely long and sound more instrumental than vocal; the musical ideas are complex and not easily accessible on first hearing; the poetry, although it tells a story, is nevertheless subordinate to the development of Brahms's musical ideas. The songs require the talents of a fine pianist and an exceptional vocal artist who possesses a beautiful voice and a magnetic personality. The continuousness of the songs as well as their lengthiness and broad, lyrical character should be approached in Wagnerian terms, and a performance should include a clear plot synopsis in the program. These songs are ironically the antithesis of the folk song that Brahms loved so much.

With all his harmonic brilliance and excellent craftsmanship, Brahms confines himself to a more narrow emotional scale than did Schubert or Wolf. He shows us beauty, passion, melancholy, love, and humor, but he keeps us at a distance. This is in character with Brahms, the private man. Wolf bares his soul: he despairs and laughs and ridicules; he shows us his anguish and we feel our own. Only at the end of his life does Brahms reveal something of his inner core, with songs such as "O Tod, wie bitter bist du" of the *Vier ernste Gesänge*.

To point out that Brahms restricted himself to poetry with a more limited emotional range than did Wolf, however, is perhaps ignoring what distinguishes the two men's contrasting musical messages. Wolf was not interested in writing in the musically abstract style that characterized Brahms's songs. We might stretch Nietzsche's terminology from *The Birth of Tragedy* and say that Brahms was an Apollonian composer who stressed serene proportion while Wolf represented the Dionysian forces of passion (although Brahms could also capture the intense emotion of a poem when it touched him). Brahms was generally more cautious in his writing style and rarely indulged in such ingenious piano figurations as Wolf and Schubert tailored to each new poem. Brahms's reliance on more traditional forms and on figurations that are often similar to one another sometimes obscures the sweep of his great harmonic range, and his music is often so subtle and understated that his songs may elude many listeners. But his melodic gift, so gloriously illustrated in songs such as "Dein blaues Auge" (Your Blue Eyes), is rarely matched by Wolf.

All the major song composers—Schubert, Schumann, Brahms, and Wolf—are performed on the recital stage with a stock selection of songs that represent only a small fraction of their magnificent repertory. The majority of their songs are never heard. Singers have the marvelous opportunity of introducing audiences to a treasure-trove of little-known song that will surprise and thrill them.

Figure 14-1. Hugo Wolf. Half-tone reproduction. Courtesy of the Library of Congress.

CHAPTER FOURTEEN

Hugo Wolf

One could search the works of Strauss, of Mahler, of Hugo Wolf, without finding a melody which has a truly original value in its own right, apart from its application to a text or to a literary idea and from its harmonic development.
—from the correspondence of Romain Rolland[1]

The musical reputation of Hugo Wolf (1860–1903) rests primarily on his 245 published songs. He was a post-Wagnerian composer who had at his disposal a highly colorful, expressive harmonic palette: dissonant, chromatic, tenuously retaining its tonal orientation. He had also assimilated Wagner's philosophical justifications for the synthesis of text and music and was able to translate these ideas into his song composition. His refined literary taste and genius for musically matching the nuances of words has never been surpassed. In fact, Wolf's respect for poetry led him to place the name of the poet ahead of his own in his first collections of song, and at public concerts he would read aloud each poem before it was sung. He was the most successful of the lieder composers in portraying a variety of characters and subjects and, at the same time, was an astonishing master of humor. "Storchenbotschaft" (The Storks' Message), "Nimmersatte Liebe" (Insatiable Love), "Selbstgeständnis" (Self-Confession), "Abschied" (Farewell), and "Auftrag" (The Commission) are just a few of his many lighthearted songs. He captured the essence of a wide variety of subjects and poetic moods, ranging from profound religious supplication to slapstick humor.

While Wolf's songs are considered by many to represent the

pinnacle of song, they are also the least-known works of all the great lieder composers. Because his music is so closely linked to the poetry, his songs require a clear understanding of the German words in order to appreciate how subtly he has translated meanings into musical sound, finding the exact inflection and drama inherent in each word. In the delicate balancing of text and music, it is the text that controls the direction of his music.

Most of his songs are through-composed but unified by rhythmic or melodic motives, or both, as well as by recurring figurations in the accompaniment. Although these songs are intensely beautiful, this beauty is rarely the result of traditional melodic loveliness. His melodies have no "logic" in themselves and can rarely stand alone, for the subordination of text to melodic development is not a part of Wolf's musical technique; vocal lines are molded to the text.

Although Wolf wrote no song cycles, he did organize all his published works into collections. His first two collections, consisting of six songs each and representing a compilation of early songs, were published in 1887 with the aid of his friend Friedrich Eckstein. Two of these songs, "Mausfallensprüchlein" (A Little Maxim About the Mouse) and "Zur Ruh, zur Ruh!" are prophetic of the inspired works that poured forth in the following years.

In 1888, Wolf began to write songs in a white heat, inspired by the poems of the great German poet Eduard Mörike (1804–1875). His fifty-three Mörike songs were followed by settings of Joseph von Eichendorff (twenty songs) and Goethe (fifty-one songs). Wolf then composed the music for translations by Paul Heyse (1830–1914) and Emanuel Geibel (1815–1884) of forty-four Spanish poems—ten sacred texts and thirty-four secular. He then set six poems by Gottfried Keller (1819–1890), which were followed by Paul Heyse's translations of forty-six Italian poems. Wolf allowed five years to elapse between his setting of the first twenty-two songs of the Italian Songbook and the last twenty-four. He also set translations of three poems by Ibsen, three by Michelangelo, one by Shakespeare, and one by Byron.

Hugo Wolf had much in common with his slightly younger French contemporary Claude Debussy (1862–1918). Because of Richard Wagner's influence, both Wolf and Debussy wrote with a heightened sensitivity to poetic and musical synthesis. Their efforts to compose music that allied itself closely to the intimate nuances of text resulted in melody that, though not always beautiful, was exquisitely molded to the inflections of each composer's own language. Although their melodies are of dissimilar character because the accentual demands of German and French are quite different, they often have in common a lack of elemental rhythmic drive because the melody is subordinated to the expression of textual subtleties and because the rhythms of the accompaniment are so independent from both the text and meter of the song. In Wolf's "Sterb' ich so hüllt in Blumen meine Glieder" (If I Die, Cover Me with Flowers), while the right-hand piano part coincides with the prescribed 12/8 meter, the tied notes in the voice line and the left hand of the piano accompaniment set up metrical accents quite at variance with this (Example 14-1a). Debussy's "La flûte de Pan" (Pan's Flute) from the *Chansons de Bilitis* concludes with a chanted voice line that is metrically neutralized, as is the piano part, through the fluid shifts of two against three (the beat is sometimes subdivided into three or six) and by the grace-note figure in the left-hand piano part of the interlude that precedes the final section of the song (Example 14-1b).

Both Wolf and Debussy often negated the basic meter of the piece in order to allow textual inflection to dominate. In the accompaniment of Wolf's "Nachtzauber" (Night Magic) from the Eichendorff songs and in Debussy's "Les Ingénus" (The Ingenues)

Example 14-1a. Wolf, "Sterb' ich so hüllt in Blumen meine Glieder" (If I Die, Cover Me with Flowers), mm. 1–4.

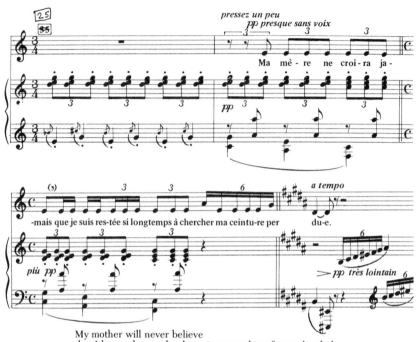

Example 14-1b. Debussy, "La flûte de Pan" (Pan's Flute), in *Chansons de Bilitis* (The Songs of Bilitis), mm. 25–28.

from the *Fêtes galantes II*, for example, both composers imply two different metrical schemes at the same time, while the voice part floats independently over the accompaniment. The metrical implication of a melodic figuration in the right hand of the accompaniment is contradicted by a separate rhythmic scheme in the left hand. The result is a complex rhythmic scheme that negates a sense of meter or dominant rhythmic pattern (Example 14-2a and Example 14-2b). Wolf's right-hand melody is a three-note motive that appears in various guises as it falls on a different part of each sixteenth-note division of the beat. Its shape is "contrary" to the 3/4 meter of the song (Example 14-3). Despite the stark independence of accompaniment and voice part, neither makes sense without the other. Occasionally, Wolf writes an accompaniment that can stand alone, in "Mein Liebster singt" (My Lover Sings) from the Italian songbook, for example, but this is the exception rather than the rule. When Debussy or Wolf decided to employ a strong rhythmic pulse, it was often a dance rhythm as in the Habanera of Wolf's "Auftrag" or the ancient Provençal tambourin of Debussy's "Le Faune" (The Faun).

Softly drifting down from the mountains,
awaken the ancient songs,

Example 14-2a. Wolf, "Nachtzauber" (Night Magic), mm. 18–21.

Example 14-2b. Debussy, "Les Ingénus" (The Ingenues), in *Fêtes galantes II* (Elegant Festivals), mm. 3–6.

Example 14-3. Wolf, "Nachtzauber," mm. 1–3.

Debussy and Wolf further explored the colorful harmonic vocabulary that Wagner had pursued in his operas. Each composer had his own methods for blurring the boundaries of tonality, frequently relying on pedal point as a primary link with key. Debussy also used the whole-tone scale, the pentatonic scale, and other scale patterns, whereas Wolf relied on chromaticism and nonfunctional harmonic progressions, all of which contributed to the disintegration of tonality.

Wolf, like Schumann, was a music critic. Unlike Schumann, however, Wolf was caustic, sarcastic, and did little to foster or encourage other young musicians. For three years, starting at the end of 1883, he wrote for the *Wiener Salonblatt*, a Viennese Sunday journal. The German musical world at this time was unsettled by those who supported Brahms's music and despised Wagner's or vice versa. Wolf's admiration for Wagner, coupled with his own volatile, outspoken nature, brought him prominently into the fray. He used his position as critic at the *Salonblatt* to launch a vendetta against Brahms. One of his classic attacks on Brahms follows:

> A musical menu spiced by two Brahms compositions cannot but make us thoroughly ill. To avoid that misfortune . . . we heard only the "Ständchen," sung by Herr Winkelmann. What with Herr Winkelmann's distinct enunciation, it was not surprising that we lost the sense of the poem. The lover, presumably, is complaining to his beloved about his boredom, his despair, and his toothache. Herr Brahms, who has hardly a rival when it comes to the characterization of such moods and afflictions, has again given a brilliant example of his eminent ability to master a situation with a few short strokes. How beautifully, in this "Ständchen," is boredom expressed! How eloquent is its language! The effect was also surprising. One yawned to one's heart's content. And with what mastery was the transition from boredom to despair prepared and executed! One would have liked to tear one's hair out by the roots in sheer delight. Now despair, now boredom, and this in a degree of perfection possibly [*sic*] only with a master of Brahms's significance.[2]

Wolf did not limit his scathing criticism to the music of Brahms, however, and ultimately he made many powerful enemies. When he requested that the well-known Rosé Quartet perform his D Minor String Quartet, he was refused. The Quartet's violist, Sigismund Bachrich, who had been mortally wounded by Wolf's review of his opera, returned the favor. Bachrich was also an influential member of the Philharmonic Orchestra. When it rehearsed Wolf's symphonic poem *Penthesilea*, the orchestra members made such critical remarks about the work that Wolf was cut to the quick.

It is curious to note the frenzy of inspiration that seems to have been basic to the creative songwriting process for Schubert, Schumann, and Wolf. Each of these composers had at least one year in which he composed more than one hundred songs. Both Schumann and Wolf expressed amazement at the way in which the creative impulse would dominate them, yielding one beautiful song after another while seeming to be a force unto itself, separate from their individual will. The inspiration of the muses was embodied in their songwriting, for they admired their creations as though these songs were the work of a third party who held them captive.

> On Saturday I composed, without having intended to do so, "Das verlassene Mägdlein," already set to music by Schumann in a heavenly way.... It happened almost against my will.[3]

In the Mörike lieder, Wolf was unquestionably in the power of the muse, and he was filled with pride and wonder as he wrote.

> March 20—Today... I created my masterpiece. "Erstes Liebeslied eines Mädchens"... is by far the best thing that I have done up to now.

> March 21—I retract the opinion that the "Erstes Liebeslied eines Mädchens" is my best thing, for what I wrote this morning, "Fussreise,"... is a million times better.[4]

The Mörike lieder contain some of Wolf's best-known and most popular songs: "Fussreise," "Verborgenheit" (Seclusion), "Nimmersatte Liebe," "Er ist's," "Der Gärtner" (The Gardener), and "Das verlassene Mägdlein" are all standard concert fare. But there are many other beautiful songs in this collection that are seldom performed: "Der Genesene an die Hoffnung" (Address to Hope), "Begegnung," "Im Frühling" (In Spring), "Um Mitternacht" (About Midnight), "An die Geliebte" (To the Beloved), "Erstes Liebeslied eines Mädchens," "Lied eines Verliebten" (Song of the Lover).

One of these less-known but lovely songs, "Zum neuen Jahr—Kirchengesang" (For the New Year—A Hymn), illustrates characteristics that could be considered not only typical of Wolf's songs but, at the same time, unique to this particular song. The text is a gentle prayer of thanks, praise, and a request for guidance in the new year. Wolf creates an atmosphere of worship, trust, and faith by writing a relatively linear vocal part and an accompaniment that is harmonically consonant and rhythmically simple. In fact, the figuration of the accompaniment in the first and last sections is filled with parallel thirds in both hands. The steady progression of the accompaniment creates the feeling of a procession or of walking, something that occurs in a number of Wolf's songs such as "Nun wandre, Maria" (Now Walk On, Mary) from the *Spanisches Liederbuch*. The song, divided into three sections, is in a very free ABA' form since the last section returns with the parallel thirds of the first. Wolf, however, adds the open fifths from the B section at the beginning of the first six bars of the final section, cleverly uniting all segments of the song and lending a new stability to the parallel thirds of the first section as the voice affirms "Lord, may all things be laid in Thy hands, the beginning and the end." Two open fifths are moved to the bass clef in the postlude to add a warmth and depth to the conclusion of the song.

The accompaniment for both A sections lies primarily in the treble clef; Wolf seems to have preferred the high, bell-like sound of the piano for religious ecstasy or the peaceful contemplation of Heaven. The colors of the piano's upper register are often used to suggest religious experiences, delicate images, or unusual characters such as the fairies in "Nixe Binsefuss" (The Water Sprite Binsefuss). Transposition of these songs into lower keys is questionable since Wolf's sense of sound coloration here is so keen.

Wolf often uses sudden shifts of register in the piano to set off a new thought or section of his music. In "Zum neuen Jahr," he has the right hand of the accompaniment move down an octave to introduce the B section. He also establishes this new section with a sudden change of key, moving from B major to G major. Such mediant key shifts are typical for Wolf, just as they were for all the nineteenth-century song composers. His song "In der Frühe" (In the Early Morning) exemplifies constant mediant shifts: in measure 14, he moves suddenly from E major to G major, in measure 16 from G major to B-flat major, and in measure 18 he heads for home by shifting from B-flat major to D major, the parallel key to the opening key of D minor.

Both "In der Frühe" and "Zum neuen Jahr" illustrate another aspect of Wolf's musical vocabulary—syncopation. The open fifth drone in the left hand of the accompaniment at the beginning of the B section of "Zum neuen Jahr" occurs in many of Wolf's songs, frequently in moments of contemplation. In the inward looking "Verborgenheit," Wolf begins and ends with a dronelike figure (Example 14-4). Other examples occur in "Auf einer Wanderung"

Example 14-4. Wolf, "Verborgenheit" (Seclusion), mm. 1–4.

(On a Walking-Tour) and "In der Frühe."

The tessitura of the vocal line in "Zum neuen Jahr" is high as well as expansive, covering the range of an octave and a sixth. Although it moves in tandem with the accompaniment at the beginning of the song, it is completely independent of the accompaniment from the B section to the end, freely declaiming the text in the final section. The voice line is through-composed while the accompaniment is a freely organized ABA' form. The voice part also includes some word-painting—a long note on "Alles" (everything), for example. Wolf, considered the greatest textual purist of the lieder composers, did not hesitate to repeat words when it suited the structure of his song. The two repeated phrases in "Zum neuen Jahr" are his rather than Mörike's.

Unlike Schubert and Brahms, Wolf was very specific in giving directions to the singer. Throughout the nineteenth and twentieth centuries the trend has been to increase expressive markings and directions to the performer—culminating in electronic music, a medium that is totally controlled by the composer.

Although it is possible to recognize a basic musical vocabulary that appears in all his songs, Wolf composed with exceptional individuality, tailoring his music to each poem. For example, in the playful, humorous song, "Auftrag," Wolf incorporated a Habanera rhythm in the accompaniment that also carries over to the voice part. The simplicity of the dance rhythm dominates the song and highlights its comic effect. In "Er ist's," Wolf wrote a twenty-one-bar postlude that parallels the excitement and profuseness of spring. Yet he included no postlude for "Verborgenheit," since the song is artistically complete when the last words are sung. Wolf sometimes chose to write an accompaniment that is completely independent of the voice and sometimes completely subordinate to the voice. The piano part to "Gesang Weylas" (Weyla's Song), for example, imitates the strumming of a harp, with arpeggiated chords as background for the chanted vocal line. The slow harmonic rhythm at the beginning of the song shifts from tonic to dominant to subdominant and back to tonic before moving to the mediant key, all of which lends dignity, strength, and timelessness to Mörike's mystical poem. In "Der Gärtner," voice and accompaniment are independent of each other: the prancing figure of the piano symbolizes the dancing white horse upon which a young princess rides; the graceful vocal line reveals the admiring glances of a humble gardener who watches the young princess (Example 14-5). The rhythmic motive of the first four beats in the introduction provides the foundation for the entire song.

On her horse, as white as snow,

Example 14-5. Wolf, "Der Gärtner" (The Gardener), mm. 1–8.

In the introduction of "Lied eines Verliebten," Wolf fashions one of his longer melodic figures, constructed from a short two-sectioned motive, reminiscent of Schubert's "Die Krähe" from *Winterreise*. This melody serves as the basis of both voice and accompaniment for the entire song (Example 14-6). Unlike the poor, desperate character in "Die Krähe," Wolf's young man is a humorous figure of regret.

He wrote a beautiful melody in the piano part of "Mein Liebster singt" in the *Italienisches Liederbuch*. Here Wolf was able to construct a lengthy melody that extends beyond a few measures. This is one of the few examples in Wolf's lieder where the accompaniment is able to stand alone as a piano solo.

Example 14-6. Wolf, "Lied eines Verliebten" (Song of a Lover), mm. 1–2.

Most of Wolf's vocal lines are vitalized and defined by the harmonies of the accompaniment. Piano and voice, even when presenting totally independent material, are essential to one another for completeness. In Example 14-7, the vocal line is uninteresting by itself, and only in combination with the two motives over a pedal point does the individuality of the song unfold (Examples 14-7a and 14-7b). This example illustrates the difficulty of discussing melody, harmony, and rhythm as separate entities when the composer has totally integrated all the musical elements.

Wolf's musical vocabulary for expressing humorous ideas is quite varied. In "Storchenbotschaft," he uses dissonance for comic effect (Example 14-8). Dissonance is more often Wolf's tool for conveying

Und steht Ihr früh am Morgen auf vom Bette, scheucht Ihr vom Himmel al-le Wol-ken fort,
And when you get up in the morning from your bed, you chase all the clouds from the sky,

Example 14-7a. Wolf, "Und steht Ihr früh am Morgen auf" (And When You Get Up Early in the Morning), mm. 2–5.

Example 14-7b. Wolf, "Und steht Ihr früh am Morgen auf," m 2.

Example 14-8. Wolf, "Storchenbotschaft" (The Storks' Message), m. 1.

anger, tension, or states of misery, and although there are many examples in the Mörike lieder, the gentle, reflective Mörike does not elicit the high density of dissonance that is generated by the religious flagellants in the *Spanisches Liederbuch*. Wolf also interpreted Goethe's *Wilhelm Meister* characters—the girl Mignon in "Mignon" (which is the famous "Kennst du das Land"), "Mignon I" ("Heiss mich nicht reden"), "Mignon II" ("Nur wer die Sehnsucht kennt"), and "Mignon III" ("So lasst mich scheinen"), and her father the harper in "Harfenspieler I" ("Wer sich der Einsamkeit ergibt"), "Harfenspieler II" ("An die Türen will ich schleichen"), and "Harfenspieler III" ("Wer nie sein Brot mit Tränen ass")—with a fin de siècle psychological complexity and musical tension that has made them inaccessible to the general public.

Chromaticism is a basic element of Wolf's musical vocabulary. He uses it as embellishment to his melodic lines and as part of his functional harmonic scheme. Augmented thirds (diminished fourths) and augmented fourths (diminished fifths) are also regular features of Wolf songs and are more prevalent in moments of great intensity (see "Verborgenheit" or "Das verlassene Mägdlein" from the Mörike lieder). In the song "In der Frühe," Wolf opens with a diminished fourth in the melody followed by an augmented fourth in the next phrase in his quest to express the anxiety and discomfort of the speaker. The tortured melody of the first half of the song changes to perfect fourths and octaves in the second part, while the key shifts from minor to major as the speaker finds strength, hope, and comfort.

Wolf presented a wide variety of moods and colors in his twenty Eichendorff lieder. Joseph Freiherr von Eichendorff had developed many of the popular romantic themes in his poetry—longing for the past, the mystery of the forest, moonlight, love of wandering—and Schumann set a number of these beautiful, lyric poems in his *Liederkreis*, Op. 39. Wolf chose not just the atmospheric poems but also some of Eichendorff's humorous character pieces. He created charming, cheerful settings of "Der Musikant," "Der Soldat I" (The Soldier), "Der Scholar" (The Scholar), and "Unfall" (The Disaster). His "Die Zigeunerin" is a tour de force on a popular theme in the nineteenth century—gypsies. The nonsense melismatic ending to each stanza is somewhat unusual for Wolf—although other examples occur in the Goethe lieder: "Die Spröde" (The Unyielding) and "Die Bekehrte" (The Convert)—but it is totally in character for the mood of the song (Example 14-9).

Each poet and poem commanded an individual response from

Example 14-9. Wolf, "Die Zigeunerin" (The Gypsy), mm. 11–14.

Wolf; that is why his Goethe lieder are subtly, often inexplicably, different from his Mörike lieder. By immersing himself in the works of
one writer at a time, he achieved a unique understanding of and
intimacy with the poet.

Wolf did not like to compose music for poems that he believed
had been successfully treated by other composers. Since Schubert
had set so many of Goethe's poems, Wolf looked for some of Goethe's
less well known poetry. He also tackled a number of poems that he
felt had not been definitively interpreted by Schubert or Schumann.
Despite the restrictions he placed upon himself, he was still able to
find fifty-three Goethe poems that inspired him; he set fifty-one
between October of 1888 and October of 1889 (the other two were
included in the second volume of Wolf's earliest publication). His
setting of ten poems from Goethe's *Wilhelm Meister* are the most
controversial of his Goethe lieder, partly because these poems had
already been set by Schubert and Schumann and partly because,
despite Wolf's intention of presenting an accurate depiction of the
characters as they appeared in Goethe's novel, his complex portrayal
of Mignon seems to contradict Goethe's picture of a naïve, suffering
youth. Yet Wolf is a product of his time. Could we expect less from a
composer who was heir to the musical vocabulary of Wagner and

shared a time frame with Nietzsche, Freud (1856–1939), and Darwin (1809–1882)? Actually, the piano figurations for the first three Mignon songs are restrained, unobtrusive, and relatively simple. In "Mignon I," the voice part is, at times, almost a chant, with little range or inflection. These songs, however, like those of the Harper, are very dramatic because of Wolf's most dissonant writing; the harmonically unstable chromatic music is used to reflect the misery of each speaker. "Mignon II" begins with a melodic motive which is supported by harmonically varied underpinnings for each appearance (Example 14-10). The intensity of the text is reflected in the non-functional harmonies and chromaticism.

Example 14-10. Wolf, "Mignon II," mm. 1–4.

The plodding, circular music of "Mignon III" anticipates the static style that will later develop in the music of Webern. Even the chromaticism in the voice part foreshadows early Webern, although Wolf retains a tonal structure.

It is Wolf's "Mignon" ("Kennst du das Land"), however, which is the most dramatic of his Mignon songs. The scale of this song, like his "Geh', Geliebter, geh' jetzt!" (Go, Beloved, Go Now), is orchestral; in fact, Wolf did orchestrate this masterpiece. With a two-octave range for the voice and almost a five-octave range for the piano (incorporating many octave doublings, thick chords, and dynamics ranging from *ppp* to *ff*), this song is a grand tour de force. Goethe's three stanzas of poetry are paralleled with three musical sections, which are themselves subdivided into a piano prelude, a stanza for voice and piano, and a refrain for voice and piano that is divided into two sections. This basic shape is retained for all three stanzas of poetic text. The melodic line of the voice part is freely varied within each stanza and contributes significantly to the rising tension of the third stanza as it continually moves upward. Wolf's shift to a tremolo in the accompaniment as well as his move to F-sharp minor instead of the G-flat major of the previous stanza acts to intensify the drama. His use of various syncopated figurations throughout adds to the restlessness of the song. A motive consisting of B-flat, C-flat, B-flat—the first three notes in the right hand of the piano part—permeates the entire song. The slight change of figure between the first and second stanzas contributes to the rising intensity.

The poems of Goethe's *West-östlicher Divan* were patterned after the works of the Persian poet Hafiz and are both philosophical and conversational in style. Wolf's settings are less dissonant than his *Wilhelm Meister* songs. "Als ich auf dem Euphrat schiffte" (As I Was Sailing on the Euphrates), for example, has a lyrical vocal line and a conjunct descending bass line in the accompaniment that is repeated throughout most of the song like a ground bass (Example 14-11). The

As I was sailing on the Euphrates,

Example 14-11. Wolf, "Als ich auf dem Euphrat schiffte" (As I Was Sailing on the Euphrates), mm. 1–2.

consonant harmonies, as well as a rocking figure in the accompaniment, complement the picture of sailing on the Euphrates and the dream image of the poem. Written in 12/8, this barcarolle joins a number of other art songs in the barcarolle literature: Schubert's "Auf dem Wasser zu singen," Schumann's "Venetianische Lieder" in *Myrten*, Fanny Mendelssohn Hensel's "Gondellied," and Mendelssohn's "Venetianisches Gondellied." "Als ich auf dem Euphrat schiffte" begins in A major but drops to A-flat major (enharmonically through G-sharp major) as the text describes the ring dropping into the water. The final section of the song returns to A major as the character Suleika addresses her lover Hatem (representing Marianne von Willemer and Goethe himself); the voice rises and the final chord remains unresolved on the dominant of the relative minor as the poem ends with a question from Suleika to her lover, "Was bedeutet dieser Traum?" ("What does this dream mean?")

The next song, "Dies zu deuten bin erbötig" (I Am Willing to Interpret This), provides Hatem's answer. (Apparently people were interpreting their dreams long before Freud!). Returning to the key of A major, Wolf uses a melodic figure in the left hand of the accompaniment that resembles an ascending version of the previous song's bass-line theme, then returns to the bass-line figure of "Als ich auf dem Euphrat schiffte," followed by both motives, which appear in various guises throughout the rest of the song.

The most famous of the Goethe lieder, "Anakreons Grab" (Anacreon's Grave), like "Gleich und Gleich" and "Blumengruss" (Flower Greeting), is a delicate masterpiece. Its extreme chromaticism, particularly in mm. 8–9, anticipates the move to atonality among the next generation of composers. The harmonic uncertainty of the middle section mirrors the question, "whose grave is this?" in the text. The instability is resolved with the answer, "it is Anacreon's resting place," as the music moves to G major. "Anakreons Grab" is unified by the elegiac mood that permeates the entire song and by several short motives, the most prominent being the two half-step motives, one ascending and the other descending, that first appear in the opening measure. In the interlude before the final two stanzas of text, the piano's introduction is repeated a perfect fourth above its original appearance, but harmonically altered so the music can modulate back to the key of D major; the accompaniment to the final lines of text parallels the piano part for the first two lines of text, with only the slightest variances in harmony and figuration until the final measure. The descending chromatic postlude represents an interesting contrast to the rising chromatic middle section of the song.

The German love for southern Europe is reflected in Wolf's Spanish and Italian songbooks. Goethe, Wagner, Fanny and Felix Mendelssohn, Nietzsche, Wolf, and Brahms had all traveled to Italy. There was a fascination for southern themes and dance rhythms in European song and opera—Brahms's and Schumann's songs based on Spanish translations, Bizet's *Carmen*, Ravel's *Bolero*, and both of Wolf's operas, *Der Corregidor* and his unfinished *Manuel Venegas*, are centered on Spanish topics. For the *Spanisches Liederbuch*, Wolf selected ten sacred and thirty-four secular translations by the poet-translators Heyse and Geibel, and although Wolf does use some Spanish dance rhythms and guitar imitations, these songs are thoroughly German in character. As a group, however, they are the most passionate of all his songs.

The first six of the sacred songs focus on Jesus' family, particularly his mother Mary. The first two songs are intense pleas to the Virgin Mary—the second, "Die du Gott gebarst" (You Who Bore God), translates verbal pleas into a musical plea that permeates the entire structure of the song. The voice part, plodding in 2/2 against the 6/4 of the accompaniment, is at first chanted in a deathlike monotony (Example 14-12). The octave doublings that are so prevalent in the *Spanisches Liederbuch* and the tremendous concentration of dissonance in many places point to the style of Scriabin. Wolf combines a variation of his plea motive in m. 19 with a dissonant octave doubling of C and D that becomes a tone-cluster of B-flat, C, D, E-flat on the words "Herrin, ganz zu dir mich wende" (Lady, I turn entirely to you). While the pleading motive is played softly, sforzandos on the repeated octaves of C and D create a sense of foreboding. (Example 14-13).

You who bore God, Immaculate one,

Example 14-12. Wolf, "Die du Gott gebarst" (You, Who Bore God), mm. 1–4.

Lady, I turn entirely to you,

Example 14-13. Wolf, "Die du Gott gebarst," mm. 17–20.

The gentle "Nun wandre Maria" follows. Like Brahms's "O wüsst ich doch den Weg zurück" (Oh, That I Knew the Way Back), this song complements the image of wandering with continuous motion in the accompaniment, in this case rhythmically steady thirds that perhaps symbolize Mary and Joseph walking slowly together.

The secular Spanish songs, like the sacred, are highly passionate, but this passion is spent on human love instead of love of God. Wolf chose poems of misery, anger, delight, and humor for this varied group.

Probably the most famous of the Spanish songs, "In dem Schatten meiner Locken" (In the Shadow of My Tresses), illustrates the dance rhythms and the feel of castanets that Wolf uses in so many of these songs. A young woman contemplates the playful nature of her love and her lover who is sleeping in the shadow of her hair. The inflection of her question, "Weck' ich ihn nun auf?" (Shall I wake him?), is captured in the rise of the vocal line and the sense of anticipation created in the accompaniment with the rising minor thirds in the right hand; the answer, "Ach nein!" (Ah, no!), is reflected in the harmonic shift from D major to D-flat major and the dropping vocal line (Example 14-14).

Example 14-14. Wolf, "In dem Schatten meiner Locken" (In the Shadow of My Tresses), mm. 6–12.

In "Mögen alle bösen Zungen" (Let All the Evil Tongues), Wolf uses a lighthearted musical theme to portray the carefree girl of the song who refuses to bow to the wicked gossips around her. A staccato melody and a "clucking" figure represent the wagging tongues of the gossips in this charming and very tightly organized song.

In "Alle gingen, Herz, zur Ruh" (All Have Gone to Rest, Heart), a text also set by Robert Schumann, the poet sadly addresses his heart. Wolf begins with a repeated C in the bass of the accompaniment, which Eric Sams calls the "uneasy throb of the sorrowing heart."[5] The complexity of this rhythmic figure, which permeates the entire song (Example 14-15), masks any basic rhythmic pulse (a fairly frequent technique with Wolf, as was mentioned earlier). The misery of the poet is reflected by the music in the middle of the song through a thickening texture in the accompaniment, an extended, disjunct vocal line, and highly dissonant harmonies that anticipate the style of the Russian composers Scriabin and Medtner. As the poet's misery subsides to a dull acceptance, the vocal line moves to longer rhythmic values; the accompaniment becomes more consonant and has a thinner texture, as the melody of the opening vocal line is combined with the throbbing rhythm of the prelude.

Example 14-15. Wolf, "Alle gingen, Herz, zur Ruh" (All Have Gone to Rest, Heart), m. 1.

The beautiful "Bedeckt mich mit Blumen" (Cover Me with Flowers) is one of many poems that links flowers, love, and death. The poem, attributed to Maria Doceo, states that the poet is dying of love and asks that jasmine and lilies be used to cover her grave. In the nineteenth century, the lily, traditionally a symbol of purity, love and death, was a favorite flower of British writers such as Oscar Wilde, John Ruskin (*The Stones of Venice*), and Gilbert and Sullivan (who parodied the lily in *Patience*); of French symbolist poets such as Lahor ("L'extase" [Ecstasy], set by Duparc) and Debussy ("De Fleurs" from *Proses Lyriques*, set by Debussy); and of the German poet Heine ("Die Rose, die Lilie" and "Ich will meine Seele tauchen" set by Schumann in *Dichterliebe*). Also, the act of love as a kind of dying and dying for love have frequently been popular images in both music and literature (John Dowland's "Come Again, Sweet Love Doth Now Invite").

"Bedeckt mich mit Blumen" is organized around a melodic motive that appears in the introduction (Example 14-16). The entire rhythmic portion of the motive is presented in the top line of the piano part in mm. 1–2, and the melodic motive in m. 1 is maintained

Cover me with flowers,

Example 14-16. Wolf, "Bedeckt mich mit Blumen" (Cover Me with Flowers), mm. 1–3.

throughout the song. The Wagnerian harmonies and insistent repetition of chords lends a Scriabin-like ecstasy to this lovely song. The chromatic vocal line, which sensually melts downward at the beginning of the song, is completely independent of the accompaniment; the languid movements of voice and accompaniment, combined with hemiola and rests that precede many of the repeated chords in the accompaniment, act to negate the pulse of the 6/4 meter. Wolf's musical rhythm is often guided by textual rhythms and nuances, which then become motives that are musically expanded.

"Sie blasen zum Abmarsch" (The Bugles Sound for Departure) tells the story of a girl who is left behind when her sweetheart is sent to war. Wolf graphically portrays the departing soldiers with march music, bugle calls, and drumrolls. The girl's sadness is reflected in her vocal line, which contrasts forlornly with the brisk, impersonal accompaniment. As she describes her misery, her strange vocal line is punctuated with drumroll imitations in the accompaniment. The voice part droops erratically as she states that she only wishes to converse with her pain.

The *Spanisches Liederbuch* concludes with a song of epic proportions—"Geh', Geliebter, geh' jetzt!" (Go, Beloved, Go Now)—in which a woman fervently tells her lover to leave as the dawn breaks because she is afraid they will be discovered by their neighbors. Organized in rondo form, the music continually returns to the urgent refrain, "Geh', Geliebter . . ." or the variant "Drum, Geliebter, geh' jetzt! Sieh, der Morgen dämmert" (Go Beloved, go now! See, morning is dawning). The prelude immediately communicates overwhelming urgency and stress through both rhythm and harmony: the rests in the right-hand octaves of the accompaniment lend a breathless quality to the music, as do the pressing left-hand eighth-notes followed by a rest, the chromatic movement away from the unresolved dominant seventh chord, and finally the release into a passionate resolution to F-sharp major, with a torrent of descending octaves that return throughout the song (Example 14-17). After the vocal and piano refrain, the voice dissonantly begins a half-step higher than the pedal point of the accompaniment; the 3/4 meter of the voice is pitted against the 9/8 of the piano as the awakening marketplace is described (mm. 12–15). The anxiety of the woman is again expressed with a return of the urgent opening theme; in a sudden change of mood, the music becomes calm and shifts to relatively consonant harmonies as the woman describes the morning dew, which symbolizes her tears (Example 14-18). On the third

Go, beloved, go now! See, the morning is dawning.

Example 14-17. Wolf, "Geh', Geliebter, geh' jetzt!" (Go, Beloved, Go Now!), mm. 1–7.

When the sun, shining in the sky, chases the clear pearls from the field,

Example 14-18. Wolf, "Geh', Geliebter, geh' jetzt!," mm. 37–40.

appearance of the refrain, the tension of the music continues to rise as the vocal line moves upward and the harmonies remain unresolved for three more measures. Wolf's passionate music that follows in "Fliehe denn aus meinen Armen!" (Fly then from my arms!) matches the sexual tension and release in Wagner's *Tristan und Isolde*. The song ends with the refrain, made less pressing in the piano postlude; the urgent theme of the beginning fades to a dronelike figure on the tonic in the left hand, the right hand finally arrives at F-sharp major in what sounds like "Farewell," and the rhythmic energy is dissipated by triplets alternating with two groups of duplets tied together.

The *Spanisches Liederbuch* was followed by six songs on the poems of the Swiss poet, Gottfried Keller (1819–1890). All six poems have women as their subject. The final song of the set, "Wie glänzt der helle Mond" is one of Wolf's most beautiful and touching. It paints the picture of a devout old woman who, as she gazes at the night sky, reflects that her life is over; youth has passed forever and is as far from her as the distant moon. Her picturesque view of her journey to Paradise ends with a description of St. Peter mending shoes at the gates of Heaven. Wolf envelops this poem in a mystical shroud, using the upper register of the piano to create a crystalline coldness that is enhanced by the square, hypnotically repeated chords in 8/4, at first without a third in the chord (Example 14-19). Here, again, Wolf has used the treble of the piano for the painting of a mystical scene. The old woman's journey to Heaven seems strangely graphic when Wolf shifts the accompaniment to the lower register of the piano and changes the figuration to the slow outlining of triads in the left hand. Almost every phrase of the stagnant voice part begins with a series of repeated notes, merely reciting on pitch; suddenly the voice part becomes tonal and moves up as the old woman raises her eyes to God the Father and the Holy Ghost (symbolized as a dove eating corn from the hand of God). Wolf briefly brings back the opening piano figuration, thereby suggesting an ABA' form, although he gives the voice new material; then he concludes with a rolling figure in the accompaniment to imitate St. Peter's mending shoes (mm. 29–32). The opening section of the song hovers around G minor, with the inner voice of the right-hand accompaniment primarily establishing the eerie, ethereal harmonies in the treble of the piano; Wolf then moves to F-sharp major at the end of the A sec-

How brilliantly the moon shines, so cold and distant,

Example 14-19. Wolf, "Wie glänzt der helle Mond" (How Brilliantly the Moon Shines), mm. 1–2.

tion and uses the tonic of F-sharp to shift suddenly to the key of D major in the middle register of the piano. The entire B section moves through a multitude of keys, continuing the sense of flux despite the static vocal line, to suggest the movement of the old woman up to Heaven. The final section implies A' as the music returns to the upper register of the piano, although Wolf then incorporates new musical material and concludes in G major as St. Peter appears on the scene.

Wolf's next group of songs were set to Italian poems, which had been translated into German by Paul Heyse. Like the Spanish song-book, many of these songs have texts obviously intended for a male singer, others for a female. It is considered ironic by some historians that Wolf, a composer so sensitive to fine poetry, was willing to set translations. Yet these translations are beautifully done, and in some cases they become new poems in the hands of their poet-translators. It is also sometimes suggested that Wolf was freed from his sub-ordination to the poet when he began to set these translations. "Wolf . . . at this stage of his development, after a comparative subser-vience to Mörike and Goethe, needed a lesser genre of poetry that his music could assimilate and even dominate."[6]

Certainly the Italian poems provided Wolf with some of his most charming visions! All the songs are miniatures, usually two pages in length, and most are based on poems of 8 to 10 lines. These poems, like the Spanish poetry, are direct, usually first-person points of view. Wolf's settings are a wonderful distillation of his style: thin-textured, dissonant, and expressive.

Most of the vocal melodies of the Italian songbook are repre-sentative of Wolf's melodic style—one does not walk away humming the vocal line. The voice part is independent of the accompaniment, yet incomplete without it. In fact, this melodic line, with its unexpected intervallic skips of augmented fourths, augmented and diminished fifths, minor ninths, and elevenths as well as its chromatic movements, might seem more characteristic of Webern than of a nineteenth-century song composer were it not for Wolf's harmonic definition of the melodic line. The absence of the long-lined melody, so characteristic of Schubert's style, is puzzling to many listeners. Yet the greatness and beauty of Wolf's songs are the result of a totality of parts. His harmonic originality defines his melodies and combines with his motivic organization in a truly inexplicable way to produce songs of profound loveliness.

The *Italienisches Liederbuch* appropriately begins with "Auch kleine Dinge· können uns entzücken" (Even Little Things Can

Enchant Us). This charming little song is organized around a descending scale in the left hand of the accompaniment and an arpeggiated figuration in the right hand, which is transformed into a music-box-like figure when the voice enters.

There is a conversational quality about the Italian songbook because the poetry is in the first person and the vocal line is tightly linked to word inflections. Wolf uses word-painting generously throughout this collection. Sometimes he may only imply an image. In the accompaniment of the beautiful "O wär' dein Haus durchsichtig wie ein Glas" (Oh, If Your House Were As Transparent As Glass), the delicate tinkling of glass, or perhaps even rain (another image in the poem), is suggested. At other times, particularly in moments of humor, Wolf was completely graphic, as for example, in his imitation of a donkey in "Schweig' einmal still" (Be Quiet!) (Example 14-20).

I prefer the serenade of a donkey.

Example 14-20. Wolf, "Schweig' einmal still" (Be Quiet!), mm. 18–21.

There is much variety in the *Italienisches Liederbuch*'s approach to love: humor in "Mein Liebster hat zu Tische mich geladen" (My Lover Has Invited Me to Dinner) and "Ich esse nun mein Brot" (Now I Eat My Bread); serenade in "Ein Ständchen Euch zu bringen" (I Have Come to Serenade You); misery in "Mir ward gesagt" (I Was Told); reconciliation in "Nun lass uns Frieden schliessen" (Now Let Us Make Peace); and adulation of the beloved, in "Dass doch gemalt all' deine Reize wären" (If All of Your Charms Were Painted).

One of the most beautiful songs of the collection is "Wie viele Zeit verlor ich," a song of deceptive simplicity. The short, contemplative thoughts of the speaker, which reveal his misery, are matched by short musical phrases that are constantly interrupted, either by changes in musical texture, shifts of register, or changes of key. The final phrase of text is eloquently delivered in simple recitative. It, like "Was für ein Lied" (What Song?) and "Wohl kenn' ich Euern Stand"

(How Well I Know Your Station), is a musical meditation on the text.

The very lovely "Der Mond hat eine schwere Klag erhoben" (The Moon Has Raised a Heavy Complaint) has a chanted vocal line against a chaconne-like accompaniment. The stationary vocal line and the repetitive accompaniment form many interesting dissonances.

Wolf has a marvelous vocabulary for humor. In "Wie lange schon" (How Long Already), for example, he writes a long, awkward postlude that reveals what a pitiful musician a young girl's lover is. And in the frolicking, frenetic "Ich hab in Penna einen Liebsten wohnen" (I Have One Lover Who Lives in Penna), he composes for women his own version of Mozart's catalogue aria from *Don Giovanni*.

The synthesis of poetry and music is, of course, at the heart of art song composition, and Wolf's own sensitivities weighed in on the side of text. As has already been stated, the nineteenth century was a verbal age in music. Wolf embodies the culmination of this movement, for his songs are most closely linked to a representation of poetic meaning and mood. But his treatment of text and music is not a return to the pleasant, musically nondescript settings of Reichardt or Zelter, who also granted text a dominant rôle in their songs. The originality of Wolf's music and musical characterizations is unparalleled. It is not until Maurice Ravel wrote his *Histoires naturelles* that we are again presented with such living musical portraits in song. Wolf wrote some of the most unusual works in the entire song repertory, songs that are sometimes difficult for the audience as well as the performer. Because there is rarely a predictable musical phrase or an amiably superficial melody, he demands a great deal from his audience. His works produced no school of followers, but his uncompromising music found spiritual heirs among the iconoclasts Schoenberg, Webern, and Berg.

Figure 15-1. Gustav Mahler. Photograph by A. Dupont, N.Y., 1909. Courtesy of the Library of Congress.

CHAPTER FIFTEEN

The End of an Era: Gustav Mahler and Richard Strauss

In the great German tradition two towering personalities stood at the fatal cross-roads—Gustav Mahler and Strauss.
—Norman Del Mar[1]

The lied influenced and was affected by natural and inevitable changes in the musical climate of the nineteenth century. As its grace and beauty drew it from the home into the concert hall, song became a welcome addition to the eclectic programs that were then in vogue.

But midway in the century, composers began to orchestrate a few songs of their own and of earlier composers. Liszt orchestrated not only several of his own more dramatic songs, such as "Die Loreley" and "Die drei Zigeuner," but also six of Schubert's songs including "Erlkönig" and "Der Doppelgänger." Berlioz wrote an orchestral arrangement of Schubert's "Erlkönig" and orchestrated a group of his own songs—*Nuits d'été* (Summer Nights). Brahms orchestrated several of Schubert's songs for Julius Stockhausen, who, like so many nineteenth-century performers of the lied, was an opera singer whose voice could easily project over the sound of an orchestra.

Although Hugo Wolf orchestrated some twenty-five of his songs, only a few—such as the dramatic "Prometheus"—seemed suited for any medium other than piano and voice. His songs were so idiomatically conceived for an intimate setting that his orchestrations, completed at least a year after his piano-and-voice versions,

309

appear to have been inspired by his desire to find a wider audience for his music.[2] Most of his orchestrated songs were published after he lost his sanity or after he died.

Both Gustav Mahler and Richard Strauss, following in the footsteps of Richard Wagner, wrote in a grand style that was highly suited to the voluptuous sounds and colors of the orchestra. They also happened to be two of the most prominent orchestral conductors at the turn of the century. Having the resources of the orchestra at their disposal and possessing great skills in orchestration, they quite naturally chose to orchestrate some of their songs.

GUSTAV MAHLER

For Gustav Mahler (1860–1911), song was at the core of his grand orchestral concepts. Not only did he orchestrate over half of his more than forty songs,[3] but he used song material and singing throughout his symphonic works. His First Symphony, for example, has themes from his song cycle *Lieder eines fahrenden Gesellen*, his Symphonies No. 2 and No. 3 have song material as themes, Symphonies No. 5 and No. 6 were inspired by the *Kindertotenlieder*, and Symphonies No. 2, No. 3, No. 4, and No. 8 are written for orchestra and voice—soloists, chorus, or both. *Das Lied von der Erde*, written in 1908–09 for orchestra, tenor soloist, and either contralto or baritone soloist, falls into its own unique category, symphonic in concept but united with solo voices singing Chinese poetry from the *Chinesische Flöte*, translated by Hans Bethge.

The lied as an intimate genre for home and recital hall was supplanted in most of Mahler's work by song that was designed for large concert halls. His romantic wanderer in *Lieder eines fahrenden Gesellen* transfers personal suffering to a cosmic level and requires grand forces to transmit the message. Mahler's songs reveal many new paths that were being explored at the end of the century, paths that ultimately led to the end of the romantic lied.

Most of Mahler's earliest songs, written between 1880 and 1890, were for piano and voice. Three of these for tenor were settings of Mahler's own poems and called, simply, *Lieder*. A more extensive group, *Lieder und Gesänge*, a random collection of manuscripts renamed later by Mahler's publisher as *Lieder und Gesänge aus der Jugendzeit*, consisted mostly of poetry from *Des Knaben Wunderhorn*, with one poem by Mahler, two poems by R. Leander, and two translations from Tirso de Molina's *Don Juan*.[4] The Wunderhorn poetry was to permeate Mahler's music for almost seventeen years: in another group of songs for voice and orchestra, *Lieder aus "Des Knaben Wunderhorn"* (1892–98); in two separate songs for voice and orchestra, "Revelge" and "Der Tamboursg'sell"; in his Symphonies No. 2, No. 3, and No. 4; and in the famous orchestral cycle *Lieder eines fahrenden Gesellen* (1883–96). Even the text of this cycle, written mainly by Mahler, begins with poetry from *Des Knaben Wunderhorn*, which Mahler dredged from his childhood memory.[5]

After 1891, Mahler composed most of his songs with orchestral accompaniments, obviously realizing that the enlarged scope provided by the orchestra was more suited to his ideas. These songs include the *Kindertotenlieder* (poems by Rückert)' and four of five other lieder on Rückert poetry (1901–04). "Liebst du um Schönheit," one of the five Rückert lieder, was not orchestrated by Mahler but by Max Puttmann. While all of these songs exist in scores with piano accompaniment that were prepared by Mahler, their artistic intent is obviously fulfilled in their orchestral form.

Mahler's songs for voice and piano present the map of a future landscape. His piano accompaniments, like Wagner's, are not always idiomatically written for the piano and even call for the imitation of sounds the piano does not produce. Some of the monotony in a few of these songs is the result of his doubling the voice part with the piano and of his chordal figurations that rhythmically lock the piano to the vocal line.

His most successful songs are those in which he gives the piano its own musical material. The lyrical accompaniment of "Frühlingsmorgen" (Spring Morning), for example, delicately sets the scene for a fragrant spring morning, with the linden tree tapping gently on the window of a sleeping girl while birds sing and bees buzz (Example 15-1). This lovely through-composed song is unified by material from the introduction recurring in the song's interlude and postlude.

In Mahler's playful "Ablösung im Sommer" (Relief in Summer), each of two birds, the cuckoo and the nightingale, has a separate piano figuration that defines its character: the cuckoo, who has just died, is given an accompaniment in a minor key that is melodically disjunct with a distinct rhythmic motive; the nightingale is portrayed with sparkling scale figurations in a major key to emphasize its beautiful voice. The cuckoo's motive unifies this through-composed song, reappearing in various rhythmic and melodic guises. The voice also

The linden tree knocks on the window with its branches, blossoms [hanging]

Example 15-1. Mahler, "Frühlingsmorgen" (Spring Morning), mm. 5–8.

imitates the cuckoo with the interval of a minor third sung staccato on the word "Kukuk!" The cuckoo was a popular bird in the Wunderhorn poetry and is imitated frequently with major and minor thirds in Mahler's songs. In "Lob des hohen Verstandes" (Praise of Superior Wit), Mahler brings back the cuckoo and nightingale but also includes a humorous imitation of the donkey's bray in the vocal line with the interval of a seventeenth!

Word-painting was an important expressive device for Mahler in all his songs, whether accompanied by piano or orchestra. As the previous examples indicate, word-painting can be highly graphic, as in the donkey's bray, or merely suggestive, as in the delicate scale passages of the nightingale's piano part. He created an interesting array of bird sounds that were delegated to either the piano or the voice. Like many other composers, he sometimes resorted to a simple trill (Example 15-2). In Example 15-3 from "Wenn mein Schatz Hochzeit mach" (When My Sweetheart Has Her Wedding Day), from the *Lieder eines fahrenden Gesellen,* he combined a trill in the accompaniment with a bird call in the voice.

The lark is awake,

Example 15-2. Mahler, "Frühlingsmorgen," mm. 15–18.

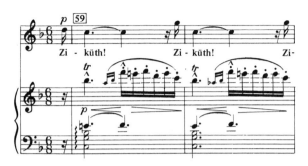

Example 15-3. Mahler, "Wenn mein Schatz Hochzeit macht" (When My Sweetheart Has Her Wedding Day), in *Lieder eines fahrenden Gesellen* (Songs of a Wayfarer), mm. 59–60.

His Wunderhorn writing is rhythmically strong, with many square rhythmic figures and dance meters occurring throughout, along with highly graphic word-painting. Many of these poems are about soldiers and war, represented by drumrolls, bugles, and marching music: "Aus! Aus!" (Out! Out!), "Zu Strassburg auf der Schanz'" (At Strassburg on the Entrenchments), "Revelge," "Der Tamboursg'sell," "Trost im Unglück" (Comfort in Misfortune) (Example 15-4). In "Scheiden und Meiden" (Parting and Avoiding), he adds yet another version of the galloping horse to the nineteenth-century repertoire (Example 15-5).

Mahler reveals his sense of the piano's restrictions in songs where he asks the pianist to imitate the sound of other musical instruments. In "Zu Strassburg auf der Schanz'," the opening phrase is to be played as if it were a shawm or alphorn: the piano is imitating a shepherd's pipe that lures a young soldier to desert his post and return home. In "Phantasie" (Fantasy), Mahler directs the pianist to sound like a harp (Example 15-6). It was a small step for Mahler to forget the piano

Example 15-4. Mahler, "Der Tamboursg'sell" (The Drummer Boy), mm. 3–5.

Three horsemen rode out to the gate! Farewell!

Example 15-5. Mahler, "Scheiden und Meiden" (Parting and Avoiding), mm. 5–7.

Example 15-6. Mahler, "Phantasie" (Fantasy), mm. 1–2.

altogether and score his songs for harp or whatever other instrumental colors he needed. (Certain figurations in the piano-accompanied songs lend themselves to predictable instruments in Mahler's orchestrations. In "Zu Strassburg auf der Schanz'," the arpeggios in mm. 43–46 would most likely be given to the harp if this song were orchestrated.)

Mahler took an Austrian country dance, the Ländler, as the foundation for "Hans und Grete," a robust, charming folk song that also appears in the second movement of his First Symphony. He successfully captured the Gemütlichkeit of the text with his slightly varied strophic setting and disjunct melody for the voice, which ends each stanza with a yodel. While anchoring the music to the tonic chord, Mahler had both piano and voice proceed in simple, strictly rhythmic gestures to paint the picture of a stylized country dance. He also used the Ländler in his symphonies and in several of the Wunderhorn settings such as the silly, humorous song, "Selbstgefühl" (Self-confidence).

Not only did many of Mahler's songs reappear in his symphonies; material from one song might also be used in another. His "Nicht wiedersehen!" (Never to see you again!) is oddly similar to "Die zwei blauen Augen" (The Two Blue Eyes) from *Lieder eines fahrenden*

Gesellen. The subject of death seems to have suggested the same dirgelike repetition of octaves moving up and down a perfect fourth in the accompaniment as the young lover says good-bye to his sweetheart in the cemetery. In "Zu Strassburg auf der Schanz'," a song in which a young deserter realizes that he will be shot, the music also has elements of the more famous "Die zwei blauen Augen"; a death march is suggested by halting rhythmic figures in both songs.

Mahler's imitation of nature, choice of folk poetry, and implied folk style impart a hardy, rustic character to many of his songs from the Wunderhorn period. In "Ich ging mit Lust durch einen grünen Wald" (I Went with Delight Through the Green Forest), he uses the piano to reinforce a lovely bucolic picture, with bird songs in the right hand and open fifths in the left hand that become drones when he precedes them with grace notes. Even the sophisticated second song of *Lieder eines fahrenden Gesellen* mimics the folk idiom: its simple, direct rhythms, a vocal line that is pushed squarely forward, a drone figure, and graphic word-painting (see Example 15-3) create a mood of robust cheerfulness.

Mahler's vocal lines are generally demanding, covering a wide range, and are often operatic in their expansive sweep. "Die zwei blauen Augen" (*Lieder eines fahrenden Gesellen*), for example, encompasses a range of nearly two octaves. A surprising number of his songs cover a vocal range of at least an octave and a sixth, even among the unorchestrated songs such as "Selbstgefühl" and "Hans und Grete," both of which have two-octave ranges.

A great many nineteenth-century musical currents converge in the works of Mahler. Beethoven's use of soloists and chorus in the Ninth Symphony, Berlioz's orchestration of his songs *Nuits d'été*, Schubert's dramatic setting of "Prometheus," Wagner's broadening of the orchestral rôle—all find transformation in Mahler's music. Even Brahms and Wagner are reconciled to some extent here. Mahler coupled Wagner's expansive orchestral writing and highly expressive grand style with a Brahmsian lyricism. Like Brahms, Mahler molded folk material into emotional, sophisticated music, and both composers found great inspiration in Brentano and Arnim's folk collection *Des Knaben Wunderhorn*.

One of Mahler's most famous songs, "Ich ging mit Lust durch einen grünen Wald," has a triadic melody that is very reminiscent of Brahms's vocal lines (Example 15-7). Another early song, "Erinnerung" (Memory), 1889, represents a beautiful linking of the styles of Brahms and Wolf. Its lyrical voice part, triple meter, and

Ich ging mit Lust durch ei-nen grü-nen Wald, ich hört' die Vög-lein sin - gen.
I went with joy through a green forest, I heard the birds singing.

Example 15-7. Mahler, "Ich ging mit Lust" (I Went with Delight), in *Des Knaben Wunderhorn* (The Youth's Magic Horn), mm. 1–6.

pedal point accompaniment, filled with Viennese melancholy, is highly reminiscent of Brahms's songs. Yet its chromatic vocal line and passionate, dissonant harmonies are Mahler's own adaptation of Wolf's style.

Mahler, one of the great opera conductors of his time, published no operas, although he tried writing for this medium early in his career. He found the symphony a more sympathetic vehicle for his dramatic ideas, although he had to stretch the definitions of traditional symphonic form to meet his own requirements. His decision to incorporate song material into the symphony is an interesting one. Song, particularly folk song, is almost the antithesis of the sophisticated symphony. But Mahler, like Brahms, while filled with highly complex musical ideas, was also attracted to the simple folk song. The intimacy, tunefulness, and honest emotion of the folk song was obviously important to Mahler, who returned again and again to this source of inspiration.

Unlike Hugo Wolf or Robert Schumann, Mahler did not choose to set the finest poetry to music. In fact, as the quote from his wife, Alma, indicated in Chapter 1 "Poetry and Music," he believed that great poetry was an independent entity that would be marred and desecrated if it were set to music. Also, while he was directly inspired by words, he was often at a loss to find words other than his own that suited his aims (as he himself stated in the excerpt from a letter to Arthur Seidl quoted in Chapter 1). Yet in 1901 Mahler turned his attention to the poetry of Friedrich Rückert, a poet and professor of Oriental languages. This resulted in ten settings of Rückert's poems and appears to be the beginning of Mahler's growing appreciation for Eastern mysticism that culminated in *Das Lied von der Erde*.[6]

Mahler covered a great range of subjects in his Wunderhorn lieder: love, spring, soldiers going to war, death, and cheerful, humorous poems such as "Um schlimme Kinder artig zu machen (In Order to Make Bad Children Good), "Des Antonius von Padua Fischpredigt," and "Hans und Grete." His *Lieder eines fahrenden Gesellen*, which come from this same period, tell a tragic story of lost love. The lover finally finds peace under the linden tree, a peace that is symbolically defined with a musical dirge.

Gradually, poems of sadness and resignation began to dominate Mahler's texts. His fascination for morose, melancholy topics and musical themes has generated much discussion among scholars. Mahler, like Schubert, came from a family where many of his brothers and sisters died in childhood. Richard Kravitt points out that Mahler's close brush with death in 1901 added to his preoccupation with death and immortality.[7] Yet Mahler's decision to use poetry about the death of children—the *Kindertotenlieder* on the poems of Rückert—even when understood as a manifestation of his preoccupation with death, is strangely morbid. He stated that he found the inspiration for these songs when "I placed myself in the situation that a child of mine had died."[8] Rückert's touching outpouring of grief over the death of his own two children resulted in more than four hundred poems, a natural, spontaneous response to his personal tragedy. But Mahler's choice of this topic is more difficult to comprehend: why try to imagine such tragedy, and how can one sing about the death of children? Death, of course, was a topic of interest to many song composers; but their musical treatment of a text usually allowed a degree of distance and "artistic" abstraction that Mahler's highly personalized contemplation of death does not. Brahms used a metaphor to explain death: "Der Tod, das ist die kühle Nacht" (Death Is the Cool Night); Schubert's "Erlkönig" merely symbolizes death, and even his "Der Tod und das Mädchen" allows the listener the space of observing the confrontation of a young girl and death. But Mahler's meeting with death is in the first person: "Das Unglück geschah nur mir allein" (The grief happened to me alone) and "Wenn dein Mütterlein tritt zur Tür herein . . . fällt auf ihr Gesicht erst der Blick mir nicht, sondern auf die Stelle . . . wo würde dein lieb Gesichtchen sein . . . O du, o du, des Vaters Zelle" (When your mother walks in the door, at first I do not see her face but look at the place where your beloved little face would be . . . oh you, your father's cell.) Many singers choke on these words. This view of death comes from the eyes of the bereaved. Mahler was later to look on these songs quite differently after he lost his own beloved child: "When I really lost my daughter, I could not have written these songs anymore." He could no longer allow himself "to study or to conduct the *Kindertotenlieder*."[9]

Mahler considered his orchestral songs as part of the lied tradi-

tion, calling performances of his songs "Lieder-Abende mit
Orchester."[10] But he was working with a larger concept of sound than
his contemporary Hugo Wolf or the earlier composers of the art song.
This required a realignment of musical elements so that the illusion of
intimacy could be maintained in the face of the increased forces of
the orchestra. In the dramatic songs such as "Ich hab' ein glühend
Messer" (I Have a Gleaming Knife) from *Lieder eines fahrenden
Gesellen*, the balance between voice and orchestra is not always
successfully achieved, sometimes shifting too far in favor of the
orchestra. Some words are lost, for example, in the performance of
the loud, rapidly sung phrase "Nicht bei Tag, nicht bei Nacht, wenn
ich schlief!" (Not by day, not by night when I sleep) and in the
growing frenzy of the section "wenn ich aus dem Traum auffahr' "
(When I start up from my dream). Even the great *Das Lied von der
Erde* does not always keep a successful balance between voice and
orchestra, a problem partly resolved by absolutely obeying the
dynamic markings of the score to keep the orchestral sound from
overwhelming the voices (most halls do not have the resources of
Bayreuth with its covered pit) and by relying on extremely large,
focused voices.

Mahler's orchestration of the Rückert songs avoids these difficulties through his contrapuntal writing and careful balancing of instruments and voice. The beginning of "Nun will die Sonn' so hell
aufgehn!" (Now Will the Sun Rise As Brightly) from *Kindertotenlieder* illustrates this most clearly with its sparse scoring for two horns,
oboe, bassoon, and voice. The independence of each instrument's
musical line (including the voice) also permits the greatest clarity
and interplay of sound. "In diesem Wetter!" (In This Weather!) is the
only song from *Kindertotenlieder* in which the successful balancing
of forces depends on a meticulous conductor. Here the voice can be
swallowed up as it chants the words "In diesem Wetter" in a low part
of the vocal range against the dramatic brass instruments.

Mahler, like Schumann, gave his songs many preludes,
interludes, and postludes. These instrumental sections are used to
complete musical ideas, introduce new material, and increase levels
of dramatic intensity by raising dynamic levels beyond those possible when the voice is present. But the most obvious shift in Mahler's
songs from the traditional vocabulary of the romantic lied is his use of
instrumental colors to further his interpretation. Mahler's piano
scores of the orchestrated songs, while beautiful, are simply incomplete without his palette of orchestral color. In fact, many of his

musical figurations are obviously conceived for some instrument other than the piano, and the piano sound is pale in comparison to the orchestrated versions. In *Lieder eines fahrenden Gesellen*, for example, Mahler's use of harp from measure 37 to the end of "Die zwei blauen Augen" clarifies the importance of the triplet figuration in measure 39 and acts to reveal his complete idea. Likewise, in "Ich hab' ein glühend Messer," he achieves a cutting sound with brass and woodwinds, reflecting more dramatically than in the piano version the image of the knife in the breast of the wayfarer. His use of the glockenspiel in the *Kindertotenlieder* unifies the cycle by appearing in the first and last song and serves as a suggestion of bells.[11]

Melody and lyricism are fundamental in all of Mahler's works. Many of the Wunderhorn melodies have both disjunct and linear features, conveying a robust quality that complements their folk song roots. But the ten Rückert lieder are totally concentrated in their lyricism. The vocal lines—long and soaring—combine with an accompaniment in which instrumental lines are woven together into one fabric along with the voice. Voice and accompaniment carry melodic material with equal responsibility as melodic ideas move freely between them.

Hans Joachim Moser's statement about Schumann's piano writing applies equally well to Mahler's orchestral writing: he uses the orchestra to "express the inexpressible, voicing a meaning that the words of the poet can only suggest." Mahler had an exquisite understanding of instrumental colors, which he combined with the human voice to produce the most personal, emotional sounds in all of song literature. One has only to compare the piano and orchestral versions of "Ich bin der Welt abhanden gekommen" (I Am Lost to the World) to understand that the piano was not part of Mahler's ideal sound. He depended on the sustaining powers of the woodwinds and the strings, on the deep resonance of the harp and the muffled brilliance of the French horn, on a variety of voices and colors.

Most of Mahler's songs lie outside the stylistic boundaries of the art song as an intimate poetic genre for voice and piano. His orchestration of song altered the nature of what the nineteenth-century song had been. Yet all of his music represents an unusual cross-relationship between song and symphonic writing; he moved the lied into a creative world that was uniquely his own.

Figure 15-2. Richard Strauss, age 24, when he was appointed third Kapellmeister of the Munich Court opera. Reproduction of photograph. Courtesy of the Library of Congress.

RICHARD STRAUSS

My first attempts at composition (at the age of six) consisted of a Christmas carol, for which I "painted" the notes myself, but my mother wrote the words below the notes since I could not then write small enough.

—Richard Strauss[12]

The most powerful of them [the new German composers] is Strauss: he is a volcano, too. His music burns, smokes, sputters, stinks, and mows down everthing before it. He is the decadent Attila of German music.

—Romain Rolland[13]

Songs such as "Allerseelen" (1883), "Ständchen" (1887), and the wonderfully evocative "Traum durch die Dämmerung" (1895) prove that Strauss is one of the masters of the nineteenth-century Lied.

—Donald Jay Grout[14]

The long life of Richard Strauss (1864–1949) takes him beyond the time span alotted to the nineteenth-century lied, yet much of his songwriting reflects romantic aesthetic ideals. Of his more than two hundred songs, nearly half were written by 1900 and are the most popular of his lieder, with the exception of the *Vier letzte Lieder* (Four Last Songs). This discussion will focus on his early works up to Op. 48 (written in 1900).

Although songwriting was often of secondary interest for Strauss, songs, nevertheless, mark several important periods in his life. At the age of six, Strauss wrote his first composition—a song; many of his most popular songs today were those which he wrote for his wife in the early years of their marriage; and his last compositions were songs—the *Vier letzte Lieder*. Songs were a useful medium for Strauss during the years of his wife's career as a singer, for she devoted herself to his vocal music, and he accompanied her at the piano and with the orchestras he conducted. His orchestrating of song seems inevitable in light of the fact that he was a famous conductor, a magnificent orchestrator, and was married to a singer who often traveled with him when he conducted.

From its inception at the end of the eighteenth century, the art song changed and adapted to the musical and social conditions of the times. The grandeur of Strauss's writing is consistent with the music that marked the end of the century. Wagner's expansion of the tonal vocabulary influenced all composers in the second half of the century, and his use of grand themes and large orchestras became the starting point for other composers. Both Wolf and Strauss reflected Wagner's influence, although each followed those ideals along different paths.

Strauss blurred the line between art song and opera with his expansive vocal lines, frequent reliance on coloratura, and dramatic demands on the voice. In fact, his music illustrates several important trends that became obvious at the end of the nineteenth century. First, traditional musical forms of the eighteenth and early nineteenth centuries were so freely manipulated by late nineteenth-century composers that many of these forms became unrecognizable or were completely discarded. Then, too, the vocabulary of tonality had continued to expand in the works of the late nineteenth-century composers. And many composers found it perfectly acceptable, even desirable, to compose songs with orchestral accompaniments. The orchestra itself reached epic proportions by the end of the century, a trend reflected in the symphonic works of Strauss, Mahler, and Bruckner. When we look at Mahler's *Das Lied von der Erde* or Strauss's Op. 33, songs with lush orchestral accompaniments, we see that the art song, even in its demise, is a barometer of the nineteenth century, revealing many changes in the musical world. Finally, concert programs became more uniform in their offerings at the end of the century, so that symphonic concerts less frequently presented songs for voice and piano but instead offered orchestrated vocal works.

Richard Strauss is the only nineteenth-century song composer who also wrote successful operas. Perhaps he was successful in both because he blurred the line between these two mediums. Many styles and forms had merged and lost their distinctive character by the end of the nineteenth century. Still, at his best, Strauss made subtle distinctions between opera and song, retaining the spirit of each: his audacious flamboyance in *Salome* exploits the ultimate drama of opera, yet he was able to realize great intimacy in songs such as "Morgen" (Tomorrow) and "Die Nacht" (Night) and to balance the dramatic and the intimate in "Befreit" (Release) and "Wie sollten wir geheim sie halten" (How Can We Keep [our love] a Secret?).

Composers such as Wolf and Schumann could achieve the most profound intimacy in their lieder but were unable to shift to the dramatic demands of opera. Wolf's failure to understand the difference between these mediums is exemplified by his inclusion of art songs such as "In dem Schatten meiner Locken" in his opera *Der Corregidor*, with decidedly undramatic results.

Occasionally, stylistic material from one genre appeared to merge with Strauss's other genre: the excessive use of coloratura in "Amor" (Cupid), Op. 68, No. 5 (1918) echoes the demanding style of Zerbinetta's role in *Ariadne auf Naxos* (1916). The virtuosic talent of the performer becomes an end in itself and a hindrance to the unity of word and tone, although the coloratura is sometimes used to highlight such words as "Flamme" (flame). The elements that were so fundamental to the nineteenth-century lied become sidetracked in the athletic display of the voice in preference to the intimate coordination of musical and textual meaning and mood (Example 15-8).

Example 15-8. Strauss, "Amor" (Cupid), mm. 56–59.

Strauss's songwriting finds many harmonic and stylistic counterparts in his operatic compositions as, for example, in the generous use of parallel thirds in the high register of the piano in "Heimkehr" (Homecoming) (1886), which calls to mind sections of *Der Rosenkavalier* (1911). Only occasionally did the literal transfer of material occur, as in the melody from "O lieber Künstler" (Oh Dear Artist), Op. 66, No. 6 (1918), which appears in his opera *Capriccio* (1942).

Music historian Alfred Orel, who once turned pages when Strauss was accompanying Elisabeth Schumann in a recital of his songs during the 1920s, offered an interesting account of how genuine the connection between song and opera was for Strauss. Orel recounts that Strauss often not only expanded the musical material that appeared on the printed page but improvised between songs while Ms. Schumann was acknowledging the audience's applause.

> It was always passages from his operas with which he made the transition to the new song, and specifically passages which were musically·closely related to the song in question, but revealed that close relationship only now in the way he played them. Thus

before "Du meines Herzens Kroenelein" he played very softly—
apparently entirely for himself—the famous closing duet from
Der Rosenkavalier. . . . It was an irrefutable demonstration of the
great unity which encompasses Richard Strauss's total oeuvre.[15]

Strauss's songs are a staple of the modern recital program,
favored by singers and audiences alike. Opera singers who appear
frequently as recitalists, often mix genres, including opera arias on
their programs. For them, Strauss's songs represent the best of both
worlds.

A haphazardness in the quality of Strauss's songs, ranging from
the superb to the indifferent, was recognized by a distinguished contemporary of Strauss, composer Alban Berg: "some very nice, some
cheap stuff."[16] Critic Ernest Newman seems not to have liked
Strauss's songs at all, stating in his biography of Richard Strauss that
"comparatively few of [Strauss's] Lieder have much chance of
survival. . . . There is a superfluity of this pretentious emptiness in
Strauss's songs—pounds upon pounds of notes from which we can
hardly squeeze a half-ounce of feeling or even of meaning."[17]

A few music historians exclude Strauss from their discussion of
the nineteenth-century art song, partly because he sometimes set
second-rate poetry (as if he were the only one!) and was casual in his
handling of the poetic text in his early years. A more valid problem
centers on the same issue that has been discussed in connection with
Mahler: his orchestration of song, which removed the lied from the
intimacy of the recital hall to the grandeur of the concert hall. Even
those of his songs which were not orchestrated are frequently so
dramatic that they easily lend themselves to orchestration.

Actually, the majority of Strauss's songs are for voice and piano,
not voice and orchestra. Approximately one-fifth of these he later
orchestrated, some many years after their piano-accompanied versions. But his songs do lend themselves to orchestration, and
numerous arrangements and orchestrations of Strauss's songs have
been made by other composers. In fact, the popular "Zueignung"
(Dedication) was orchestrated by conductor Robert Heger in 1932,
and Strauss used this version on a number of occasions when he
conducted. Strauss's own orchestral version of "Zueignung" did not
appear until 1940, an arrangement that alters the ending to incorporate the words "du wunderschöne Helena" (you, beautiful
Helena) in honor of the Czech soprano Viorica Ursuleac, who sang
the role of Helen in his opera *Die ägyptische Helena* and to whom
Strauss dedicated several songs.

Some of the vitality of Strauss's songs can be attributed to his frequent use of poetry that was written by his contemporaries such as Richard Dehmel (1863–1920), Detlev von Liliencron (1844–1909), and Hermann Hesse (1877–1962). His taste in poetry, like that of Brahms, was unrefined. When he was young, Strauss appears to have sometimes superimposed his preexistent musical ideas onto poetry, but as he matured, he found his initial inspiration in the poetry he was setting. His most famous statement about song inspiration is one that was elicited by writer Friedrich von Hausegger, who had sent Strauss and other artists a questionnaire concerning artistic inspiration.

> I will have had no desire to compose for months; suddenly one evening I will pick up a volume of poetry, leaf through it care-lessly; then a poem will jolt me, and a musical idea for it will come to me, often before I've finished reading it properly: I sit down; the whole song is finished in ten minutes. . . . If I should happen, at a time when the vessel is full to the brim, so to speak, on a poem whose content is even only roughly appropriate, the opus is there in a jiffy. If the poem—all too often, alas—does not present itself, then the urge to produce something is still satisfied, and any poem that strikes me as in the least suitable gets set to music—but then it's slow work, a lot of artifice goes into it, the melody flows dourly, I have to summon up all my technical skill in order to produce something which will stand up to my own strict self-criticism.[18]

Strauss's supporters have observed that his choice of poets and poetic settings improved as he grew older. Ironically, his later songs, with the exception of the *Vier letzte Lieder*, are his least well known. Many of his early, unpublished songs, as well as many of the songs written later in his life, are based on well-known poetry. Strauss used poetry from a wide range of sources, extending from Michelangelo Buonarroti (1475–1564) to Hermann Hesse (1877–1962). But his name is linked more closely with his contemporaries, lesser poets such as John Henry Mackay (1864–1933), Karl Henckell (1864–1929), Adolf Friedrich von Schack (1815–1894), and Otto Julius Bier-baum (1865–1910). Because of Strauss's prominence, a number of his contemporaries sought to have him set their poetry to music. The poet Richard Dehmel, for example, was quite happy to have Strauss set his poetry to music but then spoke slightingly of Strauss's setting of "Befreit." After this was reported to Strauss, he stopped setting Dehmel's poetry.[19] Some historians postulate that disagreeable situa-tions of this sort, as well as Strauss's growing interest in opera, eventually caused him to lose interest in songwriting. His wife's retirement from the concert stage may also have affected his shift away from songwriting.

Unlike some of the composers whose style was influenced by Wagner, such as Cornelius and Mahler, Strauss wrote none of the poetry he set to music. He did make slight changes in some of the poetry he used, and he frequently repeated words to suit his musical phrases. In "Kling!" (Sound), for example, there is a generous repetition of "Klings" and "Sings". He is generally successful in preserving the textual accents within the musical setting and does this within the context of highly varied vocal lines. Notice, for example, the recitative-like flexibility of "Ruhe, meine Seele" and the fluid patterns of "Die Nacht." "Die Nacht" begins with a melodic line that does not reveal a clear metrical pattern; because the second beat of the 3/4 measure is emphasized with a long-held note, the first two eighth-notes of the vocal line could be perceived by the listener as an anacrusis rather than as the first beat of the measure. Furthermore, the repeated eighth-notes of the piano in the first three measures do not define the meter, either (Example 15-9). Strauss cleverly catches the listener off guard with unexpectedly irregular phrase lengths, creating a kind of musical enjambment, an interesting technique that he used often (mm. 18–27). In "Zueignung" he also extends the musical phrase at the words "Und beschworst darin die Bösen, bis ich" (and you banished the evil from it, until I) to heighten the grandeur of the final stanza.

Out of the forest comes the night,

Example 15-9. Strauss, "Die Nacht" (The Night), mm. 1–3.

Strauss's determination to compose even when he was not inspired surely played a major rôle in determining the uneven quality of his songs. A few of his early songs such as "Geduld" (Patience), Op. 10, provide his critics with some examples of improper musical accents and a lack of subtlety in differentiating important and unimportant words in phrases.

Still, words were of consequence in Strauss's musical vision. He spent an entire opera, *Capriccio* (1940–42), debating the significance of words versus music (an opera that was never widely appreciated by audiences) and carried on a lengthy correspondence with writer-scholar Romain Rolland concerning correct declamation during his setting of Oscar Wilde's French version of *Salomé*.[20] But in the correspondence between Strauss and Rolland, Strauss, in discussing Debussy's *Pelléas et Mélisande*, does come out on the side of music:

> So far as I'm concerned, I'm a musician above everything else. Once there's music in a work, I want it to be the master, I don't want it to be subordinate to anything else. That's too humble. I don't say that poetry is inferior to music. But the true poetic dramas: Schiller, Goethe, Shakespeare, are self-sufficient: they don't need music. Where there is music, it must carry all before it; it must not come after the poetry.[21]

In his writings, he often referred to the necessity for good diction from the singer. He even used chamber orchestration in some of his late operas to insure that the orchestra would not outweigh the singer. But he also stated that singers must emphasize consonants to insure that they can be understood.[22] He concluded that this might mean that his metronomic markings would not be absolute "in order to enable the singer to attain an unimpeded, clear pronunciation of the text according to his vocal and musical qualities, and in order to allow for the size and acoustic properties of the theatre and the distance between actor and listener."[23] Although this statement is made with respect to his operas, there is ample evidence to show that it applies to his songs as well.

In Chapter 4, "Composers, Performers, and Performances," Strauss was quoted as believing himself to be a good accompanist, "in the free manner, never entirely faithful to the music." He was also very sparing in his interpretive markings, allowing the performer considerable latitude in musical expression. He sometimes begins a song by simply implying a tempo and a dynamic level and then leaves the rest to the performer. This is certainly the case in "Zueignung." Although the pedaling is carefully marked throughout, the nebulous tempo indication, *moderato*, that governs "Zueignung" often elicits strange results from young performers who, failing to read "Zueignung's" poem, choose a tempo bordering on allegro.

Strauss had written over forty songs by 1887 when he published his first collection. Completed in 1885 when he was twenty-one years old, Op. 10 contains three of his most popular lieder: "Zueignung," "Die Nacht," and "Allerseelen" (All Souls' Day), as well as several others that are almost never performed. The texts of these songs were by a nineteenth-century poet, Hermann von Gilm zu Rosenegg (1812–1864), who is now remembered only because of Strauss's settings. All the poems in this collection have love as the basic theme, incorporating images of night, flowers, and nature—all respectable romantic subjects. Strauss was most successful in songs such as "Zueignung" that present a positive view of love; he seems to have been attracted to the happiness and contentment in love rather than to themes of despair and loss. Sometimes his poetic choices verge on the sentimental, as in his highly popular "Allerseelen." Yet "Die Zeitlose" (Meadow Saffron) is a unique poem and song in which the beautiful but poisonous flower of the saffron is equated with late love: they are both deadly!

Op. 10 is not a cycle but a collection of eight songs written for high voice, as are many of Strauss's songs. Although Strauss considered the popular "Zueignung" to be ideally suited for tenor voice, it is sung today in every imaginable range by every conceivable type of voice. Written in 1885, "Zueignung" is a worthy successor to the sublime ecstacy of Wagner's music with all the grandeur of his "Schmerzen" (Anguish) from the Wesendonk lieder. The range of "Zueignung," an octave and a fourth, is the minimum range requirement of the complete opus. Strauss not only uses this range at the climax of "Zueignung," but he word-paints at the same time, placing *heilig* (holy) on the highest note of the song and *sank* (sank) on the lowest note (Example 15-10).[24] The dramatic skip from d^2 to e^1 not only plays into the meaning of the word *sank* but is a fairly common device for Strauss in highlighting words. There are numerous

holy, holy sank on your heart

Example 15-10. Strauss, "Zueignung" (Dedication), mm. 25–26.

examples of large intervallic leaps both up and down in the vocal lines of Strauss's songs to accent important words. "Ach Lieb, ich muss nun scheiden" (Ah Love, I Must Depart) from Op. 21, is based almost entirely on a linear voice part but incorporates an odd set of wide intervals in the final section to emphasize the word *Beiden* (both). There is an athletic charm in the sprightly octave leaps in the vocal line of "Ständchen," from Op. 17 on the words "Mach auf, mach auf" (Open up, open up) (Example 15-11). In two songs from Op. 36, "Für fünfzehn Pfennige" (For Fifteen Cents) and "Hat gesagt— bleibt's nicht dabei" (He Has Said, It Will Not Stop at That), large melodic leaps are used to enhance the humorous nature of the text. In "Für fünfzehn Pfennige," Strauss plays with the words "fünfzehn Pfennige" with silly melismatic phrases that become longer and longer, including ludicrous skips that reach an octave and a seventh by the end of the song.

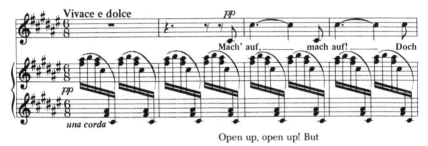

Example 15-11. Strauss, "Ständchen" (Serenade), mm. 1–4.

Strauss shows a preference, particularly in his later songs, for the high soprano voice. "Kling!" Op. 48, No. 3; "Schlagende Herzen" (Beating Hearts), Op.29, No 2; "Ich schwebe" (I Float), Op. 48, No. 2; and "Amor," Op. 68, No. 5—all are staples in the lyric soprano reper- toire and require ethereal, floating tone for their most successful realization. "Kling," with a range of an octave and a fourth extending up to high C (c^3), also has an extremely high tessitura. But certainly there are also a number of songs written specifically for low voice: both Op. 44 and Op. 51 are orchestral lieder for low voice, and Op. 51, dedicated to and premiered by Paul Knüpfer, is specifically for the bass voice.

Strauss included a variety of vocal styles in his songs as can be seen in the *Walküre*-like writing of "Wie sollten wir geheim sie halten," with its generous use of portamenti in the vocal line, its pulsing accompaniment, and the ecstatic mood of the music. But he is probably remembered more for his linear writing than for the disjunct melodic lines that are also part of his style. His long vocal lines, sometimes with melismata, and his accompaniments with their long, sustained notes and numerous harmonic shifts are memorable features of his best-loved songs (e.g., "Befreit"). Of course, his last works, the *Vier letzte Lieder*, are wonderful examples of long, sustained vocal lines that soar above their orchestral accompaniment.

The vocal line in a Strauss song is highly varied, even within a relatively short works such as "Breit über mein Haupt" (Spread over My Head). He begins with recitative-like writing for the voice and ends with coloratura (Example 15-12a and Example 15-12b). Strauss may use coloratura both for its own sake, to extend a musical phrase, and also for word-painting, as in the florid little thoughts with which the lover greets his sweetheart in "All mein Gedanken" (All My Thoughts), mm. 23–24, echoed by the piano in its postlude mm. 29–31. The extreme use of coloratura that occurs in "Amor" is also matched by pure vocalise in songs such as "Ich schwebe," which opens with an arpeggiated vocal line that covers an octave and a

Spread your black hair over my head, bend your face to me,

Example 15-12a. Strauss, "Breit' über mein Haupt" (Spread over My Head), mm. 1–4.

and the brilliance of your glance.

Example 15-12b. Strauss, "Breit' über mein Haupt," mm. 15–16.

fourth. He moves away from the lied tradition in those songs whose vocal virtuosity commands the listener's attention.

Strauss rarely relied on simple strophic form after his childhood compositions. "Zueignung," for example, is organized as a strophic variation with the rhythm of the poem's refrain, "Habe Dank" (thanks), also acting as a unifying element. Other songs, such as "Ich trage meine Minne" (I Bear My Love), fall clearly into an ABA form with material from the B section so suggestive of the A material that it is more like a mini development of A material. "Wie sollten wir geheim sie halten" is more loosely organized in an ABA' structure, while songs such as "Du meines Herzens Krönelein" (You, the Crown of My Heart), are through-composed and held together by occasional references to the opening motive (Example 15-13).

You, the crown of my heart, you

Example 15-13. Strauss, "Du meines Herzens Krönelein" (You, the Crown of My Heart), mm. 1–2.

"Allerseelen" is very loosely structured around the opening musical material of the piano (in E-flat major), which recurs at the beginning of each stanza before moving in new directions. At the beginning of stanza two, the introductory theme is syncopated and transposed briefly to D-flat over a six-four chord before moving to C minor. In its third appearance, the theme again begins in E-flat major, and the vocal part for the first time joins the piano in presenting the theme.

Strauss's "Das Rosenband" (The Rose Ribbon) is closely molded to the content of Klopstock's poem. Strauss uses an ABA'B' musical structure to reflect Klopstock's linking of the first and third stanzas of the poem through their references to a chain of roses that a young man uses to bind his sweetheart, and the linking of the second and fourth stanzas through their parallel texts, "I looked at her; my life hung on that gaze" and "she looked at me; her life hung on that gaze." The piano introduction and the first and third stanzas begin with similar music, except that stanza three moves down a whole step to G major instead of the A major of stanza one. Stanzas two and four begin with similar music, too, but also in different keys (E-flat and A major), thereby emphasizing their parallel text.

Strauss's Op. 27, his wedding gift to Pauline, includes the beautiful "Morgen!", 1894. Here he uses the accompaniment as the organizing force, brilliantly holding the song together with its AAB-coda form. The voice part, completely independent of the accompaniment, begins in mid-thought; Strauss captured this musically by having the voice part begin on the second half of a weak beat. The voice line moves at a different pace from the accompaniment, much in the style of Fauré's "Clair de lune" (Moonlight), 1887. Like "Clair de lune," the long piano introduction is the centerpiece of the song, establishing a mood of exquisite delicacy and reflectiveness. In the final section, the voice shifts to recitative as the chordal accompaniment of the piano supports the murmurs of the voice. The dynamic markings are sparse and move within the narrow range between *piano* and *pianissimo*.

"Zueignung" illustrates Strauss's progressive harmonic vocabulary, for it begins, not with the tonic or dominant, but with a mediant six-four chord in C major. Strauss exploits a harmonic virtuosity in his songs that is obviously a legacy of the Wagnerian era with its rich harmonic language; in this language, Strauss creates some of his most exalted moments. In "Kling!" for example, Strauss's music is consonant when the poet speaks of the soul's pure tone (Example 15-14a), but he uses nonfunctional, dissonant harmonies to parallel the words "von dem wütenden Harme wilder Zeiten zerrissen schon" (to have been ravished by the raging, wild times) (Example 15-14b). The song concludes with a dazzling harmonic display on the words "Kling! Sing! Kling!"—all on e^2 in the voice, using E as the third in an arpeggiated C major chord, the fifth in an A major chord, the root in an E major chord, and then again as the third of a C major chord.

The illusion of modest harmonic stability in "Du meines Herzens Krönelein" is quickly dispelled when Strauss contrasts other women to the quiet simplicity of his sweetheart. (This image is certainly out of step with our picture of Strauss's wife, Pauline.) He introduces a repeated-note figure when contrasting the artifice of others to his lover. The resulting pedal point of the repeated notes not only creates major- and minor-second dissonances with the voice but enhances the image of the beloved's openness and generosity when the accompaniment changes to an expansive arpeggio against a

Sound! My soul gives a pure tone,

Example 15-14a. Strauss, "Kling!" (Sound!), mm. 1–3.

And I already imagined the poor one to have been ravished by the raging, wild times.

Example 15-14b. Strauss, "Kling!" mm. 4–7.

The others seek love and kindness with a thousand false words, you

Example 15-15. Strauss, "Du meines Herzens Krönelein," mm. 17–20.

sustained high G-flat in the voice. In fact, G-flat, the highest note in the song, is always used when referring to the beloved (Example 15-15). Strauss's enharmonic chord spellings, shifting from G-flat major to D major and then later using a diminished seventh to move back to G-flat major, are typical tools in his tonal arsenal, as is the chromatic bass line as he approaches the end of the song. In the period preceding *Salome* (1904), Strauss's harmonic vocabulary boldly moved outside the bounds of conventional tonality. As the complexity of his harmonic setting increased, the voice part was more defined by and dependent on its harmonic foundation. The voice line is often filled with unexpected wide intervallic leaps that have been generated by unusual chord progressions. These songs obviously must be sung by singers with "good ears" and excellent vocal technique.

Ernest Newman's statement that Strauss used "pounds upon pounds" of superfluous notes is refuted in his best songs. He uses a simple, arpeggiated accompaniment in "Morgen!"; and in "Die Nacht," the restrained repetition of one note, joined by a second note, then a third, then a fourth, is one of the most beautiful accompaniments in the lieder repertoire. Even the constantly repeated eighth-note figuration that underlies "Die Nacht" enhances the image of inexorable, inescapable, ominous night (symbolizing death), which comes to steal the beloved. The stark restraint of the music highlights the rhythmic reappearance of the dotted-eighth–sixteenth-note motive; the contrary motion of voice and accompaniment in phrases such as "Nimmt vom Kupferdach des Doms" (takes from the copper roof of the cathedral) is also highly effective.

Strauss could hardly be accused of using "pounds of notes" in the recitative-like accompaniment of "Breit' über mein Haupt," or the chordal "All mein Gedanken." He relies on a simple, rocking figure in "Traum durch die Dämmerung" (Dream Through the Twilight), which enhances the dreaminess and pensive beauty of the poem and song. There is a lovely wedding of text and music in this song as the lover is drawn slowly, reflectively to his sweetheart—"Ich gehe nicht schnell, ich eile nicht" (I do not go quickly, I do not hurry). The dynamics of the music never go beyond *pianissimo*, and although Strauss word-paints in the phrase "nun geh' ich hin zu der schönsten Frau" (now I go to the most beautiul woman), with a shift of key from F-sharp major to B-flat major and a soaring vocal line, this is truly mood-painting rather than exploitation of individual words. He allows his musical ideas to dominate throughout and resists word-painting in phrases such as "Die Sonne verglomm, die Sterne ziehn" (The sun fades, the stars come out), where the melodic line does not go down for the sunset nor does it go up when the stars rise. In the haunting conclusion of the song, Strauss repeats three of the last four lines of text but uses music that began five lines from the end of the poem to create a new coordination of text and music.

Strauss's accompaniments are designed to support and highlight the voice in a grand style. Many of the piano figurations are arpeggiations of the song's harmonies, some of which, like those in "Kling!" are simple arpeggiations and others, such as those in "Ständchen," are distinctively shaped. He also uses chordal figurations, such as the repetitive triplets of "Wie sollten wir geheim," that are totally subordinate to the voice but completely essential to the driving energy that permeates the song. Because of Strauss's unexpected harmonic changes, the piano part provides the essential direction for the vocal line.

Word-painting is a common feature in the early songs, particularly the animated ones. In "All mein Gedanken," the lover's knocks and calls are graphically depicted (Example 15-16). At times his word-painting is so startling that it may even detract from the mood of the poem as, for example, in the bellowing oxen and the crying Christ Child within the placid "Die heiligen drei Könige aus Morgenland" (The Three Holy Kings from the East).

und klop-fen   und ru   -   -   fen:

and knock and call:

Example 15-16. Strauss, "All mein Gedanken" (All My Thoughts), mm. 17–18.

Some of the songs that Strauss later orchestrated manage to retain a sense of intimacy in his superb orchestration. This is certainly true of "Ruhe, meine Seele," written in 1894 but not orchestrated until 1948 while he was working on the *Vier letzte Lieder*. The orchestral version is actually an improvement on the original piano score because the orchestra sustains and colors the slow chordal changes of the accompaniment. But even the piano version, although highly static, is harmonically and formally so interesting that it is worth performing if the singer has no orchestra available. Strauss, who never limited himself in performance to what he had written, kept the piano sonorities from completely dying away by repeating them even when no repetition was indicated and increasing the tempo at the end of the song.[25]

During the nineteenth century the romantic lied appeared, flourished, and was then transformed into something new. Early in the century composers had started with a combination of voice, piano, and poetry, usually choosing to emphasize one or more of these elements, sometimes at the expense of the others. Yet song was always defined within the context of chamber music. By the end of the century, however, composers were writing works that were less intimate and more sumptuous in scale than earlier songs, more appropriate for large concert halls. This often meant that composers were writing in a style that was highly suited to orchestral accompaniment. Both Mahler and Strauss participated in this trend, moving the lied closer to an operatic style in its grandeur and vocal display. Later, when song returned to the stage as chamber music at the beginning of the twentieth century, Schoenberg's and Webern's handling of text would launch German song onto a new path.

Chronology

Chronology

Decade	Social, Political, and Artistic Events	Poets and Philosophers	Song Composers
1720s		Friedrich Gottlieb Klopstock (1724–1803) Immanuel Kant (1724–1804) Gotthold Ephraim Lessing (1729–1781)	
1730s			Joseph Haydn (1732–1809)
1740s	Reign of Maria Theresa of Austria (1740–1780) Reign of Frederick II of Prussia (1740–1786) Montesquieu's *Spirit of Laws* (1748)	Johann Gottfried Herder (1744–1803) Ludwig Christoph Heinrich Hölty (1748–1776) Johann Wolfgang von Goethe (1749–1832)	
1750s	French *Encyclopédie* (1751–1772) Seven Years' War (1756–1763)	Friedrich von Schiller (1759–1805)	Johann Friedrich Reichardt (1752–1814) Wolfgang Amadeus Mozart (1756–1791) Carl Friedrich Zelter (1758–1832)
1760s	Rousseau's *Social Contract* (1761)	J. G. Fichte (1762–1814) Johann Paul Friedrich Richter (1763–1825) August Wilhelm von Schlegel (1767–1845) Friedrich Schleiermacher (1768–1834)	Johann Zumsteeg (1760–1802)
1770s	*Stimmen der Völker in Liedern* (1778–1779)	Georg Wilhelm Friedrich Hegel (1770–1831) Novalis (1772–1801) Karl Wilhelm Friedrich von Schlegel (1772–1829) Ludwig Tieck (1773–1853) Clemens Brentano (1778–1842)	Ludwig van Beethoven (1770–1827) Luise Reichardt (1779–1826)

	Events	Writers	Composers
1780s	Reign of Joseph II of Austria (1780–1790) French Revolution (1789)	Achim von Arnim (1781–1831) Adelbert von Chamisso (1781–1838) Justinus Kerner (1786–1862) Johann Ludwig Uhland (1787–1862) Joseph Freiherr von Eichendorff (1788–1857) Friedrich Rückert (1788–1866) Johann Mayrhofer (1787–1836) George Gordon Noel Lord Byron (1788–1824) Arthur Schopenhauer (1788–1860)	Louis Spohr (1784–1859) Carl Maria von Weber (1786–1826)
1790s	Revolutionary and Napoleonic Wars (1792–1815) Shakespeare's plays translated into German (1797–1833) *Athenäum* 1798–1800 Napoleon's First Consulate (1799–1804)	Wilhelm Müller (1794–1827) August Graf von Platen (1796–1835) Heinrich Heine (1797–1856) Ludwig Rellstab (1799–1860)	Carl Loewe (1796–1869) Franz Schubert (1797–1828)
1800s	Napoleon's Empire (1804–1814) *Des Knaben Wunderhorn* (1805–1808) End of the Holy Roman Empire (1806) Confederation of the Rhine (1806)	Georg Friedrich Daumer (1800–1875) Nikolaus Lenau (1802–1850) Eduard Mörike (1804–1875) Robert Reinick (1805–1852)	Fanny Mendelssohn Hensel (1805–1847) Felix Mendelssohn-Bartholdy (1809–1847)
1810s	*Grimm's Fairy Tales* (1812) German War of Liberation (1813–1814) Congress of Vienna (1814–1815) Carlsbad Decrees (1819)	Hermann von Gilm zu Rossenegg (1812–1864) Emanuel Geibel (1815–1884) Adolf Friedrich Graf von Schack (1815–1894) Gottfried Keller (1819–1890) Klaus Groth (1819–1899)	Robert Schumann (1810–1856) Franz Liszt (1811–1886) Richard Wagner (1813–1883) Josefine Lang (1815–1880) Robert Franz (1815–1892) Clara Wieck Schumann (1819–1896)

Decade	Social, Political, and Artistic Events	Poets and Philosophers	Song Composers
1820s		Conrad Ferdinand Meyer (1825–1898), Mathilde Wesendonk (1828–1902)	Peter Cornelius (1824–1874)
1830s	Unrest in German Principalities (1830), Revolution in France (1830)	Paul von Heyse (1830–1914)	Johannes Brahms (1833–1897)
1840s	Revolutions in German States, Austria, and France (1848), Frankfurt Assembly (1848), Communist Manifesto (1848)	Friedrich Nietzsche (1844–1900), Detlev Freiherr von Liliencron (1844–1909)	
1850s	Darwin's *Origin of the Species* (1859)		
1860s	Unification of Germany (1866–1871)	Richard Dehmel (1862–1920), John Henry Mackay (1864–1933), Otto Julius Bierbaum (1865–1910)	Hugo Wolf (1860–1903), Gustav Mahler (1860–1911), Richard Strauss (1864–1949)
1870s	Franco-Prussian War (1870)		Arnold Schoenberg (1874–1951)
1880s	Reign of William II of Germany (1888–1918)		Anton Webern (1883–1945), Alban Berg (1885–1935)
1890s	Freud's *Interpretation of Dreams* 1900		

Performance Editions of Songs by Lesser-known Composers

Vocal scores for the most famous composers of song—Schubert, Schumann, Mendelssohn, Brahms, Wolf, Mahler, Strauss—are readily available to the singer. The following list includes some of the commercially available scores for some of the less well known composers.

Lang, Josephine. 1982. *Selected Songs*. Ed. Judith Tick. New York: Da Capo Press.

Reichardt, Luise. 1981. *Songs*. Intro. & col. Nancy B. Reich. New York: Da Capo Press.

Schumann, Clara Wieck. 1990. *Sämtliche Lieder für Singstimme und Klavier*. 2 vols. Wiesbaden: Breitkopf und Härtel.

Most of Fanny Mendelssohn Hensel's songs are not yet commercially available. Singers may wish to write to the Mendelssohn Archive at the Staatsbibliothek Preussischer Kulturbesitz in Berlin, the Bodleian Library at Oxford University, or the Goethe Museum or the Heinrich Heine Institut in Düsseldorf for microfilm of Hensel's unpublished manuscripts or to contact the Library of Congress and the New York Public Library, which have some of the published song editions. The following scores are available:

Hensel, Fanny Mendelssohn. 1985. *Lieder*, Op. 1 and Op. 7. Berlin: Bote und Bock.

———. 1991. Ausgewählte Lieder. Wiesbaden: Breithopf und Härtel.

Five of the six early songs that were published under Felix Mendelssohn's name are included in

Felix Mendelssohn. *Seventy-nine Songs*. Melville, New York: Belwin Mills.

Lang's "Frühzeitiger Frühling," Hensel's "Schwanenlied," and C. Schumann's "Liebst du um Schönheit" are included in

Briscoe, James R., ed. 1987. *Historical Anthology of Music by Women.* Bloomington, Indiana: Indiana University Press.

The following listing of commercially available editions includes collections by three early songwriters in addition to some editions of the composers discussed in Chapter 11, "The Supporting Cast." A number of songs such as "Ein Ton" by Cornelius and "Widmung" by Franz also appear in various other song collections.

Cornelius, Peter. *Brautlieder.* New York: International Music.

———. *Lieder für eine Singstimme mit Pianofortebegleitung.* Ed. Max Friedländer. Leipzig: C. F. Peters.

———. *Weihnachtslieder.* New York: International Music.

Franz, Robert. 1964. *50 Ausgewählte Lieder.* Ed. Wilhelm Weismann. Leipzig: C. F. Peters.

Loewe, Carl. 1968. *Balladen und Lieder.* 2 vols. Ed. Hans Joachim Moser. Frankfurt: C. F. Peters.

Reichardt, Johann Friedrich. 1984. *Goethe Lieder, Oden, Balladen und Romanzen.* Huntsville, Texas: Recital Publications.

Spohr, Louis. 1971. *Deutsche Lieder.* Kassel: Bärenreiter.

Zelter, Carl Friedrich. 1932. *Fünfzig Lieder.* Ed. Ludwig Landshoff. Mainz: B. Schotts Söhne.

Zumsteeg, Johann Rudolf. 1969. *Kleine Balladen und Lieder mit Klavierbegleitung.* England: Gregg International.

APPENDIX 3

Program Planning

PREPARING RECITAL PROGRAMS

Performers confront a vast array of choices when they plan a song recital. Most successful programs are constructed with the principles of unity and variety in mind. A performer may choose to focus on a particular poet (lieder on poetry by Goethe, Eichendorff, Heine, etc.) or theme (spring, night, ghosts, gypsies) as a starting point and then flesh out the program with a sufficient variety of subjects, mood, tempi, form, key, and meter to stimulate audience interest.

The longer song cycles such as Schubert's *Winterreise* or *Die schöne Müllerin* are complete recitals in themselves. Other cycles such as Schumann's *Dichterliebe* and *Frauenliebe und -leben* are not long enough to occupy a complete evening and are sometimes performed on the same recital, usually by a male and female singer.

The following suggestions are merely a starting point in program planning.

Program 1

The first program works well for male voices because of the subject matter of the poetry; it mixes the familiar with some less familiar repertoire and is suitable for any recital audience.

Ludwig van Beethoven
  "Ich liebe dich"
  "Neue Liebe, neues Leben"
  "Aus Goethes Faust"
  "Adelaide"
Franz Schubert
  "An Silvia"
  "Seligkeit"
  "Der Musensohn"
  "Der Jüngling an der Quelle"
  "Der Atlas"

Richard Wagner
    "Les deux Grenadiers"
Robert Schumann
    "Die beiden Grenadiere"
Johannes Brahms
    "O liebliche Wangen"
    "Dein blaues Auge"
    "Meine Liebe ist grün"
    "Von ewiger Liebe"
Carl Loewe
    "Erlkönig"
Franz Schubert
    "Erlkönig"
Hugo Wolf
    from the Mörike Lieder
        "Fussreise"
        "Verborgenheit"
        "Der Feuerreiter"
Richard Strauss
    "Traum durch die Dämmerung"
    "Ständchen"
    "Du meines Herzens Krönelein"
    "Befreit"

Program 2

The next recital consists of songs that are suited for the female voice or are subjects that are considered to represent a feminine point of view.

Franz Schubert
    "Ariette der Claudine"
    "Die junge Nonne"
    "Ave Maria"
    "Gretchen am Spinnrade"
Carl Loewe
    "Edward"
Peter Cornelius
    Brautlieder
        "Ein Myrtenreis"
        "Der Liebe Lohn"
        "Vorabend"
        "Erwachen"
        "Aus dem hohen Lied"
        "Erfüllung"
Franz Schubert
    "Der Hirt auf dem Felsen" (for soprano and clarinet)
        or, if the recital is being performed by a contralto
Johannes Brahms
    "Zwei Gesänge," Op. 91 (for contralto and viola)

Hugo Wolf
from the *Italienisches Liederbuch*
"Mein Liebster ist so klein"
"Mein Liebster singt am Haus"
"O wär dein Haus"
"Ich hab in Penna"

Program 3

The song texts in the next program would work well for either male or female singers. All the music in this group, except for Fanny Hensel's songs, can be found in a variety of keys.

Franz Schubert
"An die Musik"
"Nacht und Träume"
"Lachen und Weinen"
"Die Forelle"
Robert Schumann
Der arme Peter
"Der Hans und die Grete tanzen
"In meiner Brust"
"Der arme Peter"
Franz Liszt
"Es muss ein Wunderbares sein"
"Ihr Glocken von Marling"
"Die drei Zigeuner"
Fanny Mendelssohn Hensel
"Gondellied"
"Frühling"
"Nachtwanderer"
"Dein ist mein Herz"
Richard Strauss
"Die Nacht"
"Ständchen"
"Allerseelen"
"Zueignung"
"Morgen"

Program 4

Many wonderful lieder are rarely performed. The next recital includes many beautiful songs that are not familiar to most audiences.

Franz Schubert
"An den Mond" (Geuss, lieber Mond)
"Alinde"
"Gruppe aus dem Tartarus"
"An Schwager Kronos"

Felix Mendelssohn
  "Neue Liebe"
  "Die Liebende schreibt"
  "Suleika" (Ach, um deine . . .)
  "And'res Maienlied"
Johannes Brahms
  "Auf dem Kirchhofe"
  "Nicht mehr zu dir zu gehen"
  "Regenlied"
  "Dämmrung senkte sich von oben"
  "Unüberwindlich"
Clara Wieck Schumann
  "Er ist gekommen"
  "Liebst du um Schönheit"
  "Ich hab' in deinem Auge"
  "Das ist ein Tag"
Hugo Wolf
  "Begegnung"
  "Um Mitternacht'
  "Auftrag"
  "An die Geliebte"
  "Storchenbotschaft"

Program 5

The following program is unified by using folk material as its basis: folk poetry, folk melodies, or music that imitates folk style.

Luise Reichardt
  "Betteley der Vögel"
  "Hier liegt ein Spielmann begraben"
Franz Schubert
  "Heidenröslein"
  "Die Vögel"
  "Fischerweise"
Carl Loewe
  "Edward"
Robert Schumann
  "Erstes Grün"
  "Volksliedchen"
  "Der Sandmann"
  "Marienwürmchen"
Johannes Brahms
  "Der Jäger"
  "Der Gang zum Liebchen"
  "Vergebliches Ständchen"
  "Sonntag"

Gustav Mahler
from *Des Knaben Wunderhorn*
"Ich ging mit Lust"
"Des Antonius von Padua Fischpredigt"
"Das irdische Leben"
"Wo die schönen Trompeten blasen"
"Wer hat dies Liedlein erdacht?"
Richard Strauss
from *Des Knaben Wunderhorn*
"Mein Vater hat gesagt"
"Für fünfzehn Pfennige"

Program 6 (Select from the following)

Interesting song groups can focus on particular subjects such as lullabies, gypsy songs, barcaroles, serenades and other night songs, or songs of spring.

Lullabies
Brahms
"Wiegenlied"
"Geistliches Wiegenlied"
Schubert
"Schlafe, schlafe"
"Wie sich der Äuglein"
Spohr
"Wiegenlied"
Mendelssohn
"Bei der Wieg"
Schumann
"Der Sandmann"
Strauss
"Wiegenlied"

Gypsy Songs
Spohr
"Zigeunerlied"
Schumann
"Zigeunerliedchen" I & II
Liszt
"Die drei Zigeuner"
Wolf
"Die Zigeunerin"
Brahms
Zigeunerlieder
"He, Zigeuner"
"Hochgetürmte Rimaflut"
"Wisst ihr"
"Lieber Gott, du weisst"

"Brauner Bursche"
"Röslein dreie in der Reihe"
"Kommt dir manchmal in den Sinn"
"Rote Abendwolken ziehn am Firmament"

Barcaroles
Schubert
"Auf dem Wasser zu singen"
Mendelssohn
"Wenn durch die Piazetta"
Hensel
"Gondellied"
Schumann
"Zwei Venetianische Lieder"
Wolf
"Als ich auf dem Euphrat"

Serenades
Schubert
"Ständchen" (Leise flehen)
"Ständchen" (Horch, horch, die Lerch)
Schumann
"Ständchen" (Komm' in die stille)
Brahms
"Ständchen" (Der Mond steht)
"Serenade" (Liebliches Kind)
"Vergebliches Ständchen"
Wolf
"Ein Ständchen Euch"
Strauss
"Ständchen" (Mach auf)

Songs of Spring
Hensel
"Frühling"
"Die Mainacht"
"Mayenlied"
Schubert
"Frühlingsglaube"
"Im Frühling"
Mendelssohn
"Altdeutsches Frühlingslied"
"Frühlingslied" (Durch den Wald)
Lang
"Frühzeitiger Frühling
Schumann
"Frühlingsnacht"
Brahms
"Die Mainacht"

Wolf
  "Er ist's"
  "Im Frühling"
Strauss
  "Frühling"

Songs of Night and Celestial Bodies
Schubert
  "Nacht und Träume"
  "An den Mond"
Hensel
  "Die frühen Gräber"
  "Nachtwanderer"
R. Schumann
  "Mein schöner Stern"
  "Mondnacht"
C. Schumann
  "Der Mond kommt still gegangen"
Franz
  "Selige Nacht"
Cornelius
  "Komm, wir wandeln zusammen im Mondschein"
Wolf
  "Die Nacht"
Strauss
  "Die Nacht"
  "An die Nacht"

Program 7

Sometimes recital music is selected for special occasions. Women's History Week, for example, is celebrated each year in March, and a Liederabend can easily be constructed with songs by Luise Reichardt, Fanny Mendelssohn Hensel, Clara Schumann, Josephine Lang, and Alma Mahler. Certainly the songs of these composers should also be included on standard recitals.

CHAMBER MUSIC PROGRAMS

Chamber music concerts provide the opportunity for great variety in programming. A singer could include any of the following:

Schubert
> "Der Tod und das Mädchen"
> String Quartet No. 14 in D minor, D. 810 ("Death and the Maiden"),
>> second movement.
>> Brahms
> "Regenlied"
> "Nachklang"
> Violin Sonata in G Major, Op. 78 (which has the "Regenlied" theme in
>> the third movement).

Liszt
> *Tre sonetti di Petrarca* (songs)
> *Tre sonetti del Petrarca* (for piano)

Loewe
> "Edward"

Schubert
> "Eine Altschottische Ballade—Edward"

Brahms
> "Edward" (duet for contralto and tenor)
> *Four Ballades, d'Edward,'* Op. 10 (for piano)

Loewe
> "Erlkönig"

Schubert
> "Erlkönig"

Spohr
> "Erlkönig" (for voice and violin), Op. 154.

Notes

Introduction

1. Nietzsche 1924, 63.
2. Sams 1975, 171.
3. Austen 1950, 136–137.

Chapter One

1. Schoenberg 1950, 4.
2. Schoenberg 1950, 6.
3. Lang 1941, 780–781.
4. Plantinga 1967, 175.
5. Plantinga 1967, 177.
6. Medtner 1951, 124–125.
7. Newman 1907/Rev. ed. 1966, 156.
8. Mahler 1979, 212.
9. Werfel 1969, 93.
10. Harrison 1972, 112–113.
11. Schumann 1877, 136.
12. Schumann 1971, 130. Although he set poems by Goethe, Schiller, and other great writers, Zumsteeg was also capable of setting virtually anything to music as he proved with his setting of the following poem:

> *Schön röthlich die Kartoffeln sind*
> *Und weiss wie Alabaster*
> *Sie dau'n sich lieblich und geschwind*
> *Und sind für Mann und Weib und Kind,*
> *Geschweige denn für Schwein und Rind*
> *Ein rechtes Magenpflaster!*

> The potatoes are beautifully red
> And white as alabaster.
> They are easily and quickly digested

And are for man, woman, and child,
Not to mention for pigs and cows,
A balm to the stomach.

(In *Kleine Balladen und Lieder mit Klavierbegleitung* by J. R. Zumsteeg. Leipzig: Breitkopf und Härtel, vol. 5, 30.), c. 1821.

13. Schumann 1971, 131.
14. Harrison 1972, 113.
15. Auden 1955, *xvi–xvii.*
16. Richard Wagner also set "Gretchen am Spinnrade" to music but did not tamper with Goethe's ending.
17. Stein 1971, 100.
18. Stein 1971, 89.
19. Brody 1971, 97.
20. Osborne 1974, 49.
21. Walker 1951, 295.

Chapter Two

1. Nietzsche 1987, 48–49.
2. Fischer-Dieskau 1988, 217.
3. Nietzsche 1987, 41.
4. Letter from Ludwig van Beethoven to Bettina von Arnim, August 15, 1812. Hugo 1964, 605.
5. Kravitt 1960, 4.
6. Rousseau 1985, 1.
7. Dahlhaus 1987, 25.
8. Schlegel translated seventeen plays [1797–1810]; Dorothea Tieck and Graf W. H. Baudissin completed the remaining translations [1825–1833].
9. Mitchell 1985, 3:128.
10. Miller 1966, 265.
11. Feise 1958, 14.
12. Schumann 1927, 128.
13. Nietzsche 1987, 61.
14. Nietzsche 1987, 48.
15. Nietzsche 1968, 681.
16. Nietzsche n.d., 82–83.
17. Strauss 1977, 99.

Chapter Three

1. Sumner 1966, 148.
2. Plantinga 1967, 172.
3. Ripin et al. 1984, 72.
4. Ehrlich 1976, 14.

5. Loesser 1954, 45.
6. Winter 1988, 6:285.
7. Neuls-Bates 1982, *xiii.*
8. Loesser 1954, 150.
9. Loesser 1954, 131
10. Reichardt 1981, *ix–x.*
11. Deutsch 1946, 44.
12. Sumner 1966, 149, 167.
13. Sumner 1966, 148–150, & plate 19.
14. Plantinga 1967, 220.
15. Ripin et al. 1984, 89.
16. Litzmann 1913, 1:194.
17. Litzmann 1913, 1:198.
18. Litzmann 1913, 1:200.
19. Litzmann 1913, 1:257–258.
20. Schumann 1877, 240–241.

Chapter Four

1. Litzmann 1913, 1:284.
2. Schünemann 1936, 51–52.
3. Deutsch 1958, 233.
4. Deutsch 1946, 76.
5. Deutsch 1946, 906.
6. Deutsch 1946, 420.
7. Liszt 1877, 96. Also, see Chapter 6 on Schubert for further discussion of Nourrit's rôle in introducing Schubert's songs to France.
8. Walker 1951, 318.
9. Walker 1951, 306.
10. Walker 1951, 206.
11. Deutsch 1946, 162. Also, see the discussion in Chapter 6 about the quartet performance of "Erlkönig."
12. Friedländer 1976, 188–189.
13. Litzmann 1913, 1:393.
14. Wagner 1983, 37.
15. Wagner 1983, 37.
16. Mendelssohn 1863, 221–222.
17. Werner 1963, 321
18. Kehler 1982, 1:763.
19. Kehler 1982, 1:763–764.
20. Kehler 1982, 2:1311.
21. Kravitt 1960, 28–35.
22. Litzmann 1913, 2:160.
23. Litzmann 1913, 2:168.
24. Litzmann 1913, 1:416.
25. Litzmann 1913, 1:417.
26. Litzmann 1913, 1:468.
27. Litzmann 1913, 1:468–469.

28. Kehler 1982, 2:1186.
29. Litzmann 1913, 1:331. The programs given in Litzmann and in Kehler differ on several pieces.
30. Litzmann 1927, 2:45.
31. Barkan 1957, 50.
32. Schumann 1927, 186.
33. Pleasants 1979, 275.
34. Kravitt 1960, 5.
35. Kravitt 1960, 6.
36. Wirth 1927, 226.
37. Wirth 1927, 497.
38. Kravitt 1960, 7.
39. Litzmann 1913, 2:289–290.
40. Grove 1954, 8:93–94.
41. Newman 1907/Rev. ed. 1966, 79.
42. Pleasants 1979, 272.
43. Pleasants 1979, 235.
44. Pleasants 1979, 272.
45. Litzmann 1913, 1:416.
46. Walker 1951, 337.
47. Walker 1951, 339.
48. Peterson 1980, 149.
49. Kravitt 1960, 31.
50. Mitchell 1985, 40.
51. Peterson 1980, 152.
52. Peterson 1980, 142.
53. Strauss 1953, 135.
54. Schuh 1982, 454.
55. Schuh 1982, 454.
56. Strauss 1953, 134.
57. Schuh 1982, 456–457.
58. Schuh 1982, 219.
59. Peterson 1980, 154.
60. Werfel 1975, 28.

Chapter Five

1. Tovey 1910, 3:650.
2. Miller 1966, 172.
3. McNaught 1954, 1:570.
4. He is word-painting on the lengthy repetitions of "lange."
5. Stein 1971, 51–52. Stein is quoting a discovery by Ernst Bücken.

Chapter Six

1. Deutsch 1958, 128.
2. Sams 1975, *viii.*
3. Deutsch 1946, 603.
4. Plantinga 1967, 219–220.

5. Brown 1961, 1.
6. Deutsch 1946, 946.
7. Deutsch 1946, 876–878.
8. Deutsch 1946, 877.
9. Deutsch 1958, 140.
10. Spohr 1878, 205.
11. Citron 1980, 61:24.
12. Noske 1970, 34.
13. Deutsch 1946, 178.
14. Challier 1885.
15. Brody 1971, 38.
16. Deutsch 1946, 122.
17. Deutsch 1958, 203. Deutsch claimed that Randhartinger exaggerated his relationship with Schubert as he got older.
18. Deutsch 1946, 690.
19. Noske 1970, 26–28.
20. Noske 1970, 415.
21. Noske 1970, 34. See Frits Noske's discussion of "Schubert and the German Lied," in *French Song from Berlioz to Duparc* 1970, 25–34.
22. Brown 1961, 324.
23. Kravitt 1965, 209.
24. Kravitt 1965, 211–213.
25. Deutsch 1946, 162.
26. Frost 1881, 8.
27. Deutsch 1958, 34.
28. Deutsch 1946, 476.
29. Deutsch 1946, 574.
30. Deutsch 1946, 867.
31. Deutsch 1958, 337–338.
32. Reich 1971, 202–204.
33. Capell 1957, 256–257.
34. For a detailed discussion of both Schubert song cycles, see Feil 1988, 21–151.
34. John Reed states that a walking pace is suggested by the steady movement of the first song but is not a literal imitation of a walking tempo. Reed 1985, 182.
35. Deutsch 1946, 613.
36. Reich 1971, 212, 214.
37. Deutsch 1946, 795.
38. Deutsch 1958, 233.

Chapter Seven

1. Litzmann 1913, 1:280.
2. Plantinga 1967, 183.
3. Barkan 1957, 227.
4. Plantinga 1967, 171.
5. Litzmann 1913, 1:283–284.

6. Plantinga 1967, 63.
7. Abraham 1977, 9.
8. Pleasants 1965, 164–166.
9. Litzmann 1913, 1:291.
10. Litzmann 1913, 1:280.
11. Schumann 1877, 136.
12. Schumann 1877, 136.
13. Plantinga 1967, 176–177.
14. Pleasants 1965, 189–190.
15. Stein 1971, 175.
16. Abraham 1977, 100–101.
17. Plantinga 1967, 174.
18. Moser 1937, 165.
19. Miller 1966, 190.
20. Plantinga 1967, 268.
21. Miller 1966, 47.
22. Of course, many figurations, such as that of Example 7-10a, are so general that the nature of what they are "painting" evokes various interpretations. Arthur Komar believes that the piano figuration in "Hör ich das Liedchen klingen" suggests the strumming of an instrument that is accompanying the voice. Schumann 1971, 85.
23. For a detailed analysis of *Dichterliebe* that posits an overall key plan, see Arthur Komar's essay in Schumann 1971, 63–93.
24. Abraham 1977, 104.
25. Fischer-Dieskau 1988, 89.
26. Wirth 1927, 497.
27. Nietzsche, in "The Case of Wagner," extols the opera *Carmen* and says, "That love which is war in its means, and at bottom the deadly hatred of the sexes!—I know no case where the tragic joke that constitutes the essence of love is expressed so strictly, translated with equal terror into a formula, as in Don José's last cry, which concludes the work: 'Yes. I have killed her, I—my adored Carmen!'" Nietzsche 1968, 615.
28. Pleasants 1967, p. 62.
29. Fischer-Dieskau 1988, 218.
30. Fischer-Dieskau 1988, 155.

Chapter Eight

1. Rousseau 1911, 322, 331, 333, 340, 357.
2. Hensel 1881, 2:260.
3. Citron 1980, 21.
4. Citron 1980, 16.
5. Citron 1980, 21.
6. Citron 1980, 24.
7. Citron 1980, 22.
8. Reichardt 1922, *vii.*
9. Reich 1980, 707–708.
10. Reich 1980, 707–708
11. Lang 1982, Introduction.

12. Lang 1982, Introduction.
13. Lang 1982, Introduction.
14. Lang 1982, Introduction.
15. Exceptions were Goethe's "Nähe des Geliebten" (Op. 5, No. 1) and Heine's "Und wüssten's die Blumen" (Op. 40, No. 5).
16. Schumann 1927, 196.
17. Litzmann 1913, 1:150.
18. Schumann 1927, 196–197.
19. Litzmann 1913, 1:314–315.
20. Litzmann 1913, 1:259.
21. Litzmann 1913, 1:318–319.
22. Reich 1985, 297–306.
23. Litzmann 1913, 1:429–430.
24. Litzmann 1913, 1:429.

Chapter Nine

1. Miller 1892, 152.
2. Hensel 1881, 1:73.
3. Elvers 1975, 218.
4. Devrient 1972, 3.
5. Hensel 1986, *vi.*
6. Hensel 1881, 1:92.
7. Werner 1947, 329.
8. Werner 1947, 331.
9. Hensel 1986, *vi.*
10. Hensel 1881, 1:219.
11. Werner 1947, 327.
12. Miller 1966, 106–107.
13. Hensel 1881, 2:169–170.
14. Hensel 1980, *vii.*
15. Hensel 1881, 1:173. "Heine is here, and I do not like him at all, he is so affected.... He gives himself sentimental airs, is affectedly affected, talks incessantly of himself, and all the while looks at you to see whether you look at him.... And though for ten times you may be inclined to despise him, the eleventh time you cannot help confessing that he is a poet, a true poet! How he manages the words! What a feeling he has for nature, such as only a real poet has!"
16. Grove 1896, 2:254.
17. Hensel 1881, 1:82.
18. Hensel 1881, 1:84.
19. Citron 1983, 573.
20. Gounod 1896, 90–91.
21. Hensel 1881, 2:30.
22. Mendelssohn-Bartholdy 1863, 113–114.
23. Hensel 1881, 2:326.
24. Grove 1896, 2:253.
25. Citron 1983, 576.
26. Hensel 1881, 2:31.

27. Hensel 1881, 2:38.
28. Hensel 1881, 2:32.
29. Krautwurst 1973, 658–662.
30. Hensel 1986, *vi.*
31. Her manuscripts give the impression that she was frequently working under the pressure of limited time. In her part songs, for example, she sometimes only copied the text into the soprano voice part. Some of her music must have been written hurriedly for her Sunday concerts.

Chapter Ten

1. Devrient 1972, 114, 258–260.
2. Litzmann 1913, 1:293.
3. Litzmann 1913, 1:370.
4. Werner 1963, 123.
5. Finson 1984, 5.
6. Werner 1963, 320.
7. Litzmann 1913, 1:368.

Chapter Eleven

1. For an extended discussion on the songs of Louis Spohr, see Gorrell, 1978, 31–38.
2. *Allgemeine musikalische Zeitung* 1818, 647.
3. Rellstab 1841, 47–48, 105–106.
4. The popularity of collections containing six songs can be judged by the large number of these listed in the Whistling-Hofmeister *Handbuch der musikalischen Literatur*, 1828, and continued by Adolph Hofmeister, 1828–1879.
5. Spohr 1878, 205.
6. Spohr 1878, 218.
7. Redlich 1949, 313.
8. Brown 1969, 110:359.
9. See discussion of the original Scottish poem in Brody 1971, 187–188.
10. Kleemann 1915, 497.
11. Kleemann 1915, 499.

Chapter Twelve

1. Litzmann 1913, 1:149–150, 1:275, 1:288.
2. Noske 1970, 125–126.
3. Liszt 1877, 92.
4. Quoted in Noske 1970, 254, 426.

Chapter Thirteen

1. Schumann 1946, 253.
2. Schumann 1927, 173.

3. Schumann 1927, 173.
4. Barkan 1957, 229.
5. Barkan 1957, 248.
6. *Deutsche Volkslieder mit ihren Original-Weisen* (1838–40, 2 vols.). The full title is "Deutsche Volkslieder mit ihren Original-Weisen. Unter Mitwirkung des Herrn Professor Dr. Massmann in München, des Herrn von Zuccalmaglio in Warschau und mehrerer anderer Freunde der Volks-Poesie, nach handschriftlichen Quellen herausgegeben und mit Anmerkungen versehen von A. Kretzschmer, Königlichem Geheimen Kriegsrate und Ritter usw. (Erster Teil. Berlin, 1840); and Deutsche Volkslieder mit ihren Original-Weisen. Unter Mitwirkung des Herrn Professor Dr. E. Baumstark und mehrerer anderer Freunde der Volks-Dichtung, als Fortsetzung des A. Kretzschmerschen Werkes, gesammelt und mit Anmerkungen versehen von A. Wilh. v. Zuccalmaglio" (Zweiter Teil. Berlin, 1840).
7. Friedländer 1976, 140–141.
8. Friedländer 1976, 221.
9. Selk 1961, 1450–1451. Nicolai alienated both Herder and Goethe with his parody, *Freuden des jungen Werthers* (The Pleasures of Young Werther). While Herder believed that folk collections should be a selection of the best works, Nicolai wanted folk song to be presented as it was, represented by both good and bad. Songs from his *Almanach* reappeared later not only in the Zuccalmalglio/Kretzschmer collection but in *Des Knaben Wunderhorn* and in Brahms's *Volkslieder* of 1894.
10. Friedländer 1976, 204–206.
11. Litzmann 1913, 2:162–164.
12. Over half of the forty-nine folk songs are strophic variations; the children's songs (1858) and the folk songs that were published after his death are all strophic.
13. See Friedländer 1976, 79.
14. Friedländer 1976, 194.
15. Friedländer 1976, 136.
16. Schumann 1927, 147–148.
17. Friedländer 1976, 199–200.
18. Brahms 1980, Introduction, *xiii*. The original manuscript is in the Preussische Staatsbibliothek in Berlin, but the songs have been published in Dover's complete edition of Brahms songs.
19. Friedländer 1976, 32.
20. Latham 1962, 151.
21. Geiringer 1933, 19:58–68.
22. Friedländer 1976, 5. Philip Miller, 1966, also notes several examples of Brahms's use of poetry that reproduce Schubert's and Schumann's changes; 34, 138–139, 141–142.
23. Geiringer 1933, 19:58–68.
24. Geiringer 1933, 159.
25. Harrison 1972, 35.
26. Friedländer 1976, v.

Chapter Fourteen

1. Strauss 1968, 214.
2. Pleasants 1979, 173.
3. Walker 1951, 203–204.
4. Walker 1951, 203.
5. Sams 1975, 287.
6. Sams 1975, 250. This same idea is developed by Walker and is quoted in Chapter 1, "Poetry and Music."

Chapter Fifteen

1. Del Mar 1962, 1.
2. Interestingly enough, Wolf was highly dissatisfied with his orchestral version of "Prometheus." In 1894 he wrote, "I have been looking at the Prometheus score I wrote years ago and am convinced that the orchestration is worth absolutely nothing. The instrumentation is terribly overloaded and completely crushes the voice." Wolf 1982, *vii–viii.* He also made two orchestrated versions of the dramatic "Kennst du das Land" and two orchestrations of "Anakreons Grab," one of which is lost. His orchestrations of "Geh, Geliebter, jetzt!" and "Ganymed" are also lost. Four of the five orchestrated songs from the *Spanisches Liederbuch* were to be included in his two operas, *Der Corregidor* and the unfinished *Manuel Venegas.*
3. He composed forty-five songs plus *Das Lied von der Erde*, often called Mahler's tenth symphony, although his actual tenth symphony was not completed.
4. These last two songs appear to be much later than the other songs in the collection.
5. Werfel 1969, xxii.
6. Kravitt 1978, 64:349.
7. Kravitt 1978, 64:331.
8. Kravitt 1978, 64;333.
9. Kravitt 1978, 64:353.
10. Donald Mitchell includes the program for a 29 January 1905 orchestral performance of Mahler's *Kindertotenlieder*, his four other orchestrated Rückert songs, and seven songs from *Des Knaben Wunderhorn* in a concert conducted by Mahler in Vienna. Mitchell 1985, 3:40.
11. Mitchell 1985, 3:78.
12. Strauss 1953, 134.
13. Strauss 1968, 158. Strauss incurred the wrath of many critics at the beginning of his career by appearing too avant-garde and too decadently erotic in operas like *Salome* and *Elektra.* He was criticized at the end of his long career for being too conservative.
14. Grout and Palisca 1988, 763–764.
15. Berg 1971, 249.
16. Newman 1908, 89, 96.
17. Schuh 1982, 457.

18. Schuh 1982, 455.
19. Peterson 1980, 32.
20. Strauss 1953, 100.
21. Strauss 1968, 29–87. Richard Kravitt discusses Strauss's care in setting German text. Kravitt 1960.
22. Strauss 1968, 151–152.
23. Strauss 1968, 101.
24. "Zueignung" and Strauss's songs in general elicit strong responses, both positive and negative. Anneliese Landau describes "Zueignung" as concluding with "a sickening theatrical pathos, an almost visible operatic gesture." Landau 1980, 101.
25. Peterson 1980, 157–158.

Bibliography

Abraham, Gerald, ed. 1977. *Schumann: A Symposium*. Westport, Conn.: Greenwood Press.

Asprey, Robert B. 1986. *Frederick the Great*. New York: Ticknor & Fields.

Auden, W. H. and Chester Kallman. 1955. *An Elizabethan Song Book*. Garden City, New York: Doubleday.

Austen, Jane. 1950. *Pride and Prejudice*. New York: Modern Library. Orig. publ. 1813.

Bach, Albert B. 1891. *The Art Ballad*. Edinburgh and London: William Blackwood & Sons.

Barkan, Hans, ed. 1957. *Johannes Brahms and Theodore Billroth: Letters from a Musical Friendship*. Norman, Oklahoma: University of Oklahoma Press.

Berg, Alban. 1971. *Letters to His Wife*. Ed. & trans. Bernard Grun. New York: St. Martin's Press.

Blume, Friedrich. 1947. *Two Centuries of Bach*. Trans. Stanley Godman. London: Oxford University Press.

Bowers, Jane and Judith Tick. 1986. *Women Making Music*. Urbana, Illinois: University of Illinois Press.

Briscoe, James R., ed. 1987. *Historical Anthology of Music by Women*. Bloomington, Indiana: Indiana University Press.

Brody, Elaine and Robert Fowkes. 1971. *The German Lied and Its Poetry*. New York: New York University Press.

Brown, Maurice. 1961. *Schubert: A Critical Biography*. London: Macmillan.

_____. 1966. *Essays on Schubert*. New York: St. Martin's Press.

_____. 1969. "Carl Loewe." *Musical Times* 110:357–359.

Capell, Richard. n.d. *Schubert's Songs*. New York: E. P. Dutton.

Carner, Mosco. 1982. *Hugo Wolf Songs*. London: British Broadcasting Corporation.

Challier, Ernst. 1885. *Grosser Lieder-Katalog*. Berlin: Ernst Challier's Selbstverlag.

Chissell, Joan. 1983. *Clara Schumann: A Dedicated Spirit*. New York: Taplinger.

Christiansen, Rupert. 1984. *Prima Donna: A History*. Middlesex, England: Penguin Books.

Citron, Marcia. 1980. "Corona Schröter: Singer, Composer, Actress." *Music and Letters* 61:15–27.

———. 1983. "The Lieder of Fanny Mendelssohn Hensel." *The Musical Quarterly* 69:570–593.

———. 1987. *The Letters of Fanny Hensel to Felix Mendelssohn*. New York: Pendragon Press.

Dahlhaus, Carl. 1987. *Nineteenth-Century Music*. Trans. J. Bradford Robinson. Berkeley: University of California Press.

David, Hans T. and Arthur Mendel. 1945. *The Bach Reader*. New York: W. W. Norton.

Del Mar, Norman. 1962–1972. *Richard Strauss: A Critical Commentary on His Life and Works*. 3 vols. London: Chilton Books.

Deutsch, Otto, ed. 1928. *Franz Schubert's Letters and other Writings*. Trans. Venetia Savile. New York: Alfred A. Knopf.

———. 1946. *Schubert: A Documentary Biography*. London: J. M. Dent.

———. 1958. *Schubert: Memoirs by his Friends*. London: Adam & Charles Black.

Devrient, Eduard. 1972. *My Recollections of Felix Mendelssohn-Bartholdy, and His Letters to Me*. Trans. Natalia MacFarren. New York: Vienna House. Orig. publ. 1869.

Ehrlich, Cyril. 1976. *The Piano: A History*. London: J. M. Dent.

Elvers, Rudolf. 1972. "Verzeichnis der Musik-Autographen von Fanny Hensel im Mendelssohn-Archiv zu Berlin." In *Mendelssohn Studien*, vol. 1. Ed. Cécile Lowenthal Hensel. Berlin: Ducker & Humblot. 169–174.

———. 1975. "Weitere Quellen zu den Werken von Fanny Hensel." In *Mendelssohn Studien*, vol 2. Ed. Cécile Lowenthal Hensel. Berlin: Duncker & Humblot. 215–220.

———, ed. 1986. *Felix Mendelssohn: A Life in Letters*. Trans. Craig Tomlinson. New York: Fromm International.

Feil, Arnold. 1988. *Franz Schubert*. Trans. Ann C. Sherwin. Porland, Oregon: Amadeus Press. Orig. publ. 1975.

Feise, Ernst and Harry Steinhauer. 1958. *German Literature Since Goethe*. Boston: Houghton Mifflin.

Felber, Rudolf. 1940. "Schumann's Place in German Song." *The Musical Quarterly* 26:340–354.

Finson, Jon W. and R. Larry Todd, ed. 1984. *Mendelssohn and Schumann*. Durham, North Carolina: Duke University Press.

Fischer-Dieskau, Dietrich. 1976. *Wagner and Nietzsche*. New York: The Seabury Press.

———. 1977. *Schubert's Songs*. New York: Alfred A. Knopf.

———. 1988. *Robert Schumann: Words and Music*. Trans. Reinhard G. Pauly. Portland, Oregon: Amadeus Press. Orig. publ. 1981.

Friedländer, Max. 1976. *Brahms's Lieder*. Trans. C. Leonard Leese. New York: American Musicological Society Press. Orig. publ. 1928.

Frost, H. F. 1881. *Schubert*. New York: Scribner & Welford.

Fuller-Maitland, J. A. 1911. *Brahms*. Rpt. 1972. New York: Kennikat Press.

Gay, Peter. 1988. *Freud. A Life for Our Time*. New York: W. W. Norton.

Geiringer, Karl. 1933. "Brahms as a Reader and Collector." *The Musical Quarterly* 19:58–68.

———. 1963. *Brahms: His Life and Work*. 2nd ed. London: Allen and Unwin.

Gorrell, Lorraine. 1978. "The Songs of Louis Spohr." *The Music Review* 39:31–38.

———. 1986. "Fanny Mendelssohn and Her Songs." *The National Association of Teachers of Singing Journal*. 42:6–11.

———. 1989. "Composers and Singers." *Music and Musicians, International* 37:59–60.

Gounod, Charles. 1896. *Autobiographical Reminiscences with Family Letters and Notes on Music*. Trans. W. Hely Hutchinson. London: William Heinemann.

Grout, Jonald Jay, and Claude V. Palisca. 1988. *A History of Western Music*. New York: W. W. Norton.

Grove, Sir George. 1896. "Hensel, Fanny Cecile." *Dictionary of Music*, vol. 1. London: MacMillan.

———. 1896. "Mendelssohn, Jakob Ludwig Felix Mendelssohn-Bartholdy." *Dictionary of Music*, vol. 2. London: MacMillan.

———. "Stockhausen, Julius." 1954. *Grove's Dictionary of Music and Musicians*. 5th edition, vol. 8. Rev. H. C. Colles. New York: St. Martin's Press.

Hall, James. 1953. *The Art Song*. Norman: Oklahoma University Press.

Hanslick, Eduard. 1950. *Vienna's Golden Years of Music*. Trans. & ed. Henry Pleasants. New York: Simon & Schuster.

Harding, Rosamond E. M. 1973. *The Piano-forte: Its History Traced to the Great Exhibition of 1851*. New York: Da Capo Press.

Harrison, Max. 1972. *The Lieder of Brahms*. New York: Praeger Publishers.

Hensel, Fanny Mendelssohn. 1980. *Trio in D minor*. Intro. Victoria Ressmeyer Sirota. New York: Da Capo.

———. 1986. *Ausgewählte Klavierwerke*. Intro. Rudolf Elvers. Munich: Henle.

Hensel, Sebastian. 1881. *The Mendelssohn Family (1729–1847) from Letters and Journals*. 2 vols. Trans. Carl Klingemann. New York: Harper & Brothers.

Hofmeister, Adolph. 1844–1868. *Handbuch der musikalischen Literatur*. Leipzig: Friedrich Hofmeister.

Hugo, Howard E., ed. 1964. *The Portable Romantic Reader*. New York: The Viking Press.

Jefferson, Alan. 1971. *The Lieder of Richard Strauss*. New York: Praeger Publishers.

Kehler, George, ed. 1982. *The Piano in Concert*. 2 vols. Metuchen, New Jersey: Scarecrow Press.

Kleeman, Hans. 1915. "Robert Franz: The Liedermeister." *The Musical Quarterly*, 497.

Köhler, Karl-Heinz. 1980. "Mendelssohn (-Bartholdy) [Hensel], Fanny (Cäcilie)." *The New Grove Dictionary of Music and Musicians*, vol. 8. London: MacMillan.

Krautwurst, Franz. 1979. "Hensel, Fanny Caecilia." *Die Musik in Geschichte und Gegenwart*, Supplement. Kassel: Bärenreiter.

Kravitt, Edward F. 1960. *The Late Romantic Lied: Performance, the Literary Approach, and the Naturalistic Movement*. Ph.D. Dissertation, New York University.
_____. 1962. "The Influence of Theatrical Declamation upon Composers of the Late Romantic Lied." *Acta Musicologica*. 34:18–28.
_____. 1965. "The Lied in 19th Century Concert Life." *Journal of the American Musicological Society*. 18:207–218.
_____. 1978. "Mahler's Dirges for his Death: February 24, 1901." *The Musical Quarterly* 64:349
_____. 1988. "The Lieder of Alma Maria Schindler-Mahler." *The Music Review*. (August) 49:190–204.
Landau, Anneliese. 1980. *The Lied. The Unfolding of Its Style*. Lanham: University Press of America.
Lang, Josephine. 1982. *Selected Songs*. Ed. Judith Tick. New York: Da Capo Press.
Lang, Paul Henry. 1941. *Music in Western Civilization*. New York: Norton.
Latham, Peter. 1962. *Johannes Brahms*. Rev. New York: Farrar, Strauss and Cudaky. Orig. publ. 1948.
Liess, Andreas. 1954. *Johann Michael Vogl*. Graz-Köln: Hermann Böhlaus.
Liszt, Franz. 1877. *Frederick Chopin*. Trans. Martha Walker Cooke. Boston: Oliver Ditson.
_____. 1872. *Robert Franz*. Leipzig: F. E. C. Leuckart.
Litzmann, Berthold, ed. *Clara Schumann: An Artist's Life*. Trans. Grace E. Hadow. 2 vols. London: Macmillan. Orig. publ. in 3 vols., 1902–1908.
_____, ed. 1927. *Letters of Clara Schumann and Johannes Brahms, 1853–1896*. 2 vols. London: Edward Arnold.
Loesser, Arthur. 1954. *Men, Women and Pianos. A Social History*. New York: Simon and Schuster.
Loewe, Carl. 1872. *Selbstbiographie*. Berlin: Wilhelm Müller.
McNaught, William. 1954. "Beethoven." *Grove's Dictionary of Music and Musicians*. 5th edition. Vol. 1. New York: St. Martin's Press.
Mahler, Alma. See Alma Mahler Werfel.
Mahler, Gustav. 1979. *Selected Letters of Gustav Mahler*. Ed. Knud Martner. Original ed. Alma Mahler. Trans. Wilkins, Kaiser, & Hopkins. New York: Garrar/Straus/Giroux.
Mandyczewski, Eusebius, ed. 1980. *The Complete Songs for Solo Voice and Piano by Johannes Brahms*. 4 vols. Trans. Stanley Appelbaum. New York: Dover.
Marek, George R. 1967. *Richard Strauss: The Life of a Non-Hero*. New York: Simon and Schuster.
May, Florence. 1905. *The Life of Johannes Brahms*. London: William Reeves.
Medtner, Nicolay. 1951. *The Muse and the Fashion*. Trans. A. J. Swan. Haverford, Pennsylvania: Haverford College Bookstore.
Mendelssohn Bartholdy, Felix. 1863. *Letters from 1833–1847*. Ed. Paul Mendelssohn Bartholdy & Carl Mendelssohn Bartholdy. Trans. Lady Wallace. Boston: Oliver Ditson.
Mendelssohn Bartholdy, Karl. 1974. *Goethe and Mendelssohn*. Trans. M. E. von Glen. London: Macmillan.

Miller, Florence Fenwick. 1892. *In Ladies Company: Six Interesting Women*. London: Ward and Downey.

Miller, Philip L. 1966. *The Ring of Words*. Garden City, New York: Anchor Books.

Mitchell, Donald. 1958. *Gustav Mahler: The Early Years*. London: Rockliff.

_____. 1976. *Gustav Mahler: The Wunderhorn Years*. Boulder, Colorado: Westview Press.

_____. 1985. *Gustav Mahler: Songs and Symphonies of Life and Death*. Vol. 3. Berkeley: University of California Press.

Moser, Hans Joachim. 1937. *Das Deutsche Lied*. 2 vols. Berlin: Atlantis Verlag.

_____. 1958. *The German Solo Song and the Ballad*. Ed. K. G. Fellerer. Köln: Arno Volk Verlag.

Neuls-Bates, Carol. 1982. *Women in Music: An Anthology of Source Readings from the Middle Ages to the Present*. New York: Harper & Row.

_____. 1983. "Creating a College Curriculum for the Study of Women in Music." *The Musical Woman: An International Perspective*. Ed. Judith Lang Zaimont. Westport, Connecticut: Greenwood Press.

Newman, Ernest. 1907. *Hugo Wolf*. Rev. ed. 1966. New York: Dover Publications.

_____. 1908. *Richard Strauss*. London: John Lane, The Bodley Head.

Nietzsche, Friedrich. 1924. Nietzsche contra Wagner. *The Works of Friedrich Nietzsche*. Ed. Alexander Tille. Trans. Thomas Common. Vol. 8. New York: MacMillan.

_____ 1968. *Basic Writings of Nietzsche*. Trans. & ed. Walter Kaufmann. New York: The Modern Library.

_____. 1987. *The Portable Nietzsche*. Trans. & ed. Walter Kaufmann. New York: Penguin Books.

_____. n.d. *Thus Spake Zarathustra*. New York: Modern Library.

Noske, Frits. 1970. *French Song from Berlioz to Duparc*. Trans. Rita Benton. 2nd ed. New York: Dover.

Osborne, Charles. 1974. *The Concert Song Companion*. New York: Da Capo Press.

Palmer, R. R. 1959. *A History of the Modern World*. 2nd ed. Rev. Joel Colton. New York: Alfred A. Knopf.

Petersen, Barbara A. 1980. *Ton und Wort. The Lieder of Richard Strauss*. Ann Arbor, Michigan: University Microfilm International Research Press.

Plantinga, Leon. 1967. *Schumann as Critic*. New Haven & London: Yale University Press.

_____. 1984. *Romantic Music*. New York: W. W. Norton.

Pleasants, Henry, ed. 1965. *The Musical World of Robert Schumann*. New York: St. Martin's Press.

_____, ed. 1979. *The Music Criticism of Hugo Wolf*. New York: Holmes & Meier Publishers.

Redlich, Hans F. 1949. "Spohr: A Forgotten Romantic." *The Music Review*. 10:313.

Reed, John. 1985. *The Schubert song companion*. New York: Universe Books.

Reich, Nancy B. 1980. "Louise Reichardt." *The New Grove Dictionary*. Vol.

15. London: MacMillan.

———. 1985. *Clara Schumann: The Artist and the Woman*. Ithaca, New York: Cornell University Press.

Reich, Willi, ed. 1971. *Franz Schubert: Im eigenen Wirken und den Betrachtungen seiner Freunde*. Zürich: Manesse Verlag.

Reichardt, Louise. 1922. *Ausgewählte Lieder*. Ed. Gerty Rheinhardt. Munich: Drei masken Verlag.

———. 1981. *Songs*. Intro. by Nancy B. Reich. New York: Da Capo Press.

Rellstab, Ludwig. 1841. *Iris im Gebiete der Tonkunst*. Vol. 12: 47–48, 105–106. Berlin.

Ripin, Edwin M., Philip R. Belt, Maribel Meisel, Derek Adlam, William J. Conner, Rosamond E. M. Harding, and Cyril Ehrlich. 1984. "Piano." *The New Grove Dictionary of Musical Instruments*. Vol. 3. London: MacMillan.

Rousseau, Jean-Jacques. 1911. *Émile, or Education*. Tran. Barbara Foxley. London: J. M. Dent; New York: E. P. Dutton. Orig. publ. 1760.

———. 1985. *The Confessions*. Trans. J. M. Cohen. Great Britain: Penguin Books.

Sammlung von Musik Stücken alter und neuer Zeit. 1838/1967. Vol. 4. Rpt. Scarsdale, New York: Annemarie Schnase.

Sams, Eric. 1975. *The Songs of Robert Schumann*. London: Eulenburg Books.

———. 1983. *The Songs of Hugo Wolf*. 2nd ed. London: Eulenburg Books, 1983.

Schoenberg, Arnold. 1950. *Style and Idea*. New York: Philosophical Library.

Schünemann, Georg. 1936. *Erinnerungen an Schubert-Josef von Spauns erste Lebensbeschreibung*. Berlin: Atlantis Verlag.

Schuh, Willi. 1982. *Richard Strauss: A Chronicle of the Early Years 1864–1898*. Trans. Mary Whittall. Cambridge: Cambridge University Press.

Schumann, Eugenie. 1927. *The Schumanns and Johannes Brahms*. Trans. Marie Busch. New York: The Dial Press.

Schumann, Robert. 1877. *Music and Musicians*. Trans. Fanny Raymond Ritter. New York: Edward Schuberth.

———. 1946. *On Music and Musicians*. Ed. Konrad Wolff. Trans. Paul Rosenfeld. New York: McGraw-Hill.

———. 1971. *Dichterliebe*, ed. Arthur Komar. New York: W. W. Norton.

Selk, Günter. 1961. "Nicolai, Christoph Friedrich." *Die Musik in Geschichte und Gegenwart*. Vol. 9. Kassel: Bärenreiter.

Sirota, Victoria Ressmeyer. 1981. *The Life and Works of Fanny Mendelssohn Hensel*. Ph.D. Dissertation, Boston University School for the Arts.

Smeed, J. W. 1987. *German Song and its Poetry 1740–1900*. London: Croom Helm.

"Spohr," *Allgemeine musikalische Zeitung*. 1818. 20:647. Leipzig.

Spohr, Louis. 1878. *Autobiography*. London.

Stein, Jack M. 1971. *Poems and Music in the German Lied from Gluck to Hugo Wolf*. Cambridge: Harvard University Press.

———. 1973. *Richard Wagner and the Synthesis of the Arts*. Connecticut: Greenwood Press.

Sternfeld, Frederick W. 1979. *Goethe and Music*. New York: Da Capo Press.

Stevens, Denis, ed. 1960. *A History of Song*. New York: Norton.

Strauss. Richard. 1953. *Recollections and Reflections*. Ed. Willi Schuh. Trans. J. L. Lawrence. London: Boosey & Hawkes.

———. 1968. *Richard Strauss & Romain Rolland: Correspondence*. Ed. Rollo Myers. Berkeley: University of California Press.

———. 1977. *A Confidential Matter: The Letters of Richard Strauss and Stefan Zweig, 1931–1935*. Trans. Max Knight. Berkeley: University of California Press.

Sumner, W. L. 1966. *The Pianoforte*. London: Macdonald.

Taylor, Ronald. 1982. *Robert Schumann: His Life and Work*. New York: Universe Books.

Tovey, Donald Francis. 1910. "Beethoven." *The Encyclopedia Britannica*. 11th ed., vol. 3. New York: Encyclopaedia Britannica.

Wagner, Richard. 1983. *My Life*. Trans. Andrew Gray. Cambridge: Cambridge University Press.

Walker, Frank. 1951. *Hugo Wolf*. London: J. M. Dent & Sons.

Werba, Erik. 1984. *Hugo Wolf und seine Lieder*. Vienna: Österreichischer Bundesverlag.

Werfel, Alma Mahler. 1958. *And the Bridge is Love*. New York: Harcourt & Brace.

———. 1969. *Gustav Mahler: Memories and Letters*. Ed. Donald Mitchell. Trans. Basil Creighton. New York: Viking Press. Orig. publ. 1946.

———. 1975. *Gustav Mahler: Memories and Letters*. 3rd rev. & enl. ed., Ed. Donald Mitchell and Knud Martner. Trans. Basil Creighton. Seattle: University of Washington Press.

Werner, Eric. 1960. "Levy, Sara." *Die Musik in Geschichte und Gegenwart*. Vol. 8. Kassel: Bärenreiter.

———. 1963. *Mendelssohn. A New Image of the Composer and His Age*. Trans. Dika Newlin. London: The Free Press of Glencoe, Collier-MacMillan.

Werner, Jack. 1947. "Felix and Fanny Mendelssohn." *Music and Letters* 28:303–337.

Winter, Robert S. 1988. "Striking It Rich: The Significance of Striking Points in the Evolution of the Romantic Piano." *The Journal of Musicology* 6:267–292.

Wirth, Julia. 1927. *Julius Stockhausen der Sänger des Deutschen Liedes*. Frankfurt am Main: Im Verlag Englert und Schlosser.

Wolf, Hugo. 1982. *Gesamtausgabe: Lieder mit Orchesterbegleitung*. Ed. Hans Jancik. Vienna: Musikwissenschaftlicher Verlag.

Song Index: Listing by Title

Song Index: Listing by Composer

CLARA WIECK SCHUMANN (1819–1896)

ROBERT SCHUMANN (1810–1856)

Subject Index